SINGAPORE
AND
SWITZERLAND

Secrets to Small State Success

SINGAPORE

AND

SWITZERLAND

Secrets to Small State Success

Editors

Yvonne Guo
Lee Kuan Yew School of Public Policy
National University of Singapore

J. J. Woo
School of Humanities and Social Sciences
Nanyang Technological University, Singapore

World Scientific

NEW JERSEY · LONDON · SINGAPORE · BEIJING · SHANGHAI · HONG KONG · TAIPEI · CHENNAI · TOKYO

Published by

World Scientific Publishing Co. Pte. Ltd.
5 Toh Tuck Link, Singapore 596224
USA office: 27 Warren Street, Suite 401-402, Hackensack, NJ 07601
UK office: 57 Shelton Street, Covent Garden, London WC2H 9HE

Library of Congress Cataloging-in-Publication Data
Names: Guo, Yvonne, author. | Woo, J. J. (Jun Jie) author.
Title: Singapore and Switzerland : secrets to small state success / Yvonne Guo, J. J. Woo.
Description: New Jersey : World Scientific, 2015.
Identifiers: LCCN 2015031765| ISBN 9789814651394 | ISBN 9814651397
Subjects: LCSH: States, Small--Case studies. | States, Small--Politics and government. |
    Singapore--Politics and government. | Switzerland--Politics and government.
Classification: LCC JC365 .G86 2015 | DDC 330.9494--dc23
LC record available at http://lccn.loc.gov/2015031765

British Library Cataloguing-in-Publication Data
A catalogue record for this book is available from the British Library.

Desk Editor: Karimah Samsudin

Printed in Singapore

Contents

Foreword

By Ambassador Thomas Kupfer

I was very pleased to hear that Yvonne Guo, an alumna of the University of St. Gallen in Switzerland, and Jun Jie Woo, Assistant Professor at the Nanyang Technological University (NTU) in Singapore, intended to publish a book about Switzerland and Singapore. I have met Ms Guo several times and have had the opportunity to listen to some of her presentations about her studies. Within the framework of her PhD thesis about small state responses to international financial regulatory pressures, she is concentrating on the cases of Singapore and Switzerland. As a Singaporean, she knows the local framework very well, and participating in regular study visits to Switzerland has given her important insights into Switzerland and its political system. Furthermore, with the involvement of Swiss and Singaporean authors, the book gives a deep and informative insight into the nature of two small states which are very similar and yet very different.

Switzerland and Singapore indeed enjoy excellent bilateral relations. Even before the establishment of diplomatic relations on 11 October 1967, the two countries have maintained significant ties, dating back to well before Singapore's independence. Already during the mid-19th century, Swiss traders and merchandisers were selling watches and textiles to Singapore and working for Dutch, German or English trading houses in Singapore. Since then, the economic and financial cooperation between both countries has grown continuously. Singapore became Switzerland's main trading partner in Southeast Asia and Switzerland the fifth-largest investor in Singapore. Singapore was the first Asian country with which Switzerland concluded a Free Trade Agreement through the EFTA

ix

(European Free Trade Association) in 2003. Over the years, there have been numerous visits of Swiss and Singaporean politicians to both countries. One of the important highlights was to receive Singapore President Dr Tony Tan in Berne in May 2014 for his first Presidential visit to Switzerland.

As many things are, size is relative. Switzerland and Singapore are considered to be small states. However it is, in fact, a question of perspective. Compared to the land surface of their respective neighbours, Switzerland at 42,000 square kilometres and Singapore at 720 square kilometres are defined as being small. The same applies for the size of the populations living in the two states. With eight million in Switzerland, and 5.5 million in Singapore, both countries are considered small relative to other countries in the world. In contrast, the picture of 'small and big countries' is completely different in terms of economic and financial power. Being among the most important financial centers, Switzerland and Singapore are two of the major players worldwide. Is it a coincidence that they are both so small in terms of area and citizens and yet have such successful economies? Well, both countries indeed share distinct features such as a business-friendly regulatory framework and low taxes. Actually, they are generally very similar in many ways. Besides political stability, both states focus on high quality products and have export-oriented economies. Additionally, as a result of their small local populations, Switzerland and Singapore are both dependent on foreign labour. Interestingly, concerns related to foreigners and immigration feature heavily in political debates in both countries. The populations in both countries are concerned about competition by immigrants in the job market and potential strains on existing infrastructure. Although this fear may not be fully rational due to both countries' dependence on immigration, it continues to influence large parts of the population, as evidenced by the Swiss approval in February 2014 of a popular initiative on reducing mass immigration, and debates prior to the Singapore General Elections in September 2015.

These concerns with rising immigration belie the fact that both countries have strong traditions of a high degree of internationality and with it multiculturalism and multilingualism. The mother tongue of about 65% of the inhabitants in Switzerland is German, 20% speak French, 5% Italian, less than 1% speak Romansh, its fourth national language, and the rest speak a different language. This percentage division is similar to Singapore where 23% of Singapore residents primarily speak English, 59% Chinese, 14% Malay, 3% Tamil and 1% other languages.

Today, Switzerland and Singapore have serious challenges to face, some of which are common to both countries. In terms of economy, the lack of natural resources makes them import-dependent and export-oriented. To increase and maintain a high level of prosperity, a dynamic and proactive international economic outlook is essential. Michel Anliker, a Trade Senior Manager at Pricewaterhouse Coopers (PwC) who worked for three years in Singapore, is focusing on this issue in his chapter, and gives an interesting insight into how the two countries manage to reach this goal. The relationship with surrounding countries has to be kept on a good bilateral level. Switzerland tries to balance its position within the EU; although it is not a member, it remains strongly connected to the EU and part of the EU internal market. Especially now, as Europe is in the middle of a refugee crisis, Switzerland's behaviour and interaction within the EU is important. Singapore's challenge, on the other hand, lies in keeping up strong ties with the ASEAN states and being an active member of the ASEAN Economic Community, just launched in December 2015.

Another topic of great relevance to both our countries is science and education. The universities of both countries have done well and hold top positions in international rankings. In the QS World University Rankings 2015–2016, the Swiss Federal Institute of Technology (ETH) Zurich was ranked as the ninth best university in the world, the first out of non-English-speaking countries, while the Ecole Polytechnique Fédérale de Lausanne (EPFL) ranks 14th. The National University of Singapore (NUS) and the Nanyang Technological University (NTU) in Singapore are ranked as the best Asian universities in the 12th and 13th positions.

Ten years ago, *swissnex* Singapore was established as a Swiss governmental platform for Science and Education, and it has recently been integrated in the Embassy as a Science and Technology Office. It has played, over the years, a pioneering role to promote exchanges on Swiss and Singaporean education and research. Suzanne Hraba-Renevey and Yvonne Guo provide a valuable insight to this success story, discussing how both countries are managing in different ways to sustain a knowledge-based economy through strongly investing in education. Today, three important Swiss public universities have an office in the city-state: The ETH Zurich with its Singapore ETH-Centre (SEC) for Research within the CREATE (Campus for Research Excellence And Technological Enterprise), the newly-established Ecole Hôtelière de Lausanne and the University of St. Gallen with the St. Gallen Institute of Management in Asia, where editor Yvonne Guo and chapter author Dr. Manuel Baeuml carried out part of their doctoral research. In his article, Dr. Baeuml focuses on the importance and role of SMEs in both Switzerland and Singapore, and the different regulatory frameworks that govern them. Today, Singaporean policymakers have expressed great interest in the highly-developed and well-established Swiss vocational training system, and a lot of expert exchanges and discussions are going on. I am very optimistic that the fruitful cooperation in research and education between the Swiss and Singaporeans will be successfully continued as a mutual learning process.

Although there are many similarities between Switzerland and Singapore, some differences obviously exist as well. Most of them, besides being located at opposite sides of the world with very different climates, are related to the different historical backgrounds of the two countries. The historical Switzerland was founded in the year 1291 and is now over 700 years old. Many cultural habits and traditions have developed ever since. The modern Switzerland was established in 1848 with its current political system of federalism, divided into 26 cantons, each with its own constitution, government and parliament. The National Government involves both representatives of the population, the National Council, and representatives of the states, the Council of States. The collective Government of seven Federal Councillors, elected by the Parliament from different parties with a yearly rotating President, is a very unique system and adequate to Swiss political culture. Additionally, with direct democracy, Swiss citizens have the power to make important decisions through popular initiatives and referenda. It is self-evident that this Swiss political mechanism needs a longer time for decision-making as the citizens are directly involved. This makes Switzerland an essentially bottom-up system. Andreas Ladner, Professor at the Swiss Graduate School of Public Administration (IDHEAP) of the University of Lausanne, discusses further in his article, co-authored with Yvonne Guo, what the political system of Switzerland is about and how it differs from the more centralised Singapore system. The Singaporean Government, run by the Prime Minister and his Cabinet, clearly works differently. One main party, the People's Action Party, has governed the city-state successfully since Singapore's independence. This so-called 'meritocracy' is a top-down way of politics.

A product of both countries' different histories is their different developmental strategies and governance styles. Having just celebrated its 50 years' Jubilee, Singapore is still relatively young. But interestingly, whether they are arrived at through a bottom-up or top-down process, the solutions found to the same issues are often quite similar. Many of those questions were discussed in detail at two seminars, inspired by an idea of Professor Tommy Koh and supported by the Swiss Embassy, organised by the Institute of Policy Studies (IPS) in Singapore and Avenir Suisse, a Swiss think tank. The seminars were held in October 2013 in Singapore and in May 2014 in Switzerland on the occasion of President Dr Tony Tan's visit to Switzerland under the theme: "Singapore — Switzerland: Learning from Each Other".

The Editors' work is a very useful contribution to the Swiss–Singaporean relationship and I was happily expecting the release of this final book. The comparison of the small states Switzerland and Singapore, examined by many competent Singaporean and Swiss authors, will fill a gap in the bookshelves of many politically interested Swiss and Singaporeans. With currently about 5,000 Swiss citizens, 400 Swiss companies and an increasing number of Swiss universities in the city-state, the book already addresses a substantial audience. The community is growing, and with it, the exchanges between both countries. The various articles are a very valuable contribution to the discussion of the similarities and differences between Singapore and Switzerland, those two rather small but successful states. And the book will help to find answers to the interesting question: What can we learn from each other to do better in the future?

I wish you an enjoyable read!

Thomas Kupfer
Ambassador of Switzerland, Singapore
April 2016

Foreword

By Ambassador Tommy Koh

I congratulate Yvonne Guo and Jun Jie Woo for having taken the initiative to co-edit this important book comparing and contrasting Switzerland and Singapore.

Switzerland occupies a very special place in the minds of Singaporeans. The former Prime Minister of Singapore, Mr Goh Chok Tong, had singled out Switzerland as a role model and benchmark for Singapore. Mr Goh had urged Singaporeans, in 1984, to work hard so that we could achieve the standard of living of Switzerland by 1999.

Why do I admire Switzerland?

I admire Switzerland for many reasons. Let me just mention three of them. First, Switzerland is one of the richest and most prosperous countries in the world in spite of the fact that it has no natural resources. The World Economic Forum regularly ranks Switzerland as one of the world's most competitive economies. Switzerland's strengths include its good education system, including its famous apprenticeship scheme; its strong work ethic; its spirit of innovation and enterprise; its social harmony, and the rule of law. Switzerland is a model of sustainable development. The environment is kept in a pristine condition. It is also a model of inclusive growth. Its GINI coefficient is a salutary 0.33.

Second, Switzerland is a small country with a population of 7.5 million. Contrary to conventional wisdom that small countries lack the scale to be able to produce global champions in business, there are 15 Swiss companies in the Fortune Global 500. This is a formidable achievement. The companies span the spectrum from food (Nestlé), to financial services (UBS, Credit Suisse, Zurich Insurance), pharmaceuticals (Novartis, Roche), and engineering and construction (ABB). The achievement of Switzerland gives me hope that Singapore too could produce global champions in business beyond our beloved Singapore Airlines.

Third, I admire Switzerland because it has made two strategic contributions to the world, namely, the International Committee of the Red Cross (ICRC) and the World Economic Forum (WEF). On the occasion of the ICRC's 150th anniversary, I described it as a "unique and indispensable international organisation". Its most important role is to be the custodian and promoter of international humanitarian law. The founder of the WEF, Dr Klaus Schwab, is a genius. He has succeeded in making the WEF a thought leader, a convener, and a meeting place for the world's elite. The annual summit in Davos is second in importance only to the UN General Assembly.

On the 26th of November 2013, I had the great pleasure and honour of launching the beautiful book, *The Swiss in Singapore* by Andreas Zangger, at the residence of Ambassador Thomas Kupfer. I am therefore pleased that Ambassador Kupfer and I have contributed a foreword each for this book.

Tommy Koh
Ambassador-At-Large
Ministry of Foreign Affairs
Singapore
April 2016

Preface

The idea for this book grew out of a series of articles on Singapore and Switzerland published by both editors in several newspapers, discussions held during the Swiss–Asian Summer School organised by the Lee Kuan Yew School of Public Policy in July 2013, and the "Switzerland and Singapore: Learning from Each Other" conferences jointly organised by the Institute of Policy Studies and Avenir Suisse in October 2013 and May 2014. The seminars discussed the management of policy challenges that Singapore and Switzerland had in common, and explored opportunities for further collaboration among academics and think-tanks in the two countries.

Singapore and Switzerland are both small states which have topped international rankings in a dazzling array of policy areas, from economic competitiveness to education to governance. Yet their pathways to success could not be more different. While Singapore is the archetypal developmental state, whose success can be attributed to strong political leadership and long-term planning, Switzerland's success is a more organic process, due to the propitious convergence of strong industries and a resilient citizenry. Yet throughout the course of their development, both countries have had to deal with the dual challenges of a culturally heterogeneous population and an unstable regional context. Indeed, both have experienced internal conflict as well as occupation by external powers.

Both countries pride themselves of being models of 'exceptionalism' in having surmounted the odds. While such claims should be subjected to greater scrutiny, it is clear that the Swiss model has served as an invaluable reference for Singapore in its development. In school, Singaporean children were taught how the Swiss model of multilingualism served as an example for Singapore policymakers in preserving harmony among its diverse communities. In addition to this, both countries have emphasised trade, finance and service industries, carving out niches for themselves in these areas within an international system dominated by bigger powers.

Apart from their convergences, what also makes Singapore and Switzerland fascinating are their divergences. While the Singapore government prides itself on having a custom-made, carefully calibrated policy solution to most problems, the Swiss government does not exercise the same degree of control, having delegated many of its competencies to its cantons and communes, and even bestowed upon its citizens the power to directly influence the policymaking process through direct democracy mechanisms. Its bottom-up approach to governance stands in stark contrast to Singapore's resolutely top-down approach.

The cases of Singapore and Switzerland thus present a fascinating puzzle: how have both small states achieved similar levels of success through divergent pathways? Are both approaches equally sustainable, and what lessons do they hold for each other? If Switzerland, in Minister S Iswaran's words, represents "what might lie on the frontier of possibilities for Singapore" , then what could Singapore possibly represent for Switzerland in a globalised world where both countries are confronted with increasingly similar challenges?

Drawing on the contributions of authors whose research focuses on specific policy sectors in Singapore and Switzerland, including foreign policy, finance, small and medium-sized enterprises (SMEs), immigration policy, language policy, and public administration, this volume provides an insight into the policy challenges faced by both countries, as well as their policy solutions. As such, it provides a useful resource for policymakers and scholars in Singapore and Switzerland, or for anyone curious about how two small states have accomplished so much out of so little.

For the successful realisation of this book, the editors would like to acknowledge the generous support of our graduate institution, the Lee Kuan Yew School of Public Policy at the National University of Singapore, and thank our colleagues and our Dean, Professor Kishore Mahbubani, for encouraging us in this endeavour. We are also very much indebted to the Institute of Policy Studies (IPS), to Avenir Suisse, as well as to Credit

Suisse, Swiss Re and Singapore Airlines for their organisation and generous support of the Singapore–Switzerland seminars in 2013 and 2014. Finally, we would like to express our gratitude to our friends and colleagues at the St. Gallen Institute of Management in Asia, the Swiss Graduate School of Public Administration (IDHEAP), the Swiss School of Management in Fribourg, and the Embassy of Switzerland in Singapore, whose contributions to this book are testimony to the tremendous potential for academic collaboration that exists between both our countries.

Yvonne Guo
J. J. Woo
April 2016

Introduction and Background: The Trajectories of History, Politics and Economics

What makes a small state succeed? This question was first posed by Peter Katzenstein in his well-known 1985 book *Small States in World Markets*. Katzenstein argued that the small states in Europe had succeeded due to their ability to "adjust to economic change through a carefully calibrated balance of economic flexibility and political stability"[1]. Though Katzenstein's analysis focused on small states in Europe, his central argument — that small states succeed because of their ability to be improvise — is just as relevant to small states in other parts of the world.

What this book adds to Katzenstein's argument is an in-depth exploration of the forces that drive this improvisation: market or state? Here, Singapore, a 'developmental' state characterised by high levels of political control, is contrasted with Switzerland, a classic 'liberal corporatiset' state. The point here is that there is no 'perfect balance' between the market and the state. Rather, the challenge is how to design market mechanisms flexibly, in tandem with state policy objectives, while making sure that they reflect the general will of the people. The pages of this book will explore how Singapore and Switzerland have negotiated this 'trilemma' between political leadership, international pressures and domestic demands.

---

[1] Katzenstein, Peter J, *Small States in World Markets: Industrial Policy in Europe*. Ithaca, N.Y.: Cornell University Press, 1985.

This chapter will present a broad overview of both countries' historical, political and economic contexts to provide a context for subsequent chapters.

History of Singapore

Although Singapore and Switzerland are located in different geopolitical regions, they share a number of common characteristics. Firstly, as small states, they both share the same sense of vulnerability relative to their neighbours, and have in fact experienced occupation by external powers for a number of years. Owing to this, both states have well-established citizen militaries and relatively independent foreign policy stances. Secondly, their rise can be attributed to their strategic locations along important trading routes. This has allowed both states to emerge as economic and financial powerhouses, as advanced producer services and other supporting industries flourished on the back of vibrant trading activities. However, the historical origins of Singapore and Switzerland could not have been more different.

Singapore's tumultuous historical origins also reflect the city's vulnerability to external political and economic forces. Singapore's early history can be traced back to the early 13th century, when settlements were first established in 1298 and the island was then known as *Temasek*. At that point, Singapore was already a major trade hub with strong connections with Yuan and Ming Dynasty China[2]. It was subsequently renamed *Singapura* or the 'Lion City' in the 14th century by a prince from Palembang, Sang Nila Utama, who had spotted a lion on a hunting trip on the island. Owing to its strategic geographical location, Singapore grew to become a major trading post for ships plying the various sea routes that converged at the island.

However, Singapore's modern history only began when the British Empire, under Sir Stamford Raffles, established a colony on the island in the 19th century and made it a major entrepôt trade hub. As a result, there was massive immigration from China, India, and the Malay Peninsula.

---

[2] Kwa Chong Guan, Derek Heng, and Tan Tai Yong, *Singapore: A 700-year History — From Early Emporium to World City* (Singapore: National Archives of Singapore, 2009).

This early wave of immigration played an important role in cementing Singapore's existing ethnic make-up, with the Chinese, Indians and Malays continuing to make up the city's major ethnic groups.

During this period, Singapore's banking and commercial sectors began to take root as the city continued to grow as a major entrepôt hub serving British trade interests within the broader Commonwealth zone. To address the city's increasing ethnic diversity and burgeoning commercial needs, Raffles initiated large-scale urban planning, ethnic segregation, and infrastructural development through the Raffles Town Plan. The Raffles Town Plan would continue to define subsequent efforts at urban planning, as it clearly demarcated civic, commercial, and ethnically-segregated residential areas[3].

However, Singapore's economic and social development was disrupted when Japanese forces invaded the island during the Second World War. On 15 February 1942, Allied forces on the island surrendered to the Japanese, and Singapore was renamed *Syonan-to* under Japanese rule. The war-time violence associated with the Japanese Occupation would prove traumatic for Singapore, weighing heavily on the psyche of future policy-makers, and causing the city to take on a 'siege mentality' approach to foreign and defense policy that was centered on a perceived vulnerability to external threats well into the late 1990s[4]. With the end of the Japanese occupation in 1945, Singapore reverted to British rule and subsequently became a British Crown Colony.

However, this spate of British rule was short-lived. Emerging anti-colonialist and nationalist sentiments prompted a shift towards self-government and a gradual withdrawal of British influence over domestic policy, although the British retained control over security, defence and foreign affairs. This period of limited self-government was highly unstable, as communist sentiments in various quarters of society sparked off the Hock Lee Bus riots in 1955 and Chinese student riots in 1956. Full self-government was established after Singapore's first general elections in 1959, with the

---

[3] Bonny Tan, "Raffles Town Plan", *Singapore Infopedia*, 2002 http://eresources.nlb.gov.sg/infopedia/articles/SIP_658_2005-01-07.html
[4] Michael Leifer, *Singapore's Foreign Policy: Coping with Vulnerability* (London: Routledge, 2000).

People's Action Party (PAP) securing 43 of the 51 seats contested and party leader Lee Kuan Yew becoming Singapore's first Prime Minister.

Under early PAP rule, Singapore developed many of the socio-cultural markers of a modern state. These included a national flag, crest, and anthem, while English and Malay were designated national languages[5]. Under the leadership of Minister of Finance Goh Keng Swee, Singapore also embarked on a spate of rapid economic development by providing industry incentives and developing western Singapore as an industrial estate. The Housing and Development Board (HDB) was also established in 1960 to facilitate the rapid construction of new housing units and resettlement of slums. Yet despite these efforts at economic development, early PAP leaders believed that Singapore's economic survival required a merger with Malaysia.

Singapore's merger with Malaysia was finalised in 1963 under the Malaysia Agreement, although this resulted in a split within the ranks of the PAP. Despite the formation of the Barisan Sosialis by rebel PAP assemblymen, the PAP eventually consolidated its authority and obtained a parliamentary majority in the 1963 elections. However, the merger with Malaysia brought Singapore to the forefront of a diplomatic stand-off between Malaysia and Indonesia, known as *Konfrontasi*. Internally, Singapore faced a serious of communal riots involving clashes between Malays and Chinese; these allegedly arose from political tensions between the PAP and the United Malays National Organisation (UMNO) over special rights for Malays as well as provocateurs from Indonesia[6].

Escalating political tensions would ultimately result in Singapore's separation from Malaysia on 9 August 1965. Singapore's separation would spark off an intense period of urban, economic and social development. Recognising the need for economic independence, the government identified key sectors such as manufacturing, finance and services as potential areas of growth and focused on their development. In

---

[5] Barbara Leitch LePoer, *Singapore: A Country Study* (Washington: Federal Research Division of the Library of Congress, 1989).

[6] Jamie Han, "Communal riots of 1964", *Singapore Infopedia*, 18 September 2014 http://eresources.nlb.gov.sg/infopedia/articles/SIP_45_2005-01-06.html; Albert Lau, *A Moment of Anguish: Singapore and Malaysia and the Politics of Disengagement* (Singapore: Eastern Universities Press, 2003).

particular, this involved opening up Singapore's economy to multinational corporations (MNCs) and attracting greater foreign participation in the economy. This required the availability of a pool of skilled workers, which was developed through the formation of a rigorous education system.

As a newly-sovereign state, there was also a need to develop defence capabilities and forge strong relations and alliances with other nations. With the aid of Israel, a national service programme was established, forming a citizen army based on conscription of healthy eighteen-year-old males. This was particularly important with the full withdrawal of British forces in 1971. Singapore also established strong diplomatic relations with other countries, co-forming and participating in multilateral organisations such as the Association of South East Asian Nations (ASEAN), the Non-Aligned Movement and the World Trade Organisation.

These policy trajectories continued to guide Singapore's development well into the 2000s, with policymakers remaining focused on spurring economic development and fostering diplomatic ties. It is striking that Singapore's policy directions have not changed significantly since independence, although it has enjoyed increasing levels of success across various areas. As a consequence, Singapore has established itself as a major global city, financial centre and maritime hub. However, it is also beginning to face new and emerging political and economic instabilities arising from both external and internal sources. While Singapore's post-independence historical development has featured political stability and policy consistency, the city continues to be exposed to the vagaries of an increasingly globalised socio-economic context.

History of Switzerland

Switzerland started out as a loose confederation of independent small states, also known as cantons. Its political history dates back to the foundation of the Swiss Confederation in 1291. Legend has it that the leaders of the cantons of Uri, Schwyz and Unterwalden gathered on the Rutli meadow in the heart of Switzerland and swore an alliance between them, known as the "Oath of Rutli", to defend each other against a common enemy. While the exact date remains open to historical scrutiny, we know that the Swiss Federal Charter, which dates to the same year, documents the union of these three cantons.

Initially, the three cantons were not actually independent, but largely autonomous, due to having been granted *reichfrei* status by the Holy Roman emperors, meaning they were under the direct authority of the emperors. This special status was due to their strategic location: the cantons were located along important trade routes in the Central Alps, particularly the Gotthard Pass, which the emperors wanted control over. However, their *reichfrei* status came under increasing threat by the rise of the Habsburg dynasty, which tried to bring them under their rule. It was in this context — in defending their independence — that the Swiss Confederacy was born.

With the Habsburgs still seeking to assert sovereignty over the region, the Confederacy gradually expanded, signing alliances with city-states like Lucerne, Zurich and Berne, and conquering other territories, such as Glarus and Zug. With the entry of Berne in 1353, the alliance comprised eight members (*Bund der Acht Orte*), held together by a loose network of treaties. By the end of the century, the states had signed their first treaty together, assuring that wars could only be started with each other's mutual consent.

Over the next two centuries, notwithstanding internal tensions between the cantons, the eight states of the Confederacy continued to expand their territories. Some of these states (Aargau, Thurgau, Ticino) were conquered by force, while others (Fribourg, Appenzell, Schaffhausen, St. Gallen, the Grisons and the Valais) opted to join as 'associates' to the Confederacy. At the end of the Burgundy and Swabian wars, Fribourg, Solothurn, Basel, Schaffhausen and finally Appenzell joined the original eight cantons, forming a federation of thirteen cantons (*Dreizehn Orte*). The Confederacy's period of rapid expansion came to an end with its defeat at the Battle of Marignano in 1515.

Although they still considered themselves as sovereign territories bonded by a loose military alliance, the states formed a federal assembly, the *Tagsatzung*, during the 15th century. Both cantons and associate states were represented in this assembly, which helped to decide inter-cantonal affairs and settle disputes between the states. The *Tagsatzung* played an important stabilising role during the Thirty Years' War in Europe by creating a consensus against direct military involvement, supported by the fact that religious differences between the cantons made any common foreign policy impossible. At the Peace of Westphalia in 1648, the independence of the Swiss Confederacy was formally recognised.

However, the newly-independent Swiss Confederation grew increasingly reliant on its powerful neighbour France, creating further tensions between Catholic and Protestant cantons, since the French emperor had withdrawn certain rights to Protestants in the Edict of Nantes. Initially, France recognised Swiss independence in its treaties with the Confederation; however, in March 1798, France invaded Switzerland on the grounds that it was 'liberating' the Swiss people from its 'feudal' system of decentralised governance[7]. In its place, the French occupiers established a centralised state known as the Helvetic Republic, which they proclaimed would be "One and Indivisible".

The new regime encountered much resistance. Three cantons — Uri, Schwyz and Nidwalden — tried to fight back with an army of 10,000 men, but their resistance was soon crushed. Embattled by coups and disputes among pro-centralisation *Unitaires* and pro-decentralisation *Federalistes,* and burdened by increasing debt, the Helvetic Republic descended into instability and civil war and eventually collapsed.

Summoning representatives of the *Unitaires* and *Federalistes* to a conference in Paris, Napoleon Bonaparte, then First Consul of France, acknowledged that "Switzerland is not like any other state, whether in regard to the events that have occurred there in the past several centuries, or in regard to its geographical situation, or in regard to the great differences between the customs of its various parts. Nature has made your state a federal one, and no wise man would want to flout her"[8].

With the 1803 Act of Mediation, Napoleon restored the cantons, thus forming the Swiss Confederation, which established 19 cantons, with equal rights, under the old Federal Diet (*Tagsatzung*), the assembly of the cantons' representatives. The Conservatives managed to restore many of the old laws. The cities again dominated their rural vicinity, but not as absolutely as before: The 1815 Treaty of Vienna further increased the number of cantons to 22 (with the addition of Valais, Neuchatel and Geneva) and established Swiss permanent neutrality. During the French

---

[7] Interestingly, Swiss farmers quite welcomed the French because they seemed to promise a more equal society and the same was the case with the more enlightened citizens in the towns. The French invaders encountered probably the strongest resistance from troops of the canton of Berne which lost the final battle at "Grauholz" on March 5, 1798.

[8] Napoleon I (1769–1821) Letter to the delegates of the Swiss cantons, 1802.

July Revolution of 1830, however, a liberal renewal movement, called regeneration, swept over the country, demanding full democratic rights and equality between citizens in cities and from the countryside.

At the beginning of the 1840, the predominantly Liberal and Protestant cantons obtained a majority in the Federal Diet. This enabled them to create a modern, more centralised nation state, abolishing borders between cantons, introducing a common currency, unifying metric measurements and weight systems, also to promote economic development. The conservative cantons preferred the loosely knit Confederation of cantons. To this was added the dispute over the closure of monasteries in the canton of Aargau and role of the Jesuits in the canton of Lucerne.

In 1848, at the end of a month-long civil war (the *Sonderbundskrieg*) between Liberals and the Catholic cantons which had formed a separate alliance (the *Sonderbund*), the first Federal Constitution was formed, creating the institutions of the Swiss Confederation, a federalist nation-state, which exists to this day. The Federal Assembly was divided into the Council of States (representing the cantons) and the National Council (representing the Swiss people). Swiss citizenship came into existence, and was conferred upon the inhabitants of Switzerland alongside their cantonal citizenship. In 1874, the referendum system was introduced to ensure that any laws introduced were supported by popular approval. The popular initiative, the possibility to amend the constitution from outside the parliament, was introduced in 1891.

Throughout the two World Wars, Switzerland kept to a stance of armed neutrality, reaffirmed both by the Treaty of Versailles and by the Swiss Federal Council's own proclamations. For this reason, Switzerland was reluctant to join the United Nations, doing so only in 2002. Switzerland was even more reluctant to join the European Union, rejecting membership of the European Economic Area (EEA) in 1992, and refusing to open talks regarding EU membership in 2001.

Politics

It is in their political systems that Singapore and Switzerland differ most markedly, and challenge most profoundly, the orthodoxy of representative democracy as it is often practiced. While both countries can be considered representative democracies, the highly decentralised Switzerland relies heavily on multi-party consensus government and on the political innovation of direct democracy in policymaking, where decisions are taken as closely to the people as possible; Singapore, on the other hand, has been ruled by a single party since its independence and decisions are usually taken by a centralised government. However, beneath these differences lie surprising similarities, one of which is the stability of the governing executive of both countries. It is widely known that Singapore has been ruled by the same party since 1959; perhaps less widely known is that Switzerland, too, was ruled by the same governing coalition between 1959 and 2003, in an arrangement known as the 'magic formula'.

Singapore: Political institutions and innovations

Singapore's political system strongly reflects its British colonial history. This is most evident in its unicameral Westminster parliamentary system, albeit with modifications put in place over the years. Similar to the British political system, the Singapore government is led by the Prime Minister and a cabinet of ministers, all of whom are elected members of parliament (MPs), with all MPs elected into parliament through popular vote. Given that the cabinet is drawn from parliamentary MPs, there is thus an overlap between the executive and legislative bodies. In other words, the government of the day is typically selected from the pool of elected MPs, usually those from the ruling party.

This conflation of political decision-making and law-making is further reinforced by Singapore's majoritarian first-past-the-post electoral system, another vestige of British colonial rule. Under a typical majoritarian system, the party that obtains a parliamentary majority in an election forms the government. Given that party members are subject to the discipline of the party whip, MPs from the ruling party typically vote along party lines. The result of this is an expedited decision-making process and greater consensus in parliament, although scholars of electoral processes have argued that a majoritarian system tends to be less representative of minority views in its focus on effective governance[9].

It is also impossible to discuss Singapore's political system without addressing the ruling PAP. Formed in 1954, the PAP has won every election since 1959 and hence dominates Singapore's political landscape as its longstanding ruling party. More importantly, the PAP has, over the years, forged close relations with bureaucratic and industry actors, forming a policy 'governing elite'[10]. Indeed, the PAP has been described as a "political class" whose influence extends to the civil service as well as government-linked enterprises through either direct linkages or indirect co-optation[11]. The PAP's dominance of political competition has also been aided by a weak opposition. This combination of a majoritarian parliamentary system and the longevity of PAP rule has served to ensure Singapore's political stability and policy expediency.

However, this is not to say that political development in Singapore has remained static. The Republic has, over the years, made several significant political innovations that have served to expand parliamentary representation and encourage greater diversity in political participation. The most significant political innovation is the introduction of Group Representation Constituencies (GRCs). GRCs are electoral divisions in which MPs are collectively elected into parliament as a group. Encompassing a significantly larger geographical area than Single Member Constituencies (SMCs), voters in GRCs have to choose between two or more contesting 'teams' of MPs.

Importantly, the Constitution stipulates that there must be at least one MP from an ethnic minority group in any given GRC. This includes Indians, Malays, Eurasians, or any other minority ethnic groups. The rationale for this was to ensure ethnic minority representation in

---

[9]Arend Lijphart, *Patterns of Democracy: Government Forms and Performance in Thirty-Six Countries* (New Haven: Yale University Press, 1999); Pippa Norris, "Choosing Electoral Systems: Proportional, Majoritarian and Mixed Systems", *International Political Science Review* 18, no. 3 (1997): 301.

[10]Natasha Hamilton-Hart, "The Singapore state revisited", *The Pacific Review* 13, no. 2 (2000): 195–216.

[11]Kenneth Paul Tan, "Meritocracy and Elitism in a Global City: Ideological Shifts in Singapore", *International Political Science Review* 29, no. 1 (2008): 11–17.

parliament. GRCs have also been seen as disadvantageous to opposition parties due the immense financial and logistical resources required for contesting in a GRC[12]. However, the loss of two cabinet ministers from the defeat of Aljunied GRC to the opposition Workers' Party in the 2011 General Elections (GE2011) has shown how GRCs may prove disadvantageous to the ruling party as well.

Two other political innovations were similarly implemented to introduce greater parliamentary diversity. First, the Non-Constituency Member of Parliament (NCMP) scheme was introduced in 1984. Under this scheme, losing opposition candidates with the highest vote-shares can be offered seats in parliament as NCMPs. Singapore's Parliamentary Act and Constitution requires a minimum of nine opposition MPs in parliament. This means that if there are less than nine opposition MPs elected to parliament, the shortfall will be made up by other opposition candidates with the highest percentage of votes. However, NCMPs cannot vote on constitutional amendments, motions of 'no confidence' in the government or budgetary and supply bills. While opposition parties had initially derided the NCMP scheme as a means for the PAP to strengthen its rule by negating the need for citizens to actually vote in opposition MPs since they are already represented, opposition representatives have since taken up NCMP seats.

Similarly, the Nominated Member of Parliament (NMP) scheme aims to increase parliamentary diversity by appointing nonpartisan individuals representing various spheres of Singaporean society into parliament. Given that NMPs are typically appointed by the President on the recommendation of a special committee typically comprising MPs from the ruling party, questions have been raised over the independence of NMPs. However, NMPs have contributed to parliamentary debate and often questioned PAP polices. After a constitutional amendment bill in 1997, the maximum number of NMPs was raised from six to nine. Similar to NCMPs, NMPs cannot vote on constitutional amendments, budgetary bills or motions of 'no confidence' in the government.

---

[12]Hussin Mutalib, "Constitutional-Electoral Reforms and Politics in Singapore", *Legislative Studies Quarterly* 27, no. 4 (2002): 665–667.

A final piece of political innovation in Singapore is the elected presidency. This was established in 1991, and was aimed at providing an elected President with a custodial role over Singapore's national reserves. This is part of a 'two-key' system, with the prime minister and president each holding one key to Singapore's national reserves. This gives the president blocking power over the government's use of national reserves. Furthermore, the president is also able to veto the appointment of key public officials. The elected presidency was implemented to prevent the irresponsible usage of national reserves or appointments of public officials by the government. However, the government can still remove the president's blocking powers through a national referendum while the Supreme Court has the authority to remove the president should he or she be found incompetent or incapable of performing his duties[13].

In sum, all four political innovations discussed above serve to increase the diversity of views and representation in parliament as well as to introduce checks and balances to the government, particularly in the areas of national reserves utilisation and the appointment of public officials. While these political innovations were introduced in response to a weak opposition presence, critics have pointed out that these innovations have instead proven disadvantageous to opposition parties and served to further strengthen PAP rule. However, gains by the Opposition during the watershed GE2011 suggest that these criticisms may be unfounded. During the elections, the PAP's vote-share fell to a low of 60.1 percent while the Opposition managed to win a GRC for the first time. While Singapore's success has depended in large part on its political stability, the city–state is now facing increasing instability as it seeks to re-establish a political consensus in this "new normal".

Switzerland: Executive, legislative and judicial bodies

Switzerland is one of only four states in the world[14] headed by a collective rather than unitary head of state — the Swiss Federal Council, which is

---

[13]Government of Singapore, *Constitutional Amendments to Safeguard Financial Assets and the Integrity of the Public Services* (Singapore: Singapore National Printers, 1988).
[14]The three others are Bosnia and Herzegovina, Andorra and San Marino.

Figure 1: The 'magic formula' reflecting party seat allocation in the Swiss Federal Council between 1959 and 2003

The 'magic formula'
Free Democratic Party (FDP): 2 members,
Christian Democratic People's Party (CVP): 2 members,
Social Democratic Party (SP): 2 members,
Swiss People's Party (SVP): 1 member.

---

also the head of government. The seven members that comprise the Federal Council, known as Federal Councillors, head the seven federal executive departments in Switzerland, and adopt the position of President and Vice-President on a rotating basis. Particularly fascinating is the fact that the party composition of Federal Councillors stayed the same for 44 years, in an agreement known as the 'magic formula'. Seats were accorded as seen in Figure 1.

In 2003, the SVP became Switzerland's largest party by votes, winning 29 percent of the popular vote, and taking over one of the CVP seats. At the end of an internal struggle between the SVP Federal Councillors and their party, the Conservative Democratic Party of Switzerland (BDP) was established. The BDP held one of the SVP's two seats between 2008 and 2015. However, in December 2015, the SVP regained its second seat in the Federal Council.

Given the Federal Council's inclusion of opposing parties and its need to seek consensus between them, the Council has to abide by principles such as collegiality (displaying public support for all decisions adopted by the Council), and secrecy (results of votes taken by the Council are not open to the public; records are only visible after 50 years).

The Swiss parliament — the Federal Assembly — is bicameral, consisting of the National Council (200 seats) and the Council of States (46 seats). While the National Council represents the Swiss population and seats are accorded proportionally to each canton based on population and elected in a proportional representation system, the Council of States represents the cantons, with every canton receiving two seats except for six 'half-cantons' which receive one seat each.

Including the five parties listed above, there are eleven political parties represented in the Federal Assembly. Changing majorities in parliamentary decisions are not infrequent and are seen to be beneficial for the political system. The judicial branch is represented by the Federal Supreme Court, with judges elected by the Federal Assembly for six-year terms.

Switzerland: Political innovations

The most unique feature of the Swiss political system lies in its frequent use of direct democracy as a policy instrument, through mandatory referendums, optional referendums, and popular initiatives. Referendums are mandatory for changes in the Swiss Constitution and optional for changes in Swiss laws. If a Swiss citizen, or more often a group of citizens, an interest group or a party, wants a new law to be submitted to a referendum, they have to gather 50,000 signatures within 100 days of the publication of the law. Popular initiatives are used to propose amendments to the Constitution. For an initiative to be launched, 100,000 signatures must be collected within 18 months, and voters can decide on whether or not to accept the proposed amendment. Direct democracy processes take place at all three levels: national, cantonal, and municipal.

The scope of Swiss federal referendums is noteworthy, encompassing a wide range of policy areas, such as foreign policy, defense policy, social policy, economic policy and so on. In particular, the use of popular initiatives has been gaining ground as a bottom-up policymaking tool, arguably with an increasingly nationalistic flavour. Notable popular initiatives in recent years have included the so-called 'Minder' initiative, to indirectly cap the salary of executives of listed companies by giving shareholder assemblies a stronger say (2013, accepted); the initiative against the construction of minarets (2009, accepted); the initiative to introduce a minimum wage (2014, rejected); initiatives to abolish the Swiss army or to end compulsory military service (1989, rejected; 2001, rejected; 2013, rejected); the initiative to join the United Nations (2002, accepted) and the initiative 'against mass immigration' (2014, accepted).

Economics

Despite differences in their historical and political development, a key aspect of convergence for Singapore and Switzerland is their economic success. Switzerland and Singapore are respectively ranked first and second in the WEF Global Competitiveness Index 2014–2015, first and second in Deloitte's Wealth Management Centre Ranking, and second and first in the Business Environment Risk Intelligence (BERI)'s ranking of cities with the most investment potential. Despite differences in their financial governance models which have stemmed from their different historical and political backgrounds, both nations have firmly established themselves as leading wealth management centres, although Singapore has been predicted to overtake Switzerland as the world's top wealth management centre by the end of the decade[15].

Singapore and Switzerland share many similarities in their fundamental approach to economic development. These include having low taxes, being open to trade, and having a diversified economy. The similarities between their economic outcomes are even more astonishing given their radically different evolutionary paths: while Singapore's economic success was the fruit of a carefully-planned national vision drawn up and sequentially implemented by experts, Switzerland's was a more organic process, the felicitous coincidence of cantonal competition, but like Singapore, undergirded by a strong rule of law and work ethic.

Both countries started out as poor, small states with a lack of natural resources (with the exception of water in the Swiss case); what they did have, however, is a strategic location and heterogeneous populations. Switzerland was situated at the heart of important Alpine trade routes linking northern and southern Europe; Singapore is located on the key trade route between China and India. Both countries have consequently benefited significantly from migration flows throughout the centuries, and served as magnets for regional and global talent.

---

[15]Wilson, Schwarz. "Singapore Expected to Dislodge Switzerland as World's Wealth Management Capital." AsiaOne Business, May 12, 2014. http://business.asiaone.com/news/singapore-expected-dislodge-switzerland-worlds-wealth-management-capital.

The difference is that industrial planning was politically centralised in Singapore while it was decentralised in Switzerland. Swiss cantons played to their industrial and competitive advantages, offering sets of incentives to attract investors, a pattern that continues to this day notably through the offering of different tax regimes. One of the legacies of this state-led versus industry-led economic structure is that government-linked companies (GLCs) continue to play a big role in Singapore's economy, while small-and-medium enterprises (SMEs) play a bigger role in Switzerland. This is linked to the fact that many SMEs in Switzerland started out in separate cantons, enabling each separate area to develop its own specialisation[16], while in Singapore, promising companies were given strong support by the state, allowing them to play a dominant role in the local economy.

Singapore: Economic development and strategies

In Singapore, two names are often associated with the planning and execution of modern Singapore's economic strategy: Albert Winsemius, a Dutch consultant who was Singapore's economic advisor from 1961 to 1984, and Goh Keng Swee, the second Deputy Prime Minister of Singapore. Both men were highly instrumental in Singapore's early industrialisation as well as its subsequent transition to a service economy. Under their guidance, three significant policy innovations were instituted in 1960s post-independence Singapore. These were the formation of the Jurong Industrial Estate, Economic Development Board (EDB) and the Asian Dollar Market.

The Jurong Industrial Estate was formed to drive industrialisation and provide employment during a time of high unemployment and labour unrest. This was particularly crucial with the withdrawal of British troops from their military bases in Singapore, which contributed to more than 20 percent of Singapore's GDP then and provided employment to 25,000 people. The British withdrawal provided the impetus for Singapore's rapid

---

[16]Breiding, R. James, *Swiss Made: The Untold Story Behind Switzerland's Success*. Profile Books, 2013.

industrialisation, with $900 million spent on urban renewal and infrastructural projects.

An important aspect of Singapore's industrialisation drive in the 1960s was attracting foreign investors and companies to set up businesses and factories in Singapore. Such an approach ran counter to that of other regional economies, which were operating instead from an import-substitution model of economic development that required extensive protectionism and favoured domestic firms. In contrast, Singapore was focused on attracting MNCs and other foreign businesses as its policymakers believed that the skills and expertise necessary for running successful businesses were lacking in newly-independent Singapore.

To this end, the EDB was established in 1961 as Singapore's lead government agency for planning and executing strategies to enhance the city-state's global economic position. This firmly established Singapore's adherence to a 'developmental state model' that placed the onus of driving Singapore's economic development on the EDB, with the state deriving the basis of its authority from a growth-centred "performance legitimacy"[17]. This adherence to performance legitimacy also affected Singapore's political development, as the election of political leaders into power came to be associated with their ability to provide continued economic growth. Given their strong track record in these areas, the PAP was thus able to secure its long tenure in office.

The third policy innovation that was introduced during this period and which would have profound implications for Singapore's subsequent development was the Asian Dollar Market (ADM). Established in 1968, the ADM was built on Singapore's time zone advantage, allowing it to bridge the "gap between the close of markets in the United States and the reopening of business the next day in Europe"[18]. Along with subsequent

---

[17]W.G. Huff, "The Developmental State, Government, and Singapore's Economic Development since 1960", *World Development* 23, no. 8 (August 1995): 1421–38; Martin Perry, *Singapore: A Developmental City State* (Chichester: Wiley, 1997); Linda Low, "The Singapore Developmental State in the New Economy and Polity", *The Pacific Review* 14, no. 3 (2001): 411–41.

[18]Ong Chong Tee, *Singapore's Policy of Non-Internationalisation of the Singapore Dollar and the Asian Dollar Market*, BIS Papers chapters (Bank for International Settlements, 2003), 96, http://econpapers.repec.org/bookchap/bisbisbpc/15-11.htm.

moves to abolish a withholding tax on interest income from non-resident foreign currency deposits in 1968 and other efforts to attract financial institutions, the ADM was a crucial foundation for Singapore's subsequent growth as a global financial centre.

As part of its "two-pronged strategy", the Singapore government had identified financial services as a key sector that could both support the development of existing industries and become a growth industry in its own right[19]. As a result, financial sector development did not fall under the purview of the EDB, but was managed by the Monetary Authority of Singapore (MAS), which was established in 1971 as the lead agency for regulating and developing Singapore's financial services sector.

These early policy innovations would come to define Singapore's future economic trajectory. Under the guidance of the EDB and with the success of Jurong Industrial Estate, manufacturing flourished in Singapore through the 1970s and 1980s. More importantly, more sophisticated products were being manufactured, such as computer parts, silicon wafers and electronics. This was largely driven by the government's emphasis on education and training, which had facilitated the emergence of a highly skilled and competitive workforce. As a result, more MNCs began locating their headquarters and research and development (R&D) functions in Singapore. The growth of manufacturing bode well for Singapore's exports and contributed immensely to the city's economic expansion. However, manufacturing was only part of the story.

With the success of the ADM, the formation of Singapore's stock exchange, and under the guidance of the MAS, Singapore's financial services sector began to take off in the 1970s. A 10-year development plan unveiled in 1975 explicitly articulated the government's desire to turn Singapore into a leading international financial centre and provided the guiding framework for subsequent policy measures adopted in the development of Singapore's financial services sector[20]. Like its

---

[19] Manuel F. Montes, "Tokyo, Hong Kong and Singapore as Competing Financial Centres", *Journal of Asian Business* 18, no. 1 (1999): 153–68.

[20] Kam-Hon Lee and Ilan Vertinsky, "Strategic Adjustment of International Financial Centres (IFCs) in Small Economies: A Comparative Study of Hong Kong and Singapore", *Journal of Business Administration* 17, no. 1–2 (1988–1987): 161.

industrialisation and the development of its manufacturing sector, the emergence of Singapore's financial services sector was driven and planned by the state.

However, it was only in the 1980s that Singapore's financial services sector took on an international character, with its banking, equity, asset management and foreign exchange sectors thriving under a robust legal-regulatory infrastructure and relative socio-political stability. Incentives unveiled in the 1993 Budget further sought to "develop an external economy" and "attract offshore activities to Singapore"[21]. This stimulated both the manufacturing and services sectors, as Singapore sought to extend beyond its limited domestic markets and leverage on burgeoning global demand.

As Singapore entered the new millennium, it continued to leverage on its existing strengths in manufacturing, technology and financial services. In recognition of the global growth of the technology sector, Singapore also announced plans to develop an 'information economy' by establishing a strong intellectual property (IP) protection regime. It has also announced plans to become a 'smart nation' by leveraging on emerging data analytics and sensor technologies. This focus on technology reflects the government's desire to reduce Singapore's reliance on foreign workers — a bugbear of GE2011 — and a need to identify and develop new emerging industries, as other emerging economies in Asia move up the value chain.

Like its political development, Singapore is facing a period of flux in its economic development. As other emerging economies industrialise and establish their strengths in manufacturing, Singapore is looking to expand its strengths in services and technology. However, Singapore's approach to economic governance remains largely unchanged. It is still seeking to develop exportable goods and services as sources of economic growth, under the aegis of lead agencies such as the EDB and MAS. Nonetheless, it is doing so from a position of relative strength.

---

[21] Chwee Huat Tan, *Financial Markets and Institutions in Singapore*, Tenth (Singapore: Singapore University Press, 1999), 15.

Switzerland: Economic development and strategies

A number of factors have been cited to explain the Swiss economic miracle: social mobility, urban self-government, Calvinism and Protestantism, high levels of education, the presence of an innovative class of entrepreneurs, managers, engineers, and a *laissez-faire*, free trade economic structure[22]. However, it is also important to bear in mind two caveats to the general narrative of Switzerland's successful bottom-up economic development in the last two centuries.

Firstly, and somewhat paradoxically, a number of the major reforms in Switzerland, which set the context for its economic success, were the direct result of the French invasion of Switzerland. For example, the French abolished taxes and tithes that farmers had to pay to landowners, weakening feudal dependency, and also abolished 'subjugated' regions placing all the cantons on an equal footing[23]. This set the stage for reform and cooperation across cantons in agriculture, and also in other sectors.

Secondly, despite Swiss agriculture and industry having developed relatively successfully in the 18th and 19th centuries, what we know today as the "Swiss miracle"[24] is very much a product of the late 20th century driven by the dizzying rise of the Swiss financial centre. Using data of Swiss real wages and prices in comparison with other European countries, Studer argued that "the rise of Swiss living standards to take a top position internationally was clearly a phenomenon of the short twentieth century"[25].

With these two caveats in mind, it is nevertheless important to present briefly the Swiss experience in industrial and economic development. Bergier spoke of unique aspects of the "Swiss model of

---

[22] Pollard, Sidney, and Richard S. Tedlow, *Economic History*. London: Routledge, 2002.

[23] Gerster, Richard, "Switzerland as an Emerging Economy: How Switzerland Became Rich". Richterswil, 2011. http://www.gersterconsulting.ch/docs/switzerland_as_an_emerging_economy_final.pdf.

[24] Studer, Roman, "When did the Swiss get so rich? Comparing Living Standards in Switzerland and Europe, 1800–1913".

[25] Studer, "When did the Swiss get so rich? Comparing Living Standards in Switzerland and Europe, 1800–1913". *Journal of European Economic History* 37, no. 2 (2008): 405–452.

industrialisation"[26]. Compared to other European countries, Switzerland was an early industrialiser[27]. With the influence of the French revolution, popular education had become widespread at the beginning of the 19th century, giving rise to a highly-skilled labour force that was fairly cheap, working out of small factories in rural settings, sometimes complemented by foreign labour.

These two advantages, coupled with Switzerland's early industrialisation, gave rise to Switzerland's comparative advantage of being able to process and add value to the resources it imported. For instance, Switzerland initially produced high quality silks, printed cottons and watches[28]. Swiss industrialisation was kickstarted by the textile industry at the end of the 18th century. With the help of steam machines, and shielded from English competition until 1815, Switzerland rose to become the second producer of cotton textiles. Although long since obsolete, the cotton manufacturing industry contributed indirectly to the growth of the chemical industry and the machine-making industry[29].

Switzerland also pursued the strategy of searching for niche markets, thereby converting its comparative advantage into absolute advantage in sectors as diverse as food, tourism, and banking[30] in addition to watchmaking and textiles, all with the reputation of high standards of quality. Another key characteristic of Swiss manufacturing was its inherently export-oriented character, which compensated for its small domestic market. Swiss companies capitalised on the opportunities opened up by other colonial powers to pursue overseas business opportunities[31].

The Swiss finance industry grew in tandem with the country's industrialisation. Switzerland's location as a trading hub in the heart of Europe meant that trading firms in Swiss city-states had to develop their

[26] Bergier, Jean-François, *Die Wirtschaftsgeschichte der Schweiz: von den Anfängen bis zur Gegenwart*. Benziger, 1990.
[27] Tortella, Gabriel, *The Origins of the Twenty First Century*. Routledge, 2009.
[28] Pollard, Sidney, and Richard S Tedlow, *Economic History*. London: Routledge, 2002.
[29] Gerster, "Switzerland as an Emerging Economy: How Switzerland Became Rich".
[30] Tortella, Gabriel, *The Origins of the Twenty First Century*. Routledge, 2009.
[31] Gerster, "Switzerland as an Emerging Economy: How Switzerland Became Rich".

own expertise in finance. Many private banking houses in St. Gallen, Basel, Zurich and Geneva originated from larger trading firms or were established from a particular industry, such as the textile industry in St. Gallen. The growth of the Swiss banking industry was further stimulated by the immigration of refugees from neighbouring states, a number of whom were financial specialists[32]. During the two world wars, Switzerland was a safe haven for capital and emerged relatively unscathed due to its neutrality.

Switzerland's transition to a service economy took place after the 1950s, when traditional industries such as the textile and metal industries came under the pressures of globalisation and the emergence of cheaper international competitors. Today, services such as banking, tourism and insurance make up 72.5 percent of Switzerland's GDP, compared to 26.8 percent for industry and 0.7 percent for agriculture[33]. Interestingly, 99 percent of companies in the Swiss economic landscape are small and medium-sized enterprises (SMEs), with less than 250 employees[34]. Finally, certain areas are associated with a particular industrial specialisation; for example the watch industry is centered around Jura in the northwest, IT companies in the Zurich–Lake Constance area in the northeast, financial services in the urban agglomerations of Zurich, Geneva, Basel and Lugano, and biotechnology clusters in Basel, Zurich, around Lake Geneva and Ticino[35].

Plan of the Book

The rest of this book articulates the arguments presented in this chapter in greater detail and granularity. Chapter 1 by Yvonne Guo and Andreas Ladner delineates and compares the public administration systems of the

---

[32] Woo Jun Jie and Yvonne Guo, "Wealth management for all seasons?" *The Straits Times*. 3 December 2013.
[33] CIA World Factbook, 2014. https://www.cia.gov/library/publications/the-world-factbook/geos/sz.html
[34] Swiss Federal Department of Trade and Investment Promotion. "Swiss Investment Handbook". 2012.
[35] *Ibid.*

two nations. Despite attaining similar levels of success and reputations of administrative efficiency, the authors argue that Switzerland's public administration is characterised by "input legitimacy" while that of Singapore is characterised by "output legitimacy". This assessment of the internal administrative intricacies of the two nations provides a solid foundation for subsequent policy-oriented chapters.

In Chapter 2, Yvonne Guo and J. J. Woo compare and contrast the foreign policy stances of the two nations, noting in particular that both exist in a context of small state vulnerability with the result being a continual need to balance or engage with other greater powers as well as to uphold neutrality amidst international disputes. Such engagement with the international environment is further explored by Michel Anliker in Chapter 3, as he addresses Singapore and Switzerland's approaches to trade liberalisation, focusing in particular on their participation in bilateral and international trade agreements.

Given their important positions as nodes of global financial and capital flows, Chapter 4 studies financial sector policy in Singapore and Switzerland. Despite differing state-industry configurations of financial governance, Yvonne Guo and J. J. Woo argue that Singapore and Switzerland are facing similar pressures as financial centres, and discuss the implications these portend. Delving deeper into state infrastructure and how it has shaped transport policy, Bruno Wildermuth compares the urban transport policies of both nations in Chapter 5.

Both Singapore and Switzerland are also known for being attractive business and education hubs. In this perspective, Manuel Baeuml discusses the SME landscape in the two nations in Chapter 6, focusing in particular on the key market factors that have driven their divergent SME trajectories. Philippe Régnier and Pascal Wild compare Singapore and Switzerland's economic profiles in Chapter 7, with reference to the Global Entrepreneurship Monitor reports. Chapter 8 by Suzanne Hraba-Renevey and Yvonne Guo discusses both nations' education policies and their evolution towards being knowledge-based societies.

Subsequent chapters focus less on the economy and more on the socio-cultural landscape. Specifically, Chapter 9 by Yvonne Guo compares the ways in which Singapore and Switzerland manage ethnic and linguistic diversity through 'consocialism' in the former and 'multiculturalism' in the latter. In a similar vein, Chapter 10 by Hui Weng Tat and Cindy Helfer discuss how Singapore and Switzerland address the challenges arising from labour migration, focusing specifically on the lessons that Singapore may draw from Swiss policy successes and failures in its migration and labour market policies. Mehmet Kerem Çoban seeks to explain rising inequality in Singapore and Switzerland from a power-resource perspective in Chapter 11. Finally, the editors conclude by returning to the core questions that have stimulated the conception of this book: what can Singapore and Switzerland learn from each other? And what do the divergent success strategies of both countries tell us about good governance in small states?

References

Bergier, J.-F. *Die Wirtschaftsgeschichte der Schweiz: von den Anfängen bis zur Gegenwart.* Benziger, 1990.

Breiding, R. James, and G. Schwarz. *Swiss Made: The Untold Story Behind Switzerland's Success.* Profile Books, 2013.

Brouwer, G. D., and W. Pupphavesa. *Asia-Pacific Financial Deregulation.* Routledge, 2002.

Department of Trade and Investment Promotion. "Swiss Investment Handbook," 2002.

Fossedal, G. A. *Direct Democracy in Switzerland.* Transaction Publishers, 2005.

Gerster, R. "Switzerland as an Emerging Economy: How Switzerland Became Rich." Richterswil, 2011. http://www.gersterconsulting.ch/docs/switzerland_as_an_emerging_economy_final.pdf.

Government of Singapore. *Constitutional Amendments to Safeguard Financial Assets and the Integrity of the Public Services.* Singapore National Printers, 1988.

Guo, Y., and J. J. Woo. "Wealth Management for All Seasons?," December 5, 2013. http://business.asiaone.com/news/wealth-management-all-seasons.

Hamilton-Hart, N. "The Singapore State Revisited." *The Pacific Review* 13, no. 2 (January 2000): 195–216. doi:10.1080/095127400363550.

Han, J. "Communal Riots of 1964." *National Library Board*, September 18, 2014. http://eresources.nlb.gov.sg/infopedia/articles/SIP_45_2005-01-06.html.

Huff, W. G. "The Developmental State, Government, and Singapore's Economic Development since 1960." *World Development* 23, no. 8 (August 1995): 1421–38. doi:10.1016/0305-750X(95)00043-C.

Katzenstein, P. J. *Small States in World Markets: Industrial Policy in Europe.* Cornell Studies in Political Economy. Ithaca, NY: Cornell University Press, 1985.

Kwa, C. G., D. Thiam Soon Heng, and Tai Y. T. *Singapore, a 700-Year History: From Early Emporium to World City.* National Archives of Singapore, 2009.

Lau, A. *A Moment of Anguish: Singapore in Malaysia and the Politics of Disengagement.* Eastern Universities Press, 2003.

Lee, K.-H., and I. Vertinsky, "Strategic Adjustment of International Financial Centres (IFCs) in Small Economies: A Comparative Study of Hong Kong and Singapore," *Journal of Business Administration* 17, no. 1–2 (1988 1987): 161.

Leifer, M. *Singapore's Foreign Policy: Coping with Vulnerability.* Psychology Press, 2000.

LePoer, B. L. *Singapore: A Country Study.* Library of Congress, Federal Research Division, 1989.

Lijphart, A. *Patterns of Democracy: Government Forms and Performance in Thirty-Six Countries.* Yale University Press, 1999.

Low, L. "The Singapore Developmental State in the New Economy and Polity." *The Pacific Review* 14, no. 3 (January 2001): 411–41. doi:10.1080/09512740110064848.

Montes, M. F. "Tokyo, Hong Kong and Singapore as Competing Financial Centres," *Journal of Asian Business* 18, no. 1 (1999): 153–68.

Mutalib, H. "Constitutional-Electoral Reforms and Politics in Singapore." *Legislative Studies Quarterly* 27, no. 4 (2002): 659–672.

Norris, P. "Choosing Electoral Systems: Proportional, Majoritarian and Mixed Systems." *International Political Science Review* 18, no. 3 (July 1, 1997): 297–312. doi:10.1177/019251297018003005.

Ong, C. T. "Singapore's Policy of Non-Internationalisation of the Singapore Dollar and the Asian Dollar Market." BIS Papers chapters. Bank for International Settlements, 2003. https://ideas.repec.org/h/bis/bisbpc/15-11.html.

Pang, Y.-N. "Crisis Narratives in Political Discourse in Singapore," 2005. http://scholarbank.nus.edu.sg/handle/10635/14442.

Perry, M., L. Kong, and B. S. A. Yeoh. *Singapore: A Developmental City State.* Wiley, 1997.

Pollard, S., and R. S. Tedlow. *Economic History*. London: Routledge, 2002.

Studer, R. "When did the Swiss get so rich? Comparing Living Standards in Switzerland and Europe, 1800–1913." *Journal of European Economic History* 37, no. 2 (2008): 405-452.

Tan, B. "Raffles Town Plan." *National Library Board*, 2002. http://eresources.nlb.gov.sg/infopedia/articles/SIP_658_2005-01-07.html.

Tan, C. H. *Financial Markets and Institutions in Singapore*. Singapore: Singapore University Press, 1999.

Tan, L. Y. "The Next Lap." *National Library Board*. Accessed April 19, 2016. http://eresources.nlb.gov.sg/infopedia/articles/SIP_165_2004-12-23.html.

Tan, K. P. "Meritocracy and Elitism in a Global City: Ideological Shifts in Singapore", *International Political Science Review* 29, no. 1 (2008): 11–17.

"The World Factbook." *Central Intelligence Agency*, March 24, 2016. https://www.cia.gov/library/publications/the-world-factbook/geos/sz.html.

Tortajada, C., and A. K. Biswas. *Asian Perspectives on Water Policy*. Routledge, 2013.

Tortella, G. *The Origins of the Twenty First Century*. Routledge, 2009.

Vertinsky, I. and K.-H. Lee. *Strategic Adjustment of International Financial Centres (IFCs) in Small Economies: A Comparative Study of Hong Kong and Singapore*. Vancouver: University of British Columbia, Faculty of Commerce and Business Administration, 1988.

Wilson, S. "Singapore Expected to Dislodge Switzerland as World's Wealth Management Capital." *AsiaOne Business*, May 12, 2014. http://business.asiaone.com/news/singapore-expected-dislodge-switzerland-worlds-wealth-management-capital.

Chapter 1

Public Administration in Singapore and Switzerland

Yvonne Guo and Andreas Ladner

Introduction: Comparing Countries and Administrative Systems

"Both Singapore and Switzerland exist as extreme acts of political will," declared former head of the Singapore civil service, Mr Lim Siong Guan, during a seminar in Zurich in May 2014. The 'political will' he was referring to, however, springs from different sources in both countries. When the Swiss describe themselves as a *'Willensnation'*, they refer to the unity of their nation by free will, the voluntary coming together of linguistically diverse cantons.[1] When Singaporeans talk about 'political will', however, they are referring to an 'elite' will[2] to achieve a set of predetermined objectives.

As discussed in the previous chapter, Singapore and Switzerland are politically and institutionally very different. One is a highly centralised state led by a single party and characterised by "top-down" governance, while the other is a highly decentralised state led by a coalition of political parties and characterised by "bottom-up" governance. Yet both Singapore and Switzerland have achieved high standards of public facilities and services, and have an effective civil service and high state capacities. Thus

---

[1] Fossedal, Gregory A, *Direct Democracy in Switzerland.* Transaction Publishers, 2005.
[2] Yen-Ning, Pang, "Crisis Narratives in Political Discourse in Singapore", 2005. http://scholarbank.nus.edu.sg/handle/10635/14442. See also Tortajada, Cecilia, and Asit K. Biswas. *Asian Perspectives on Water Policy.* Routledge, 2013.

they are interesting cases for comparison using a most-different-systems design. This chapter seeks to pin down why two systems that are structurally so different work for their citizens. Using Scharpf's concept of "input" and "output" legitimacy, it argues that Switzerland is characterised by "input legitimacy", while Singapore is characterised by "output legitimacy".

Role of the administration in society

Public administration plays a crucial role in any society. The civil service keeps the state running and provides the facilities and services needed by citizens. It is here where a government's decisions and policies are implemented and executed. The way this is done as well as the relationship between the civil service, politicians and citizens, however, varies over time and between countries.

From the perspective of citizens, it is important that they are satisfied with the services provided by their civil service, that they trust in its efficiency and in its impartiality, and that they feel that the civil service is here for them and not the other way round. In Switzerland, despite recurrent claims for reforms and improvements, this is generally the way the civil service is perceived. In Switzerland, 76 percent of citizens reported having confidence in their national government in 2012,[3] and comparative studies show that, on the local level, confidence is even higher than in other high-trust countries such as Denmark, Norway and the Netherlands.[4] In Singapore, 67 percent of citizens reported high trust levels.[5] According to the Asia Barometer, institutions such as the police, military, government, law courts and civil service enjoy high levels of public trust in Singapore.[6] Notwithstanding this,

---

[3] OECD "Switzerland Fact Sheet", 2013. Accessed from http://www.oecd.org/gov/ GAAG2013_CFS_CHE.pdf

[4] Deters, Bas, Michael Goldsmith, Andreas Ladner, Poul Erik Mouritzen and Lawrence E. Rose (2014). *Size and Local Democracy*. Cheltenham: Edward Elgar.

[5] "2013 Edelman Trust Barometer". *Edelman*. Accessed from http://www.edelman.com/ insights/intellectual-property/trust-2013/.

[6] "Public Governance and Public Trust — Part 2." www.cscollege.gov.sg, April 7, 2012. https://www.cscollege.gov.sg/Knowledge/Pages/Public-Governance-and-Public-Trust-Part-2.aspx

political commentators have noted the existence of 'blurred lines' between the civil service and politics in Singapore,[7] with former civil servants frequently running for political office.

A second distinctive element is the recruitment of civil servants. Are they life-time bureaucrats with particular privileges or are they simple employees of the state without extensive additional benefits? Are civil servants recruited on the basis of merit, do they have to pass specific exams, or are they simply employed by different departments on the basis of their competences? Swiss civil servants can best be described as employees of the public sector, generally recruited by their hierarchical superiors in different departments and services.[8] The civil service is open and based on merit or competencies. No special diplomas or entrance exams are required. Salaries and benefits do not differ considerably from the private sector other than being a bit higher in the lower brackets and considerably lower in the top brackets. In Singapore, the recruitment of most of its 60,000 civil servants is done by individual ministries as well. However, within the civil service exists a group of about 270 Administrative Officers who are rotated throughout different ministries and work closely with the political leadership to formulate policies.[9] These 'top-tier' civil servants undergo a stringent selection procedure. Many of them are selected just after completing their 'A' levels, and given full scholarships to pursue their tertiary studies at prestigious universities in Singapore and around the world. In return, they are bonded to the civil service for a period of up to six years. Salaries in the Singapore civil service are also comparable with those in the private sector. However, the salaries of senior civil servants, known as Administrative Officers, are

---

[7] "Civil Service: Keeping It a Success Factor". *TODAYonline*. Accessed March 4, 2015. http://m.todayonline.com/singapore/civil-service-keeping-it-success-factor.

[8] Emery, Yves (2013). "Neue Politiken und Prozesse im Personalmanagement", in: Ladner, Andreas, Jean-Loup Chappelet, Yves Emery, Peter Knoepfel, Luzius Mader, Nils Soguel und Frédéric Varone (Hrsg.). *Handbuch der öffentlichen Verwaltung in der Schweiz.* Zürich: NZZ libro. S. pp. 479–498.

[9] "The Singapore Public Service: A Development-Oriented Promotion System". www.cscollege.gov.sg, December 11, 2013. https://www.cscollege.gov.sg/Knowledge/Ethos/Ethos%20Issue%201,%202002/Pages/The%20Singapore%20Public%20Service%20A%20Development-Oriented%20Promotion%20System.aspx

pegged to two-thirds the median salary among the top eight earners from six professions (bankers, lawyers, engineers, accountants, employees of MNCs and local manufacturers). This was justified on the grounds of attracting the best talent and avoiding corruption.

A third element concerns the functioning of the administration and more particularly its internal processes. Especially since the emergence of New Public Management (NPM) — the concept that ideas used in the private sector can be successful in the public sector — the question has been whether public administration functions according to prescriptions, rules and specific resources allocated to different activities or whether there are more output-oriented forms of steering using global budgeting and performance contracts. Although Switzerland started NPM reforms relatively late, they had quite an impact on the functioning of the civil service. Without leaving the traditional Weberian model of bureaucracy completely behind, new NPM-based forms of organising internal processes have considerably influenced the civil service. Similarly, NPM reforms in Singapore's civil service had an impact on the country's "developmental state" strategy emphasising national economic development based on state ownership and economic control. The NPM reforms introduced led to the privatisation of state enterprises, the contracting out of services, and the liberalisation of sectors such as finance, telecommunications and utilities.[10]

A final distinctive element is the relationship between administration and politics. Throughout the history of public administration there has been debates about whether the administration is really an independent body acting according to laws and regulations, or whether the administration is more closely linked to the political leaders or parties in power. In the latter case, a change of the party in power would automatically lead to a replacement of top-level civil servants with civil servants politically close to the new party in power. Additionally, the question of the autonomy of civil servants is often raised: do civil servants simply execute political decisions or do they also shape and influence them and become political actors themselves?

---

[10] Haque, M.S., "Governance and Bureaucracy in Singapore: Contemporary Reforms and Implications". *International Political Science Review* 25, no. 2 (April 1, 2004): 227–40. doi:10.1177/0192512104042314.

In this regard, the Swiss civil service is not political but politically influential. Other than for positions very close to the minister, party membership is not a decisive element for promotion and a new minister from a different party does not necessarily lead to top-level civil servants of his party. Civil servants, nowadays, are well-trained experts in their domains. Many solutions to complex problems have to be sought, and especially where international coordination is needed, this information gap tends to play into the hands of civil servants. In Singapore, the close relationship between politicians and civil servants and the frequent movement of civil servants into politics, accentuated by the fact that Singapore has been governed by the same party since 1959, has led to the perception that there is no clear distinction between political and administrative elites. Chan Heng Chee, a political scientist who later became Singapore's ambassador to the United States, conceptualised Singapore as an 'administrative state',[11] describing Singapore's style of government as one which emphasised "the elimination of politics" in favour of placing "trust in experts and expertise in planning and implementation"[12] although this is difficult to prove. In such a context, "senior bureaucrats… are regarded as the natural allies and successors to political leadership".[13]

Different state and administrative traditions

Governing from the bottom-up in Switzerland

Swiss public administration does not perfectly fit into the common European typologies of administrative systems and is sometimes called a hybrid containing elements of the Scandinavian, the Napoleonic and the Anglo-Saxon models.[14] Characteristic elements are the strong decentralisation giving considerable discretion to the lower state units, the lack of a clear separation between the state and the private sector, and an accessible public service considered to be on eye-level with the citizens.

---

[11] Chan, Heng Chee, *Politics in an Administrative State: Where Has the Politics Gone?*. University of Singapore, Department of Political Science, 1975.
[12] Saw, Swee-Hock, and R.S. Bhathal, *Singapore Towards the Year 2000*. NUS Press, 1981.
[13] Ibid.
[14] Kuhlmann, Sabine and Hellmut Wollmann (2014). Introduction to Comparative Public Administration. Administrative Systems and Reforms in Europe. Cheltenham: Edward Elgar. p. 21.

The history of Swiss bottom-up nation building prevented the formation of a strong nation-state with a large and powerful administration.[15] All the competences the national government and its administration possess today had to be transferred to them through the consent of the people and the cantons at the polls. The cantons jealously guarded their competences and, with them, their particularities in important domains such as education, health and many others, and only reluctantly accepted attempts to harmonise legislation for the whole country. They were, not astonishingly, particularly hesitant to grant the national government the right to levy tax on income and wealth as well as to collect value-added tax (VAT). The highest possible tax rates are written down in the Constitution and cannot be changed without the direct democratic consent of the cantons and the citizens. Where nationwide programs are needed, the national government is responsible for regulatory activities, while the implementation and execution of the programs remain in the hands of the lower units. Swiss federalism can thus best be described as a cooperative, leaving room for tailor-made solutions. The political system remains characterised by diversity, with far-reaching competences of the lower state units. There are considerably more civil servants working for the 26 cantons and the more than 2,300 municipalities and cities than there are for the national government.

The small size of many of the cantons, together with a larger number of very small municipalities, also hampered the formation of a large and strong state sector. Very much in line with the predominant doctrine of liberalism, and because of Switzerland's territorial organisation, a close cooperation with the private sector was inevitable. Especially on the local level, the outsourcing of specific tasks, such as road maintenance or the assessment of working permits, was practiced long before New Public Management asked for it. The main reason for this was the small size of most of the municipalities, resulting in their inability to run a large professional administration. The ratio of public

---

[15] Ladner, Andreas (2013). "Der Schweizer Staat, politisches Systems und Aufgabenerbringung", in: Ladner, Andreas, Jean-Loup Chappelet, Yves Emery, Peter Knoepfel, Luzius Mader, Nils Soguel und Frédéric Varone (Hrsg.). *Handbuch der öffentlichen Verwaltung in der Schweiz*. Zürich: NZZ libro. S. 23–46.

spending to gross national product (GNP) in Switzerland is comparatively low, not because services and facilities do not exist but because they are provided for in a mixed system together with the private sector and do not enter the state budget, similar to the compulsory health insurance or an important part of the old age pension scheme. In a similar vein, only very few politicians are full-time politicians. Most Members of Parliament fulfill their mandate on a part-time basis and usually have another professional engagement. This is even more so the case at the lower levels and it is commonly referred to as the "militia system" (*Milizsystem*). Apart from saving costs, the main advantage of such a system is that politicians do not lose touch with society and the private sector, and this is meant to bring politics closer to the people.

Another distinct characteristic is the autonomy of the lower-level units when it comes to their budget. In general, cantons and municipalities are responsible for their expenditures and have to cover them through their own income. The amount of transfers from the central government is rather low, but in exchange, they collect the larger part of the tax on income and wealth, which is the major tax in Switzerland. Here, they also set the tax rate which can vary considerably from one municipality to another and from one canton to another. As predicted by the theory of fiscal federalism, this puts pressure on the lower level units, the cantons and the municipalities, to provide their services efficiently and to cut unnecessary costs for the administration. An increase in expenditure due to overambitious projects or an inefficient administration is likely to cause an increase in the tax rate which then might lead to the loss of taxpayers if they choose to 'vote with their feet'. Since opportunities are unequally distributed over the country and there are huge differences between the financial centers such as Zurich and Geneva and the mountainous areas in the Alps, there is a redistribution scheme which operates not only vertically from the central government to the poorer cantons, but also horizontally from the richer to the poorer cantons. It guarantees minimal standard living conditions for the disadvantaged areas.

In a nutshell, all the principles which can be found on the reform agenda of New Public Management — such as decentralisation, cooperation with the private sector, fiscal equivalence and citizen orientation — are not particularly new for Switzerland but rather the result of bottom-up nation building and the lack of a strong central power or emperor in the past. Cultural diversity has led to the acceptance of pragmatic solutions, often combining elements of different schools and theories. Switzerland has neither a presidential nor a parliamentary system, it is a hybrid of both. It is neither a Scandinavian welfare state nor is it a liberal country like the United States. It fosters competition between the lower levels but it has an elaborate system of equalising differences. It promotes self-responsibility but it has an inclusive system of social security, old age pension, unemployment benefits and health insurance.

Governing from the top-down in Singapore

Like Switzerland, Singapore has been described as a 'hybrid' of various types of administrative traditions in the sense that it displays characteristics of the colonial-bureaucratic, the developmental, and the new public management 'Southeast Asian' models.[16] Its colonial-bureaucratic heritage is evident in the way it has adopted the British model of parliamentary democracy and institutions such as the Public Service Commission, driven by principles such as meritocracy, efficiency and pragmatism. Civil servants are clearly subordinate to political leaders in accordance with Weberian principles. Singapore also adheres to the development administration model, in the sense that the Singapore public service was primarily responsible for the planning and implementation of Singapore's long-term economic development. Singapore chose to do so by establishing government-linked companies and forming partnerships with investors. In this sense, new public management is also compatible with Singapore because market-based principles have been at the core of Singapore's developmental strategy since independence. Features of NPM are present in key public service initiatives, such as PS21 (Public Service for the 21st Century), which emphasised innovation, greater ministerial autonomy and the importance

---

[16] Haque, M. Shamsul, "Theory and Practice of Public Administration in Southeast Asia: Traditions, Directions, and Impacts". *International Journal of Public Administration* 30, no. 12–14 (November 9, 2007): 1297–1326. doi:10.1080/01900690701229434.

of attracting talent, but crucially did not question the leading role of the state.[17] According to Martin Painter, "corporatisation and privatisation have been pursued, but not to the extent of undermining control of these corporations by the political and bureaucratic elites." Unlike the other 'Asian Tigers', the Singapore government owns its biggest companies.[18]

Thus in Singapore, it is the state that is guided by the logic of pragmatism, rationality and efficiency. The description of Singapore being run like a corporation — "Singapore Inc" (used to refer to the combination of government and government-linked corporations) — remains in vogue; the government remains very much committed to fiscal prudence. Public spending in Singapore was a mere 14.2 percent of GDP in 2013,[19] and limited welfare provisions mean that self-reliance is encouraged, with social assistance only offered as a last resort.

Therefore, the principles of New Public Management exist in Singapore and even predated the movement itself, but were precisely the product of a deliberate state strategy to seek partnerships with the private sector and embrace internationalisation at a time when poor countries looked at multinational corporations with much suspicion. However, Singapore has adopted the means and methods of NPM but not its fundamental assumption — that the private sector can do a better job than the state itself. Rather, Singapore prides itself on a careful blend of state-managed capitalism and indirect forms of control, guided foremost by the twin tenets of meritocracy and pragmatism.

Public administration in Singapore is very much characterised by the idea of merit-driven elite governance; both civil servants and politicians are selected on the basis of achievement criteria, and the public service actively competes with the private sector for the best

---

[17] McLaughlin, Kathleen, Ewan Ferlie, Professor and Head of Department the School of Management Ewan Ferlie, and Stephen Osborne P, *New Public Management: Current Trends and Future Prospects.* Routledge, 2005.

[18] "Whither Singapore Inc?" *The Economist*, November 28, 2002. http://www.economist.com/node/1465814.

[19] Singapore Budget 2014. http://www.singaporebudget.gov.sg/data/budget_2014/download/FY2014_Analysis_of_Revenue_and_Expenditure.pdf

talent.[20] Singapore's improbable economic success has often been attributed to the vision and foresight of its team of legendary first-generation leaders. Wedded to this is the belief that an equally talented and capable leadership is needed to sustain Singapore's economic miracle. To this end, a number of policies in Singapore are devoted to recruiting the best possible talents for civil service jobs, such as giving out prestigious government scholarships to finance the university education of top students, or paying competitive salaries to top civil service and political office holders that are pegged to that of the private sector. For example, meritocracy is taken to its logical end through the creation of the Management Associates Programme, the elite scheme within the Singapore civil service. The civil servants who are part of this programme are groomed to take on leadership positions in the civil service; they are rotated through different ministries in order to hone their management skills, and are occasionally 'seconded' out to other government-linked organisations or companies. They are also rigorously evaluated by their peers and superiors on a regular basis, using a rubric based on Shell's human resource methodology emphasising HAIR qualities — *helicopter* ability, power of *analysis*, their sense of *imagination* and their sense of *reality*.

Singapore and Switzerland: Similar in Output Legitimacy, Different in Input Legitimacy

The concepts of input and output legitimacy are very helpful in understanding the similarities and differences between the two countries. In 1970, using the case study of the European Union, Scharpf theorised democratic legitimacy in two dimensions, which he referred to as the 'inputs' and the 'outputs' of a political system. Alluding to Lincoln's famous assertion about democracy, Scharpf suggested that input legitimacy was political participation 'by' the people, while output legitimacy referred to effective governing 'for' the people. In other words, input legitimacy referred to the existence of 'mechanisms or procedures' that

---

[20] Quah, Jon S.T., *Public Administration Singapore–Style*. Emerald Group Publishing, 2010.

linked political decisions with citizens' preferences, while output legitimacy referred to 'achieving the goals that citizens collectively care about'. Institutions had to 'work', 'perform', or be able to 'deliver the goods', because if democratic processes were not able to produce effective outcomes, democracy would be an 'empty ritual'.[21]

Other authors added that input legitimacy focused on democratic elements of decision making, emphasising consent and 'what to do' rather than on 'what to obtain',[22] and the process of gaining citizen consent by making sure that their preferences were taken into account through participation channels.[23] Output legitimacy, on the other hand, focused on outcomes, or the "utilitarian/welfare-economics-oriented criterion of the best possible attempt to achieve a particular political goal".[24]

In 1999, Scharpf clarified his definition by arguing that input legitimacy referred to the participatory quality of the process leading to laws and rules as ensured by the 'majoritarian' institutions of electoral representation, while output legitimacy was concerned with the problem-solving quality of the laws and rules, and was guaranteed by a range of institutional mechanisms. He found that both input and output legitimacy were necessary for democratic legitimisation, but stated that in the case of the EU, both forms of legitimacy were facing serious challenges.

The debate in the literature has also focused on the notion of a trade-off between 'input' and 'output' legitimacy, which has also been related to

---

[21] Boedeltje, Mijke, and Juul Cornips, *Input and Output Legitimacy in Interactive Governance*. NIG Annual Work Conference 2004 Rotterdam, October 19, 2004. http://repub.eur.nl/res/pub/1750/

[22] Beisheim, Marianne, and Klaus Dingwerth, "Procedural Legitimacy and Private Transnational Governance", 2008. http://www.edocs.fu-berlin.de/docs/receive/FUDOCS_document_000000000337.

[23] Lieberherr, Eva, "The Role of Throughput in the Input-Output Legitimacy Debate: Insights from Public and Private Governance Modes in the Swiss and". Accessed March 4, 2015. http://icpublicpolicy.web2.mezcalito.net/IMG/pdf/panel_39_s2_lieberherr.pdf.

[24] Wolf, Klaus Dieter, "Contextualizing Normative Standards for Legitimate Governance beyond the State". In *Participatory Governance*, edited by Jürgen R. Grote and Bernard Gbikpi, 35–50. VS Verlag für Sozialwissenschaften, 2002. http://link.springer.com/chapter/10.1007/978-3-663-11003-3_2.

the notion of the 'democratic dilemma'[25] or the conflict between system capacity and citizen effectiveness as described by Dahl and Tufte.[26] An emphasis on output could lead to a 'democratic deficit' if citizens' preferences were not taken into consideration. However, an emphasis on input could result in a lower output due to longer decision-making processes, or because citizens might not act in favour of the common good.[27] There are various ways to measure output legitimacy. At the core of the concept is the performance of a given government or of the political system as such.

Following Scharpf, there are three types of requirements for output-related democratic legitimacy: economic prosperity, realisation of the common good and prevention of tyranny.[28] The first requirement is quite easy to measure but falls only to some extent into the responsibility of the national government and its administration. Nevertheless, as we have seen, both Singapore and Switzerland constantly rank in the top group when it comes to the gross domestic product (GDP) per capita.[29] According to other indicators which more directly capture government effectiveness and performance,[30] Switzerland and Singapore have performed remarkably well. They were ranked 5th and 7th worldwide on the Corruption Perception Index (2014), and 1st and 2nd worldwide in the Global Competitiveness Index.

---

[25] Dahl, Robert A, "A Democratic Dilemma: System Effectiveness versus Citizen Participation". *Political Science Quarterly* 109, no. 1 (April 1, 1994): 23–34. doi:10.2307/2151659.

[26] Dahl, Robert Alan, and Edward R. Tufte, *Size and Democracy*. Stanford University Press, 1973.

[27] Lieberherr, Eva, "The Role of Throughput in the Input-Output Legitimacy Debate: Insights from Public and Private Governance Modes". Accessed March 4, 2015. http://icpublicpolicy.web2.mezcalito.net/IMG/pdf/panel_39_s2_lieberherr.pdf.

[28] Scharpf, F.W. (1970). *Demokratietheorie zwischen Utopie und Anpassung*. Konstanz: Universitätsverlag.

[29] See for example http://data.worldbank.org/indicator/NY.GDP.PCAP.PP.CD/countries?display=default. Accessed March 19, 2015.

[30] Zweifel, Thomas D, *International Organizations and Democracy: Accountability, Politics, and Power*. Swiss Consulting Group, Inc., 2006.

Table 1: Corruption Perception Index (2014)

Country	Score	Rank
Singapore	84	7
Switzerland	86	5

Source: "How Corrupt Is Your Country?" Accessed March 4, 2015. http://www.transparency.org/cpi2014/infographic.

Table 2: Global Competitiveness Index (2014)

Country	Score	Rank
Singapore	5.6	2
Switzerland	5.7	1

Source: "Global Competitiveness Report 2014–2015". *World Economic Forum*. Accessed March 4, 2015. http://reports.weforum.org/global-competitiveness-report-2014-2015/.

The Worldwide Governance Indicators (2013) provides a more telling breakdown of different areas of governance: voice and accountability, political stability, government effectiveness, regulatory quality, rule of law and control of corruption. Here, Switzerland scored above the 90th percentile for all indicators, while Singapore scored above the 90th percentile for all indicators except Voice and Accountability, where it scored only in the 52nd percentile. Voice and Accountability measures the 'input' side of legitimacy, while the other five indicators measure the 'output' side of legitimacy. The rankings suggest that both countries are globally acknowledged to be models of good governance in terms of 'output' legitimacy. In terms of 'input' legitimacy, however, Switzerland is perceived to be more accountable to its citizens.

Rankings that explicitly take 'input legitimacy' indicators into account, such as the Economist Intelligence Unit's Democracy Index, illustrate a substantial gap between Singapore and Switzerland across

Table 3:   Worldwide Governance Indicators (2013)

Country	Voice and Accountability	Political Stability	Government Effectiveness	Regulatory Quality	Rule of Law	Control of Corruption
Singapore	52.1	95.7	99.5	100	96.3	96.7
Switzerland	96.6	97.6	97.6	94.3	96.7	97.6

Source: "World Governance Indicators 2013". Accessed March 4, 2015. http://info.worldbank.org/governance/wgi/index.aspx#home.

Table 4:   *The Economist Intelligence Unit* Democracy Index (2013)

Country	Rank	Score	Electoral Process and Pluralism	Functioning Government	Political Participation	Political Culture	Civil Liberties
Singapore	80	5.89	4.33	7.14	3.89	6.88	7.35
Switzerland	7	9.09	9.58	9.29	7.78	9.38	9.41

Source: "Democracy Index 2013". *Economist Intelligence Unit.* Accessed March 4, 2015. http://www.eiu.com/public/topical_report.aspx?campaignid=Democracy0814.

indicators such as electoral process and political participation. The Democracy Index gave Singapore fairly high scores in terms of functioning government, political culture and civil liberties, but seemed to suggest that institutional factors were to account for the lack of citizen 'input' in the electoral and political process. A closer look at the methodology for the Democracy Index suggests that factors such as the limited presence of opposition members in Singapore's government as well as restrictions on the press and public demonstrations could have explained its score.

How to Bring the People in: Direct Democracy vs. Public Consultation

Indicators may be a useful guide, but they merely provide a one-dimensional and rather simplistic snapshot of input legitimacy in Singapore and Switzerland. If input legitimacy is "government by the people", the question is: To what extent are the citizens really able to make them heard and to influence their government's policies? Here, the two countries — as we will see in this section — build upon two completely different concepts: direct democracy in Switzerland and public consultation in Singapore.

Chart I: Forms of consultation

	Method of selection			
Public opinion	1. Self-selection	2. Non-random sample	3. Random sample	4. "Everyone"
A. Raw	1A. SLOPs	2A. Some polls	3A. Most polls	4. Referendum democracy
B. Refined	1B. Discussion groups	2B. Citizens' juries, etc.	3B. Deliberative polls	4B. 'Deliberation Day'

Source: Fishkin, James, *When the People Speak: Deliberative Democracy and Public Consultation*. Oxford University Press, 2009.
(*Note*: SLOPs refer to 'Self-Selected Listener Opinion Poll'). Chart taken from Fishkin (2009)

Applying Fishkin's eight methods of Public Consultation (Fishkin, 2009)[31] to Switzerland and Singapore illustrates the significant differences between both countries. While the practice of referendum democracy is highly ingrained in Switzerland, public consultation in Singapore generally relies on the practice of convening self-selected discussion groups or publishing public consultation papers regarding proposed policy changes on government websites for the public to respond to.

Direct democracy: Institutionalised public decision making in Switzerland

When people reflect on direct democracy in Switzerland, they usually only look at the tip of the iceberg, at referendums and initiatives on the national level. Of course, there have been some spectacular decisions that resulted from this process: when Swiss citizens refused to abolish the army in 1989, refused to join the European Economic Area in 1992, prohibited the construction of minarets in 2009, or refused to extend holidays to six weeks a year in 2012. However, the bulk of decisions take place at lower levels and they are, by far, not as spectacular. In his/her active political life, a Swiss citizen is called for up to 1500 decisions at the polls on a huge variety of questions. They concern smaller or larger adjustments of the constitution

---

[31] Fishkin, James. *When the People Speak: Deliberative Democracy and Public Consultation*. Oxford University Press, 2009.

and laws, new legislation, and very often, costly projects such as new tramways, parks, school buildings, museums, football grounds and such.

Most importantly, Swiss direct democracy has little to do with citizen participation as it is discussed in many other countries nowadays. Of course, it offers citizens additional possibilities to participate politically but it is, above all, about binding political decisions that have to be implemented. The government does not want to know what the people want; it is told what it has to do. For instance, the government wanted to join the European Economic Area but the people refused. Similarly, it did not want to prohibit the construction of minarets, but the citizens wanted such a ban and thus the Constitution was amended accordingly.

It is also important to state that direct democracy was not simply given to the citizens because the parties in power wanted to let them participate in the decision-making process. The concept has its origin in the French Revolution which emphasised the sovereignty of the people. As the prominent Swiss philosopher Jean-Jacques Rousseau has mentioned, the sovereignty of the people is best exercised directly and not through representatives in Parliament. Starting off with a very minimalistic Constitution in 1848, the mandatory referendum was the price to pay for getting a more ambitious constitution accepted, giving more competences to the central state. The initiative for a partial revision of the constitution granted in 1891 was also a means to safeguard the existing constitution in its totality. On a lower level, the ideas of the French Revolution fell on even more fertile grounds. Referendums and initiatives were introduced earlier and were met with already existing means of local self-government in the form of citizens' assemblies.

Often the question arises on whether Swiss direct democracy can be practised in other countries. It is not the place here to enter into this debate; however, it has to be kept in mind that direct democracy also has an impact on other elements of the political system. To prevent strong parties from obstructing the decisions of government and parliament by the means of a referendum, they have to be integrated into governmental responsibilities. This mechanism, at least to some extent, helps to explain Swiss multi-party government. Besides, following Lijphart, power sharing and consensus democracy is not uncommon for small and heterogeneous societies.[32]

---

[32] Lijphart, Arend, "The Southern European Examples of Democratization: Six Lessons for Latin America". *Government and Opposition* 25, no. 01 (January 1990): 68–84. doi:10.1111/j.1477-7053.1990.tb00747.x.

Direct democracy definitely changes the relationship between citizens, the state and its administration. It is not a question of "we" and "them" from the perspective of the citizens. Citizens are directly involved in the most important decisions, and such decisions, regardless of whether they are good or bad, right or wrong, have a very high legitimacy. For politicians and for the administration, direct democracy makes them — sometimes very painfully — aware that they are the agents and not the principal. For important projects, policymakers need the approval of the citizens and the same is true for important expenditures.

Probably most important is the direct link between direct democracy and the tax level which is particularly salient on the local level, and, to some extent, on the cantonal level. Municipalities have to cover most of the public expenditures with their own resources because there are — as we have seen — very little transfers from higher levels. Citizens are well aware that the costly projects might lead to a tax increase. Given the fact that they have the final say, they think twice before accepting a project. The government therefore needs good arguments to justify its projects. The citizens, on the other side, learn to take up responsibilities for their community. They often say 'yes' to spending money on new schools, sports facilities, tramways and parks even if they do not personally benefit from them, knowing that they are also likely to be dependent on the understanding and benevolence of others in time to come.

Ad-hoc public consultation in Singapore: A history of consultative exercises

Citizen participation in Singapore has often been characterised by ad-hoc public consultations but they are now increasingly formalised in the political process. Although governing in Singapore remains, by and large, a top-down process mainly controlled by politicians and bureaucrats, public feedback has increasingly been taken into account when making policy decisions, especially in recent years. This gradual evolution was facilitated by the rise of social media and the growth of civil society, enabling the expression of more diverse opinions on social and political issues. The Singapore government has made several notable and large-scale attempts to engage citizens through ground-up public consultations, in tandem with conducting their own polls and opinion surveys. Such consultative exercises, such as *The Next Lap* in 1991, *Singapore 21* in 1999, and *Remaking Singapore* in 2003, tended to take place after critical periods in Singapore's history, such as political or economic crises.[33] A number of scholars have commented that such exercises were attempts to channel dissent and educate the public, without genuinely viewing citizens as equal partners. In particular, Garry Rodan argued that far from weakening the PAP state, participation enabled an expansion of the state; it promoted "co-option" rather than contestation, reinforcing regime stability; and it was circumscribed by certain limits. It could not, for example, 'undermine the government's standing'.[34]

Past attempts at consultation were also shaped by the political context of the time — what Chan Heng Chee called an 'administrative state' characterised by PAP hegemony and devoid of 'real' politics.[35] It was also what Chua Beng Huat called a 'communitarian' state, with the government trying to maintain power by being the arbiter between different communities.[36] Within this context, consultation initiatives were also influenced by specific events. Firstly, the election results in 1984 which saw the end of the PAP monopoly in parliament preceded the setting up of the *Feedback Unit* in 1985. In 1987, Government Parliamentary Committees (GPCs) were set up to enable PAP MPs to play a more active role in questioning government policies.

Soon after the 1988 elections, the government set up the National Agenda, an intra-party attempt to better engage citizens. In 1989, a Cabinet sub-committee was tasked to develop a broad agenda, known as

---

[33] Kenneth Paul Tan, *Our Singapore Conversation: Telling National Stories*, in *Global-is-Asian*, October 2013.

[34] 'Singapore "Exceptionalism"? Authoritarian Rule and State Transformation' in Joseph Wong and Edward Friedman (editors), *Political Transitions in Dominant Party Systems: Learning to Lose* (New York: Routledge, 2008, pp. 231–51). See also Chua, Beng Huat. "The Relative Autonomies of State and Civil Society in Singapore". *State-Society Relations in Singapore* (2000): 62–76.

[35] Chan, Heng Chee, *Politics in an Administrative State: Where has the Politics Gone?*. Singapore: Department of Political Science, University of Singapore, 1975.

[36] Chua, Beng-Huat, *Communitarian Ideology and Democracy in Singapore*. Vol. 10. Routledge, 2002.

The Next Lap, for Singapore's long-term development. It drew on the ideas put forth in the past by government and private groups.[37] In total, 1,000 people were consulted, culminating in a 160-page book, *The Next Lap*, that mapped out plans for the next 20 to 30 years.

In 1990, Goh Chok Tong became the second Prime Minister of Singapore. He promised a more consultative style of governance, and public consultation attempts under his leadership could be seen as an attempt to establish his credibility. This new inclusiveness was manifested in a variety of ways, such as the adoption of a national ideology known as the Shared Values,[38] and the setting up of the NCMP and NMP schemes[39] and Government Parliamentary Committees (GPCs).[40] Such institutional innovations provided 'alternative voices' in Parliament while co-opting civil society groups and the public, thus reinforcing the PAP's political longevity. Moreover, institutions such as the GRC (Group Representation Constituencies) system and the Elected Presidency served to consolidate the PAP's hold on power while making symbolic appeals to 'inclusiveness'.

After the 1997 and 2001 elections, two public consultation attempts were launched: *Singapore 21* (S21)[41] and *Remaking Singapore,* which consulted 6,000 people and 10,000 people respectively on competing visions for Singapore, and how to make Singapore less materialistic. Academics commented that these exercises appeared to have a pre-set agenda and appeared to be exercises in "pseudo-participation".[42]

---

[37] Tan, Lay Yuen. "The Next Lap." *National Library Board*. Accessed March 4, 2015. Accessed from http://infopedia.nl.sg/articles/SIP_165_2004-12-23.html.

[38] Lim, Tin Seng. "Shared Values." *National Library Board*, July 13, 2015. Accessed from http://infopedia.nl.sg/articles/SIP_542_2004-12-18.html.

[39] The NCMP (Non-Constituency Member of Parliament) scheme allowed the 'best losers' from opposition parties to enter the Parliament, while the NMP (Nominated Member of Parliament) scheme created a category of parliamentarians who were representatives of civil society organisations and other interest groups.

[40] GPCs examine the policies, programmes and proposed legislation of a particular government ministry, provides the ministry with feedback and suggestions, and is consulted by the ministry on issues of public interest. They are backed by resource panels that members of the public are invited to join.

[41] Terence Lee, *Media, Cultural Control and Government in Singapore* (Oxon: Routledge), 2010, p. 89.

[42] Ibid.

The most recent exercise, *Our Singapore Conversation* (OSC), was the most ambitious of such consultative initiatives. Convened in 2012, and headed by a group of civil servants determined to break away from the mould of the past, the OSC exercise was innovative in its own right and established useful innovations in public engagement. Involving more than 47,000 participants through dialogue sessions in seven languages and dialects, OSC was divided into two phases and a survey involving 4,000 respondents. Phase 1 was an 'agenda-building' phase focused on the question "What would you like to see in 2030?". Phase 2 was focused on specific themes which were inductively drawn from the first phase, and involved certain ministries, such as the housing, education, manpower and transport ministries.

By using an open-ended format[43] and small focus-group discussions, the OSC avoided being just an exercise in testing or 'rubber-stamping' government agendas, and provided an additional instrument for ministries to include in their toolbox of public engagement. Moreover, although the OSC's consideration to reach out to vulnerable and voiceless groups could be seen as legitimising the 'silent majority' concept, it could also be interpreted as contributing to the exercise's democratic legitimacy in including previously-unheard groups.

However, the tangible contributions of the OSC notwithstanding, one must be careful not to overstate its impact. The OSC Committee was made up of Members of Parliament as well as selected members of civil society, with the exclusion of the opposition and other critical voices, casting doubt on its inclusiveness.[44] The Committee's preference for self-selected focus groups as a method of engagement suggested that only people comfortable with this form of engagement would participate.

Besides the OSC and other public consultation exercises, individual ministries in Singapore have developed their own consultation processes to gather public feedback on proposed new legislation or amendments to existing legislation. These processes take place before new policies are rolled out. Consultation papers are published on government ministries'

---

[43] As cited in an interview with Kenneth Paul Tan, 19 September 2013.
[44] Tan, "Our Singapore Conversation: Telling National Stories."

websites and interested parties are invited to submit written comments, ensuring that feedback from the public is taken into account — albeit in a non-binding way — during the policymaking process.

Therefore, while Switzerland has a formal and institutionalised form of public consultation in the form of direct democracy, Singapore is still experimenting with different ways of integrating public feedback into policy-making. Input legitimacy in Switzerland is high because citizens have the final say in policy-making, while in Singapore, despite the evolution of public consultation towards greater participation and inclusiveness, the government retains the final say.[45]

Discussion

As small states with diverse populations, both Singapore and Switzerland face additional hurdles to balancing input and output legitimacy. Besides having to balance the needs of different groups within society, both governments have to negotiate the trade-offs between domestic and international demands. While in Switzerland, the referendum appears to be a handy political instrument to mediate between these groups, it is not without its limitations. The 2009 Swiss minaret referendum is only one out of a growing number of referendums championed by nationalist parties which have appeared to stigmatise a minority group using a perfectly legitimate political process. In recent years, much debate in Switzerland has focused on whether the fact that referendums are becoming increasingly nationalistic and taking place more often justifies reforms to the system of direct democracy. Some voices demand raising the threshold of the number of signatures needed to call a national referendum. More importantly, there are also demands to search for mechanisms (for example, a constitutional court) to declare proposals

---

[45] Interestingly enough, Singapore's constitution does have provisions for the use of referenda for specific purposes, such as constitutional amendments. A referendum was carried out only once in Singapore's history — to decide on the terms of merger with Malaysia in 1962. Even so, the referendum did not give citizens a choice on whether merger should take place — the vote was on how much autonomy Singapore would retain post-merger.

invalid when they infringe guaranteed international human rights and contradict the core values of the Swiss Federal Constitution.

Another feature of direct democracy is the fact that it appears to operate in a vacuum of presumed popular sovereignty. The underlying assumption is that the will of the people *is* the national interest. Unlike in Singapore, where diplomats are fond of saying that "domestic politics should stop at the water's edge",[46] foreign and defence policy is a fixture of Swiss referenda, from the numerous votes on European integration and the abolishment of military service to the proposed acquisition of 22 Gripen fighter aircraft. In recent years, however, there have been instances of conflict between Switzerland's international obligations and the results of its domestic referenda. A good example is the Swiss immigration referendum in February 2014, which aimed to limit immigration through quotas. After it was accepted with a razor-thin margin of 0.3 percent, the European Union signalled that the existing and new collaborations it had with Switzerland, especially in the areas of research and education, could be adversely affected. The people had spoken, but they would also have to pay a price for their decision. In other words, high input legitimacy does not guarantee that the decision taken is a good one and that there will be no problems on the output side.

In Singapore, however, the non-binding nature of public consultation has given rise to doubts about how seriously the government takes public feedback into account. In the case of "Our Singapore Conversation", the government took pains to emphasise that it was a 'learning journey', and the views expressed would inform policy reviews — but also that they would need to balance the 'trade-offs' between the needs of different groups, and also the challenges of staying competitive internationally. While general elections every five years act as a barometer of public satisfaction towards government policies, the power of individual citizens to decisively influence the outcome of specific policies remains limited.

The debate over input and output legitimacy has to be reframed as a debate between international and domestic demands. In many cases,

---

[46] Kausikan, Bilahari. "Lee Kuan Yew Played Chess, Not Draughts: Bilahari." *Singapolitics*. Accessed March 4, 2015. http://news.asiaone.com/news/singapore/mr-lee-kuan-yew-played-chess-not-draughts-bilahari.

the bottom line of policy-making in Singapore remains the survival imperative: Singaporean policymakers often attribute the country's success to the fact that it is an open and trusted destination of international investment, and by that token, domestic demands (such as curbs on immigration, higher social spending or a minimum wage) which would have an impact on Singapore's international competitiveness would threaten the country's very survival. Output legitimacy — defined in terms of international economic relevance — would always take precedence over input legitimacy.

In Switzerland, although tensions between domestic and international pressures are keenly felt, the people's will is usually respected, with the consequence that the results of a popular vote often forms the starting point of subsequent international negotiations, as was the case with the immigration referendum. In rare cases of perceived crisis — notably when Switzerland was threatened by the United States over cases of suspected tax evasion — the Swiss government took the step of turning over account information to the USA, in possible violation of the country's bank secrecy laws.[47] No amount of popular sovereignty rhetoric could protect Switzerland from what was to be a long-drawn onslaught on its cherished ideal of banking secrecy. Small countries may have to accept that they may not always have the power to withstand international pressure, especially if there is also resistance this position within the country, as it was the case in Switzerland where the left was also fighting against banking secrecy.

Meanwhile, in Singapore, what author Catherine Lim calls a 'great affective divide', and more recently, a 'crisis of trust', continues to loom over the government-citizen relationship.[48] Social commentator Alex Au noted the persistence of a 'petitionary state',[49] in which citizens got into the habit of proposing 'wishlists' to a paternalistic government, rather than taking the initiative to effect social change on their own.

---

[47] "Swiss Banks to Divulge Names of Wealthy US Tax Avoiders, Pay Billions in Fines". Accessed March 4, 2015. http://rt.com/business/swiss-banks-disclose-assets-196/.

[48] "An Open Letter to the Prime Minister". *Catherinelim.sg*. Accessed March 4, 2015. http://catherinelim.sg/2014/06/07/an-open-letter-to-the-prime-minster/.

[49] "The Conversation Isn't Getting Very Far." *Yawning Bread*. Accessed March 4, 2015. https://yawningbread.wordpress.com/2012/12/17/the-conversation-isnt-getting-very-far/.

In conclusion, while globally admired for their reliability and efficiency, decision-making in Singapore and Switzerland is guided by two different forces: one by the long-term vision of a strong government, the other by the collective will of its citizenry. Both are driven by close collaboration with the private sector, a highly pragmatic, results-driven work culture, and low levels of corruption. But in the long run, both systems will have to adapt to a changing international context. There is no iron law stating a trade-off between output and input legitimacy as the Swiss example shows, but to achieve and maintain high levels on both components of legitimacy in a globalised world is quite a challenge. Singapore will have to do more to systematically integrate citizen input into its policy process, while Switzerland has to make sure that its institutions of direct democracy can be reconciled with its international obligations, and are not taken hostage by domestic forces which may threaten its foundations.

References

"2013 Edelman Trust Barometer." *Edelman*. Accessed March 4, 2015. http://www.edelman.com/insights/intellectual-property/trust-2013/.

Au, A. "The Conversation Isn't Getting Very Far." *Yawning Bread*. Accessed March 4, 2015. https://yawningbread.wordpress.com/2012/12/17/the-conversation-isnt-getting-very-far/.

Beisheim, M., and K. Dingwerth. "Procedural Legitimacy and Private Transnational Governance," 2008. http://www.edocs.fu-berlin.de/docs/receive/FUDOCS_document_000000000337.

Boedeltje, M., and J. Cornips. "Input and Output Legitimacy in Interactive Governance." NIG Annual Work Conference 2004 Rotterdam, October 19, 2004. http://repub.eur.nl/pub/1750/.

Chan, H. C. *Politics in an Administrative State: Where Has the Politics Gone?*. University of Singapore, Department of Political Science, 1975.

Chua, B.-H. "The Relative Autonomies of State and Civil Society in Singapore." In *State-Society Relations in Singapore*, 62–76. Institute of Policy Studies, 2000.

Dahl, R. A. "A Democratic Dilemma: System Effectiveness versus Citizen Participation." *Political Science Quarterly* 109, no. 1 (April 1, 1994): 23–34. doi:10.2307/2151659.

Dahl, R. A., and E. R. Tufte. *Size and Democracy*. Stanford University Press, 1973.

"Democracy Index 2013." *Economist Intelligence Unit*. Accessed March 4, 2015. http://www.eiu.com/public/topical_report.aspx?campaignid=Democracy0814.

Denters, B., M. Goldsmith, A. Ladner, P. E. Mouritzen, and L. E. Rose. *Size and Local Democracy*. Cheltenham UK: Edward Elgar Pub, 2014.

Emery, Y. "Neue Politiken und Prozesse im Personalmanagement." In *Handbuch der öffentlichen Verwaltung in der Schweiz*, 479–98. Neue Zürcher Zeitung NZZ Libro, 2012.

Fishkin, J. *When the People Speak: Deliberative Democracy and Public Consultation*. Oxford University Press, 2009.

"Global Competitiveness Report 2014-2015." *World Economic Forum*. Accessed March 4, 2015. http://reports.weforum.org/global-competitiveness-report-2014-2015/.

Government of Singapore. "Singapore Budget 2014." Accessed May 4, 2015. http://www.singaporebudget.gov.sg/data/budget_2014/download/FY2014_Analysis_of_Revenue_and_Expenditure.pdf

Haque, M. S. "Governance and Bureaucracy in Singapore: Contemporary Reforms and Implications." *International Political Science Review* 25, no. 2 (April 1, 2004): 227–40. doi:10.1177/0192512104042314.

Haque, M. S. "Theory and Practice of Public Administration in Southeast Asia: Traditions, Directions, and Impacts." *International Journal of Public Administration* 30, no. 12–14 (November 9, 2007): 1297–1326. doi:10.1080/01900690701229434.

"How Corrupt Is Your Country?" *Transparency International*. Accessed March 4, 2015. http://www.transparency.org/cpi2014/infographic.

Kausikan, B. "Lee Kuan Yew Played Chess, Not Draughts: Bilahari." *Singapolitics*. Accessed March 4, 2015. http://news.asiaone.com/news/singapore/mr-lee-kuan-yew-played-chess-not-draughts-bilahari.

Kuhlmann, S., and H. Wollmann. *Introduction to Comparative Public Administration: Administrative Systems and Reforms in Europe*. Edward Elgar Publishing, 2014.

Krishnadas, D. "Civil Service: Keeping It a Success Factor." *TODAYonline*. Accessed March 4, 2015. http://m.todayonline.com/singapore/civil-service-keeping-it-success-factor.

Ladner, A. "Der Schweizer Staat, politisches Systems und Aufgabenerbringung." In *Handbuch der öffentlichen Verwaltung in der Schweiz*, 23–46. Neue Zürcher Zeitung NZZ Libro, 2012.

Lee, T. *The Media, Cultural Control and Government in Singapore*. Routledge, 2010.

Lieberherr, E. "The Role of Throughput in the Input-Output Legitimacy Debate: Insights from Public and Private Governance Modes in the Swiss and." Accessed July 2, 2014. http://icpublicpolicy.web2.mezcalito.net/IMG/pdf/panel_39_s2_lieberherr.pdf.

Lijphart, A. "The Southern European Examples of Democratization: Six Lessons for Latin America." *Government and Opposition* 25, no. 01 (January 1990): 68–84. doi:10.1111/j.1477-7053.1990.tb00747.x.

Lim, C. "An Open Letter to the Prime Minister." Accessed March 4, 2015. http://catherinelim.sg/2014/06/07/an-open-letter-to-the-prime-minster/.

Lim, T. S. "Shared Values." *National Library Board*, July 13, 2015. http://eresources.nlb.gov.sg/infopedia/articles/SIP_542_2004-12-18.html.

Low, D., and S. T. Vadaketh. *Hard Choices: Challenging the Singapore Consensus*. Singapore: NUS Press, 2014.

Low, J. "Public Governance and Public Trust — Part 2." *Civil Service College, Singapore*, April 7, 2012. https://www.cscollege.gov.sg/Knowledge/Pages/Public-Governance-and-Public-Trust-Part-2.aspx.

McLaughlin, K., E. Ferlie, and Stephen Osborne P. *New Public Management: Current Trends and Future Prospects*. Routledge, 2005.

OECD. "Switzerland Fact Sheet," 2013. Accessed from http://www.oecd.org/gov/GAAG2013_CFS_CHE.pdf

Quah, J. S. T. *Public Administration Singapore-Style*. Emerald Group Publishing, 2010.

"Swiss Banks to Divulge Names of Wealthy US Tax Avoiders, Pay Billions in Fines." *Russia Today*, Accessed March 4, 2015. http://rt.com/business/swiss-banks-disclose-assets-196/.

Rodan, G. "Singapore 'Exceptionalism'? Authoritarian Rule and State Transformation." In *Political Transitions in Dominant Party Systems: Learning to Lose*, 231–51. Routledge, 2008.

Saw, S.-H., and R. S. Bhathal. *Singapore Towards the Year 2000*. NUS Press, 1981.

Scharpf, F. W. *Demokratietheorie zwischen Utopie und Anpassung*. Konstanz: Universitätsverlag, 1970.

Tan, K. P. Interview, September 19, 2013.

Tan, K. P. "Meritocracy and Elitism in a Global City: Ideological Shifts in Singapore." *International Political Science Review* 29, no. 1 (January 1, 2008): 7–27. doi:10.1177/0192512107083445.

Tan, K. P. "Our Singapore Conversation: Telling National Stories." *Global-is-Asian*, October 2013.

Tan, L. Y. "The Next Lap." *National Library Board*. Accessed March 4, 2015. http://eresources.nlb.gov.sg/infopedia/articles/SIP_165_2004-12-23.html.

Tay, Simon S. C., ed. *A Mandarin and the Making of Public Policy: Reflections by Ngiam Tong Dow*. Singapore: NUS Press, 2007.

Teo, E. "The Singapore Public Service: A Development-Oriented Promotion System." *Civil Service College, Singapore*, December 11, 2013. https://www.cscollege.gov.sg/Knowledge/Ethos/Ethos%20Issue%201,%202002/Pages/The%20Singapore%20Public%20Service%20A%20Development-Oriented%20Promotion%20System.aspx.

"Worldwide Governance Indicators 2013." *World Bank*, Accessed March 4, 2015. http://info.worldbank.org/governance/wgi/index.aspx#home.

"Whither Singapore Inc?" *The Economist*, November 28, 2002. http://www.economist.com/node/1465814.

Wolf, K. D. "Contextualizing Normative Standards for Legitimate Governance beyond the State." In *Participatory Governance*, edited by Jürgen R. Grote and Bernard Gbikpi, 35–50. VS Verlag für Sozialwissenschaften, 2002. http://link.springer.com/chapter/10.1007/978-3-663-11003-3_2.

Zweifel, T. D. *International Organizations and Democracy: Accountability, Politics, and Power*. Swiss Consulting Group, Inc., 2006.

Chapter 2

Neutrality, Balancing or Engagement? Comparing the Singaporean and Swiss Approaches in Small–State Diplomacy

Yvonne Guo and J.J. Woo

Introduction

In 2009, Singapore's former Prime Minister and then-Minister Mentor, Lee Kuan Yew, remarked that "small countries have little power to alter the region, let alone the world. A small country must seek a maximum number of friends, while maintaining the freedom to be itself as a sovereign and independent nation... We must make ourselves relevant so that other countries have an interest in our continued survival and prosperity as a sovereign and independent nation".[1] Such a formula for survival is commonly known in the international relations literature as 'small state diplomacy' and is hence not unique to Singapore. Other small states, most notably Switzerland, have engaged in similar practices.

At their cores, the foreign policies of Singapore and Switzerland have been driven by the same concerns of survival and vulnerability. Their objectives are similar: to safeguard independence, autonomy and sovereignty in a world dominated by larger powers. Both occupy unique positions in their respective regions as they are significantly smaller and

---

[1] Speech by Mr Lee Kuan Yew, Minister Mentor delivered at *The S. Rajaratnam Lecture*, 09 April 2009, 5:30 PM at Shangri-La Hotel, Singapore.

richer than their immediate neighbours, and both have sought to protect their "unaligned" characteristics amidst instances of regional political turbulence. Although Singapore and Switzerland describe their foreign policies using the varying concepts of "balancing" and "neutrality" that are tied to their different role conceptions relative to their historical and regional contexts, they employ, in practice, similar strategies to mitigate their vulnerability and ensure their survival in a world dominated by greater powers.

For Switzerland, neutrality is a permanent policy position that is variously a legal obligation, a realist survival strategy, and — viewed through a constructivist lens — an integral part of Swiss national identity. However, a more subtle, and often neglected, corollary of Swiss neutrality is engagement. Since the post-war years, under the façade of neutrality, Swiss foreign policy has also been driven by trade, with the top managers in Switzerland's trade division in the Federal Department of Economic Affairs described as "the real foreign ministers of Switzerland".[2] Neutrality, in this sense, was described as a cover for engagement: "with their stereotypical reference to neutrality, the elites believed they could remove themselves from accountability for their real activities".[3] Moreover, in recent years, Switzerland has engaged in a limited form of political engagement, evidenced in Swiss participation in various international fora and even in select groupings in the United Nations, some of which — like the Forum of Small States (FOSS) and the Global Governance Group (3G) were initiated by Singapore.

For Singapore, the need to balance between hostile neighbours, regional powers and global powers was preordained from the start. Singapore's early leaders, and particularly its former Prime Minister, Lee Kuan Yew, saw Singapore as "the small fish eternally caught between the medium and the big fish", and concluded that the best recourse was "to be friends with both the medium and the big fish".[4] This statement encapsulates the idea that for Singapore, balancing and engagement are

---

[2] Goetschel, Laurent, Magdalena Bernath and Daniel Schwarz (2005): Swiss Foreign Policy. Foundations and possibilities. Oxon/New York: Routledge, p. 19.

[3] *Ibid.*

[4] Ang, Cheng Guan, *Lee Kuan Yew's Strategic Thought*. Routledge, 2013, p. 25.

two sides of the same coin, with engagement — political as well as economic — as the means to optimising its chances for survival in a hostile region through the formation of alliances. This laid the groundwork for closer regional economic and political integration, culminating in the formation of ASEAN.

In this chapter, we provide a systematic analysis of the different foreign policy strategies employed by Singapore and Switzerland, attempting in particular to separate the official discourses of "neutrality" and "balancing" from an implicit strategy of engagement in both countries. We base our analysis on primary data in the form of official documents and releases as well as in-depth interviews with foreign policy officials at the ministerial and ambassadorial levels. This analysis of the explicit and implicit dimensions of "balancing" and "neutrality" with their corollary of "engagement" demonstrates that small state foreign policies are more complex and multi-dimensional than the existing literature and policy discourse would lead us to believe.

Existing understandings of foreign policy that dichotomise engagement and balancing, or over-emphasise and hence sharpen the differences between realist and liberal approaches, tend to over-simplify the picture. In reality and as the rest of this chapter will show, foreign policy is a complex and multi-faceted endeavour that cuts across traditional theoretical conceptual frames, defying easy categorisation and by implication, requiring a more nuanced and multi-frame analysis. While our analysis provides a clearer picture of the different ways in which small state foreign policies may be practiced, more research is required to gain a fuller understanding of the panoply of small state strategies in foreign policy.

Review of the Literature

The study of small states originated in 19th-century Europe and was dominated by German-speaking scholars, but lost its popularity with the rise of the nation-state and German unification. Following the First World War, small states saw hope in the creation of the League of Nations and the development of international law and multilateral organisation. However, with the rise of fascism and the outbreak of the Second World

War, realism became a more popular international relations theory and the focus shifted to great power relations.[5] Only in the late 1950s did a genuine school of small state studies develop, with Baker Fox's study of small states' wartime diplomacy.[6] This focused on a few issues: firstly, the definition of a "small state"; secondly, the survival of small states among the big powers; and thirdly, explaining small state strategies using a system level of analysis.[7]

How is a small state defined? A state can be small in terms of its population size, level of development, degree of overt and legal recognition, and actual or potential military power,[8] or in terms of political power and having to depend on alliances.[9] Or smallness can be *relational*,[10] relative to other states.

Acting alone, small states face high costs.[11] Thus they make use of a variety of strategies to guarantee their own security, such as alliance formation.[12] This often involves harnessing the potential of joint actions by joining regional and international institutions.[13] Small states have also

---

[5] Ingebritsen, Christine, *Small States in International Relations*. University of Iceland Press, 2006, p.7–8.

[6] Fox, Annette Baker, *The Power of Small States: Diplomacy in World War II*. Chicago, Ill., U.S.A.: University of Chicago Press, 1959.

[7] Ingebritsen, *Small States in International Relations*, p. 7–8.

[8] Vital, David, *The Inequality of States. A Study of the Small Power in International Relations*. P. 198. Clarendon Press: Oxford, 1967.

[9] Rothstein, Robert L, *Alliances and Small Powers*. Columbia University Press, 1968.

[10] Selwyn, Percy, *Development Policy in Small Countries*. London: Croom Helm in association with the Institute of Development Studies, 1975; Hänggi, Heiner. *Small State as a Third State: Switzerland and Asia-Europe Inter-Regionalism*. St. Gallen: Institut für Politikwissenschaft, Hochschule St. Gallen, 1998.

[11] Vital, *The Inequality of States*.

[12] Rothstein, *Alliances and Small Powers*.

[13] Rothstein, *Alliances and Small Powers*. Keohane, Robert O, "Lilliputians' Dilemmas: Small States in International Politics". *International Organization* 23, No. 2 (March 1969): 291–310; Vital, David. *The Survival of Small States: Studies in Small Power/Great Power Conflict*. London; New York: Oxford University Press, 1971; Hey, Jeanne A.K. *Small States in World Politics: Explaining Foreign Policy Behavior*. Boulder: Lynne Rienner Publishers, 2003.

coped with an increasingly global economy by being economically open and adaptable.[14]

Since the 1990s, the literature on small states has largely focused on European states within the context of the EU,[15] neglecting both non-European states and the international context. This can be attributed to the rise of the number of small states in Europe precipitated by the fall of the Berlin Wall, accompanied by their integration into the EU. Small state literature has also been influenced by recent developments in IR theory, where social constructivism with its focus on international norms, identity and ideas has suggested that small states can add the strategy of being "norm entrepreneurs" in international politics to their existing toolkits.[16]

Neutrality

Neutrality is a multi-dimensional concept that is on the periphery of international relations theory because few states consider it to be an acceptable foreign policy position. Historically, neutrality has been associated with passive inaction and perceived to be an untenable position.[17]

---

[14] Katzenstein, Peter J, *Small States in World Markets: Industrial Policy in Europe*. Ithaca, N.Y.: Cornell University Press, 1985.

[15] Zahariadis, Nikolaos, "Nationalism and Small-State Foreign Policy: The Greek Response to the Macedonian Issue". *Political Science Quarterly* 109, No. 4 (1 October 1994): 647–67; Breuning, Marijke. "Words and Deeds: Foreign Assistance Rhetoric and Policy Behavior in the Netherlands, Belgium, and the United Kingdom". *International Studies Quarterly* 39, No. 2 (1 June 1995): 235–54; Krebs, Ronald R. "Perverse Institutionalism: NATO and the Greco-Turkish Conflict". *International Organization* 53, No. 02 (March 1999): 343–77; Hey, *Small States in World Politics*.

[16] Ingebritsen, Christine, "Norm Entrepreneurs: Scandinavia's Role in World Politics". *Cooperation and Conflict* 37, No. 1 (2002): 11–23; Björkdahl, Annika. *From Idea to Norm — Promoting Conflict Prevention*. Department of Political Science, 2002. http://lup.lub.lu.se/record/20760.

[17] In the Melian Dialogue of 416 BC, as recounted by Thucydides, the Melians' desire to remain neutral was scoffed at by the Athenians, who countered that by not attacking Melos they would be perceived as weak. See Benjamin Jowett, and Andrew P Peabody, *Thucydides*. Boston: D. Lothrop & Co., 1883.

The theoretical literature on neutrality has focused on legal definitions of neutrality, categorisations (such as "permanent" vs "traditional" neutrality) and related international relations concepts such as non-alignment. A second approach to the study of neutrality has been to focus on its practice and impact on international security.[18]

Historically, neutrality has often been defined in strict legal terms and "concerned with the formal rights and responsibilities of neutral states".[19] Neutrality re-emerged as a practice in 15th century Europe, as principalities found it to be a good strategy to keep themselves out of conflicts.[20] The concept of neutrality began to be discussed in the legal philosophy of the 16th century, amid the dawn of an international system where principles of a 'just war' were laid.[21] In the 18th century, positivist legal philosophers[22] questioned whether neutral states could truly be impartial, and weighed the rights of neutral states against those of belligerent states. It was in this context of newly sovereign states that the notion of "armed neutrality" came into prominence, with the formation of the First and Second Leagues of Armed Neutrality in 1780 and 1800. Neutrality during wartime was acknowledged as a legally justifiable strategy during the 1815 Congress of Vienna, and emphasised in the 1899 and 1907 Hague Conventions.[23]

However, the First World War demonstrated the futility of these rules. After Belgian and Norway's neutrality was violated by Germany, the

---

[18] Politis, Nicolas, *La neutralité et la paix*. Paris: Hachette, 1935; Armstrong, Hamilton Fish. "Neutrality: Varying Tunes". *Foreign Affairs*, October 1956. http://www.foreignaffairs. com/articles/71287/hamilton-fish-armstrong/neutrality-varying-tunes.

[19] Grant-Bailey, S. N. *The Law of Neutrality: Notes and Analysis*. London: Stevens, 1944. Agius, Christine, *The Social Construction of Swedish Neutrality: Challenges to Swedish Identity and Sovereignty*. Manchester University Press, 2006.

[20] Raymond, Gregory A, "Neutrality Norms and the Balance of Power". *Cooperation and Conflict. 32(2) June 1997 : 123–146*, 1997.

[21] Ørvik, Nils, *The Decline of Neutrality, 1914–1941. With Special Reference to the United States and the Northern Neutrals*. Oslo: J. Tanum, 1953; Agius, *The Social Construction of Swedish Neutrality*.

[22] de Vattel, Emer, Joseph Chitty, and Edward Duncan Ingraham, *Law of Nations*. T. & J. W. Johnson, 1852. van Bynkershoek, Cornelius. *On Questions of Public Law. Two Books, in 1 Vol. English*. Oxford: At The Clarendon Press. London: Humphrey Milford, 1930.

[23] Ørvik, *The Decline of Neutrality, 1914-1941. With Special Reference to the United States and the Northern Neutrals*; Karsh, Efraim. *Neutrality and Small States*. London; New York: Routledge, 1988.

United States abandoned neutrality, declaring that armed neutrality was "ineffectual enough at best".[24] The view of "amoral neutrality"[25] resurfaced, with neutral states being depicted as both politically and morally aberrant, "cynical actors that gain from war without incurring sacrifice".[26] During the Second World War, neutrality proved to be equally futile as the rights of belligerent states prevailed over those of neutrals, even as neutral states took seriously the concept of "armed neutrality".[27]

Much of the late 20th century literature on neutrality has focused on "neutral" state behaviour during the Cold War period and the constraints they faced.[28] In the Cold War period, neutrality was viewed with "suspicion".[29] In an age of nuclear weapons, "armed neutrality" seemed to be a futile policy, despite the practice of so-called "active neutrality" by a number of small states at the UN level.[30] After the Cold War, neutrality was seen as "obsolete… a hindrance to closer forms of security cooperation between states",[31] and rendered even more irrelevant by the end of the Cold War, European integration, and the events of September 11.[32]

---

[24] Wilson, Woodrow, "Wilson's War Message to Congress", *The World War I Document Archive*, April 2, 1917. http://wwi.lib.byu.edu/index.php/Wilson%27s_War_Message_to_ Congress.

[25] Agius, *The Social Construction of Swedish Neutrality*.

[26] *Ibid.* Michael Handel called the doctrine of neutrality "defence nihilism". Swiss author Friedrich Dürrenmatt also commented that Swiss neutrality "makes me think of a virgin who earns her living in a bordello but wants to remain chaste" (The European, 24–30/12/93).

[27] Churchill echoed this belief when he declared, "Small nations must not tie our hands when we are fighting for their rights and freedom… Humanity, rather than legality, must be our guide". (Churchill, cited in Agius, 2006, p. 22).

[28] Kruzel, Joseph, and Michael H. Haltzel, *Between the Blocs: Problems and Prospects for Europe's Neutral and Nonaligned States*. Cambridge University Press, 1989; Neuhold, Hanspeter, and Hans Thalberg, *The European Neutrals in International Affairs*. Wilhelm Braumüller, 1984.

[29] Agius, *The Social Construction of Swedish Neutrality*.

[30] Neutral states, afforded the UN platform to articulate their views, became increasingly outspoken on superpower behaviour and attempted to "directly promote international systemic change", leading to the revival of "active neutrality".

[31] Agius, *The Social Construction of Swedish Neutrality*.

[32] *Ibid.*

Balancing

The literature on balancing is derived from the realist balance of power theory. According to this theory, states in an anarchic international order, motivated by survival in a zero-sum context, seek to balance against potential hegemons, thus constraining the latter's power and dominance.

International relations scholars have distinguished between external and internal balancing.[33] In the case of external balancing, small states seek out alliances and cooperation with other states to protect against other powers, assuring at least partial deterrence, but imposing diplomatic attachments and long-term policy constraints. In the case of internal balancing, small states pursue self-reliance by maximising internal resources, but in so doing, they incur high economic and social costs.[34]

Balancing is often opposed to the concept of 'bandwagoning', which refers to states allying with major powers in order to protect themselves. Bandwagoning is seen as inherently unstable for the international system because it rewards the hegemonic behaviour of dominant powers.[35] In recent years, a literature has developed around the concept of 'soft balancing', referring to small states using diplomatic and other non-military mechanisms to balance against a dominant state.[36]

This chapter proposes another interpretation of 'balancing': it is interpreted here to mean balancing *between* the contradictory demands of several larger powers. Developed during the Cold War to explain the behaviour of states like Egypt, this strategy of balancing *between* is a way for smaller states to neutralise major powers by playing them off against each other in the framework of their rivalry to expand their spheres of influence. By balancing major powers against each other, smaller states may acquire some advantages that, absent the power struggle between

---

[33] Waltz, Kenneth Neal, *Theory of International Politics*. Addison-Wesley Pub. Co., 1979.
[34] Cohen, Stuart A, "Small States and Their Armies: Restructuring the Militia Framework of the Israel Defense Force". *Journal of Strategic Studies* 18, No. 4 (December 1995): 78–93. doi:10.1080/01402399508437620.
[35] Waltz, *Theory of International Politics.*
[36] Pape, Robert A, "Soft Balancing against the United States". *International Security* 30, No. 1 (1 July 2005): 7–45.

those powers, they would not have achieved. Thus, 'balancing' explains what a small state can do on an individual level when it is faced with the competing demands of two hegemons.

Realist and Constructivist Approaches in Small–State Diplomacy

The international relations literature details three approaches that a state can take in its foreign policy: self-dependence, balancing, or bandwagoning. However, these approaches are not mutually exclusive, since it is, in theory, possible for a state to practise all three strategies at the same time. To convey the diverse nature of small state foreign policies relative to their environment, we propose the conceptualisations of 'balancing' and 'neutrality'. Both these conceptualisations presuppose a high degree of state sovereignty and desire for autonomy. However, a state that chooses the strategy of 'balancing' is a state that has a certain degree of flexibility in foreign policy, maintaining equidistance between major powers in its region, while a state that chooses a strategy of 'neutrality' takes a fixed position and does not move relative to the positions of other states in its region. In other words, the policy of 'neutrality' is a *static* position, while the policy of balancing is a *dynamic* position. This suggests that in the long term, states with 'neutral' foreign policies will have less room to manoeuvre than states taking a dynamic foreign policy of 'balancing' between great powers. What both have in common is their refusal to explicitly take sides by formal bandwagoning, in the form of a legal alliance or other treaty with greater powers. In this regard, both 'balancing' and 'neutrality' can be seen as strategies to maximise the sovereignty of small states, but they are only effective when backed up with a credible military deterrent.

Singapore and Switzerland are archetypal examples of small states with realist foreign policies of 'balancing' and 'neutrality' respectively. Both small states chose the strategy that would best maximise their sovereignty and security. In the context of Southeast Asia, this strategy was 'balancing'; in the context of Westphalian Europe, this strategy was 'neutrality'. Both are two different forms of 'not taking sides'; one static, the other dynamic.

(a) Realist Perspectives: Traditions of Balancing and Neutrality

Singapore: Balancing

Having attained statehood by virtue of its expulsion from the Federation of Malaysia, the need for autonomy and sovereignty was impressed on the political leadership of Singapore from the earliest days of its independence. As a small state in a hostile region, Singapore emphasised the need to build up a deterrent military capacity, as well as the importance of making 'as many friends as possible' through diplomacy, which bolstered its strategy of 'balancing'.

The security imperative: Balancing as a deterrence strategy

Singapore adopted balancing as a strategy to deal with the two main 'existential' threats it faced from its neighbours Malaysia and Indonesia. Both were Muslim-majority states which perceived Chinese-majority Singapore as a potential hotbed of communism. Moreover, competition between political leaders in Singapore and Malaysia during the period of merger between both countries had led to much mutual distrust. Malaysia had threatened to cut off its supply of water to Singapore while Indonesia directly threatened Singapore with its policy of *Konfrontasi* in the 1960s, going so far as to plant bombs in the city centre that caused civilian fatalities. To achieve security, newly-independent Singapore therefore had to look beyond its regional boundaries, establishing defence arrangements with countries which were further away but were able and willing to help. One such country was Israel, which saw geopolitical similarities with Singapore in being surrounded by hostile Muslim-majority states. Israel would subsequently contribute to the setting up of the Singapore Armed Forces.

Singapore has since established defence arrangements with various other nations, with the most significant being a close defence relationship with the United States (US). This began in the late 1960s, with then-Prime Minister Lee Kuan Yew noting that Singapore needed "overwhelming power on its side"[37] as a response to perceived threats

---

[37] Leifer, Michael, Joseph Chinyong Liow, and Ralf Emmers, *Order and Security in Southeast Asia: Essays in Memory of Michael Leifer*. Psychology Press, 2006.

from its immediate neighbours as well as North Vietnam at that time. This relationship culminated in the US's plans to deploy up to four littoral combat ships to Singapore on a permanent and rotational basis. Singapore also sought to engage China, particularly through a "Four-Point Consensus" to deepen the two countries' defence relationship. Moreover, Singapore conducts joint military exercises and maintains military training bases in Australia, New Zealand, India, Thailand, Brunei, and Taiwan. Not only do such defence arrangements ensure the operational readiness of Singapore's military, they also allow Singapore to foster close ties with its allies.

The regional context in Southeast Asia facilitated the pursuit of Singapore's strategy of balancing. Southeast Asia was characterised by the lack of a 'concert of powers' structure, since great powers (such as the US and China) came from outside Southeast Asia as opposed to being located within it. Moreover, the strategy of balancing was compatible with collective security in ASEAN, which was characterised by informal norms rather than formal rules and a low level of institutionalisation and political integration. Thus, member states had much flexibility to pursue independent foreign policies. Like all the other ASEAN member states (except Myanmar), Singapore was a member of the Non-Aligned Movement, another reflection of its policy of 'balancing' between the United States and the Soviet Union during the Cold War.

The sovereignty imperative: Balancing to maximise autonomy

Finally, balancing was also a strategy to secure maximum flexibility and manoeuvring space in Singapore's foreign policy. In Southeast Asia's relatively fluid geopolitical environment, characterised also by the shifting balance of power between the United States, China, and other powers influential in the region, balancing was a strategy that helped Singapore adapt to changes easily while not having to 'take sides'. It was a pragmatic policy of flexibility, of keeping one's options open so if geopolitical winds changed, it would not be too hard to adjust. Singapore's founding fathers saw diplomatic engagement, and especially ASEAN membership, as an integral aspect of promoting peace, security and economic development in the region. Given the harsh regional environment it found itself in, Singapore also relied on its close relations with major powers external to the region for its survival, joining, for example, the FPDA (Five Power Defence Arrangements) to mitigate potential security threats. Deep-seated vulnerabilities such as a small size, the lack of a natural hinterland, and the presence of hostile neighbours have imbued Singapore's foreign policy orientation with a "siege mentality".[38] The impacts of the Cold War further fuelled Singapore's realist foreign policy approach.[39]

Switzerland: Neutrality

For Switzerland, the policy of neutrality also served the dual objectives of sovereignty and security. Neutrality has its long-term origins in the Swiss defeat at the Battle of Marignano in 1515, which temporarily ended the expansionist plans of Swiss cantons. The Treaty of Westphalia in 1648, which recognised Swiss independence, also acknowledged its neutrality. Neutrality means that the Swiss are not allowed to enter military alliances unless attacked, or take part in international conflicts, including allowing foreign forces to use Swiss territory for transit.

The security imperative: Neutrality guaranteed by international law

After being under French control from 1798 to 1803 as the 'Helvetic Republic', Switzerland formally regained its neutrality but remained under French influence. At the Congress of Vienna from 1814 to 1815, the Congress adopted a declaration relative to Switzerland on 20 March 1815 stating that the perpetual neutrality of Switzerland was in the interest of the European states and guaranteeing the integrity of the 22 cantons. Therefore, Swiss neutrality was a formal agreement between Switzerland and the 'Concert of Europe' powers who agreed to be the guarantors of this neutrality. The idea behind granting Switzerland neutrality was that this geostrategically important place should not be allowed to ally with either of the superpowers (France, Austria and the

---

[38] Leifer, Michael, *Singapore's Foreign Policy: Coping with Vulnerability*. Psychology Press, 2000.

[39] Singh, Bilveer, *The Vulnerability of Small States Revisited: A Study of Singapore's Post-Cold War Foreign Policy*. Gadjah Mada University Press, 1999.

Prussians) in Europe. Such alliances were seen as a threat to a peaceful balance of power in Europe.

Although Swiss neutrality was dictated rather than chosen at the beginning, the Swiss found that it suited their interest as a nation with diverse language communities. Neutrality meant that different language groups would not have to take sides against each other — this was particularly crucial both during the Franco–Prussian war of 1870 and during the two World Wars. Far from only guaranteeing its external security, neutrality also guaranteed Swiss internal security by eliminating a possible point of contention between the different cantons. Neutrality was also easy to reconcile with Switzerland's traditional role as a humanitarian centre for victims facing political and religious persecution. As early as 1863, the Red Cross was founded in Geneva. Swiss humanitarian work has been attributed to the belief "that a neutral nation has not only the right, but also the duty, to get involved in situations concerning justice and humanity".[40]

The sovereignty imperative: From 'armed' to 'active' neutrality

What is fascinating, however, is how Switzerland has chosen to interpret and practise neutrality, and the various types of neutrality that have emerged, from 'armed' to 'active' neutrality. Traditionally, the Swiss practice of 'armed' neutrality was associated with the capacity for self-defence, including compulsory military service. "The whole idea of armed defense is deeply rooted in the Swiss mentality. [...] Switzerland illustrates that a credible neutrality demands a high degree of military power and readiness, and serious military deterrence demands preparations lasting decades".[41] However, armed neutrality also had its costs, notably restricting the Swiss room for manoeuvre in international affairs. For example, Swiss neutrality prevents it from joining NATO or participating in UN peacekeeping forces, although Switzerland has supported international peace efforts in other ways, such as the supervision of truces.

---

[40] Kruzel and Haltzel, *Between the Blocs.*
[41] *Ibid.*

The growth of the European Union and the end of the Cold War led to an evolution of Swiss attitudes towards neutrality. Breaking from Swiss traditional isolationism under "armed neutrality", Switzerland's former foreign minister Micheline Calmy-Rey promoted what she termed "active neutrality", initiating dialogue with North Korea and Iran, and creating the Human Rights Council in Geneva. In 2002, Switzerland, which had participated in UN activities for decades, finally became a member of the UN after a referendum. However, Calmy-Rey faced criticism from right-wing conservative parties throughout her tenure, and her successors have espoused a more "traditional" form of neutrality.

Moreover, there have been limits to Swiss neutrality over the years. For the sake of its survival, Switzerland struck compromises with the Nazis during the Second World War, leading to the 'Nazi Gold' and other scandals. By virtue of its geography, Switzerland remained squarely in the Western camp during the Cold War; its 'implicit alliance' with the UK and US was demonstrated through Swiss arms sales as well as its indirect participation in NATO.

(b) Constructivist Perspectives: The Rise of Engagement

The previous section has sought to interpret neutrality and balancing within the realist framework. This section will show how their corollary — engagement — can be interpreted through a constructivist lens. Despite 'not taking sides' politically, both countries play pivotal roles as financial and business hubs, and have elaborate trade arrangements with many other countries. Such engagements typically fall under the liberal conception of international relations, with its assumption that shared interests will result in a 'complex economic interdependency' among nations, precluding armed conflict for fear of losing shared economic gains.[42] A key differentiating factor between realist and liberal conceptions of foreign policy is realism's focus on relative gains (and hence

---

[42] Keohane, Robert O., and Joseph S. Nye, *Power and Interdependence: World Politics in Transition.* Little, Brown, 1977.

competitive politics in pursuit of such gains) and liberalism's focus on positive gains (with the assumption that cooperation facilitates the sharing of gains).

While such early liberal conceptions of engagement tended to take an 'ex post' understanding of how economic integration leads to greater engagement, other liberal scholars of international relations, particularly in the vein of liberal intergovernmentalism, have also noted that states may actively seek to engage each other and exert greater influence in the international environment through a 'pooling of sovereignties'.[43] Such pooling of sovereignties continues to inspire more recent efforts at regionalism.[44] As such, engagement can be an overt attempt at securing and maintaining state sovereignty, except that it does so through cooperation rather than balancing.

However, foreign policy goals and gains are not necessarily an objective and static phenomena. As is often the case in social and political endeavours, foreign policy objectives are fundamentally based on the beliefs and values that are held by policymakers and society. The recognition of this socially motivated aspect of foreign policy gave rise to the constructivist approach to international relations, which is predicated upon the socially-constructed nature of reality and hence policy objectives.[45] Hence, a state's national interests are socially constructed and its preferences subject to socialisation in international society.[46] The constructivists' societal conception of the international arena therefore places an emphasis on cooperation over conflict and paves the way for

---

[43] Moravcsik, Andrew, "Preferences and Power in the European Community: A Liberal Intergovernmentalist Approach". *JCMS: Journal of Common Market Studies* 31, No. 4 (1 December 1993): 473–524; Moravcsik, Andrew. "Liberal Intergovernmentalism and Integration: A Rejoinder". *JCMS: Journal of Common Market Studies* 33, No. 4 (1 December 1995): 611–28.

[44] Ravenhill, J., 2008, "Regionalism", in Global Political Economy. John Ravenhill (Ed.), 172–209. Oxford: Oxford University Press.

[45] Wendt, A., 1992. "Anarchy is what States make of it: The Social Construction of Power Politics", International Organization 46 (2): 391–425.

[46] Finnemore, M., 1996. National Interests in International Society. Ithaca: Cornell University Press.

subsequent interest in 'global public policy'[47] aimed at solving shared global issues.

Singapore: Overt engagement

A key aspect of Singapore's foreign policy involves extensive economic engagement with regional and global partners. Even as issues of sovereignty continue to dominate its foreign policy discourse, Singapore is, in reality, highly integrated into the global and regional order. As such, taking a completely realist or 'realpolitik' view of Singapore's foreign policy orientation may be limiting.[48] Ganesan has noted how Singapore's realist world-view has been complemented with a need to integrate itself within the liberal international economic order, with Singapore's foreign policy orientation informed by both realist and liberal ideologies.[49] Taking a constructivist approach, Acharya has gone even further, in highlighting the ideational and institutional impacts of Singapore's foreign policies, in particular its drive towards regionalism as a means for achieving regional stability.[50]

For instance, soon after its independence, Singapore joined a large number of regional and international institutions as a way of assuring its survival and asserting its sovereignty in a hostile regional environment. At the regional level, Singapore has signed various bilateral FTAs and positioned itself squarely within regional trade arrangements such as the ASEAN FTA, ASEAN Plus Three, ASEAN-China FTA, and, more recently, the TPP and RCEP. At the international level, Singapore established the Forum of Small States in 1992 and the 3G or "Global Governance Group" (3G) in 2010, allowing it to represent other small states and participate in various G20 summits. It

---

[47] Stone, D., 2008. "Global Public Policy, Transnational Policy Communities, and their Networks", Policy Studies Journal. 36 (1): 19–38.

[48] Acharya, A., 2008. Singapore's Foreign Policy: The Search for Regional Order. Singapore: World Scientific.

[49] Ganesan, Narayanan, *Realism and Interdependence in Singapore's Foreign Policy.* Routledge, 2005.

[50] Acharya, *Singapore's Foreign Policy.*

was explicitly aimed at addressing the G20's legitimacy deficit, bridging the G20 and the UN, and putting the voices of small states on the G20's agenda.[51]

Importantly, the 3G initiative allowed Singapore to band together with other small states in order to ensure that the interests of small and hence less powerful states were heard on the international arena. Bound by shared identities and conceptions of state smallness, the 3G represents a constructivist tactic that simultaneously pools the sovereignties of the states involved and facilitates the formation of a discursively-grounded international entity. This allows small states to shape the global foreign policy discourse by ensuring their place at the table during G20 summits. Such efforts at regional and global engagement have established Singapore's position as a key international player and allowed it to pursue its interests in the greater global environment.

Switzerland: Discreet engagement

Swiss foreign policy, although more 'reserved' than Singapore's, is similarly pro-business, with a focus on ensuring cross-border trade. Swiss scholars have described how, traditionally, the trade division was in fact Switzerland's 'secret foreign ministry', with its top ministers 'the real foreign ministers of Switzerland'.[52] In Switzerland, however, a greater tension exists between the country's political neutrality and economic engagement. An example of this is the Swiss electorate's repeated votes against closer European integration, even when there already exists a complex network of treaties that bind Switzerland to Europe, giving rise to the perception of a Swiss 'free-riding' approach to European integration.

Perhaps this uncertainty over Switzerland's role can be attributed to the 'myth' of neutrality.[53] As described in the Swiss constitution, it is an

---

[51] Cooper, Andrew F., and Bessma Momani, "Re-Balancing the G-20 from Efficiency to Legitimacy: The 3G Coalition and the Practice of Global Governance." *Global Governance: A Review of Multilateralism and International Organizations* 20, no. 2 (2014): 213–32.

[52] Goetschel, Bernath, and Schwarz, *Swiss Foreign Policy*.

[53] Kruzel and Haltzel, *Between the Blocs*.

"instrument for ensuring peace," but some have interpreted it to be an end in itself. The result has been a gap between Switzerland's desire for greater economic integration and its cautious approach to taking on political commitments.

Finally, one of the arguments why Switzerland should remain neutral is the idea that the world needs a place where conflicts can be settled. As a neutral country, Switzerland is well-placed to host negotiations between parties in conflict as well as international organisations, such as the International Committee of the Red Cross (ICRC). After the Second World War, Switzerland actively tried to promote these services to the world in order to get rid of its reputation for cherry-picking the use of its neutrality (*Rosinenpickerei*). Swiss debates on neutrality today tend to focus on the country's independence, rather than power concerns or the fear of other states, as is often the case in Singapore.

Conclusion: Rhetoric and Practice in Small–State Diplomacy

In both Singapore and Switzerland, small state foreign policy was driven by pragmatism. Balancing and neutrality served as means to an end — security and sovereignty — rather than ends in themselves. Singapore used balancing pragmatically in order to secure greater flexibility in foreign policy. Neutrality would have been less effective in Southeast Asia, with the absence of the European tradition of international law.[54] Switzerland used neutrality to the same effect: not to take overt political positions which could jeopardise its economic interests. However, while the practice of foreign policy in Singapore and Switzerland has substantively changed, becoming more constructivist and emphasising engagement, the rhetoric remains one of realism, reflecting both governmental and societal visions of the small state as a permanently vulnerable entity with existential concerns. While the means have changed, the ends remain very much focused on sovereignty and survival.

There is a clear need for small state foreign policies to be adaptable. In Switzerland, declaring neutrality had a clear purpose when Europe

---

[54] Interview with Amitav Acharya, August 22, 2013.

was geopolitically unstable and Swiss survival was uncertain. However neutrality was also a myth, given the many limits in practice to Swiss neutrality. Ironically, although now neutrality has lost its *raison d'être*, the discourse of neutrality persists and has become so deeply rooted in Swiss identity that it now constrains, to some extent, Swiss government action.

Singapore has used balancing and engagement simultaneously as strategies to advance its interests. This approach is not risk-free: it might enmesh Singapore in regional conflicts. But at the same time, it is more flexible than the Swiss strategy because there is less of a dissonance between what is said and what is done. Having established close relations with both established powers such as the US and emerging powers such as China and India, Singapore has been caught in the middle of an ongoing tussle for power and influence in the Asia–Pacific, where it has had to repeatedly affirm that it is "not taking sides". Ensuring equidistant relations with all major powers requires high expenditures of political capital, while maintaining a deterrent military force entails high military expenditures. Thus, despite their conceptual divergences, both Singaporean and Swiss foreign policies are driven by similar underlying desires to survive and retain independence in an increasingly multi-polar world.

References

Acharya, A. *Singapore's Foreign Policy: The Search for Regional Order*. World Scientific, 2008.

Agius, C. *The Social Construction of Swedish Neutrality: Challenges to Swedish Identity and Sovereignty*. Manchester University Press, 2006.

Ang, C. G. *Lee Kuan Yew's Strategic Thought*. Routledge, 2013.

Armstrong, H. F. "Neutrality: Varying Tunes." *Foreign Affairs*, October 1956. http://www.foreignaffairs.com/articles/71287/hamilton-fish-armstrong/neutrality-varying-tunes.

Björkdahl, A. *From Idea to Norm — Promoting Conflict Prevention*. Department of Political Science, 2002. http://lup.lub.lu.se/record/20760.

Breuning, M. "Words and Deeds: Foreign Assistance Rhetoric and Policy Behavior in the Netherlands, Belgium, and the United Kingdom." *International Studies Quarterly* 39, no. 2 (June 1, 1995): 235–54. doi:10.2307/2600848.

Cohen, S. A. "Small States and Their Armies: Restructuring the Militia Framework of the Israel Defense Force." *Journal of Strategic Studies* 18, no. 4 (December 1995): 78–93. doi:10.1080/01402399508437620.

De Vattel, E., J. Chitty, and E. D. Ingraham. *Law of Nations*. T. & J. W. Johnson, 1852.

Finnemore, M. *National Interests in International Society*. 1st edition. Ithaca, N.Y: Cornell University Press, 1996.

Fox, A. B. *The Power of Small States: Diplomacy in World War II*. Chicago, Ill., U.S.A.: University of Chicago Press, 1959.

Ganesan, N. *Realism and Interdependence in Singapore's Foreign Policy*. Routledge, 2005.

Goetschel, L., M. Bernath, and D. Schwarz. *Swiss Foreign Policy: Foundations and Possibilities*. Psychology Press, 2005.

Grant-Bailey, S. N. *The Law of Neutrality: Notes and Analysis*. London: Stevens, 1944.

Hänggi, H. *Small State as a Third State: Switzerland and Asia-Europe Inter-Regionalism*. St. Gallen: Institut für Politikwissenschaft, Hochschule St. Gallen, 1998.

Hey, Jeanne A. K. *Small States in World Politics: Explaining Foreign Policy Behavior*. Boulder: Lynne Rienner Publishers, 2003.

Ingebritsen, C. "Norm Entrepreneurs: Scandinavia's Role in World Politics." *Cooperation and Conflict* 37, no. 1 (2002): 11–23.

Ingebritsen, C. *Small States in International Relations*. University of Iceland Press, 2006.

Jessup, P. C., F. Deák, W. A. Phillips, A. H. Reede, and E. W. Turlington. "Neutrality, Its History, Economics and Law," 1935. http://agris.fao.org/agris-search/search.do?recordID=US201300453812.

Jowett, B., and Peabody, A. P. *Thucydides*. Boston: D. Lothrop & Co., 1883.

Karsh, E. *Neutrality and Small States*. London; New York: Routledge, 1988.

Katzenstein, P. J. *Small States in World Markets: Industrial Policy in Europe*. Ithaca, N.Y.: Cornell University Press, 1985.

Keohane, R. O. "Lilliputians' Dilemmas: Small States in International Politics." *International Organization* 23, no. 02 (March 1969): 291–310. doi:10.1017/S002081830003160X.

Keohane, R. O., and J. S. Nye. *Power and Interdependence: World Politics in Transition*. Little, Brown, 1977.

Krebs, R. R. "Perverse Institutionalism: NATO and the Greco-Turkish Conflict." *International Organization* 53, no. 02 (March 1999): 343–77. doi:10.1162/002081899550904.

Kruzel, J., and M. H. Haltzel. *Between the Blocs: Problems and Prospects for Europe's Neutral and Nonaligned States.* Cambridge University Press, 1989.

Lee, K. Y. "Speech by Mr Lee Kuan Yew, Minister Mentor, Delivered at The S. Rajaratnam Lecture, 09 April 2009, 5:30 PM at Shangri-La Hotel." *Singapore Press Centre.* Accessed April 24, 2015. http://www.news.gov.sg/public/sgpc/en/media_releases/agencies/pmo/speech/S-20090409-1.html.

Leifer, M. *Singapore's Foreign Policy: Coping with Vulnerability.* Psychology Press, 2000.

Leifer, M., J. C. Liow, and R. Emmers. *Order and Security in Southeast Asia: Essays in Memory of Michael Leifer.* Psychology Press, 2006.

Moravcsik, A. "Liberal Intergovernmentalism and Integration: A Rejoinder." *JCMS: Journal of Common Market Studies* 33, no. 4 (December 1995): 611–28. doi:10.1111/j.1468-5965.1995.tb00554.x.

Moravcsik, A. "Preferences and Power in the European Community: A Liberal Intergovernmentalist Approach." *JCMS: Journal of Common Market Studies* 31, no. 4 (December 1993): 473–524. doi:10.1111/j.1468-5965.1993.tb00477.x.

Neuhold, H., and H. Thalberg. *The European Neutrals in International Affairs.* Wilhelm Braumüller, 1984.

Ogley, R. *The Theory and Practice of Neutrality in the Twentieth Century.* London: Routledge & K. Paul, 1970.

Ørvik, N. *The Decline of Neutrality, 1914-1941. With Special Reference to the United States and the Northern Neutrals.* Oslo: J. Tanum, 1953.

Pape, R. A. "Soft Balancing against the United States." *International Security* 30, no. 1 (July 1, 2005): 7–45. doi:10.1162/0162288054894607.

Politis, N. *La neutralité et la paix.* Paris: Hachette, 1935.

Ravenhill, J. "Regionalism." In *Global Political Economy*, 172–209. Oxford University Press, 2008.

Raymond, G. A. "Neutrality Norms and the Balance of Power." *Cooperation and Conflict.* 32(2) June 1997: 123-146, 1997.

Rothstein, R. L. *Alliances and Small Powers.* Columbia University Press, 1968.

Selwyn, P., ed. *Development Policy in Small Countries.* London: Croom Helm in association with the Institute of Development Studies, 1975.

Singh, B. *The Vulnerability of Small States Revisited: A Study of Singapore's Post-Cold War Foreign Policy.* Gadjah Mada University Press, 1999.

Stone, D. "Global Public Policy, Transnational Policy Communities, and Their Networks." *Policy Studies Journal* 36, no. 1 (February 1, 2008): 19–38. doi:10.1111/j.1541-0072.2007.00251.x.

Van Bynkershoek, C. *On Questions of Public Law. Two Books, in 1 Vol. English.* Oxford; At the Clarendon Press. London; Humphrey Milford, 1930. http://www.lawbookexchange.com/pages/books/29277/cornelius-van-bynker-shoek-tenney-frank-trans/on-questions-of-public-law-two-books-in-1-vol-english.

Vital, D. *The Inequality of States. A Study of the Small Power in International Relations.* Pp. 198. Clarendon Press: Oxford, 1967.

Vital, D. *The Survival of Small States: Studies in Small Power/great Power Conflict.* London; New York: Oxford University Press, 1971.

Waltz, K. N. *Theory of International Politics.* Addison-Wesley Pub. Co., 1979.

Wilson, W. "Wilson's War Message to Congress." *The World War I Document Archive*, April 2, 1917. http://wwi.lib.byu.edu/index.php/Wilson%27s_War_Message_to_Congress.

Zahariadis, N. "Nationalism and Small-State Foreign Policy: The Greek Response to the Macedonian Issue." *Political Science Quarterly* 109, no. 4 (October 1994): 647–67. doi:10.2307/2151842.

Chapter 3

Trade Policy: The *Status Quo* and The *Quo Vadis* of Trade Liberalisation

Michel Anliker[1]

Introduction

Today's economy has become highly complex and a wide range of factors play a major role in business decisions to remain competitive. Strategic decisions are not exclusively taken based on competitive tax policies and available tax incentives anymore. Businesses have an emerging interest to invest and expand in developing countries. Therefore, strategic considerations around factors such as the availability of investment opportunities, the development of infrastructure, labour standards, the integration of smooth and secure supply chains (i.e., trade facilitation), the stability of political environments, and legal certainty, are increasingly important for businesses. The entire economic framework of a country is a major factor for businesses to remain competitive in today's global trade.

In this respect, trade liberalisation, respectively Free Trade Agreements (FTAs) and Regional Trade Agreements (RTAs), has become a major topic in the world of global trade. Almost daily, newspapers carry headlines on new FTA negotiations or the signature of new FTAs, but also worrying news such as increasing protectionism through non-tariff barriers and

---

[1]This article includes the author's personal views, fact findings, experiences and conclusions. Some of the topics discussed are highly topical and their developments may have changed since the time this article was written.

trade distortions. Dispute settlements and other trade restrictions, sanctions or embargos are also frequently discussed.

In this global competition of trade liberalisation through FTAs and RTAs, two countries are playing leading roles: Singapore and Switzerland. They are often compared because of their small sizes and prosperous economies. In foreign trade, both countries pursue an open-minded and trade-facilitative approach. In the very early days, both economies realised that with their limited size and resources, the only way for them to remain competitive was to attract businesses locally and increase international trade beyond their borders.

This paper gives an overview of both countries' trade policies, focusing on their continuous and ambitious efforts to negotiate bi- and multilateral trade agreements. Section II (Singapore) and Section III (Switzerland) gives an overview of each country's FTA strategy, highlighting the motives and the importance of FTAs. Section IV will highlight the potential impacts of future "mega" FTAs such as the Transatlantic Trade and Investment Partnership (TTIP) and the Trans-Pacific Partnership (TPP) on Singapore and Switzerland. This is followed by Section V which gives a critical view of the increasing amounts of concluded FTAs and RTAs, the increasing issues observed around non-tariff barriers as well as how well FTAs are utilized. Finally, Section VI gives two examples of typical practical challenges for companies using FTAs, finalised by my conclusions in Section VII.

Singapore

Singapore is a small country with almost no natural resources. As a consequence, Singapore's trade policy direction is guided by its dependence on the global economy and is export-driven. It is estimated that 60 percent of Singapore's gross domestic product (GDP) and about 50 percent of employment is directly linked with foreign demands. In 2014, Singapore's total merchandise trade grew by 0.3 percent, in contrast to the 0.5 percent decline in the previous year. Singapore's total merchandise trade reached S$982.7 billion in 2014, higher than the previous year's achievement of S$980.2 billion. Total merchandise exports expanded by 1.1 percent in 2014 while merchandise imports declined by 0.6 percent in the same period.[2] Singapore remains one of the largest trading hubs in the world. The constraints of a small domestic market with limited natural resources is its dependence on the global economy and its dependence on free market access around the world for its economic survival and growth.[3] These are key factors for Singapore's foreign trade policy.

Hence, to maintain economic wealth, sustainable future growth and international development as well as competitiveness, Singapore is required to stay linked to global markets. Having a close connection and being tightly integrated within the region (and globally) is of major importance for Singapore. Singapore's trade policy aims are as follows:[4]

- It aims to expand the international economic space for Singapore-based companies;
- It seeks a predictable and fair trading environment for Singapore-based companies by supporting a rules-based multilateral trading system;
- It strives to minimise impediments to the flow of imports by continuously improving Singapore's trade and business environment. Singapore achieves these goals by engaging with trade partners at the multilateral, regional and bilateral levels, while working domestically to improve the flow of goods, services and investments into Singapore.

Singapore has always played an important role within the WTO for the multilateral trading system. Singapore promotes trade liberalisation and is fully committed to the Doha Development Agenda negotiations. Singapore has chaired committees and negotiating groups and is participating in regular WTO bodies and committees. However, since the Doha Round is not yet ready to be finalised, Singapore is — following

---

[2]"Review of 2014 Trade Performance." International Enterprise Singapore, February 17, 2015. http://www.iesingapore.gov.sg/Media-Centre/Media-Releases/2015/2/Review-of-2014-Trade-Performance.

[3]Liang, Margaret. "Singapore's Trade Policies: Priorities and Options." *ASEAN Economic Bulletin* 22, no. 1 (2005): 49–59

[4]"Trade Policy Review Report by Singapore." World Trade Organization, June 5, 2012, page 6. https://docs.wto.org/dol2fe/Pages/FE_Search/DDFDocuments/34513/Q/WT/TPR/G267.pdf.

the global trend — pursuing bilateral and regional trade strategies to complement its efforts at the multilateral level.

Aside from its large FTA network, which will be described later in this article, Singapore is engaged in various bodies, cooperations and associations.

Singapore is a founding member of the Asia–Pacific Economic Cooperation (APEC), which was established in 1989. The APEC strongly strives for regional economic integration initiatives and its secretariat is located in Singapore. The APEC has 21 member economies[5] promoting free trade throughout the Asia–Pacific region, aiming to strengthen regional peace and security between member economies. Singapore is a supporter of the common goals of free and open trade and investment which APEC has undertaken since the Bogor Declaration of 1994.[6] Within the APEC, Singapore's implication in the negotiations of the Free Trade Area of the Asia–Pacific (FTAAP), which started in 2006, demonstrates its policy of trade engagement to further liberalise trade.

Aside from APEC, Singapore is a founding member and an active participant of the Association of Southeast Asian Nations (ASEAN), which was established on 8 August 1967 in Bangkok (Thailand), with the signing of the ASEAN Declaration (Bangkok Declaration) together with Indonesia, Malaysia, Philippines and Thailand. ASEAN is a political and economic organisation. Singapore strongly supports ASEAN's goal of building a strong, cohesive and prosperous ASEAN.[7] Singapore signed the first FTA under the ASEAN Free Trade Area (AFTA) that came into force on 1 January 1993. The ASEAN member countries also signed an agreement on the Common Effective Preferential Tariff (CEPT) Scheme in 1992 to eliminate tariffs and non-tariff barriers in the region. In 2010, the ASEAN Trade in Goods Agreement (ATIGA) entered into

---

[5]Australia, Brunei Darussalam, Canada, Indonesia, Japan, South Korea, Malaysia, New Zealand, Philippines, Singapore, Thailand, United States, Republic of China (Taiwan), Hong Kong, People's Republic of China, Mexico, Papua New Guinea, Chile, Peru, Russian Federation Vietnam.
[6]"APEC." Ministry of Foreign Affairs, Singapore. Accessed April 28, 2016. http://www.mfa.gov.sg/content/mfa/international_organisation_initiatives/apec.html.
[7]"ASEAN." Ministry of Foreign Affairs, Singapore. Accessed April 28, 2016. http://www.mfa.gov.sg/content/mfa/international_organisation_initiatives/asean.html.

force. The ATIGA is an enhancement of the CEPT–AFTA to a more comprehensive legal instrument. With ATIGA, certain ASEAN agreements relating to trade in goods (i.e., CEPT Agreement and selected Protocols) have been superseded.[8]

At this stage, it is worth mentioning the efforts of the EU to negotiate FTAs with countries in Asia. Singapore has concluded an FTA with the EU, which is the second FTA the EU has concluded with an Asian country (the first being South Korea, and the third being Vietnam). Initially negotiations were launched in July 2007 for an ASEAN-EU FTA. However, both sides agreed to suspend the negotiations in March 2009. At the 12th ASEAN Economic Ministers (AEM)–EU Trade Commissioner Consultations on 8 March 2013 in Hanoi, the EU Trade Commissioner reiterated that the EU would pursue bilateral FTA negotiations with individual ASEAN member countries as building blocks towards the regional FTA and that the EU would consider resuming negotiations of an ASEAN–EU FTA upon the realisation of the ASEAN Economic Community (AEC) by the end of 2015. These bilateral FTAs were conceived as building blocks towards a future region-to-region agreement. Negotiations were launched with Malaysia in 2010, with Vietnam in June 2012 and with Thailand in March 2013 and with the Philippines in 2016. The European Commission finalised the negotiation of a bilateral FTA with Singapore in October 2014 and with Vietnam in August 2015. The EU remains open to starting new negotiations with other partners in the region and hopes to complete these agreements in the future with a region-to-region trade agreement.

Singapore is also engaged in the discussion on the ASEAN Economic Community (AEC). The AEC is an effort to integrate the economies of Southeast Asia through the gradual harmonisation of various policies and the gradual removal of restrictive policies. The AEC aims to transform the economies of ASEAN's 10 member states into a single market and production base which should be established by 31 December 2015.[9] A

---

[8] "Singapore's International Network of Agreements." International Enterprise Singapore. Accessed April 28, 2016. http://www.iesingapore.gov.sg/trade-from-singapore/international-agreements.

[9] The AEC consists of four pillars: Pillar 1: Single Market & Production Base, Pillar 2: Competitive Economic Region, Pillar 3: Equitable Economic Development and Pillar 4: Integration into the Global Economy.

common misunderstanding is that the AEC is not a customs union like the EU and there is no common external tariff. The customs borders between AEC countries will remain. The AEC is not a political union in any manner and there is no ASEAN parliament or other body with rule-making authority being considered at this time. However, from a pure trade-in-goods perspective, the goal of having a free flow of goods has already been achieved with ATIGA in 2010.

So far we have discussed the broad approach of Singapore through various engagements to diversify and strengthen their foreign trade policy. Let us now turn the discussion towards its FTA network.

The FTA network of Singapore includes 21 bilateral[10] and regional FTAs in force with 32 trading partners. Singapore signed an FTA with the EU and the Trans-Pacific Partnership (TPP)[11] and is currently negotiating the Regional Comprehensive Economic Partnership (RCEP).[12] Singapore's FTAs have been helpful for Singapore-based businesses in strengthening cross-border trade, eliminating or reducing import tariff rates in various partner countries, providing preferential access to services sectors, easing investment rules, improving intellectual property regulations, and opening government procurement opportunities. Being a member of ASEAN, Singapore is a signatory partner of the ASEAN FTAs with major regional economies such as Australia, China, India, Japan, Korea and New Zealand. Beyond advancing economic interests, these intra- and inter-regional FTAs help build a web of strategic linkages for Singapore within the region and with countries outside the region. These FTAs also help to

---

[10]ASEAN Free Trade Area (AFTA), ASEAN-Australia-New Zealand FTA (AANZFTA), ASEAN-China (ACFTA), ASEAN-India (AIFTA), ASEAN-Japan (AJCEP), ASEAN-Korea (AKFTA), Australia (SAFTA), China (CSFTA), Costa Rica (SCRFTA), GCC (GSFTA), General Hashemite Kingdom of Jordan (SJFTA), India (CECA), Japan (JSEPA), Korea (KSFTA), New Zealand (ANZSCEP), Panama (PSFTA), Peru (PeSFTA), Switzerland, Liechtenstein, Norway and Iceland (ESFTA), Trans-Pacific SEP (Brunei, New Zealand, Chile, Singapore), United States (USSFTA).

[11]Member countries: Australia, Brunei Darussalam, Canada, Chile, Japan, Malaysia, Mexico, New Zealand, Peru, Singapore, Vietnam and the United States.

[12]Negotiating countries: 10 ASEAN Member States and the six ASEAN FTA Partners, i.e., Australia, China, India, Japan, Republic of Korea and New Zealand.

sustain an open regional orientation and prevent the formation of inward-looking trading blocs.[13] However, the rapid development and conclusions of a large number of FTAs and RTAs are leading to more complexities, also commonly known as the "noodle bowl" or "spaghetti bowl" effect. The increasing number of applicable FTAs without harmonised rules of origin is making it difficult for businesses to use their full potential. Businesses may even give up the idea of using FTA benefits just because the large quantity of information makes it too complicated to use them. The FTAAP, and more recently the RCEP discussions, should align those large numbers of agreements, harmonising the rules of origin and promoting a large free trade area. It may, however, take some time until one of those agreements is settled and its successful conclusion will largely depend on the political will of the negotiating parties.

Not only does Singapore ambitiously conclude bilateral agreements which are designed as building blocks towards broader regional integration, which will in turn strengthen the global consensus for free and open trade,[14] Singapore is also engaged in various organisations and bodies to pursue its open foreign trade policy.

Switzerland

Switzerland is a small country which is poor in natural resources. An international economic outlook is essential for Switzerland to increase and maintain a high level of prosperity. Switzerland depends on international trade in goods and services and cross-border investment activities to maintain its level of wealth. It is a core objective of Swiss foreign economic policy to constantly improve foreign market access. The multilateral approach within the framework of the World Trade Organisation (WTO) is the best way to achieve this objective. However, since the Doha Round, progress in WTO negotiations has been slow, and the constantly growing

---

[13] "FTAs." Ministry of Foreign Affairs, Singapore. Accessed April 28, 2016. http://www.mfa.gov.sg/content/mfa/international_organisation_initiatives/ftas.html.
[14] "Trade Policy Review Report by Singapore." *World Trade Organization*, June 5, 2012, page 7. https://docs.wto.org/dol2fe/Pages/FE_Search/DDFDocuments/34513/Q/WT/TPR/G267.pdf.

number of countries which are entering into bilateral and plurilateral FTAs is a trend which Switzerland has to actively pursue to maintain its international competitiveness. By concluding and negotiating FTAs, Switzerland aims to provide its companies with a similar level of access to international markets, gain access to business opportunities and promote domestic policy reforms.[15] Switzerland has to keep pace with its most important foreign competitors, such as the European Union (EU), US and Japan, which are continuously extending their FTA networks. FTAs are an important instrument in maintaining and strengthening Switzerland's competitiveness as a business hub.[16]

At a very early stage, the Swiss government initiated the first steps towards an open-minded international trade policy, which led to Switzerland becoming one of the founding members of the European Free Trade Association (EFTA), a free trade organisation. The Stockholm Convention, which established the EFTA, was signed on 4 January 1960 in the Swedish capital by seven countries — Austria, Denmark, Norway, Portugal, Sweden, Switzerland and the United Kingdom.

Since the establishment of the European Economic Community (EEC) in 1957 (the members at that time were France, West Germany, Italy, Belgium, Luxembourg and the Netherlands), the EFTA functioned as a trade bloc-alternative to the EEC.

To prevent a split into two separate economic blocs, several FTAs were concluded in the beginning of 1970 between the EEC and members of the EFTA. In 1972, Switzerland signed an FTA with the EEC, which entered into force on 1 January 1973. This FTA allowed Switzerland to deepen its relationship with the EEC and resulted in a significant reduction of tariff barriers (import and export duties as well as certain quotas) for industrial products that were produced within the free trade zone.

With the rejection of the accession of Switzerland to the European Union (EU) on 6 December 1992, Switzerland and the EU started to negotiate a special relationship in 1994. Switzerland wanted to safeguard

---

[15] "Free Trade Agreements." *State Secretariat for Economic Affairs SECO*. Accessed April 28, 2016. https://www.secolive.admin.ch/themen/00513/00515/01330/index.html?lang=en.
[16] *Ibid.*

its economic integration with the EU. These negotiations resulted in a total of 10 treaties (the so-called Bilateral I treaties concluded in 1999 and Bilateral II treaties concluded in 2004), the sum of which makes a large share of EU law applicable to Switzerland. The Bilateral I treaties[17] have a major importance for Switzerland's economy since these various agreements regulate the abolishment of tariffs of industrial products and processed agricultural products, the facilitation of market entry through mutual recognition, and the alignment of regulations as well as Switzerland's participation in Europe's research area. As of today, the relationship between Switzerland and the EU is an important pillar in both countries' foreign trade policy.

However, this relationship has recently been tarnished with the acceptance of the federal popular initiative "against mass immigration" in February 2014. This initiative aims to limit immigration through quotas, which contradicts the principle of the free movement of people, specified in one of the agreements of the Bilateral I treaties. As a consequence, the EU could dissolve the entire set of Bilateral I treaties, since it contains a so-called "guillotine clause" (i.e., if Switzerland does not fulfil one of the agreed commitments, the clause foresees a revocation of all the Bilateral I treaties). The EU has (fortunately) not taken this step; however, in some cases Switzerland already faces more challenges in discussions with the EU. It is still too early to assess the long-term consequences of that initiative and the general impacts on Switzerland's economy. For example, in education and research, Switzerland's participation in the important Framework Program for Research and Technological Development has faced certain restrictions and it is working on alternative solutions.

Switzerland needs to carefully assess the situation and work hard to maintain its good relationship with the EU. The relationship is not only important for trade in goods between the two countries (e.g., in 2013, about 55 percent of Switzerland's exports were destined to the EU, whereas about 73 percent were imports from the EU into Switzerland), but also for a wide range of other aspects of collaboration, since the Bilateral

---

[17] The seven agreements regulate the following topics: free movement of people, air traffic, road traffic, agriculture, technical trade barriers, public procurement, and science.

I treaties constitute a broad-ranging comprehensive agreement. The EU is and remains Switzerland's most important trade partner.

Coming back to Switzerland's emerging interest to pursue its path of concluding FTAs, the Federal Council's foreign economic policy strategy adopted in 2004 — which is still applicable — established four criteria for the selection of prospective free trade partners:[18]

- The current and potential economic importance of a partner;
- The extent of existing or potential discrimination that may result from the conclusion of FTAs between the prospective partner and important competitors of Switzerland;
- The willingness of the partner to enter into negotiations, and the corresponding prospects for success;
- Other considerations such as the expected contribution of an FTA towards the economic stabilisation and development of a partner or its compatibility with Swiss foreign policy objectives in general.

As a result of this policy, Switzerland has built up a network of 28 FTAs[19] with 38 partners, excluding the FTA with the EU and with the EFTA. Switzerland usually concludes its FTAs together with its EFTA partners but also has the possibility of entering into FTAs outside the EFTA framework. Out of those 28 FTAs, 25 have been concluded within the EFTA framework. The FTAs with China, Japan and the Faroe Islands

---

[18] Abt, Marianne. "The Economic Relevance of Free Trade Agreements with Partners Outside the EU," November 5, 2010. https://www.secolive.admin.ch/themen/00513/00515/ 01330/index.html?lang=en&download=NHzLpZeg7t,lnp6I0NTU04212Z6ln1ad1IZn4Z2q ZpnO2Yuq2Z6gpJCFeYJ2fWym162epYbg2c_JjKbNoKSn6A--.

[19] EFTA-Convention, European Community, Faeroe Islands, Macedonia, Albania, Serbia, Ukraine, Montenegro, Bosnia-Herzegovina, Turkey, Israel, Palestinian Authority, Morocco, Jordan, Tunisia, Lebanon, Egypt, Mexico, Singapore, Chile, Republic of Korea, South African Custom Union (SACU: South Africa, Botswana, Lesotho, Namibia and Swaziland), Canada, Japan, Colombia, Peru, Hong Kong, Cooperation Council for the Arab States of the Gulf (GCC: Bahrain, Kuwait, Oman, Qatar, Saudi Arabia and the United Arab Emirates), China, Central American States (Costa Rica, Guatemala, Honduras and Panama). Source: http://www.seco.admin.ch/themen/00513/00515/01330/04619/index. html?lang=en.

have been concluded on a bilateral basis. This policy is underpinned by a statistical analysis of the average growth of worldwide trade versus growth with FTA partners. Between 1988 and 2008, Swiss worldwide exports have increased by an average of 5.7 percent annually whereas trade with FTA partners has grown on average more than 10.5 percent per year.[20]

The current trend of concluding FTAs seems unstoppable. The EFTA recently concluded negotiations with Guatemala. Negotiations are ongoing with Indonesia, Vietnam and India. Because of the current conflict in the Ukraine, negotiations with the Belarus–Kazakhstan–Russia Customs Union have been put on hold. The EFTA has started its first talks to enter into negotiations with Malaysia. Discussions have been continued with the Mercosur[21] Member States. Finally, a Joint Declaration on Cooperation with the Philippines has been signed to engage in further talks.

The above outlines Switzerland's efforts to pursue its plurilateral liberalisation to increase its access to other export markets and achieve economic growth. Not only is the conclusion of new FTAs a top priority on Switzerland's trade agenda, but so is the updating of concluded FTAs. The "older" FTAs have to be adapted to newer economic developments. This will strengthen Switzerland's position as an attractive business location and will maintain and increase employment. However, on this journey of trade liberalisation, certain obstacles have to be overcome. The volatility of today's global economy is accompanied by uncertainties for countries' economic development. Hence, the trade community has observed an increase in non-tariff measures. Switzerland's non-competitive sectors, such as agriculture, are under pressure and the related restrictive agricultural policy can be considered to be a barrier for trade negotiations. Agriculture is sensitive not only in Switzerland but in every country. As a result, more than 60 years of negotiations in the General Agreement on Tariffs and Trade (GATT) and in the WTO have made only modest progress towards opening agricultural markets.[22]

---

[20] Abt, Marianne. "The Economic Relevance of Free Trade Agreements with Partners Outside the EU."

[21] MERCOSUR refers to Argentina, Brazil, Paraguay, Uruguay.

[22] Elms, Deborah. "Why Is Agriculture So Difficult for Trade Deals?" Asian Trade Centre, April 28, 2015. http://www.asiantradecentre.org/talkingtrade/2015/4/28/why-is-agriculture-

Pertaining to this situation, Urata[23] emphasises that within the context of Japan's protective agricultural policy, liberalising rather than protecting the agricultural sector will help to achieve sustainable economic growth. He mentions that the inefficient use of effort as well as the misallocation of resources and its related high costs for protectionism in various forms neither encourages the promotion of FTAs nor increases economic growth. He emphasises that liberalisation would mean that governments have to find creative and proactive solutions to mitigate the impact on potential unemployment and adjustment costs.[24] In future, Switzerland should conduct further studies in that respect and will have to delicately balance its export market interests against its protective measures within the agricultural sector.[25]

Future Impact of TTIP and TPP

Hardly a day goes by without optimistic news about FTA negotiations and new trade deals. On the other hand, negative news such as politicians criticising trade agreements and people protesting against trade deals has also increased. International trade, especially free trade, is omnipresent. It has become a sensitive topic not only in itself but also as a (geo-) political instrument.

The mega-trade deals such as TTIP, TPP and RCEP will have different impacts on Singapore's and Switzerland's economies respectively. After long negotiations, on 5 October 2015, it was announced that the TPP was concluded successfully. We may recall that President Obama faced many difficulties to obtain Trade Promotion Authority (TPA), having the House and the Senate going back and forth until it was finally approved. As of today, there is uncertainty about the ratification process. The US has quite a

---

so-difficult-for-trade-deals.

[23] Urata, Shujiro. "Free Trade Agreements: A Catalyst for Japan's Economic Revitalization." *Reviving Japan's Economy*, 2005, pp. 377–410.

[24] *Ibid.*

[25] Schweizerische Bundesrat. "Bericht zur Aussenwirtschaftspolitik 2014." *Switzerland Global Enterprise*, January 14, 2015, p. 62.

time-consuming political process, and in the midst of that, there is the presidential election with a new (and possibly different) trade agenda. Most of the member countries believe that the TPP's very survival is contingent on US ratification. Future political developments will bring us the answers but there are clearly elements that create continued uncertainty and may impede the successful implementation of the TPP.

These new generations of FTAs are purported to be the "new" standard of trade agreements, as topics beyond simple tariff reduction are negotiated. Even if such trade agreements aim for comprehensiveness and include commitments to services, investment, intellectual property rights, government procurement, competition and so on, they are quite controversial. Opponents are criticising the fact that the negotiations and content of these trade agreements are kept secret, and there is fear about topics such as the Investor–State Dispute Settlement (ISDS) mechanism to circumvent state sovereignty, and its possible impacts on the cost of medicine, currency manipulation and income inequality, just to name a few.

However, independently of the actual outcome of a conclusion of those agreements, it is at this stage worthwhile to highlight what potential impacts those trade deals may have on Singapore's and Switzerland's trade landscapes.

The TTIP was initiated by the EU and the US. Singapore is not part of the TTIP negotiations. However, since Singapore has bilateral FTAs with the EU and the US, the potential negative impact might be less of a concern and it is balanced out. In contrast, Switzerland's concerns are more significant, especially potential trade diversion effects. Discriminatory effects, mainly in the agricultural sector, are expected in both the EU and the US markets. Further negative effects, aside from tariff reductions, may be encountered in the areas of services and government procurement.[26] Switzerland does not yet have an FTA with the US; related negotiations were stopped by the Federal Council in 2006 because of disagreements in the agricultural sector. It is expected that the TTIP will lead to competitive disadvantages for Switzerland.

---

[26] Schweizerische Bundesrat. "Bericht zur Aussenwirtschaftspolitik 2014," p. 59.

Having said the above, a recent study[27] has highlighted that Switzerland may still receive certain benefits of the TTIP through spillover effects. Should the agreement, for example, abolish or reduce tariffs and non-tariff barriers in a comprehensive way (so-called "deep agreement"), it is expected that through the regulatory harmonisation of non-tariff barriers, Switzerland may unilaterally move and adopt its European compatibility to a rather more focused transatlantic compatibility of standards and regulations. As a consequence, Switzerland may indirectly benefit from the TTIP. However, Switzerland will have to closely observe the ongoing negotiations and take proactive actions to encounter any trade diversion effects.

The TPP was initiated by Brunei, Chile, New Zealand and Singapore, and counts twelve member countries: Australia, Canada, Japan, Malaysia, Mexico, Peru, the US and Vietnam. For Singapore, being part of the TPP is an enormous competitive advantage to keep pace with the growing race of global free trade and to expand its global network as well as its integration in international trade. Switzerland, however, is not part of that trade deal either. As with the TTIP, the potential negative impacts of TPP are, as of today, very difficult, if not impossible, to assess. The Swiss government foresees that the impacts of the TPP can, to some extent, be balanced out, since Switzerland has existing FTAs with Chile, Canada, Japan, Mexico, Peru and Singapore, and negotiations with Malaysia and Vietnam are ongoing.[28]

Aside from the Swiss and Singapore views, some critical voices have highlighted that the TPP and RCEP are a reflection of the rivalry between the US and China. Some question if these mega-RTAs are mainly

---

[27]Cottier, Thomas, Joseph François, and CEPR. "Potential Impacts of an EU-US Free Trade Agreement on the Swiss Economy and External Economic Relations." *World Trade Institute*, July 2014. https://www.seco.admin.ch/dam/seco/en/dokumente/Aussenwirtschaft/ Wirtschaftsbeziehungen/Handel%20mit%20Dienstleistungen/Artikel_Studien/WTI_ Potential_Impacts_of_TTIP.pdf.download.pdf/13%20WTI%20-%20Potential%20 Impacts%20of%20a%20EU-US%20Free%20Trade%20Agreement%20on%20the%20 Swiss%20Economy%20and%20External%20Economic%20Relations%20-%20 Summary%20(englisch).pdf.

[28]Schweizerische Bundesrat. "Bericht zur Aussenwirtschaftspolitik 2014," p. 59.

geopolitically motivated, or if, at the end, the trade aspect still prevails. This discussion goes far beyond the current content of this article but is worthwhile considering in order to have a holistic view of the topic.

A Critical View of Increasing Trade Deals

So far, we have discussed the trade policies and developments of Singapore and Switzerland, including aspects of future developments. At this point, a critical view of the entire development seems appropriate. However, we will not be able to discuss in detail all those aspects, as the complexity may require another article with further analysis.

In February 2016, the WTO counted 419 Regional Trade Agreements (RTA) which were in force and 625 were notified.[29] This corresponds to 454 physical RTAs, of which 267 are currently in force. Because of the slow progress of WTO's Doha Round of trade negotiations, countries are seeking alternative solutions to increase global trade activities. Not only are small countries such as Singapore and Switzerland seeking to enlarge their trade activities through FTAs, but large economies such as the US and China have also put trade negotiations at the top of their trade agenda.

When the regional trade exception in Article XXIV of GATT 1994 regulating the requirements to derogate from the Most Favoured Nation (MFN) principle was implemented, few could have imagined its importance in today's trade environment. The main concern of mega-RTAs creating entire trade blocs is the loss of the WTO's fundamental spirit, which is to create a non-discriminatory and fair global trade landscape. There is a clear danger that FTAs will undermine the multilateral trade rules embodied in the GATT/WTO,[30] and that developing and least-developed countries will bear the consequences. Their limited ability to participate in

---

[29] "Regional Trade Agreements." World Trade Organization. Accessed April 28, 2016. https://www.wto.org/english/tratop_e/region_e/region_e.htm.
[30] Nakatomi, Michitaka. "Plurilateral Agreements: A Viable Alternative to the WTO." In *The Future of the World Trading System: Asian Perspectives.* Edited by Richard Baldwin, Masahiro Kawai and Ganeshan Wignaraja. Centre for Economic Policy Research, 2013. http://voxeu.org/sites/default/files/Future_World_Trading_System.pdf.

mega-RTAs will leave developing and least-developed countries behind and result in effective discriminatory effects. The discriminatory nature of such FTAs against non-WTO members may also hinder the creation of future WTO rules.[31] It is a fact that FTAs and RTAs go beyond the usual coverage of the WTO and include, in addition to trade in goods and trade in services, intellectual property topics such as labour, government procurement, environment and foreign direct investment and so on. Compared to the WTO, FTAs and RTAs are much more flexible, allowing the choice of negotiating partners and including specific issues and areas.[32] In that sense, FTAs should be complementary to the WTO. On the other hand, they should give new impulses to the WTO to broaden the topics to be negotiated and to enlarge its multilateral approach. However, the large number of WTO members (i.e., 162 countries) and their ability to decide only on the basis of consensus has hindered the progress of the WTO. This is a challenge for the WTO, which has called for reforms to get the member countries again interested in further developing and supporting WTO efforts. However, criticising the WTO is easy. Member countries are playing an important role too. It is easier to follow the (self-serving) trend of concluding a large number of FTAs than to put in a lot of effort into reforming the multilateral system of the WTO.

Although free trade has been proclaimed, it is somewhat of a contradiction that non-tariff barriers and non-tariff measures are increasing. The global economic downturn resulted in an increase in protectionism. Traditional forms of protectionism such as tariff barriers have been substituted with other — less regulated — forms of barriers.[33] In practice, companies are facing an increasing number of trade barriers in their daily operations. An article in the Swiss newspaper reported about technical barriers between Switzerland and the EU with an interesting illustration: Swissmedic (the Swiss agency for the authorisation and supervision of therapeutic products) requires an authorisation for *Fisherman's Friends*

---

[31] *Ibid.*, p. 135.

[32] *Ibid.*, p. 134.

[33] Evenett, Simon. "Is Murky Protectionism a Real Threat to Asian Trade?" In *The Future of the World Trading System: Asian Perspectives*. Edited by Richard Baldwin, Masahiro Kawai and Ganeshan Wignaraja. Centre for Economic Policy Research, 2013.

candies because they carry the indication "Lozenges for cough and hoarseness", which falls under the definition of 'medicine'.[34] Another example is the extensive information requirements in some countries when it comes to labelling of food products, typically but not only in ASEAN. Food distributed directly to consumers in Laos, for example, must carry Lao language wording in a font and size that is clearly visible.[35] In Thailand, alcoholic beverages must carry the percentage of alcohol content, and a health warning, printed in Thai, on the label or on a sticker, with specific wording.[36] Even though FTAs are in force, addressing the abolishment of non-tariff barriers, the commercial reality is different.

Last but not least, what about the utilisation rates of FTAs? Are the efforts to conclude FTAs worth the result? Numerous scientific analyses and research works have been carried out.[37] One of the biggest challenges for those studies is on what basis the utilisation rates can be determined. For example, based on published trade statistics, it might be easy to state low utilisation rates if the formula used does not consider the tariff lines which are already duty-free. If two partner countries have already unilaterally reduced 80 percent of their tariff lines to zero before signing a bilateral trade agreement, the FTA utilisation for the remaining dutiable 20 percent tariff lines for which the FTA has concluded will have to be analysed. If not, the utilisation rate will always be way below 20 percent,

---

[34]Helble, Yvonne. "Handel mit der EU: Bürokraten legen dem Freihandel Fesseln an." *Neue Zürcher Zeitung*, April 9, 2015. http://www.nzz.ch/wirtschaft/buerokraten-legen-dem-freihandel-fesseln-an-1.18518444.

[35] Elms, Deborah. "Blocking Trade with a Label." *Asian Trade Centre*, February 24, 2015. http://www.asiantradecentre.org/talkingtrade/2015/2/24/blocking-trade-with-a-label.

[36]*Ibid.*

[37]Takahashi, Katsuhide, and Shujiro Urata. "On the Use of FTAs by Japanese Firms: Further Evidence." *Business and Politics* 12, no. 1 (2010); Hayakawa, Kazunobu, Daisuke Hiratsuka, Kohei Shiino, and Seiya Sukegawa. "Who Uses FTAs?" *Economic Research Institute for ASEAN and East Asia* IDE Discussion Paper, no. 207 (July 2009); Hamanaka, Shintaro. "On the Use of FTAs: A Review of Research Methodologies." ADB Working Paper Series on Regional Economic Integration, 2013; Economist Intelligence Unit. "FTAs: Fantastic, Fine or Futile? Business Views on Trade Agreements in Asia." *The Economist*, 2014; Economist Intelligence Unit. "FTAs in South-East Asia: Towards the next Generation." The Economist, 2014; AmCham Singapore, and U.S. Chamber of Commerce. "ASEAN Business Outlook Survey 2015."

which does not reflect reality. Focused on the 20 percent, the calculation may show that 80 percent of companies do use the specific FTA benefits for the 20 percent remaining tariff lines. Recent studies seem to show that the utilisation rate of FTAs has increased but is, in some regions, still very low. A survey from the Economist's Intelligence Unit[38] shows an average utilisation rate of 26 percent.[39] Another survey[40] shows a utilisation rate of between 43 to 49 percent of ASEAN FTAs through US manufacturing businesses exporting into Australia, New Zealand, China, Korea, Japan and India. A recently-published comprehensive research study of Switzerland Global Enterprise[41] analysed the FTA usage of Swiss exporters. The FTAs in scope were the Swiss–Canada FTA, the Swiss–Mexico FTA, the Swiss–South Korea FTA and the Swiss–EU FTA. The study was based on the available data of the destination (i.e., importing) countries. Within their statistical analyses, the researchers used an "adjusted utilisation rate" of FTAs, which is an effective analysis of trade flows benefitting from preferential duty rates. Through that process, zero-rated tariff lines have been excluded from the utilisation rate calculation. The result is impressive: the utilisation rates are high (in some cases above 50 percent), depending on the industry and sector. The most impressive result is the usage of the Swiss–EU FTA, which shows utilisation rates of more than 80 percent, or even above 90 percent in some sectors.

Practical Implementation of FTAs

So far we have discussed FTAs in the broad sense, as a tool of enhancing trade. The following will show the practical application and the

---

[38] Economist Intelligence Unit. "FTAs in South-East Asia: Towards the next Generation." *The Economist*, 2014. https://globalconnections.hsbc.com/downloads/ftas_in_southeast_asia.pdf.

[39] Indonesia, Malaysia, Singapore, Vietnam.

[40] AmCham Singapore, and U.S. Chamber of Commerce. "ASEAN Business Outlook Survey 2015". https://www.uschamber.com/sites/default/files/asean_business_outlook_survey_2015.pdf.

[41] Küng, Daniel, and Alfonso Orlando. "Effektivität der Schweizer Freihandelsabkommen (FHA) weltweit, Evaluierung der FHA-Nutzung durch Schweizer-Exporteure, 2012-2013." *Switzerland Global Enterprise*, January 2014. http://www.s-ge.com/sites/default/files/private_files/Effektivit%C3%A4t%20der%20Schweizer%20Freihandelsabkommen_S-GE.pdf.

operational challenges companies are facing when using FTAs. There are various reasons companies face such challenges: for example, FTA rules do not always match the commercial reality, businesses do not understand how to benefit from FTAs and which rules have to be followed, or businesses may find the rules too complex or are not aware of existing FTAs. In some cases, businesses may feel that the administrative costs overweigh the benefits of an FTA, and some customs authorities do specifically scrutinise preferential treatment of goods, which leads to frustrations in using FTAs.

Example 1: Company ABC manufactures goods in ASEAN Country A. The finished goods are exported throughout the ASEAN region. As those goods are subject to significant customs duties in various ASEAN destination countries, company ABC seeks to use the ASEAN Trade in Goods Agreement (ATIGA). Company ABC applies for a Certificate of Origin (CoO) as the manufactured goods comply with the Rules of Origin. This CoO is stamped by the Ministry of Country A, located in region Y. The port of loading of those goods, however, is located in region Z, still in Country A. Arriving in Country B, the importing customs authority rejects the CoO and requests a retroactive verification. The main reason of the rejection is that the CoO was not stamped in the same region as where the goods have been dispatched. Country A never responds to the official request of retroactive verification. As a consequence, Country B is denied preferential treatment of the goods and company ABC is obliged to pay customs duties.

Example 2: A manufacturer X in Thailand, which is a related party to Z located in Singapore, sends finished goods to Customer Y located in China. The manufactured goods are subject to customs duties in China and, as a consequence, manufacturer X applies for a Certificate of Origin in Thailand according to the ASEAN–China FTA to benefit from preferential treatment in China (provided Rules of Origin are met). X (in Thailand) sends an invoice to Z (in Singapore) who in turn sends an invoice to Y (in China). When setting up these commercial transactions and after having looked into the various operational requirements, Z realises that the Certificate of Origin must mention the Freight On Board (FOB) price.

As a consequence, Y in China will not only see the mark-up of Z but also the name of the related manufacturing entity in Thailand. This is a business confidentiality concern for Z. Z decides to route the goods through Singapore, where the regional HQ of Z is located. As a member of the ASEAN–China FTA, this is in compliance with the direct consignment rule. According to specific rules under ASEAN–China FTA, Z can apply for an intermediate CoO in Singapore. This CoO allows Z to declare the value which is stated on the invoice to Y. Hence, the CoO allows Z to mask the price and the applied mark-up, and it does not disclose the manufacturer. Within these operations and in order to be compliant with the above rules, there are additional points to consider (e.g., which scheme is to be used for storage in the intermediate country, local requirements for trans-shipment in combination with the specific ASEAN FTA, varying documentation requirements, etc.).

The above are two simple (and simplified) practical examples which illustrate that even with FTAs, barriers at the border do still remain. It also shows the level of detail at which the provisions of an FTA need to be understood and how technical the process can become when businesses are seeking the preferential treatment of goods.

Conclusion

It is undeniable that for countries such as Singapore and Switzerland, trade liberalisation has to be at the top of their trade agenda. The increasing numbers of FTAs and RTAs indicates a shift to focused negotiations with selected partners on selected topics to push forward each country's own economic interest to increase economic growth — a consequence of the slow progress of the WTO. The large number of trade agreements will consequently add associated complexities that should be questioned by the trade community. Would it not be better to have quality instead of quantity? The feedback of the business community illustrates the difficulty of practically implementing a reasonable FTA strategy. What will the future bring in this respect? Even more agreements with more rules, none of them harmonised? The administrative costs to implement and use efficiently the raising number of FTAs will increase significantly, and, as a consequence, businesses may use them less. Non-tariff barriers are rising, and the utilisation rates of FTAs are, on average, not as high as expected. For small countries such as Singapore and Switzerland, where cross-border movements of goods and export-oriented trade policies are essential for their economic survival, FTAs and RTAs are a must to remain competitive. The difficulty of future updates to all those agreements has been underestimated and will be a future obstacle. On a long-term perspective, "back to the roots" might be the smarter way to go. The discriminatory effects of building more and more trade blocs will only raise trade distortion for non-partner countries. Countries should take a step back and push the WTO agenda again, initiating discussions on a WTO level and making the WTO a platform to address the current and future trade developments. A harmonised approach may increase global trade activities even more efficiently.

References

Abt, M. "The Economic Relevance of Free Trade Agreements with Partners Outside the EU," November 5, 2010. https://www.secolive.admin.ch/themen/ 00513/00515/01330/index.html?lang=en&download=NHzLpZeg7t,lnp6I0N TU042l2Z6ln1ad1IZn4Z2qZpnO2Yuq2Z6gpJCFeYJ2fWym162epYbg2c_ JjKbNoKSn6A--.

AmCham Singapore, and U.S. Chamber of Commerce. "ASEAN Business Outlook Survey 2015," 2015. https://www.uschamber.com/sites/default/ files/asean_business_outlook_survey_2015.pdf

"APEC." *Ministry of Foreign Affairs, Singapore.* Accessed April 28, 2016. http:// www.mfa.gov.sg/content/mfa/international_organisation_initiatives/apec. html.

"ASEAN." *Ministry of Foreign Affairs, Singapore.* Accessed April 28, 2016. http://www.mfa.gov.sg/content/mfa/international_organisation_initiatives/ asean.html.

Cottier, T., J. François, and CEPR. "Potential Impacts of an EU-US Free Trade Agreement on the Swiss Economy and External Economic Relations." *World Trade Institute*, July 2014. https://www.seco.admin.ch/dam/seco/en/ dokumente/Aussenwirtschaft/Wirtschaftsbeziehungen/Handel%20mit%20 Dienstleistungen/Artikel_Studien/WTI_Potential_Impacts_of_TTIP.pdf. download.pdf/13%20WTI%20-%20Potential%20Impacts%20of%20a%20

EU-US%20Free%20Trade%20Agreement%20on%20the%20Swiss%20
Economy%20and%20External%20Economic%20Relations%20-%20
Summary%20(englisch).pdf.

Economist Intelligence Unit. "FTAs: Fantastic, Fine or Futile? Business Views on
Trade Agreements in Asia." *The Economist*, 2014. https://globalconnections.
hsbc.com/downloads/ftas_fantastic_fine_or_futile.pdf.

————. "FTAs in South-East Asia: Towards the next Generation." *The Economist*,
2014. https://globalconnections.hsbc.com/downloads/ftas_in_southeast_
asia.pdf.

Elms, D. "Blocking Trade with a Label." *Asian Trade Centre*, February 24, 2015.
http://www.asiantradecentre.org/talkingtrade/2015/2/24/blocking-trade-
with-a-label.

————. "Talking Trade Blog Recap." *Asian Trade Centre*, June 30, 2015. http://
www.asiantradecentre.org/talkingtrade/2015/6/30/talking-trade-blog-
recap?rq=28%20april.

————. "Why Is Agriculture So Difficult for Trade Deals?" *Asian Trade Centre*,
April 28, 2015. http://www.asiantradecentre.org/talkingtrade/2015/4/28/
why-is-agriculture-so-difficult-for-trade-deals.

Evenett, S. "Is Murky Protectionism a Real Threat to Asian Trade?" In *The
Future of the World Trading System: Asian Perspectives*. Edited by Richard
Baldwin, Masahiro Kawai and Ganeshan Wignaraja. Centre for Economic
Policy Research, 2013. http://voxeu.org/sites/default/files/Future_World_
Trading_System.pdf.

"Free Trade Agreements." *State Secretariat for Economic Affairs SECO*. Accessed
April 28, 2016. https://www.secolive.admin.ch/themen/00513/00515/01330/
index.html?lang=en.

"FTAs." *Ministry of Foreign Affairs, Singapore*. Accessed April 28, 2016. http://
www.mfa.gov.sg/content/mfa/international_organisation_initiatives/ftas.
html.

Hamanaka, S. "On the Use of FTAs: A Review of Research Methodologies."
ADB Working Paper Series on Regional Economic Integration, 2013. http://
www.econstor.eu/handle/10419/109609.

Hayakawa, K., D. Hiratsuka, K. Shiino, and S. Sukegawa. "Who Uses FTAs?"
Economic Research Institute for ASEAN and East Asia, IDE Discussion
Paper, no. 207 (July 2009). http://www.ide.go.jp/English/Publish/Download/
Dp/pdf/207.pdf.

Helble, Y. "Handel mit der EU: Bürokraten legen dem Freihandel Fesseln an."
Neue Zürcher Zeitung, April 9, 2015. http://www.nzz.ch/wirtschaft/
buerokraten-legen-dem-freihandel-fesseln-an-1.18518444.

Küng, D., and A. Orlando. "Effektivität der Schweizer Freihandelsabkommen (FHA) weltweit, Evaluierung der FHA-Nutzung durch Schweizer-Exporteure, 2012-2013." *Switzerland Global Enterprise*, January 2014. http://www.s-ge.com/sites/default/files/private_files/Effektivit%C3%A4t%20der%20Schweizer%20Freihandelsabkommen_S-GE.pdf.

Liang, M. "Singapore's Trade Policies: Priorities and Options." *ASEAN Economic Bulletin* 22, no. 1 (2005): 49–59.

Nakatomi, M. "Plurilateral Agreements: A Viable Alternative to the WTO." In *The Future of the World Trading System: Asian Perspectives*. Edited by Richard Baldwin, Masahiro Kawai and Ganeshan Wignaraja. Centre for Economic Policy Research, 2013. http://voxeu.org/sites/default/files/Future_World_Trading_System.pdf.

"Regional Trade Agreements." *World Trade Organization*. Accessed April 28, 2016. https://www.wto.org/english/tratop_e/region_e/region_e.htm.

"Review of 2014 Trade Performance." *International Enterprise Singapore*, February 17, 2015. http://www.iesingapore.gov.sg/Media-Centre/Media-Releases/2015/2/Review-of-2014-Trade-Performance.

Schweizerische Bundesrat. "Bericht zur Aussenwirtschaftspolitik 2014 und Botschaften zu Wirtschaftsvereinbarungen sowie Bericht über Zolltarifarische Massnahmen im Jahr 2014." *Switzerland Global Enterprise*, January 14, 2015. http://www.news.admin.ch/NSBSubscriber/message/attachments/38087.pdf.

"Singapore's International Network of Agreements." *International Enterprise Singapore*. Accessed April 28, 2016. http://www.iesingapore.gov.sg/trade-from-singapore/international-agreements.

Takahashi, K., and S. Urata. "On the Use of FTAs by Japanese Firms: Further Evidence." *Business and Politics* 12, no. 1 (2010). http://www.degruyter.com/dg/viewarticle/j$002fbap.2010.12.1$002fbap.2010.12.1.1310$002fbap.2010.12.1.1310.xml.

"Trade Policy Review Report by Singapore." *World Trade Organization*, June 5, 2012. https://docs.wto.org/dol2fe/Pages/FE_Search/DDFDocuments/34513/Q/WT/TPR/G267.pdf.

Urata, S. "Free Trade Agreements: A Catalyst for Japan's Economic Revitalization." *Reviving Japan's Economy*, 2005, pp. 377–410.

Chapter 4

Small States as Banking Powerhouses: Financial Sector Policy in Singapore and Switzerland

Yvonne Guo and J. J. Woo

Introduction

Described as "kindred spirits" by Ravi Menon, Managing Director of the Monetary Authority of Singapore (MAS), Singapore and Switzerland have made their mark as the biggest asset management centres in Asia and Europe respectively.[1] According to the Deloitte International Wealth Management Centre Rankings 2015, Switzerland is the leading wealth management centre in the world, with US$2.0 trillion of assets booked at the end of 2014, while Singapore is sixth, with US$0.5 trillion of assets booked.[2]

A wide range of definitions on what constitutes a financial centre abound, which generally describe the role of such centres as facilitating capital exchanges between states. For example, Nadler argued that

---

[1] Grant, Jeremy, "Singapore Loosens Switzerland's Grip on Wealth Management". *Financial Times*, July 23, 2013. http://www.ft.com/intl/cms/s/2/048c3630-f39f-11e2-942f-00144feabdc0.html#axzz2aCMZjs2V.

[2] Kobler, Daniel and Jürg Frick, "The Deloitte Wealth Management Centre Ranking 2015". Switzerland: Deloitte, 2015. http://www2.deloitte.com/content/dam/Deloitte/ch/Documents/financial-services/ch-en-financial-services-the-deloitte-wealth-management-centre-ranking-2015.pdf.

financial centres act "as a bank for the entire world" and "facilitate the flow of goods, services, and capital among nations".[3] Kindleberger defined a financial centre as a "geographical agglomeration of financial intermediaries" that performs "the highly specialised functions of lending abroad and serving as a clearinghouse for payments among countries".[4] Reed noted the ability of financial centres to "effect payments and to transfer savings between places".[5] Goldberg *et al.* concluded that international financial centres were 'major urban concentrations of financial services' with significant international and domestic service components.[6] More recently, Tschoegl described international financial centres as places where capital could be 'collected, switched, disbursed and exchanged'[7] while Poon described them as "control centres of global financial flows".[8] Cassis defined a financial centre as "a place where intermediaries coordinate financial transactions and arrange for payments to be settled".[9]

Both Singapore and Switzerland share distinct features such as low taxes, low regulatory burdens, and banking confidentiality laws, and are supported by excellent infrastructure and political and economic stability. According to the MAS, 81% of Singapore's S$2.4 trillion (US$1.78 trillion)

---

[3] Marcus Nadler, *The Money Market and Its Institutions* (New York: Ronald Press Co., 1955).

[4] Charles Poor Kindleberger, *The Formation of Financial Centers: A Study in Comparative Economic History* (International Finance Section, Princeton University, 1974).

[5] Howard Curtis Reed, "The Ascent of Tokyo as an International Financial Center," *Journal of International Business Studies* 11, no. 3 (1980): 19–35, doi:10.1057/palgrave.jibs.8490620.

[6] Michael A. Goldberg, Robert W. Helsley, and Maurice D. Levi, "On the Development of International Financial Centers," *The Annals of Regional Science* 22, no. 1 (February 1, 1988): 81–94, doi:10.1007/BF01952845.

[7] Adrian E. Tschoegl, "International Banking Centers, Geography, and Foreign Banks," *Financial Markets, Institutions & Instruments* 9, no. 1 (February 1, 2000): 1–32, doi:10.1111/1468-0416.00034.

[8] Jessie P.H. Poon, "Hierarchical Tendencies of Capital Markets Among International Financial Centers," *Growth and Change* 34, no. 2 (June 1, 2003): 135–56, doi:10.1111/1468-2257.00211.

[9] Youssef Cassis, *Capitals of Capital: The Rise and Fall of International Financial Centres 1780–2009* (Cambridge University Press, 2010).

in total assets under management in 2014 came from overseas.[10] In Switzerland, the corresponding figure is $6.65 trillion CHF (US$6.93 trillion) in assets under management, with the share of foreign assets under management accounting for over 50%.[11] Several reports have even predicted that Singapore could overtake Switzerland as the largest global offshore private banking market by 2020.[12]

Institutionally, both countries share many similarities. According to a Credit Suisse report, "Singapore has built its financial centre along traditional Swiss strengths: a stable political climate, a favourable tax regime, high quality education and infrastructure as well as privacy in financial matters. Not surprisingly, Swiss banks have long used Singapore as a hub to leverage Swiss banking expertise for Asian clients".[13]

Switzerland's assets include its long tradition of private banking and its large talent pool, while Singapore has been boosted by the rapidly growing wealth of HNWI (high net worth individuals) in the Asia–Pacific.[14] "Singapore is located at the heart of a growth region, with rising income and wealth creation generating strong demand for banking products and wealth management.[15] While Switzerland's private banking sector has been hit by a number of high-profile leaks and scandals since 2008, Singapore's

---

[10]Monetary Authority of Singapore, 2014. "2014 Asset Management Survey." Available from: http://www.mas.gov.sg/~/media/MAS/News%20and%20Publications/Surveys/Asset%20Management/2014%20AM%20Survey%20Report.pdf.

[11]Swiss Bankers' Association, 2015. "2015 Banking Barometer." Available from: http://www.swissbanking.org/en/20150903-5010-all-mm-bankenbarometer.pdf.

[12]"Singapore to Overtake Switzerland as Leading Offshore Hub by 2020." Private Banker International, April 18, 2013. http://www.privatebankerinternational.com/pressrelease/singapore-to-overtake-switzerland-as-leading-offshore-hub-by-2020/. See also Wilson, Karl. "Singapore expected to dislodge Switzerland as world's wealth management capital." China Daily/Asia News Network. May 12, 2014. http://business.asiaone.com/news/singapore-expected-dislodge-switzerland-worlds-wealth-management-capital.

[13]"Switzerland as a Financial Center." Credit Suisse, September 2012. https://www.credit-suisse.com/media/production/articles/news-and-expertise/docs/2012/09/Finanzplatz/finanzplatz-en.pdf.

[14]Palma, Stefania, "Is Private Banking Shifting from Switzerland to Hong Kong and Singapore?" Accessed June 19, 2015. http://www.thebanker.com/Banking/Is-private-banking-shifting-from-Switzerland-to-Hong-Kong-and-Singapore.

[15]"Credit Suisse, "Switzerland as a Financial Center."

reputation as an up-and-coming wealth management centre has remained largely intact.

The structure and organisation of financial regulatory authorities differs between both countries. In Singapore, the Monetary Authority of Singapore (MAS) serves as both central bank and regulator, taking charge of monetary policy formulation and exchange rate management while also regulating and supervising financial institutions in Singapore. The Ministry of Finance (MOF) controls Singapore's fiscal policies, including planning government spending and collecting tax and duty revenues.[16]

In Switzerland, the Swiss Financial Market Supervisory Authority (FINMA) is the Swiss government body responsible for the regulation of financial institutions in Switzerland. Reporting directly to the Swiss parliament, FINMA is independent from the central federal administration and the Federal Department of Finance. The Swiss National Bank (SNB) is the central bank of Switzerland, responsible for the country's monetary policy. The Swiss Federal Department of Finance (FDF) deals with a wide range of tasks, including the federal budget, both national and international finance, monetary and tax matters, customs and merchandise control and the implementation of legislation on alcohol.[17]

As small states, both Singapore and Switzerland are price-takers in the international financial regulatory process, having to adapt to international guidelines rather than set the standards. They are only able to exert influence through being involved in relevant international institutions and by ensuring the universal application of new standards. However, such perceived similarities do not address the structural differences between the two nations. This chapter will discuss these differences, focusing particularly on differences in modes of financial governance. We will first trace the development of Singapore and Switzerland as financial centres and discuss the measures they have taken to remain as attractive financial centres, particularly after the 2007–2008 financial crisis.

---

[16]"Differences between the Monetary Authority of Singapore and the Ministry of Finance." AsiaOne Business, March 24, 2016. http://news.asiaone.com/news/business/differences-between-monetary-authority-singapore-and-ministry-finance.

[17]"The Federal Department of Finance (FDF)." Swiss Federal Council, January 13, 2016. https://www.admin.ch/gov/en/start/departments/department-of-finance-fdf.html.

Case of Singapore

Development as a financial centre

The historical beginnings of Singapore as a financial centre were very much tied to its founding as a sovereign independent state in 1965. Upon independence, the newly-formed government had identified financial services as a key sector that could both support other existing industries and contribute to economic growth as an industry in its own right.[18] As such, Singapore's financial sector has since become more self-propelled and less dependent on developments in the real economy.[19] The development of Singapore as a financial centre has therefore been a state-driven affair from the very beginning, with the government playing a crucial role in identifying and developing specific financial activities or sectors by providing tax and other fiscal incentives to firms and investors within these emerging sectors.[20]

An important result of this government-targeting approach was the establishment of the Asian Dollar Market (ADM) in 1968. The ADM was conceived out of a realisation that Singapore's strategic time zone advantage allows it to bridge a gap between markets in the US and Europe, as Singapore picks up trading activity after US markets close and before European markets reopen.[21] This move to insert itself within the global time-zone gap has subsequently allowed Singapore to establish itself as a major trading hub in stocks and equities, bonds, commodities, forex, futures and derivatives that it is today. The ADM therefore prefigures much of Singapore's current success as a financial hub. This early success of the ADM and subsequent growth in other financial

---

[18]Montes, M. F. Tokyo, Hong Kong and Singapore as Competing Financial Centres. *Journal of Asian Business*, 18, no. 1 (1999), pp. 153–168.

[19]Bryant, R. C. The Evolution of Singapore as a Financial Centre. In: K.S. Sandhu and P. Wheatley, eds. *Management of Success: The Moulding of Modern Singapore*. Singapore: Institute of Southeast Asian Studies, 1989, pp. 337–372.

[20]Tan, S. L. The Development of Singapore's Financial Sector: A Review and Some Thoughts on its Future Prospects. *In:* W. T. H. Koh and R. S. Mariano, eds. *The Economic Prospects of Singapore.* Singapore: Pearson Addison-Wesley, 2006, pp. 246–273.

[21]Tee, O. C. *Singapore's policy of non-internationalisation of the Singapore dollar and the Asian dollar market.* Bank for International Settlements, BIS Papers, 2003.

services necessitated greater centralization in financial regulation and governance.

This prompted the formation of the Monetary Authority of Singapore (MAS) in 1971. As Singapore's chief financial regulator, the MAS regulates and supervises financial services associated with the banking, finance, insurance, and securities markets.[22] The MAS also acts as Singapore's central bank, manages the city-state's official foreign reserves, and actively develops Singapore as a financial centre. This makes the MAS the lead agency for regulating, governing, and promoting Singapore's financial services sector. The MAS has played an important role in driving Singapore's development as a financial centre through these dual roles of stimulation/promotion and regulation/supervision,[23] allowing the state to actively promote Singapore as a financial centre.[24] As Austin has noted, the "success of Singapore as Southeast Asia's premier financial and industrial centre was the product of the State".[25]

Under the MAS's policy guidance, Singapore established its strengths in several key financial services. These include foreign exchange (forex), commodities, wealth management, and derivatives. A strong domestic banking sector was also developed, along with the formation of three major Singaporean banks: the Development Bank of Singapore (DBS), United Overseas Bank (UOB), and Overseas Chinese Banking Company (OCBC). While DBS remains largely state-owned, UOB and OCBC emerged and continue to exist as privately-held banks. More importantly, the current strength of these three banks derives from MAS' efforts at consolidating Singapore's domestic banking sector in the 1980s, which

---

[22]Tan, C. H. *Financial Services and Wealth Management in Singapore*. Updated. Singapore: Singapore University Press, 2011.

[23]Tan, C. H. Singapore as an International Financial Centre. *In: East Asia Dimensions of International Business*. Sydney: Prentice Hall, 1982, pp. 29–44.

[24]Yoon, S. P. A Comparison of Hong Kong and Singapore as Asian Financial Centres. In: P. D. Grub, C. H. Tan, K.-C. Kwan, and G. H. Rott, eds. *East Asia Dimensions of International Business*. Sydney: Prentice Hall, 1982, pp. 21–28.

[25]Austin, I. P. *Goh Keng Swee And Southeast Asian Governance*. Singapore: Marshall Cavendish Academic, 2004.

involved encouraging smaller banks to merge or be acquired by larger banks.[26]

Singapore has since grown, on the back of these strong domestic banks and the presence of major foreign financial institutions, into one of Asia's leading financial centres. While MAS remains a key policy driver for Singapore's financial sector success, the city-state has also attained a high level of economic openness, with its financial markets featuring participation by a large number of foreign financial institutions. Ranked the fourth most competitive financial centre in the world,[27] Singapore has also proven itself to be resilient, recovering rapidly from the 1997 Asian financial crisis and 2007 global financial crisis. It has furthermore established itself as a premier wealth management centre and more recently, a leading offshore Renminbi (RMB) centre, even as it retains its strengths in forex, commodities and international banking. However, this is not to say that Singapore is without its limitations or does not face challenges in its development as a financial centre.

Recent challenges faced by Singapore as a financial centre

Vulnerability to external shocks: Due to its highly open markets and capital accounts, Singapore is vulnerable to external shocks. For instance, it rapidly entered into technical recession during the GFC. While Singapore nonetheless recovered from the GFC in mid-2009 on the back of increased industrial output and improvements in financial market conditions,[28] it has become increasingly clear that the very economic openness that has contributed to Singapore's success is also its Achilles' heel. Furthermore, Singapore's position as a hub port-city that is dependent upon trade and trans-shipment flows for its economic well-being also means that it is vulnerable to a 'double-effect' during crises.

---

[26] Hamilton-Hart, N. *Asian States, Asian Bankers: Central Banking in Southeast Asia*. New York: Cornell University Press, 2002.

[27] Yeandle, M. *Global Financial Centres Index 17*. London, U.K.: Z/Yen Group and Qatar Financial Centre Authority, 2015.

[28] Monetary Authority of Singapore. *Annual Report 2009/2010*. Singapore: Monetary Authority of Singapore, 2010.

While a financial crisis may result in a drying up of foreign investments and financial market slow-downs, it may also affect Singapore's real economy through reduced trade demands from abroad. In recognition of this source of vulnerability, MAS has focused intensively on risk-based financial regulations that aim to reduce the impacts of financial contagion.[29]

Rigging of SIBOR Rates: However, tight regulations do not necessarily guarantee compliance. MAS has recently uncovered attempts by 20 banks to rig several key benchmark rates, the most significant of them being the Singapore Interbank Overnight Rate (SIBOR), with the worst offenders being the Royal Bank of Scotland (RBS), UBS and ING.[30] These three banks have since been required to increase their reserves on deposit with MAS by S$1 billion to S$1.2 billion at zero interest. Other banks ordered to increase their reserves on deposit, albeit by lower amounts, included the Bank of America, BNP Paribas, and OCBC. Such attempts to influence the SIBOR rates mirrored similar attempts to rig the London Interbank Overnight Rates, once again highlighting Singapore's vulnerability to global forces. In this instance, Singapore was vulnerable not simply to financial contagion, but the proliferation of unethical banking practices. Another significant instance of Singapore's exposure to ethical issues in global banking involves banking secrecy.

Challenges to tax and banking secrecy: In 2009, Singapore was put on the OECD's grey list of territories that had committed to the OECD Standard on Exchange of Information (EOI) but had not yet substantially implemented the standard. Singapore concluded 90 international tax agreements, including avoidance of double taxation (DTAs) and exchange of information (EOI) agreements, most of which included provisions for the exchange of information for tax purposes. In 2009, Singapore amended the Income Tax

[29]Chia, D. J. Objectives and Principles of Financial Supervision in Singapore. *In: Regulation and the Limits of Competition.* Singapore: SNP International Publishing Pte Ltd, 2007, pp. 44–58.
[30]Thompson, M. Singapore raps 20 banks for trying to rig rates [online]. *CNNMoney* June 14, 2013. Available from: http://money.cnn.com/2013/06/14/news/companies/singapore-banks-sibor/index.html Accessed June 20, 2015.

Act to allow exchange of information upon request.[31] MAS also proposed a tougher penalty regime for violations of AML/CFT (Anti-Money Laundering/Counter-Financing of Terrorism), criminalising the laundering of proceeds from tax offences, and stepping up its enforcement resources to deal with suspicious transactions reported by financial institutions.

In May 2013, it was announced that all financial institutions in Singapore had to identify accounts that are strongly suspected to be holding proceeds of fraudulent or wilful tax evasion and, where necessary, close them. On 1 July 2013, handling the proceeds of tax crimes was made a criminal offence under changes to Singapore's anti-money laundering law.[32] Singapore has also signalled its willingness to cooperate internationally by agreeing to implement the US-led FATCA (Foreign Account Taxpayers Compliance Act, which would require foreign financial institutions to report directly to the IRS information about financial accounts held by US taxpayers) and the Common Reporting Standard (CRS), also known as the OECD Standard for Automatic Exchange of Financial Account Information. Finally, Singapore has also been involved in international efforts to set global standards on automatic information exchange, particularly through its involvement as vice-chair of the Peer Review Group of the OECD's Global Forum. Moreover, Singapore has committed to implement the OECD Standard for Automatic Exchange of Financial Account Information by 2018.[33]

Case of Switzerland

Development of the Swiss financial centre

Switzerland's growth and development as a financial centre was the result of bottom-up rather than top-down processes. For example, scholars have

---

[31]"Singapore's Implementation of Global Standard for Automatic Exchange of Financial Account Information." Ministry of Finance, November 3, 2014. http://www.mof.gov.sg/news-reader/articleid/1405/parentId/59/year/2014?category=Parliamentary%20Replies.

[32]Armstrong, Rachel, Saeed Azhar, and John O'Callaghan. "Banks in Singapore Agonise over Rich Clients in Tax Evasion Clampdown." Reuters. May 5, 2013. http://www.reuters.com/article/2013/05/05/singapore-banks-crime-idUSL2N0DG05Z20130505.

[33]"Peer Review Group." OECD Global Forum on Transparency and Exchange of Information for Tax Purposes. Accessed April 28, 2016. http://www.oecd.org/tax/transparency/peerreviewgroup.htm.

argued that "the Swiss capital market was not designed; rather, it developed organically. Therefore, neither the Swiss government nor any regulatory authority deserves credit for planning the financial system's remarkable success story. On the contrary, official Switzerland has been more of an anchor than a sail, harbouring a rather skeptical attitude towards the growth of the nation's financial centre".[34]

In the early days, Switzerland's location as a trading hub in the heart of Europe meant that trading firms in Swiss city-states had to develop their own expertise in finance. Many private banking houses in St. Gallen, Basel, Zurich and Geneva originated from larger trading firms or were established from a particular industry, such as the textile industry in St. Gallen. The growth of the Swiss banking industry was further stimulated by the immigration of refugees from neighbouring states, a number of whom were financial specialists.[35]

Swiss neutrality was another factor that supported the development of the Swiss financial sector. The Battle of Marignano in 1515 had heralded the end of Swiss territorial expansion in Europe and marked the beginning of peace and stability, culminating in the declaration of Swiss neutrality in the 1815 Treaty of Vienna. Since the 16th century, Switzerland has had a surplus of investable funds, giving rise to the creation of private banks. Today, Swiss banks are still heavily focused on private banking and asset management.[36]

In 1713, banks were banned from revealing client information by the Great Council of Geneva, laying the bedrock of banking secrecy in Switzerland. This was followed by an amendment to the Swiss Banking Law of 1934, Switzerland's first federal banking law, which codified banking secrecy for the first time in history and led dozens of other countries such as Luxembourg and Austria to adopt similar laws of

---

[34]Meier, Henri B., John E. Marthinsen, and Pascal A. Gantenbein, *Swiss Finance: Capital Markets, Banking, and the Swiss Value Chain.* 1 edition. Hoboken, New Jersey: Wiley, 2012.

[35]Woo, Jun Jie, and Yvonne Guo, "Wealth Management for All Seasons?" Accessed June 19,2015.http://www.straitstimes.com/the-big-story/asia-report/opinion/story/wealth-management-all-seasons-20131203.

[36]Meier, Marthinsen, and Gantenbein, *Swiss Finance.*

banking secrecy.[37] The 1934 Banking Act also called for greater federal supervision of domestic banks. Throughout the 20th century, a major consolidation of banks occurred in Switzerland, with UBS and Credit Suisse as the two remaining 'big banks' at the end of the century.[38] In the decades after 1973, large Swiss banks internationalised by acquiring foreign banks and delving into more risky financial practices, but also functioned as training centres for smaller banks to benefit.[39]

Finally, the Swiss franc was also established as a strong and stable currency at the beginning of the 20th century. The Swiss National Bank was founded in 1907 but only gained the full range of central bank monetary tools in 1978. It operates independently from political pressure in order to maintain public confidence in monetary stability. The Swiss franc was backed by gold until 1999. After the end of the gold standard, Switzerland floated its currency and the Swiss central bank supported its appreciation. Since 2000, the Bank has focused on keeping inflation between zero and two percent. Unconventional monetary policy tools, like a cap on the appreciation of the Swiss franc, were used in order to derail the threat of deflation. Recent expansionary monetary policies have caused the SNB's balance sheet to expand.[40]

Recent challenges faced by the Swiss financial centre

"Too big to fail" banks: The spectre of "too big to fail" banks looms large in Switzerland, since the country's two biggest banks, UBS and Credit Suisse, are larger than Switzerland's GDP. Switzerland has therefore subjected its banks to more stringent layers of regulation than other countries, known as the "Swiss finish". Too-big-to-fail legislation was included in the Swiss Banking Act in September 2011, requiring systemically important banks to meet stricter capital, liquidity and organisational requirements. Based on the belief that self-regulation is the most effective and efficient way to control banking, coupled with tighter

---

[37] Guo and Woo, "Wealth Management for All Seasons?"
[38] Meier, Marthinsen, and Gantenbein, *Swiss Finance.*
[39] *Ibid.*
[40] *Ibid.*

federal supervision, Swiss banks are now the most closely regulated in the world. Switzerland's domestic banking regulations have even been copied by other countries and international organisations, such as more stringent capital requirements. Swiss domestic regulations are even stricter than Basel III, raising the question of comparative disadvantage for Swiss banks as compared to their foreign competitors.[41] Moreover, scholars have argued that the Swiss financial regulatory authority's attempt to protect its biggest banks rendered it more vulnerable to international pressure, particularly from the USA. For example, when the US Department of Justice (DoJ) threatened to indict UBS, potentially risking the bank's bankruptcy, the Swiss Financial Market Supervisory Authority (FINMA) used its emergency powers to suspend banking secrecy regulations and sent requested client files to the US Department of Justice.[42]

Challenges to tax and banking secrecy: A sea change in foreign governments' attitudes towards the worldwide transactions of their citizens has led to the end of banking secrecy for foreign account holders in Switzerland. In 2009, Switzerland was placed on the OECD's grey list for countries which had not done enough to implement OECD standards on international tax cooperation. At the same time, Swiss banks suffered from a spate of scandals as whistleblowers uncovered lists of foreign account holders in Swiss banks. UBS entered into a deferred prosecution agreement with the US Department of Justice in February 2009, paying a fine of US$780 million and disclosing the names of 250 account holders. In August 2009, under additional pressure, UBS was forced to give the US access to an additional 4,450 client files. The US authorities, perceiving the concessions made to be inadequate, did not stop there.[43] Switzerland's oldest private bank, Wegelin and Co., was indicted by the US in February 2012 for allegedly helping US citizens evade taxes amounting to US$1.2 billion, leading to the bank's collapse. More than

---

[41] *Ibid.*

[42] Emmenegger, Patrick. "Swiss Banking Secrecy and the Problem of International Cooperation in Tax Matters: A Nut Too Hard to Crack?" Regulation & Governance, 2015. doi:10.1111/rego.12106.

[43] *Ibid.*

100 Swiss private banks have since entered into a programme led by the US Department of Justice to clear up 'legacy' issues. At the same time, Switzerland has signed up to a number of double-taxation agreements and signalled its willingness to cooperate internationally by agreeing to implement the US-led FATCA and the OECD Standard for Automatic Exchange of Financial Account Information in Tax Matters.[44] In so doing, Switzerland has agreed to comply with global standards on international tax cooperation, with the understanding that it is in the interest of the Swiss financial centre to do so.

Appreciation of the Swiss franc: Economists have pointed out the Swiss franc's role as a 'safe haven currency', noting its ability to appreciate during times of global financial crisis.[45] However, such pressure on the Swiss franc has also affected the country's price competitiveness in the export market.[46] Between September 2011 and January 2015, the Swiss National Bank set a lower boundary for the euro against the Swiss franc (a peg of 1.2 francs per euro). The rate had been set to prevent the Swiss franc from climbing too high against the single currency. However, the cap on the Swiss franc was abandoned because it was deemed to be no longer sustainable ahead of planned quantitative easing by the European Central Bank and economic recovery in the USA. The appreciation of the Swiss franc after it was unpegged from the euro caused turmoil in stock and currency markets.[47] It also affected Swiss exports greatly, causing the

---

[44]"Standard for Automatic Exchange of Financial Account Information in Tax Matters." OECD Exchange of Tax Information Portal, July 21, 2014. http://www.oecd.org/ctp/exchange-of-tax-information/standard-for-automatic-exchange-of-financial-account-information-for-tax-matters-9789264216525-en.htm.

[45]Deutsche Bundesbank, "Swiss Franc and US Dollar Are 'Safe Haven' Currencies". Accessed June 19, 2015. http://www.bundesbank.de/Redaktion/EN/Topics/2014/2014_07_30_swiss_franc_and_us_dollar_are_safe_haven_currencies.html.

[46]Thangavelu, Poonkulali, "Is The Swiss Franc A Safe Haven?" *Investopedia*. Accessed June 19, 2015. http://www.investopedia.com/articles/forex/031715/swiss-franc-safe-haven.asp.

[47]Inman, Phillip, "Swiss Bank's Currency U-Turn Hurts Watchmakers, Skiers and Traders". *The Guardian*. Accessed June 19, 2015. http://www.theguardian.com/business/2015/jan/15/currency-markets-switzerland-franc.

Swiss economy to shrink 0.2 percent in the first quarter of 2015.[48] At the time of writing, continued negative interest rates mean that monetary policy options remain limited.

Discussion

When comparing the development of Singapore and Switzerland as financial centres, it is inevitable that differences between the two nations' model of governance are first highlighted. As discussed in Chapter 1, the political systems of the two nations are vastly different. This flows into their models of financial governance. Specifically, Switzerland features a more bottom-up approach to financial governance and policy-making while Singapore's approach is more top-down and state-directed.

One major difference in the area of financial policy-making in both countries is the role of domestic interest groups. In Switzerland, the citizenry is regularly consulted on major changes in financial sector policy that would require the revision of legislation. In Singapore, members of the public are able to provide feedback to policy consultation papers published online, but public feedback is non-binding. This differs significantly from the referendum system in Switzerland, where citizens have a direct impact on matters relating to financial sector policy through the referendum mechanism. For example, in recent years, referendums related to monetary policy and banking secrecy have been launched. A recent case in point was the "Swiss Gold Initiative" referendum in November 2014 which proposed a restoration of 20 percent gold backing for the Swiss Franc, but was rejected by 78 percent of voters. Therefore, the Swiss system of direct democracy implies that significant proposed changes to financial policy can only take effect with parliamentary and citizen support.[49]

Significant differences also exist between the government-industry consultation processes in both countries. In Singapore, industry

---

[48]Roth, Carolin, "The Curse of Being a Safe Haven Currency". *CNBC*. Accessed June 19, 2015. http://www.cnbc.com/id/102766787.

[49]Guo and Woo, "Wealth Management for All Seasons?"

consultation takes place through MAS's "practice of organised, industry-wide consultation through many committees and formal bodies".[50] Such consultations are enshrined within MAS's institutional framework, such as its "Principles of Good Supervision"[51] and "Tenets of Effective Regulation — particularly "Tenet 2: Shared Responsibility".[52] Such efforts at industry and stakeholder consultation form a crucial aspect of MAS's "smart regulation" approach[53] by playing two key roles in Singapore's financial governance.

First, industry consultation ensures greater regulatory compliance by financial institutions. This is achieved through collecting industry feedback on regulations and tweaking these regulations to address industry concerns. In providing industry actors with regular updates and information on regulations in the process of consultation, MAS also ensures greater policy stability. Second, MAS's industry consultations have contributed to the "co-creation" of financial policies in Singapore, with, financial policies are collaboratively formulated by MAS and its industry partners.[54] This is due to the dense "policy relations" that are formed among MAS and its industry partners in the course of regular and institutionalised consultations, facilitating the sharing of financial policy responsibilities.[55]

Informal consultation also takes place, with financial institutions approaching and interacting with MAS on a continuous and ongoing basis, as and when concerns arise or feedback is required. Both informal and formal consultation contributes to MAS's policy considerations. Given the significance of Singapore's financial sector to its economic development,

---

[50] Hamilton-Hart, N. *Asian States, Asian Bankers: Central Banking in Southeast Asia.* New York: Cornell University Press, 2002.

[51] Monetary Authority of Singapore. *Objectives and Principles of Financial Supervision in Singapore.* MAS Monograph, 2004.

[52] Monetary Authority of Singapore. *Tenets of Effective Regulation.* Singapore: Monetary Authority of Singapore, 2010.

[53] Menon, R. *Singapore's Financial Centre in the New Landscape.* Monetary Authority of Singapore, 2013.

[54] Woo, J. J. Singapore's policy style: statutory boards as policymaking units. *Journal of Asian Public Policy*, 8, no. 2 (2014), 120–133.

[55] Woo, J. J. Policy Relations and Policy Subsystems: Financial policy in Hong Kong and Singapore. *International Journal of Public Administration* (2015), Forthcoming.

industry feedback is crucial for ensuring the relevance and applicability of regulations. Such feedback is therefore often incorporated into MAS's policies. Thus while the state continues to lead consultation, industry actors have also been able to influence or shape financial policies.

In Switzerland, formal and informal consultation processes also exist between government and industry. Informally, the Swiss Banking Association has regular contact with the Swiss Federal Department of Finance on current issues and regulations and both also participate regularly in industry forums. Officially, there are also consultations required when a new law is being drafted. There exists a specific list of organisations in Switzerland which must be consulted, including the Swiss Bankers' Association, and the Association of Foreign Banks. The feedback of these organisations is collected and taken into account in the formulation of a new law before it is presented before the Swiss parliament.

As a consequence of their different models of financial governance, Singapore and Switzerland differ in terms of their strengths and weaknesses as well. This has important bearings for the two nations' future as financial centres. First, Singapore's top-down and state-directed approach to financial governance has enabled it to rapidly target and grow emerging financial markets. In 50 years, Singapore has grown from its initial forays in the ADM to become a leading forex and commodities hub. It has also successfully developed new sectors such as wealth management. This was predicated upon efficient policy-making, an advantage which arises from its majoritarian parliamentary system that expedites decision-making and legislation, and the role of MAS as lead agency.

However, strong state intervention may also result in the perception of less than vibrant financial markets by investors. State-direction may also hinder Singapore's ability to foster financial innovation, which arguably thrives in larger and more open markets. In contrast, Switzerland has proven more amenable to financial innovation, on the back of its bottom-up approach to financial governance and the role of an active citizenry engaged in direct democracy. Switzerland is also known as one of the freest financial markets in the world. Although Switzerland's private banking industry is currently bearing the brunt of international challenges to Swiss banking confidentiality laws, the strength of the

Swiss financial infrastructure, value chain and overall ecosystem continues to contribute to the country's effectiveness as a financial centre. Switzerland's strong adherence to direct democracy has also kept the Swiss National Bank independent and prohibited the country's delegation of sovereignty to supranational regulatory bodies, such as the European Monetary Union and the European Central Bank.[56] Yet as Switzerland moves forward, policymakers will also have to find ways to compensate for its deficit in institutions providing venture capital to young companies which may hold the key to the country's future as a centre for innovation.[57]

Conclusion

This chapter has discussed the development of Singapore and Switzerland as major financial hubs. In the process, we have described the various economic, policy, and historical drivers of their development and discussed more recent developments. This discussion has elucidated several important points. First, Singapore and Switzerland are rather similar in various ways. They have both developed comparable advantages in wealth management and international banking, and face similar challenges arising from increasingly globalised financial markets. For instance, both Singapore and Switzerland have faced international criticism over their potential roles as offshore financial centres, but they have since undertaken significant reforms to boost the integrity and reputation of their respective financial centres. Notably, in recent years, the legal frameworks of both countries have been subject to significant revision with the signing of major multilateral agreements on automatic information exchange.

Despite, or perhaps because of, their success as private banking hubs, significant risks to both financial centres remain. In May 2016, BSI Singapore, a private bank which was a subsidiary of Swiss-based BSI SA, was fined S$13.3 million and ordered to shut down by the Monetary

---

[56]Meier, Marthinsen, and Gantenbein, *Swiss Finance*.
[57]*Ibid.*

Authority of Singapore for serious breaches of anti-money laundering requirements, poor management oversight of bank operations, and gross misconduct by bank staff. At the same time, the Swiss Attorney-General opened criminal proceedings against parent company BSI, while Swiss regulator FINMA found the bank to be in breach of money-laundering regulations in connection with Malaysian state investment fund 1MDB and ordered the bank to pay a US$96 million fine. While such incidents illustrate the inherent vulnerability of wealth management centres to illicit financial flows, they also show how regulatory cooperation between financial authorities can play a role in maintaining the integrity of the centres.[58]

Given the differences in their geopolitical circumstances and domestic political systems, such similarities may provide potentially interesting venues for future research. This will be of interest to other financial centres that, although existing in different geopolitical and socio-cultural circumstances, seek to emulate the financial success of Singapore and Switzerland. However, and as this chapter has shown, such perceived similarities distract from the different modes of financial governance and the different mixes of financial activities that characterise the two nations.

Such differences suggest a need for more careful examination of the political-economic foundations of financial sector development. In other words, there is a need to examine the 'engine' of financial centre success. This lies fully in the realm of political economy, a theoretical discipline which both authors have employed in the course of this book. Such an endeavour will benefit from further research into the political and economic determinants of financial centre development and require more comparative studies of financial centres across national boundaries. It is our hope that this chapter (and this book) will provide the impetus for further comparative policy research. This will elucidate the drivers of policy success across different contexts and provide a useful body of work for policymakers and policy scholars alike.

---

[58]Chor, Khieng Yuit. "Can Singapore stay clean when banks play dirty for wealthy clients?" Channel NewsAsia, 7 June 2016. http://www.channelnewsasia.com/news/business/can-singapore-stay-clean/2851840.html

References

Austin, I. P. *Goh Keng Swee And Southeast Asian Governance*. Singapore: Marshall Cavendish Academic, 2004.

Bryant, R. C. The Evolution of Singapore as a Financial Centre. *In*: K.S. Sandhu and P. Wheatley, eds. *Management of Success: The Moulding of Modern Singapore*. Singapore: Institute of Southeast Asian Studies, 1989, pp. 337–372.

Chia, D. J. Objectives and Principles of Financial Supervision in Singapore. *In*: *Regulation and the Limits of Competition*. Singapore: SNP International Publishing Pte Ltd, 2007, pp. 44–58.

Chor, K. Y. "Can Singapore stay clean when banks play dirty for wealthy clients?" Channel NewsAsia, 7 June 2016. http://www.channelnewsasia. com/news/business/can-singapore-stay-clean/2851840.html

Deutsche Bundesbank. "Swiss Franc and US Dollar Are 'Safe Haven' Currencies." Accessed June 19, 2015. http://www.bundesbank.de/Redaktion/EN/Topics/ 2014/2014_07_30_swiss_franc_and_us_dollar_are_safe_haven_currencies.html.

"Differences between the Monetary Authority of Singapore and the Ministry of Finance." *AsiaOne Business*, March 24, 2016. http://news.asiaone.com/news/busi- ness/differences-between-monetary-authority-singapore-and-ministry-finance.

Emmenegger, P. "Swiss Banking Secrecy and the Problem of International Cooperation in Tax Matters: A Nut Too Hard to Crack?" *Regulation & Governance*, 2015, n/a-n/a. doi:10.1111/rego.12106.

Grant, J. "Singapore Loosens Switzerland's Grip on Wealth Management." *Financial Times*. Accessed July 23, 2013. http://www.ft.com/intl/cms/ s/2/048c3630-f39f-11e2-942f-00144feabdc0.html#axzz2aCMZjs2V.

Hamilton-Hart, N. *Asian States, Asian Bankers: Central Banking in Southeast Asia*. New York: Cornell University Press, 2002.

Inman, P. "Swiss Bank's Currency U-Turn Hurts Watchmakers, Skiers and Traders." *The Guardian*. Accessed June 19, 2015. http://www.theguardian. com/business/2015/jan/15/currency-markets-switzerland-franc.

Kobler, D., and J. Frick. "The Deloitte Wealth Management Centre Ranking 2015." Switzerland: Deloitte, 2015. http://www2.deloitte.com/content/dam/ Deloitte/ch/Documents/financial-services/ch-en-financial-services-the- deloitte-wealth-management-centre-ranking-2015.pdf.

Meier, H. B., J. E. Marthinsen and P. A. Gantenbein. *Swiss Finance: Capital Markets, Banking, and the Swiss Value Chain*. 1st edition. Hoboken, New Jersey: Wiley, 2012.

Menon, R. *Singapore's Financial Centre in the New Landscape*. Monetary Authority of Singapore, 2013.

Monetary Authority of Singapore. *Objectives and Principles of Financial Supervision in Singapore*. MAS Monograph, 2004.

Monetary Authority of Singapore. *Annual Report 2009/2010*. Singapore: Monetary Authority of Singapore, 2010.

Monetary Authority of Singapore. *Tenets of Effective Regulation*. Singapore: Monetary Authority of Singapore, 2010.

Monetary Authority of Singapore. Overview of MAS [online]. *Monetary Authority of Singapore Website*. Available from: http://www.mas.gov.sg/en/About-MAS/Overview-of-MAS.aspx. Accessed December 2, 2012.

Monetary Authority of Singapore. "2014 Asset Management Survey." Monetary Authority of Singapore, 2014. Available from: http://www.mas.gov.sg/~/media/MAS/News%20and%20Publications/Surveys/Asset%20Management/2014%20AM%20Survey%20Report.pdf.

Montes, M. F. Tokyo, Hong Kong and Singapore as Competing Financial Centres. *Journal of Asian Business*, 18, no. 1 (1999), pp. 153–168.

Palma, S. "Is Private Banking Shifting from Switzerland to Hong Kong and Singapore?" Accessed June 19, 2015. http://www.thebanker.com/Banking/Is-private-banking-shifting-from-Switzerland-to-Hong-Kong-and-Singapore.

"Peer Review Group." *OECD Global Forum on Transparency and Exchange of Information for Tax Purposes*. Accessed April 28, 2016. http://www.oecd.org/tax/transparency/peerreviewgroup.htm.

Roth, C. "The Curse of Being a Safe Haven Currency." *CNBC*. Accessed June 19, 2015. http://www.cnbc.com/id/102766787.

"Singapore's Implementation of Global Standard for Automatic Exchange of Financial Account Information." *Ministry of Finance*, November 3, 2014. http://www.mof.gov.sg/news-reader/articleid/1405/parentId/59/year/2014?category=Parliamentary%20Replies.

"Standard for Automatic Exchange of Financial Account Information in Tax Matters." *OECD Exchange of Tax Information Portal*, July 21, 2014. http://www.oecd.org/ctp/exchange-of-tax-information/standard-for-automatic-exchange-of-financial-account-information-for-tax-matters-9789264216525-en.htm.

Swiss Bankers' Association. "2015 Banking Barometer." Available from: http://www.swissbanking.org/en/20150903-5010-all-mm-bankenbarometer.pdf.

Tan, C. H. Singapore as an International Financial Centre. *In: East Asia Dimensions of International Business*. Sydney: Prentice Hall, 2002, pp. 29–44.

Tan, C. H. *Financial Services and Wealth Management in Singapore*. Updated. Singapore: Singapore University Press, 2011.

Tan, S. L. The Development of Singapore's Financial Sector: A Review and Some Thoughts on its Future Prospects. *In*: W. T. H. Koh and R. S. Mariano, eds. *The Economic Prospects of Singapore*. Singapore: Pearson Addison-Wesley, 2006, pp. 246–273.

Tee, O. C. *Singapore's policy of non-internationalisation of the Singapore dollar and the Asian dollar market*. Bank for International Settlements, BIS Papers, 2003.

Thangavelu, P. "Is The Swiss Franc A Safe Haven?" *Investopedia*. Accessed June 19, 2015. http://www.investopedia.com/articles/forex/031715/swiss-franc-safe-haven.asp.

"The Federal Department of Finance (FDF)." *Swiss Federal Council*, January 13, 2016. https://www.admin.ch/gov/en/start/departments/department-of-finance-fdf.html.

Thompson, M. Singapore raps 20 banks for trying to rig rates [online]. *CNNMoney*, 14 June 2013. Available from: http://money.cnn.com/2013/06/14/news/companies/singapore-banks-sibor/index.html Accessed June 20, 2015.

Wilson, K. "Singapore expected to dislodge Switzerland as world's wealth management capital." China Daily/Asia News Network. May 12, 2014. http://business.asiaone.com/news/singapore-expected-dislodge-switzerland-worlds-wealth-management-capital

Woo, J. J. Singapore's policy style: statutory boards as policymaking units. *Journal of Asian Public Policy*, 8, no. 2 (2014), pp. 120–133.

Woo, J. J. Beyond the Neoliberal orthodoxy: Alternative financial policy regimes in Asia's financial centres. *Critical Policy Studies* (2015), Forthcoming.

Woo, J. J. Policy Relations and Policy Subsystems: Financial policy in Hong Kong and Singapore. *International Journal of Public Administration* (2015), Forthcoming.

Woo, J. J., and Y. Guo. "Wealth Management for All Seasons?" The Straits Times, 3 December 2013. http://www.straitstimes.com/the-big-story/asia-report/opinion/story/wealth-management-all-seasons-20131203.

Yeandle, M. *Global Financial Centres Index 17*. London, U.K.: Z/Yen Group and Qatar Financial Centre Authority, 2015.

Yoon, S. P. A Comparison of Hong Kong and Singapore as Asian Financial Centres. *In*: P. D. Grub, C. H. Tan, K.-C. Kwan, and G. H. Rott, eds. *East Asia Dimensions of International Business*. Sydney: Prentice Hall, 1982, pp. 21–28.

Chapter 5

Land Transport Policy: Urban Infrastructure in Singapore and Switzerland

Bruno R. Wildermuth

Introduction

Singapore is a city–state, while Switzerland has many cities and a hinterland. This naturally has given rise to different transport policies. In addition, Singapore has only one level of government while Switzerland has multi-level governance: most cities in Switzerland are located in different cantons, each with its own local policies. Despite Switzerland's multi-level governments and even different languages, there are hardly any differences between the transport policies of different Swiss cities. This is largely the result of the Swiss attitude towards the importance of people versus motor vehicles and the understanding for the need to minimise the overall impact of motor vehicles on the environment.

However, when compared to Singapore, substantial differences exist in the urban land transport policies of the two countries. At the national level, the transport policies of Singapore and Switzerland are less different. In the case of Singapore, intercity and international land transport aspects are limited to only one neighbouring country, Malaysia. In contrast, Switzerland is surrounded by five different countries, each with somewhat different policies.

Singapore realised early in its urban development that with its limited availability of land, it could not afford to become too dependent on private, motorised transport. As a result, Singapore has adopted and implemented policies that are unique and world firsts.

This chapter will address and compare the urban transport policies of the two countries. As Singapore has only limited international land transport traffic, namely road and rail traffic with its northern neighbour Malaysia, this subject will be addressed only briefly.

Private Transport

In Singapore, the use of motorised vehicles is controlled through pricing the use of certain roads and by limiting the total number of vehicles allowed to use the roads. Both schemes are unique to Singapore.

Back in 1975, Singapore introduced the Area Licensing Scheme (ALS). This was the first urban traffic congestion scheme to be successfully implemented in the world. This scheme included all roads entering a 6-square-kilometre area in the Central Business District (CBD) called the "Restricted Zone" (RZ), which was subsequently increased to 7.25 square kilometers. Initially, the ALS was in effect between 7.30 am and 9.30 am daily, except on Sundays and public holidays. Shortly after its introduction, it was extended until 10.15 am and in 1994 until 6.30 pm. Currently, it is extended until 8.00 pm.[1] Enforcement was carried out manually by auxiliary police officers who carried out visual checks at 34 overhead gantries. The scheme was eventually replaced in 1998 by the Electronic Road Pricing (ERP) scheme, again the first in the world. The scheme has since been expanded to include many roads outside the central area, including most expressways.

Singapore has plans to introduce from 2020 a GPS-based road pricing system that will charge motorists for travelling on any congested roads and for the distance travelled. Such a system will allow a fairer approach to charging for the use of motor vehicles. It may also help to bring about the desired modal choice, namely a 75 percent usage of public transport for travel during peak periods, which is a long-term goal of the overall transport policy.[2]

---

[1] "ERP Rate Table for Passenger Cars, Taxis and Light Goods Vehicles." *One Motoring*. Accessed April 27, 2015. http://www.onemotoring.com.sg/publish/onemotoring/en/on_the_roads/ERP_Rates.html

[2] PricewaterhouseCoopers. "The Singapore Land Transport Master Plan 2013." *PwC*. Page 3. Accessed April 27, 2015. http://www.pwc.com/sg/en/publications/lta_masterplan.html.

Recognising that road pricing alone would not be sufficient to avoid heavy congestion, Singapore has also controlled the number of motorised vehicles through the introduction of a limited number of Certificates of Entitlement (COEs), a vehicle quota system. A COE represents the right to vehicle ownership and use of the limited road space for 10 years and is available through bi-monthly auctions to the highest bidders. This scheme was first implemented in May 1990 when it was determined that simply increasing the road taxes and road pricing would not sufficiently limit the number of vehicles on Singapore's roads.

In addition to the COE and import duties, Singapore also charges an Additional Registration Fee (ARF) of between 100 and 180 percent of the Open Market Value (OMV) of each car, and a Carbon Emissions-Based Vehicle Scheme (CEVS). The latter may be a discount to be offset against the ARF depending on the level of emissions of the car. This scheme has recently been revised to be more stringent. It offers the most discount to hybrid cars and to cars with Euro V compliant diesel engines.[3]

To exercise prudence during the current period of low interest rates and to further discourage Singaporeans from owning a car, in early 2013, the Monetary Authority of Singapore (MAS) limited the amount of loans for motor vehicles. The maximum loan amount allowed depends on the OMV of the motor vehicle purchased:

(i) For a motor vehicle with an OMV that does not exceed S$20,000, the maximum loan-to-value (LTV) is 60 percent of the purchase price, including relevant taxes and the price of the Certificate of Entitlement, where applicable; and

(ii) For a motor vehicle with an OMV of more than S$20,000, the maximum LTV is 50 percent of the purchase price.

In addition, the tenure of a motor vehicle loan is capped at 5 years.[4]

---

[3] "Revised Carbon Emissions-Based Vehicle Scheme (CEVS) from 1 July 2015." *Land Transport Authority.* Accessed April 27, 2015. http://www.lta.gov.sg/apps/news/page. aspx?c=2&id=8aa03b88-409f-4852-b2df-09077e101468.

[4] "MAS Imposes Financing Restrictions on Motor Vehicle Loans." *Monetary Authority of Singapore.* Accessed April 27, 2015. http://www.mas.gov.sg/news-and-publications/ media-releases/2013/mas-imposes-financing-restrictions-on-motor-vehicle-loans.aspx.

In contrast, Switzerland has no specific policies aimed at controlling or reducing the number of cars or the use of cars in urban areas. Bringing about a balanced use of public and private transport is achieved through the provision of a highly reliable, on-schedule, and convenient public transport system. At the same time, limited public parking facilities and road space fairly shared between people and vehicles helps significantly in discouraging too much private transport. Unlike Singapore, where owning a car is still an important status symbol, Switzerland, having long been a developed country, does not have such a concern. Consequently, many Swiss are perfectly happy to make use of the excellent public transport system and do not find it worthwhile to own a car, even if they can readily afford it.

In order to be fair to Singapore motorists, who pay dearly for the ownership and use of their motor vehicles, Malaysian motor vehicles travelling in Singapore are charged a daily fee of S$35 (CHF25) for cars and S$4 (CHF2.85) for motorcycles. However, each vehicle gets ten free days per year and there is no fee charged between 5.00 pm and 2.00 am on weekdays, and all day on Saturdays, Sundays and public holidays. Malaysia has announced the introduction of a similar daily scheme charging RM$20 (S$7.45, CHF5.30) per day for Singapore cars. In addition, each country charges a toll for the use of the two connecting causeways.

Switzerland has a similar charge for foreign vehicles, which require a 'Vignette' to use its main roads. Motor vehicles of up to 3.5 tonnes, including motorcycles, require vignettes valid for 14 months, from 1 December of the preceding year to 31 January of the following year at a cost of CHF40 (S$56). Vehicles above 3.5 tonnes used for commercial goods traffic are subject to a performance-based heavy vehicle fee. In return, Swiss motor vehicles travelling on Austrian, French, or Italian Expressways are required to pay tolls. For France and Italy, tolls are distance-specific, while Austria has a similar vignette system but for various durations. Germany, Switzerland's other neighbour, is currently considering the introduction of a toll system for the use of all major roads.

According to recent data, Singapore has approximately 620,000 passenger cars on its roads. This amounts to 113 passenger cars for every 1,000 people. By contrast, Switzerland has 539 passenger cars per 1,000 people. This number is quite similar to those of three of its five neighbouring countries, but lower than that for Italy or Liechtenstein.[5]

Singapore's road network totals about 3,500 kilometers and occupies about 12 percent of its land area. To preserve its limited land, Singapore has increasingly been building tunnels for its new expressways.

Rail Public Transport

While the initial road pricing scheme was introduced at a time when few Singaporeans could afford a car, it was recognised that with a growing standard of living, such measures would not be popular unless attractive alternative ways of travel were also provided. Thus, public transport needed to be upgraded substantially from the rather inadequate bus system operated by various private companies. In 1981, after an extensive debate in public and behind the closed doors of the Istana, Singapore's political leaders decided to build the initial Mass Rapid Transit (MRT) system to serve as the backbone of the public transport system. The first section was opened in November 1987 and the full initial system completed by July 1990, two years ahead of the original schedule.

While the MRT was built and financed by the Government, it is being operated by a publicly-listed company, SMRT, initially created by the Government but now almost evenly owned between Temasek Holdings, an investment company owned by the Government of Singapore, with 54 percent of the shares, and more than 50,000 private investors, holding 46 percent of its shares. Under the original leasing contract, the operator is responsible for maintaining and replacing all equipment and assets other than the basic infrastructure such as tunnels, viaducts, stations and depots. This arrangement, a form of public-private partnership, has increasingly been applied to Singapore's bus operations that were totally private until very recently.

---

[5]Eidgenössisches Departement des Innern EDI, and Bundesamt für Statistik BFS. "Mobilität und Verkehr." *Bundesamt für Statistik*, May 2, 2015. http://www.bfs.admin.ch/bfs/portal/de/index/themen/11/22/press.Document.189718.pdf.

Since the construction of the initial MRT system, several more MRT and LRT lines have been built, including two extensions to the original system. The new lines are operated either by SMRT or SBS Transit, Singapore's other public transport operator. All lines were initially operated under a similar scheme.

Under the most recent policy change, rail operators only need to provide the funds from revenue for the original costs of the operating assets, while the government will cover the difference. This has substantially lessened the burden on the rail operators. At the same time, it has allowed the government to reduce the operating licenses for rail systems to 15–19 years from the original 30–40 years. This change has also allowed the government to change the operating conditions more frequently.

The policy of privately operating public transport services has avoided the common pitfalls of creating a bottomless pit with fare revenue barely covering the operating costs, and the timely replacement of assets that keeps the system modern and attractive. So far, the Singapore model has proven largely successful, at least for rail operations. At the same time, fares, which are controlled by the Public Transport Council, continue to be very affordable by any standard.

The ease of using public transport is further enhanced through the stored value fare payment scheme. Initially, it relied on high-coercivity magnetic cards, which were replaced with contactless smart cards in 2001. Since 2010, the scheme has offered distance-based through fares for all services without any penalties for transferring between different rail and/or bus services. The stored value scheme, enhanced over time, first started operating in November 1990 as the world's first integrated urban ticketing system. The contactless smart cards are issued by the Land Transport Authority (LTA). In addition, most local banks also issue such cards as a multi-purpose bank and travel card. For added convenience, the stored value can be automatically replenished when boarding a service through the 'Auto Top-Up' facility, which links the card to the passenger's bank account.

The public–private responsibilities for public transport are fairly unique to Singapore and some other countries in Asia. In Singapore, the only shortcoming is the lack of an independent rail inspectorate which can arbitrate between the operator and the provider when issues arise. In Switzerland, by contrast, all urban public transport is the responsibility of the respective city governments. Both the provision of facilities, equipment, and rolling stock, and its operation are provided by government agencies. In addition, public transport services between suburban areas and their related cities are mainly provided by the Swiss National Railways (SBB), using largely the tracks of the intercity national railway system.

Despite the various throughfares and season tickets, public transport ticketing is less automated and less convenient in Switzerland as compared to Singapore. Correspondingly, fares based on zonal fare schemes are generally much higher compared to the distance-based fares in Singapore. For example, a short trip ticket valid for 30 minutes and a limited number of stops costs CHF2.20 and CHF2.60 (S$3.10 and S$3.60) in Zurich and Basel respectively, compared to a bus or MRT trip of 10 kilometres in Singapore for S$1.40 (CHF1.00). Similarly, a 1-hour ticket valid within the zone of the city of Zurich costs CHF4.30 (S$6.00) versus a 20-kilometres trip in Singapore for S$1.80 (CHF1.30).

Switzerland's public transport systems are fully integrated among the various municipal, regional, and national systems with respect to tariffs. In Basel, for instance, the tariff even includes travel across the border to Germany (up to four zones) and France (two zones). This is something that Singapore will have to adopt, once its MRT system is extended to the neighbouring city Johor Bahru in Malaysia, a project for which plans are currently being finalised.

Public Bus Services

Until recently, bus services in Singapore were provided by two publicly-listed companies operating government-approved routes with their own buses. The operating companies also designed the routes based on their own analysis of demand and the likely profitability. In 2008, the Government announced that it would take over the planning of bus routes.[6] However, it has yet to come up with new routes or significant

---

[6]Tan, Shin Bin, and Ching Leong. "The Evolution of Public Transport Policies in Singapore." p. 7. Accessed April 27, 2015. http://lkyspp.nus.edu.sg/wp-content/uploads/2014/01/Transport-Planning-for-Singapore.pdf.

changes to existing routes. More recently, the Government has started to purchase additional buses and provided them to the operators to augment their services. In addition, the Government has started to put up for tender limited packages of bus routes that can be operated from one or more designated bus depots. This serves to attract more bus operators and presumably will bring about a more competitive operating environment. However, the packages tendered so far have not included any newly designed or substantially modified routes. The first successful tender under the new regime was recently awarded to a United Kingdom bus operator, Tower Transit, based on its strong track record for a strong management of en-route service reliability and high quality maintenance, rather than being the lowest bidder.

Under this new regime, all revenue collected will go to the Government while the operator's profit will need to be built into the operator's bid price. The Government is expected to apply more stringent monitoring of the service reliability and actual provision. This aspect has been largely missing with on-time performance checking limited to the starting point of each route only and a tolerance of missing up to four percent of the scheduled services without a penalty, rather than zero percent as is common in most developed countries. A 100 percent service provision, of course, requires the availability of spare vehicles and, most of all, standby drivers. Given that many Singapore bus drivers are foreigners with a low wage, it is difficult to understand why back-up drivers are not a standard feature. Similarly, there is hardly a shortage of buses as many buses can be observed to be on 'tea-break' even during peak hours when their drivers take a rest. This policy appears to be an archaic practice left-over from the old days when drivers were assigned to a specific bus to monitor its potential misuse.

Undeniably, the biggest difference between the two countries for public bus services is the complete lack in Singapore of published timetables for each stop and each service, as is customary in all Swiss cities, and for that matter, in almost all cities of the developed world. Such timetables allow passengers to plan their daily journeys and waste a minimum of time waiting for their services. This naturally helps greatly to have an efficient and productive way of life. With the Singapore system, no such consistency and reliability exists, hence the constant struggle by the Government to improve productivity that has been lagging and even declining over the last few years.

In Switzerland, timetables are published and displayed for each bus, tram, and train service, even if the service operates every three minutes. Typically, timetables are the same for each day, Monday through Friday, and different for Saturdays, Sundays and public holidays. In Singapore, buses operate on a different frequency and time each day, and passengers are expected to find out about the next available service via smartphone apps or simply by waiting at their stop until the bus shows up (often two buses of the same service together, with a correspondingly long gap behind them).

Based on the following conservative assumptions — four million daily bus journey legs, an average waiting time of six minutes, and an hourly wage of S$10 — the yearly loss to Singapore amounts to a staggering S$1 billion. This lost value is a big drag on national productivity. Clearly, Singapore has a long way to go and it has many good reasons to improve its bus network.

Bus and rail services between Singapore and Malaysia are provided primarily by Malaysian operators, although a few bus services to the Johor Bahru bus terminal are operated by Singaporean bus operators SBS and SMRT.

Road Transport and Policies of Road Usage

In recent years, land transport policy for both public and private transport has been formulated by the Land Transport Authority (LTA), a statutory board under the Ministry of Transport. In the earlier days of Singapore's development, separate ministries were responsible for roads and for public transport. Given the strong emphasis of the Singapore Government on satisfying the demands of car owners, road widening, the construction of new expressways, and other improvements to roads are a standard part of the overall policy.

Singapore has essentially become a city for cars rather than people. More recently though, the Centre for Liveable Cities, which is associated with the Urban Redevelopment Authority (URA) and is a part of the Ministry for National Development, has started a campaign to plan newer development areas with more pedestrian and bicycle facilities. However, for most of the current city, pedestrians are expected to take a backseat.

Despite policymakers' awareness of changing demographics, including population ageing, the attitude of traffic planners has not changed significantly. As a result, pedestrians find it increasingly difficult to negotiate the many overhead bridges and underpasses with long ramps and stairs that have been built, presumably to speed up motorised traffic, without much concern for the convenience of pedestrians, be they elderly, physically challenged, or mothers with baby strollers.

Such treatment of the people, who should be the primary users of city streets, is very different from the standard Swiss practice where all road space is shared equally between vehicles and people. It is a very unusual sight in Switzerland to find an overhead pedestrian bridge or an underpass. At signalised intersections, pedestrians have the same rights as motor vehicles and are given sufficient time to cross along the shortest path.

In Switzerland, road transport policy is complicated by the existence of the multi-level government structure, with the national, cantonal, and city administrations all having an interest in and involvement with roads. For example, the network of national roads will naturally provide interconnections between different parts of the country and major cities and generally follow the national standard for expressways. Certain roads are under the jurisdiction of the cantons as they form the lower level connections. Yet in the end, they all have to work together to achieve the key objectives.

Parking Policies

There are naturally large differences in the parking policies of cities in Switzerland and Singapore. Swiss cities, particularly their central areas, were built long before cars became a major part of the transport scene. Consequently, many Swiss cities have relatively few parking spaces in the central areas. Singapore, on the other hand, experienced much of its development in recent times, so parking facilities in new buildings are generally adequate. Singapore was also forward-looking with a policy that essentially attempted to minimise the generation of local traffic from vehicles searching for a parking space. Thus, every new building is required to provide parking for the estimated demand based on its use. This rule is relaxed only for developments in close proximity to MRT stations to reflect the added ease of access via public transport.[7]

There are three distinct zones for parking requirements, the Central Area (essentially defined by the Restricted Zone and the Marina Bay area), other areas, and areas within 400 meters of an MRT station. Naturally, these requirements do not apply to old areas such as Chinatown where parking is largely limited to paid on-street parking where appropriate. Payment for parking on-street and in some public parking areas is still carried out via parking coupons displayed on the dashboard of the parked car. Inspectors are needed to carry out spot checks of the coupons displayed. For most other facilities, payments take place electronically via the stored value card inserted in the in-vehicle unit mounted in each vehicle for the payment of the road pricing charges.

On-street parking in Singapore is restricted to roads with designated spaces and is generally not free during the day. However, there are no restrictions that limit parking to nearby residents only. Such restrictions do, however, apply to parking facilities, both at-grade and in parking structures, associated with public housing developments where residents can purchase access to a restricted lot.

In Swiss cities, parking is substantially limited and hence poses a fairly strong deterrent for people to use their cars to travel around the cities. Apart from dedicated parking houses and purpose-built parking facilities with high hourly charges, parking along streets with marked spaces is allowed generally for one hour for non-residents by displaying a parking disc. Registered residents of the area are allowed to park without

---

[7]"Code of Practice on Vehicle Parking Provision in Development Proposals." *Land Transport Authority.* Page 8. Accessed April 27, 2015. https://www.lta.gov.sg/content/ltaweb/en/industry-matters/development-and-building-and-construction-and-utility-works/vehicle-parking.html.

time limitations. In Zurich, parking discs are available for CHF300 (S$420) per year.[8] Special full day discs, valid for non-residents, are available for CHF15 (S$21) per day.

In Zurich's central area, parking charges are as high as CHF1.10 (S$1.55) per 15 minutes with a daily maximum of CHF43.00 (S$60.00). In the suburban areas, charges are lower at CHF1.50 (S$2.10) for the first hour and CHF2.00 (S$2.80) for each additional hour with a daily maximum of CHF28.00 (S$39.00). Other Swiss cities have similar charges.

Bicycling

Substantial differences can be found between Singapore and Switzerland in the treatment of cyclists. In Singapore, unlike Switzerland, bicycles are not registered vehicles. While cyclists are allowed to use sidewalks in some parts of Singapore, they are not allowed to do the same in other parts, including the central area. This causes confusion and uncertainty. More than that, it results in motorists not being used to sharing the road space with cyclists even in the central area. Also, in Singapore, users of low-powered motorised bicycles are often found using sidewalks, like cyclists.

In Switzerland, with traffic moving on the right, cyclists are expected to use the right-most side of the right lane and indicate any turning movements with their arms and move to the right side of the turning lane, if one exists, just like motor vehicles. Some roads in Switzerland even have special cycling lanes with a slightly raised curb. These are usually narrow lanes with just enough space for overtaking another cyclist. Cyclists are expected to strictly observe the traffic rules when it comes to intersections, traffic lights, and turning. Motorised bicycles and motorcycles are expected to follow the same standard traffic rules.

Pedestrians

Perhaps the biggest difference between Singapore and Switzerland is found when it comes to pedestrians. In Singapore, pedestrians are largely

---

[8]"Parkkarten & Bewilligungen." *Stadt Zürich Polizeidepartement.* Accessed April 27, 2015. https://www.stadt-zuerich.ch/pd/de/index/dav/parkkarten_bewilligungen.html.

considered a nuisance when it comes to allocating road space. Pedestrian facilities, such as covered walkways, are provided to make it easy for people to get from housing estates to bus stops and MRT stations, as long as they do not need to cross roads. However, when it comes to crossing roads, pedestrians are often made to use overhead bridges or underpasses, so as to allow motorised traffic to move with the least amount of disruption.

Even for a major shopping street such as Orchard Road, pedestrians are largely banned from crossing at-grade and instead have to use underpasses or overhead bridges at great inconvenience. Such inconvenient crossings are even found near access points to major hospitals, such the Singapore General Hospital and Changi General Hospital, which are visited by many physically-challenged people. An exception is granted one Saturday evening a month, where pedestrians are allowed to take over Orchard Road for various planned activities. Yet, even this event does not seem to be favoured by many merchants as the activities generally distract people from shopping.

In many parts of Singapore's central area, pedestrians are required to cross via a three-legged path rather than simply straight across, presumably to speed up the turning car traffic. This concept applies even where the turning vehicles eventually end up waiting an equally long time at the next intersection, such as is the case at the intersection of Paterson Road with Orchard Road.

By contrast, pedestrians in Swiss cites have equal rights to the use of the road space and many Swiss cities have areas where motor vehicles are generally banned except for delivery services. In Zurich, for instance, the old parts of the city on both sides of the river are designated pedestrian areas, and most of the Bahnhofstrasse, a major shopping street, is reserved for trams and pedestrians only. When it comes to crossings at intersections, pedestrians are provided with the most direct path, unlike in Singapore, where they often have to take three legs to cross instead of the straightest path.

Most Swiss cities have a car-free zone, usually in the old, historic parts of the city. Zermatt, an alpine resort town near the famous Matterhorn with about 5,800 residents and many times that number of tourists, is totally car-free, with electric taxis and delivery vehicles providing essential services.

Conclusion

In summary, despite Switzerland having nearly five times as many passenger cars per population than Singapore, its cities are generally much more pedestrian-friendly than Singapore given its substantial controls on cars. One can only surmise that on this aspect Singapore's policy has been strongly influenced by the need to please car owners who are paying dearly for their privilege.

Another aspect of substantial difference is, of course, the high reliability and predictability of Switzerland's public transport services and the more restricted availability of parking that has resulted in a better balance between car and public transport usage in Switzerland. Most important, however, is the Swiss policy of sharing public road space fairly and equally between people and motor vehicles, a policy that Singapore still needs to consider and adopt.

References

"Code of Practice on Vehicle Parking Provision in Development Proposals." *Land Transport Authority*. Accessed April 27, 2015. https://www.lta.gov.sg/content/ltaweb/en/industry-matters/development-and-building-and-construction-and-utility-works/vehicle-parking.html.

Eidgenössisches Departement des Innern EDI, and Bundesamt für Statistik BFS. "Mobilität und Verkehr." *Bundesamt für Statistik*, May 2, 2015. http://www.bfs.admin.ch/bfs/portal/de/index/themen/11/22/press.Document.189718.pdf.

"ERP Rate Table for Passenger Cars, Taxis and Light Goods Vehicles." *One Motoring*. Accessed April 27, 2015. http://www.onemotoring.com.sg/publish/onemotoring/en/on_the_roads/ERP_Rates.html

"MAS Imposes Financing Restrictions on Motor Vehicle Loans." *Monetary Authority of Singapore*. Accessed April 27, 2015. http://www.mas.gov.sg/news-and-publications/media-releases/2013/mas-imposes-financing-restrictions-on-motor-vehicle-loans.aspx.

"Parkkarten & Bewilligungen." *Stadt Zürich Polizeidepartement*. Accessed April 27, 2015. https://www.stadt-zuerich.ch/pd/de/index/dav/parkkarten_bewilligungen.html.

PricewaterhouseCoopers. "The Singapore Land Transport Master Plan 2013." *PwC*. Accessed April 27, 2015. http://www.pwc.com/sg/en/publications/lta_masterplan.html.

"Revised Carbon Emissions-Based Vehicle Scheme (CEVS) from 1 July 2015." *Land Transport Authority.* Accessed April 27, 2015. http://www.lta.gov.sg/apps/news/page.aspx?c=2&id=8aa03b88-409f-4852-b2df-09077e101468.

Tan, S. B., and C. Leong. "The Evolution of Public Transport Policies in Singapore." Accessed April 27, 2015. http://lkyspp.nus.edu.sg/wp-content/uploads/2014/01/Transport-Planning-for-Singapore.pdf.

Chapter 6

SMEs: Challenges, Potential for Mutual Learning and Implications for Policymakers

Manuel Baeuml[1]

Introduction

Small and medium-sized enterprises (SMEs)[2] are important for Singapore and Switzerland because they form the economic backbone of both economies. Furthermore, SMEs are often family-owned and these firms are known to be less liable to global downturns and external shocks, therefore stabilising the overall economy. For example, these firms came out of the 2008 crisis in much better shape than non-family rivals, with less debt, more cash, and higher research and development (R&D) investment throughout the downturn. However, the leaders of small and medium-sized enterprises (SMEs) in Singapore and Switzerland emphasise the challenging business environments they are operating in. In Singapore, input factor costs such as labour and land have risen sharply in the past, putting pressure on the cost side of the profit and loss statement Swiss SMEs have undergone similar developments in the past. Today, despite having one of the highest

---

[1] This chapter is based on findings from the author's PhD dissertation at the University of St.Gallen, 2015. For a more in-depth analysis, see Baeuml, M. (2015). The Impact of Strategic Performance Management on SME performance. Dissertation, St. Gallen, 2015.
[2] The EU Commission defines SMEs as companies with less than 250 employees and having at least one of the following two criteria: an annual turnover less than S$75 mn or an annual balance sheet of less than S$30 mn. SPRING Singapore defines SMEs in a more nuanced way, as 'firms up to 200 employees' or having 'annual sales of not more than S$100 million'.

labour costs in the world, many Swiss manufacturing SMEs operate successfully in their niches and are technology leaders. Despite the challenges described, several SME leaders in Singapore remain optimistic. In the words of an owner-manager of a manufacturing SME with 110 employees, *"When I look to the technology leaders, I can still see so much space to improve. This makes me optimistic that we can still improve."*

The goal of this chapter is to analyse manufacturing SMEs in Singapore and Switzerland to identify the potential for mutual learning, both for SME managers and for policymakers. In particular, the role of SMEs in Singapore's and Switzerland's economies is outlined, followed by similarities in their business environments. Based on interviews with managing directors and owner-managers of over 90 manufacturing SMEs in Singapore and Switzerland, light is shed on the different strategic positioning of manufacturing SMEs and associated challenges. The chapter concludes with recommendations for policymakers, drawing also from several discussions with governmental bodies such as the Standards, Productivity and Innovation Board (SPRING Singapore).

Role of SMEs in the Singaporean and Swiss Economies

SMEs in Singapore and Switzerland show many similarities in terms of their roles in the economy, i.e., their contribution to the workforce and added value, export orientation, and types of industries. More than 315,000 market-oriented SMEs in the secondary and tertiary sector form the backbone of Switzerland's economy, according to data available from governmental agencies. They employ more than two-thirds of the employees of market-oriented companies. As a result of the moderate size of the domestic market, many companies have internationalised their distribution. In 2005, the export ratio of all companies in the secondary sector was 48 percent. Many Swiss SMEs have established themselves as market leaders in their niches. They are particularly strong in the fields of machine tools, medical technology, biotechnology, life sciences, watch manufacturing and clean technology. High cost pressure has forced managers to aim for a clear strategic positioning and many Swiss SMEs have gained a competitive advantage through innovative, high quality products and services in combination with high efficiency levels. As a result, Swiss SMEs compete successfully in their niches worldwide.

A common perception in Singapore is that large multinational companies drive the Singapore economy. It might be surprising to some readers that Singapore's economy also relies heavily on SMEs. They account for 99 percent of the Republic's total number of establishments, employ about 62 percent of the Singaporean workforce, and contribute 48 percent of total added value to the economy. Singaporean companies show high levels of internationalisation activities. The export ratio of manufactured goods was 64 percent in 2011. Their manufacturing focus lies in biomedical manufacturing, electronics, precision engineering, and transport engineering. Like their Swiss counterparts, managers of Singaporean SMEs face major cost challenges in factors beyond their control, such as salary hikes, rising costs of materials and rent. In addition, the 2013 and 2014 Singapore Budgets have aimed to reduce reliance on foreign workers. To avoid higher foreign worker levies, SMEs will need to replace foreign with local manpower. Responding to these challenges, SMEs need to unlock their untapped potential, e.g., by better leveraging existing resources and improving their managerial practices. Table 1 summarises the roles of SMEs in general and manufacturing SMEs in particular in both economies.

Another view commonly shared in Singapore is that manufacturing SMEs are being crowded out by larger companies, i.e., that larger firms take up vital resources, leaving SMEs behind. In fact, the share of total added value contributed by manufacturing companies with up to 300 employees has shrunk from 53 percent in 2009 to 35 percent in 2011. Against this backdrop one could argue that changes in contribution, which are particularly pro-cyclical, are in fact driven by larger and often multinational players. For example, the same group of small companies contributed 37 percent of total added value in 2006, which is close to the observed value in 2011. Regardless of this, the fact remains that SMEs are indeed crowded out when it comes to recruiting talents from local schools and universities. In the words of SME managing directors and owners interviewed, many Singaporean "youngsters", even those with technical backgrounds, perceive working for smaller companies, particularly in manufacturing and for SMEs in general, to be less attractive as compared to higher wages, a perceived better working environment, and a centrally-located workplace in larger companies operating in industries such as banking, insurance, or telecommunications. As a result, although SMEs play an important role in the overall economy, their access to (local) talents is limited.

Table 1:   SMEs Play a Similar Role in Swiss and Singaporean Economies

	Switzerland		Singapore	
	All SMEs	**SMEs[2]** (excl. micro)	**All SMEs**	**SMEs** (excl. micro)
Share of all companies,[1] in percent	99^2	13^2	99^5	n/a
SME contribution to total value add,[1] in percent	$55\text{–}65^{12}$	n/a	48^5	n/a
Share of workforce employed,[1] in percent	$67^{2,3}$	42^2	62^5	43^{11}
Export-ratios manufacturing, in percent	48^6	23 (small)[7] 38 (med.-sized)[7]	64^4	n/a
	All Companies		**All Companies**	
Contribution of manufacturing industry to total value add, in percent	19^9		32^{10}	
Major manufacturing sub-industries	Machine tools, medical tech, biomedical technology		Biomedical technology, electronics, precision engineering	
Major challenges	High labour (USD 57.8^{11}) and rental costs Limited domestic market		Rising labour (USD 24.8^{11}) and rental costs Limited domestic market	

[1] All sectors.

[2] Data for 2008; Source: Schweizer Bundesamt für Statistik (2010).

[3] Alternative source states 82 percent; Source: Schweizer Bundesamt für Statistik (2014b).

[4] All manufacturing companies; data for 2011; Source: International Enterprise Singapore (2010), SPRING Singapore (2011).

[5] Data for 2011; Source: SPRING Singapore (2011).

[6] All companies in the secondary sector; Source: Schweizer Bundesamt für Statistik (2008b).

[7] Across all industries; micro companies had an export share of 12 percent; Source: Schweizer Bundesamt für Statistik (2008a).

[9] Data for 2012 and for all manufacturing companies ("*verarbeitendes Gewerbe*"); Source: Schweizer Bundesamt für Statistik (2014a).

[10] 50 percent for SMEs from all industries; Data for 2012; Source: Singapore Ministry of Trade and Industry (2012, 2013).

[11] Total hourly compensation costs in 2012; Source: US Department of Labour (2013).

[12] Estimate based on contribution of German "Mittelstand" to total value added (57 percent of total value add; 59 percent of all employees in 2014; Source: IfM Bonn).

[3] This study does not include micro companies with less than 10 employees. The overall numbers including micro companies are shown in the table because often limited amount of data available.

Similarities in Singaporean and Swiss Business Environments

In line with the similarities in the economic role of SMEs, exogenous market factors reflecting the ease of doing business are assessed to be almost identical for both countries by local managers. According to the World Economic Forum, the two countries show almost identical scores on nine out of 12 dimensions that measure basic requirements, efficiency enhancers, innovation, and sophistication factors (Figure 1).

In particular, both countries show similarities with regards to domestic and foreign market size, the goods market, as well as labour market efficiency and technological readiness. Smaller discrepancies exist with regards to business sophistication and innovation, where Swiss companies outperform their Singaporean peers. However, Singaporean firms have easier access to loans in the area of financial market development. In addition to this high similarity in scores, Singapore and Switzerland rank among the best in the world on most of these 12 dimensions, as indicated by the ranking of 148 countries on the right-hand side of Figure 1.

Overall, regardless of differences in national culture, the Singaporean and Swiss economies feature striking similarities with regard to factors

Figure 1:   Exogenous factors affecting firm competitiveness in Singapore and Switzerland

Global Competitiveness Index, 2013-2014
Score (1-7), higher score indicates greater sophistication

Global Competitiveness Rank, 2013-2014
Rank out of 148

Basic requirements	1	3
Institutions	3	7
Infrastructure	2	6
Macroeconomic environment	18	11
Health and primary education	2	12
Efficiency enhancers	2	5
Higher education and training	2	4
Goods market efficiency	1	6
Labor market efficiency	1	2
Financial market development	2	11
Technological readiness	7	9
Market size	34	40
Innovation and sophistication factors	13	1
Business sophistication	17	2
Innovation	9	2

Source: Own illustration. Adapted from Klaus Schwab, *World Economic Forum: Global Competitiveness Report 2013–2014* (Geneva World Economic Forum).

that describe SME contributions to the economy and the conduciveness of the business environment. That said, some differences certainly exist. For example, land restrictions in Singapore result in an innate incentive for SMEs to best utilise space and hamper the development of industry sub-sectors which require plenty of ground. In contrast, Swiss SMEs, especially rural ones, have more and therefore cheaper land available to build their businesses. Looking forward, Singaporean manufacturing SMEs are likely to undergo a similar transformation as their Swiss counterparts did in the past. Given the cost and labour pressures on Singaporean SMEs, they will need to climb the value chain and position themselves as quality and technology leaders to command a higher premium on their products and services. This transformation is likely to be catalysed by the Singaporean government with its aspiration to build regional and global leaders in niche markets as indicated by Lee Kuan Yew's vision for Singapore that does not foresee low-end factories or low-tech industries.

Importance of Strategic Positioning and Employee Investment

Three archetypes of SMEs can be observed in Singapore and Switzerland facing different challenges. In the following interviews with more than 90 managing directors or owner-managers of SMEs, the effect of the business environment on each archetype of SME is detailed and the associated challenges are elaborated.

Singaporean manufacturing SMEs

Several of the managing directors and owner-managers of Singapore-based SMEs interviewed were optimistic for the local industry, but only if local SMEs were able to improve on certain key strategic dimensions: (1) strategic positioning and planning, (2) strategic alignment of employees, and (3) productivity. In the following section, current challenges and recommendations for SMEs along these three strategic dimensions are provided.

1. *Singaporean manufacturing SMEs: Strategic positioning and planning*

Three archetypes were found for Singaporean manufacturing SMEs: *Concentration-pressed*, *opportunity-trailing*, and *niche-excellence* players.[4] In contrast to Swiss SMEs and as depicted in Figure 2, the majority of Singaporean SMEs are *opportunity-trailing* and *concentration-pressed*.[5] Few can be classified as *niche-excellence* players. Several managing directors commented that Singaporean SMEs often lacked a clear strategic positioning. Consider the impression of the owner-manager of a medium-sized SME with highly specialised niche products for the aviation industry:

> *Most SMEs in Singapore don't follow Michael Porter's recommendation: if you want to be successful, you need to have a clear strategic positioning.*

Several manufacturing sub-sectors in Singapore such as electronics are stagnating or even shrinking. As the domestic market is comparably small, SMEs have experienced downward pressure on their margins. To increase the utilisation of their machines, *concentration-pressed* SMEs have tended to accept orders of any kind, leaving them with less industry or product specification. To escape the downward pressure, many SMEs have turned to product quality (58 percent of interviewed SMEs). Most of them were *opportunity-trailing* SMEs that pursued a dual strategy: high

---

[4]*Concentration-pressed* SMEs focus on the domestic market, with old assets and little innovation; *opportunity-trailing* SMEs focus on high quality orders, but also accept lower quality orders to achieve high utilisation of their machines, while *niche-excellence* SMEs specialise in their niches, aim for technological leadership, and focus on innovation and premium quality.

[5]An alternative strategy is cost leadership. Cost leadership with production in Singapore requires a high degree of automation to offset the relatively high labour costs in Singapore compared to the region. For example, in 2012, the median annual basic guaranteed salary of an engineer with 2–5 years of relevant experience was 25% of the Singaporean salary, and in the Philippines it was 72% of the Singaporean salary. Despite automation, cost disadvantages due to higher land costs remain. This is why this strategic positioning is more difficult for Singapore-based SMEs to achieve, especially if they are competing with regional players, e.g., from Malaysia or Thailand.

quality-low volume products (complex systems) and lower quality-high volume products (volume operations model). High quality products generated premiums, while the lower quality-high volume products ensured higher utilisation of machines and employees. However, this approach carries two risks. Firstly, an opportunistic intake of orders can result in a loss of focus on defined strategic goals. For example, a customer order with a significant need for customisation of the expiring product C can result in a loss of focus on products A and B which are central to the firm's strategy. Notably, financial goals may be achieved by opportunistic behaviour, but the firm is unlikely to progress (quickly) in the direction of its long-term strategic roadmap. Secondly, optimising the production system for high utilisation of single machines often leads to inefficient end-to-end processes and costly in-process inventory levels. In addition, batch sizes tend to increase, which reduces flexibility.

Next, Singaporean SMEs that are *concentration-pressed* or *opportunity-trailing* tended to fall short on strategic planning. Seventy-eight percent of SMEs interviewed focused on their (strategic) planning with a maximum of one year. As the owner-manager of a *niche-excellence* SME pointed out:

> *Planning is critical to best make use of a system and utilise it. [....]My impression is that 90 percent of local SMEs only plan for one to two years at best. This limits them as they focus only on today.*

Several managing directors claimed that the dynamic environment has caused long-term strategic planning to be useless. For example, product cycles in electronics last less than six months. An expansion of products and services to other countries is often challenging for *concentration-pressed* or *opportunity-trailing* SMEs. Compared to local players in nearby Asian markets, these Singaporean SMEs tend to have higher costs. As for serving high quality segments internationally, they often still struggle in achieving highest quality levels or at least fall short on innovation and technology levels. That said, smaller firms can benefit from strategic planning by focusing on product developments which ultimately affect firm performance positively. In addition to a focus on innovation, diversification in terms of more promising local industries such as oil and gas, aviation, or medical devices can reduce the dependency on local sunset industries.

In contrast, *niche-excellence* SMEs based in Singapore have achieved a clear strategic positioning and focused on innovative and premium products. Fourteen percent of SMEs interviewed have their strategic focus on premium quality and innovation. Their focus on foreign markets exposed them to global competition which required specialisation of their product and service offerings. All interviewees of *niche-excellence* SMEs mentioned that they were following a strategic roadmap. It typically covered 10 years and outlined development steps in terms of technology and product innovation. Finally, Singaporean *niche-excellence* players achieved superior financial and market performance despite challenging developments with regards to costs and domestic demand.

However, only 22 percent of SMEs interviewed reviewed their strategic goals systematically. Those that conducted such reviews, did so primarily on an annual basis. Consequently, the majority of managing directors did not systematically gather feedback on whether strategic goals were met. As a consequence, their company might have developed in a less planned manner.

2. Singaporean manufacturing SMEs: Strategic alignment of employees

Besides the lack of strategic planning and positioning, the majority of SMEs reported low levels of employee strategic alignment. More precisely, only 46 percent agreed that their employees were, on average, aware of the strategic direction of the company. Eighteen percent even considered their employees to be unable to derive operational goals from strategic goals. As the managing director of a small *concentration-pressed* SME pointed out:

> Most of the workers are just happy to have a job and, frankly speaking, do the job to earn money. Our lower-paid workers change on average every two years. We do not really focus on them, e.g., in terms of training, etc.

This statement also indicates the low focus on the long-term development of employee skills. In addition, it shows that employees in Singaporean SMEs seem to be highly motivated by monetary incentives. As a result, 71 percent (six percent) of SMEs interviewed had a monetary incentive scheme that tied bonuses to individual (company) performance. The average bonus for shopfloor employees was five to 18 percent of the annual salary.[6] The remaining 24 percent of companies used non-monetary incentives such as overseas training or invitations for dinner with the leadership team.[7]

To increase awareness and understanding of strategy, managing directors could focus more on managerial processes and systems, e.g., clearly defining a firm strategy, communicating strategy and targets as well as using measurement systems in an interactive way. For example, in a Singapore-based medium-sized manufacturer, the foremen, rather than the department managers, presented the department's performance in the monthly target meeting using key measures concerning financials, quality, and productivity. Through this, the managing director ensured full understanding of and commitment to the strategic goals. At the same time, she had the chance to train the foremen.

3. *Singaporean manufacturing SMEs: Productivity*

In recent years, Singaporean SMEs have focused on productivity to improve their cost structure. Rising input factor costs are particularly challenging for *concentration-pressed* SMEs. It seems that this type of SME finds it more difficult to embrace productivity and that problems are commonly solved by adding staff. Overall, in Singapore, unit business costs in the manufacturing industry have increased in total by 7.4 percent from 2005 to 2012. Strong increases in service costs (+17.1 percent) such as charges for warehousing services, transportation and rental and to a lower extent increases in governmental rates and fees (+10.0 percent)[8] were dampened by a reduction of unit labour costs (−7.4 percent).

Higher labour productivity led, in the same period, to a 27.7 percent increase in value added per hour worked in this industry. This efficiency increase reflects the industry's and government's efforts to improve productivity, e.g., through the Productivity and Innovation Credit

---

[6]Excludes 13th month salary and salary increases for the consecutive year.

[7]In comparison, only 26 percent (37 percent) of the interviewed Swiss SMEs tied bonus to individual (company) performance with an average bonus range for shopfloor employees of 2–8 percent of the annual salary. In 37 percent of SMEs, employees were rewarded by non-monetary means.

[8]The government has decreased the fee burden during the crisis to then increased towards pre-2007 levels.

Scheme (PIC). However, evidence for most Singaporean industries exists that productivity increases in the past were mainly driven by technology improvements rather than by workforce efficiency. In the words of a managing director of a medium-sized manufacturer of precision parts:

> *[…] we need to work on productivity. The government PIC has helped us to buffer some investments but ultimately it's about people. People productivity, multitasking is essential. Not all companies can automate. I think that many SMEs need to get a lot of help to get lean. It needs to start with the top leader, who needs to believe in this. Then, people need to have a mindset for continuous improvement and the leadership team needs to keep on preaching and selling a lean mindset.*

In line with this view, the value added per worker remained almost flat between 2007 and 2012 (+4.0 percent or CAGR 0.8 percent) as shown in Figure 2.

As a consequence, further potential for improvement exists. In the words of an owner-manager of a medium-sized SME:

> *When I look to the technology leaders, I can still see so much space to improve. This makes me optimistic that we can still improve.*

Figure 2: Remuneration to value added per worker grew 1.6 percent p.a. in the manufacturing industry, 2007 to 2012p

	2007	08	09	10	11	2012p	% CAGR 2007-2012
Remuneration per worker, SGD '000	41.1	40.8	40.6	43.4	44.6	46.3	2.4
Value added per worker, SGD '000	138.6	108.6	116.2	139.7	137.8	144.1	0.8
Remuneration to value added, Percent	29.6	37.5	34.9	31.1	32.4	32.1	1.6

Source: Own illustration. Data from Singapore Ministry of Trade and Industry (2012), Singapore Ministry of Manpower (2012).

Looking forward, SMEs see major cost challenges in factors beyond their control, i.e., the cost of materials, salary hikes and rent increases. This is particularly challenging because SMEs pale in levels of value added per worker compared to large enterprises. In this light, some *concentration-pressed* and *opportunity-trailing* SMEs have considered relocating to lower cost countries such as Malaysia or China. However, SME managing directors need to be aware of the total cost of production which might be higher than initially estimated. Consider the experience of a Singapore-based medium-sized manufacturer of precision injection molds:

> *I think that relocation is wrong. Focus should be on improving productivity here [in Singapore] and grow. Often firms relocate because they see labour cost advantages. However, they do not properly calculate total costs. Besides, there is often political instability. I am convinced that companies can sustain here. Even in high-cost countries such as Germany or Switzerland companies do perfectly. Every country has a certain kind of formula for success.*

SMEs that plan to serve respective foreign markets need to bear in mind that often, not only input factor costs, but also product prices in the foreign markets, are lower. Therefore, potential cost savings do not necessarily translate into higher margins.

In sum, SMEs based in Singapore operate in a challenging market environment with rapidly increasing costs for input factors. Notably, SMEs face different challenges depending on their strategic positioning in the market. According to SME leaders, there is potential to improve the sustainability of their operations in Singapore when considering the development of value added per worker over the last few years. Strategic recommendations for *niche-excellence* players focus mainly on enhancing their innovativeness and product specialisation. *Concentration-pressed* and *opportunity-trailing* SMEs are recommended to focus their strategic endeavours on three main areas: (1) strategic positioning and planning, (2) strategic alignment of employees, and (3) productivity. In sum, *concentration-pressed* and *opportunity-trailing* SMEs can learn both from Swiss and Singaporean *niche-excellence* players and improve their business models by gradually climbing the value chain towards high-end products. This allows them to serve markets globally and to command higher prices and therefore buffer against an increasing cost baseline.

Swiss manufacturing SMEs

In Switzerland, SMEs struggle with the rise of the Swiss franc which has appreciated by more than 30 percent compared to the Euro between 2007 and 2014. Only a few of the SMEs interviewed hedged against currency fluctuations, for example by sourcing primarily from foreign countries such as Germany. As a result, Swiss exports became increasingly expensive which in turn reduced the competitiveness of Swiss products abroad. Given the average export ratio of 48 percent for all manufacturing SMEs, Swiss SMEs in general experienced challenges on the pricing and ultimately on the demand side. At the same time, labour costs remained high, which put pressure on the cost structure. For example, the hourly compensation costs in Switzerland were US$58 in 2012. This was more than 2.3 times higher than the costs in Singapore (US$25). In January 2015, the Swiss franc soared by another 20 percent as a result of the Swiss National Bank's decision to end its policy of fixed exchange rates with the Euro. At the time of writing, it is unclear how well Swiss SMEs will cope with adjusting to this abrupt landslide in price competitiveness.

Despite these structural disadvantages, Swiss manufacturing SMEs have performed well. One reason for this is that most of the Swiss SMEs interviewed had a clear strategic positioning in their niches. Eighty-two percent of the managing directors of Swiss SMEs interviewed mentioned that they produced premium products and services. In the words of an owner-manager of a Swiss medium-sized manufacturer of controlling instruments:

> The infrastructure in Switzerland allows for producing the best products in the market. For this, you also need a clear strategic direction and the aspiration to produce 'premium 200 percent'.

As *niche-excellence* players they have specialised in their niches, aimed for technological leadership, and focused on innovation and premium quality. Nickel-based combustion systems for the aircraft industry that are superior to cobalt-based ones but more difficult to manufacture are an example of products produced by this type of SMEs.

A further 15 percent of interviewees somewhat agreed with this view. Often these market players have a dual strategy, focusing on high-quality orders but also accepting lower-quality orders to achieve high utilisation of their machines (*opportunity-trailing*). For example, precision engineering SMEs produce precision turned parts with highest surface quality requirements for medical device manufacturers, whilst at the same time supplying lower quality parts for basic electronics companies. Others are *concentration-pressed*, i.e., they serve primarily the domestic market, with old assets and little innovation. A product example for these players is standard springs. Three percent of SMEs interviewed had no clear strategic focus on quality. To address cost challenges, their strategic focus lay almost exclusively on productivity.

On the financial result side, 59 percent of Swiss SMEs expressed that they clearly obtained a price premium for their products. Another 23 percent somewhat agreed with this view and only nine percent of SMEs denied achieving a price premium. Figure 3 illustrates the strategic positioning of the three archetypes of SMEs that focus on product rather than cost differentiation and indicates the number of each type of player interviewed.

To build capabilities that facilitate the production of premium products, most SMEs aimed to achieve technological leadership and anchored this aspiration in their strategic goals. This view was emphasised several times across interviews. Consider the strategic orientation of the owner-manager of a small company that manufactures precision parts:

> "*...we focus every day on good work and make use of the latest technologies. Our clear focus on our core competencies helps us to be special and unique. Acquisition of new customers is a good indicator for how things are going. When we fall behind in technology, potential new customers won't buy our products. As a result, we would have to reduce our price and end up in a race to the bottom: competing on price and ultimately [gaining] no profit to reinvest in the latest technology.*"

Figure 3: Most Swiss manufacturing SMEs are clearly positioned as *niche-excellence* players

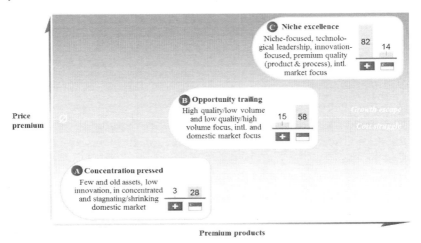

Note: This figure does not show companies that focus on a cost-leadership strategy. Please also note the relatively small sample size, especially in Singapore.

Source: Own illustration.

The ability of Swiss SMEs to invent and produce premium products has evolved over many years. Most of the managing directors interviewed emphasised that their strategic focus was predominantly on enhancing existing or developing new product niches through technological leadership and innovation. As with technological leadership, high innovativeness often does not happen by chance but is a result of strategic planning and internal mechanisms. For example, a Swiss medium-sized manufacturer of safety equipment defined the strategic goal that eight percent of the annual revenue needed to spring from products that had been implemented in the last three years. As a result, Swiss SMEs often developed their markets by producing innovative products. For example, a medium-sized manufacturer was the first to introduce electronic controls and hydraulic gears for precision machinery in its market.

However, some potential for improvement exists. Only 27 percent of the SMEs interviewed had a dedicated strategy for their major business units or departments. This is particularly important for medium-sized enterprises because they tend to have a broader product portfolio and are often serving different geographic markets. In only 32 percent of SMEs was the achievement of strategic goals evaluated systematically, i.e., strategic goals and achievements reviewed in detail by the managing director and the governing board/owner(s). This reflects the risk that market and product developments may happen rather randomly. Most of those 32 percent of SMEs with a systematic review assessed the status of achievement of strategic goals and initiatives every three to six months.

In sum, Swiss SMEs have often positioned themselves as *niche-excellence* players. Their primary focus going forward should be on enhancing their technological leadership and innovativeness. Dedicated sub-strategies for major departments, innovation accounting, and a systematic review of achievement of strategic goals contribute to this focus as sub-strategies increase the awareness of the strategic positioning of each product (line) and on detailed market trends. In addition, they should consider increasing employees' awareness and understanding of firm strategy.

Supportive Regulatory Policies for SMEs

Policymakers set the boundaries for SMEs to react to current and upcoming business challenges. For the subsequent discussion, the reader needs to bear in mind that Singapore and Switzerland follow different policy-making systems, as discussed in the introduction to this book. Where Switzerland is characterised by a decentralised system with strong governance by the regional cantons, Singapore follows a more centralised mode of decision-making. That said, the intent of this chapter is not to provide an in-depth analysis on the effects of the political systems but rather to provide recommendations to create a regulatory environment which allows SMEs to thrive. This seems legitimate, because *"political systems don't impact growth for better or worse; political leaders do"*.[9]

Switzerland has had a historical focus on SMEs. In Singapore, the government has steadily increased the number of policies focused on SMEs since the first government schemes in 1976. That said, the

---

[9] Sharma, R. *Breakout Nations — In Pursuit of the Next Economic Miracles.* W.W. Norton & Company, 2012, p. 199.

Singapore government intensified its policies towards SMEs only in the last decade. Current policies towards SMEs in Singapore focus a lot on increasing productivity to respond better to rising production factor costs and increasing overall efficiency. More recently, the focus of policy initiatives has shifted to developing long-term employee contributions. Looking ahead, innovation and technological leadership need to be promoted, and finally subsidies should be reduced to increase economic competition. This is important because it will allow for building more SMEs that successfully compete with regional and global competitors despite disadvantageous input factor costs. Figure 4 summarises a potential long-term roadmap for Singaporean policymakers towards a competitive manufacturing SME industry.

In the following, the focus lies on employee contribution (phase 2). Looking at Switzerland, three concrete initiatives seem appropriate to increase the contribution of employees in the long run: (1) long-term skills

Figure 4:   Suggested long-term policy roadmap

3 Exposure to intl. R&D
- Establish strategic partnerships with international R&D centers such as foreign engineering associations
- Promote cooperation between local and foreign companies with complementary products in promising industries such as medical devices
- Selectively attract foreign R&D expertise and technology leaders
+ Leverage internet-enabled technologies for SME marketing

4 Promote economic competition
- No incentives for persistently under-performing enterprises[1]
- Award incentives conditional upon retrospective proof of improvements
- Governmental tendering only for SMEs that proof their productivity/ innovation improvements

■ Current govern-mental focus in SIN

Goal

Leverage expertise of "type C" SMEs

2 Develop employee contribution
- Focus on people productivity
  – Long-term skill development, e.g., apprenticeship system to build (technical) talent
  – Promote brands of SME heroes to attract talent
  – Create mechanisms which allow companies to retain talent during down-turns, e.g., short-term work
  – Solve successor problem for 70s/ 80s generation, e.g., subsidized bank loan

Start

Policy roadmap

1 Promote productivity
- Current PIC scheme focus primarily on
  – Solutions: Upgrade of assets/automation
  – Consulting: Innovation, productivity, human resources, financial management

1 e.g., based on rating scheme including dimensions such as realized productivity gains (e.g., value-added per employee over last 5 years), innovativeness (e.g., revenues by products introduced in last 3 years), financial performance, strategic positioning (e.g. quality and potential of 5-10 year strategic roadmap)

Source: Own illustration.

development, (2) attracting and retaining talent, and (3) facilitating successor management.

First, when labour is expensive, SMEs need to increase the added value of each employee not only through automation but rather by viewing employees as *the* key resource for long-term success. This requires long-term skills development to train experts and increase loyalty. Retaining experts is particularly important for SMEs because know-how is often "*in the heads*" of employees rather than in processes. In Switzerland, apprenticeship systems are an important element of skills development, where employees, such as mechatronic experts, are trained for mostly four years. Many students participate in vocational schools rather than in pure academic programs. Instead of plugging away in classroom studies full-time, these students spend, for example, four days a week at a company and one day at a vocational school as part of the apprenticeship. As a positive side effect, employees tend to be proud of their industry and training. As a result, they are less likely to switch to other industries, a common pattern in Singapore. Today, an apprenticeship system is at the top of the minds of Singaporean policymakers. For example, the new university, Singapore Institute of Technology (SIT), offers applied degree programs which integrates work and study. Necessary conditions to successfully establishing apprenticeship programs include building strong links between companies and vocational schools, and encouraging employers and the community to accord equal merit to both academic and vocational career paths.

Next, to attract talents to the SME sector, the government should aim to promote the brands of SMEs. In Germany, for example, most people can easily name a handful of SMEs which have grown into global heroes, such as Bosch, Merck, and Beiersdorf. This strong branding plays a supporting role in attracting talent. Singapore's annual "*Enterprise 50*" award is a good starting point to create awareness of local heroes among Singaporeans, but requires more public promotion.

Third, to retain talents during economic downturns, SME managers need to be granted the flexibility to lower the cost base without losing talent and know-how. Short-term work has proven to be an effective mechanism to respond to lower demand in Switzerland after the collapse of Lehman Brothers in 2008. Besides flexible work-time accounts, which allowed the building up of overtime in the relatively good economic years from 2006 to 2008 and the reducing of overtime after 2008, short-term work compensation has proven to be a highly effective instrument. Short-term work is defined as the reduction in work-time of a company's employees by at least 10 percent as a result in an economic downturn. For up to six months, and in special cases for up to 24 months, government labour insurance pays the employees 80 percent of their loss of salary. This instrument is particularly important for SMEs because it allows them to adjust their workforce (and costs) to lower demand without laying off employees. As a result, SMEs retain expertise and know-how and avoid subsequent expensive recruiting activities. This was particularly important during the recent financial crisis as shown in Figure 5. This policy instrument has not only avoided massive lay-offs but also put Swiss SMEs in the front seat when the economy gained traction again.

Lastly, policymakers could think about establishing a system which supports the grooming of potential SME successors. Many Singaporean SMEs are still run by entrepreneurs of the manufacturing generation in the late 1970s and 1980s. Recent challenges in attracting young employees to the manufacturing sector in Singapore have led to critical challenges in finding *and* motivating talents to become successors, even within an entrepreneur's family, and despite well-running business models. In Germany, for example, the KfW Bank, a national bank, grants subsidised, low-interest

Figure 5:   Employees affected by short-term work in Switzerland, in counts

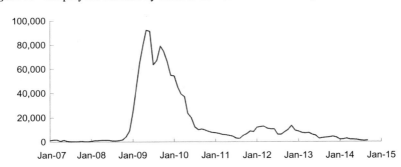

Source: Own illustration. Adapted from Governmental Office for Economy SECO Switzerland (2015).

rate loans to intermediary banks which are then passed on to SME successors. The KfW bank also takes over the default risk for the borrower, which increases the motivation of intermediary banks to grant loans.

In phase 3 of the road map, the focus could shift towards promoting research and development (R&D) to drive innovation. Rather than simply incentivising R&D with subsidies, the government could motivate SMEs to seek strategic partnerships with complementary companies or associations in Singapore or abroad. For example, a Swiss SME has entered into a strategic partnership with a Swedish engineering association to mutually share expertise and access to R&D equipment to develop spray valves. Singapore's initiatives to build competence centres, such as for aviation, are a step in this direction.

In the long term, policymakers could think about promoting economic competition during phase 4. Rather than nurturing loss-making companies, subsidies for persistently under-performing enterprises could be eliminated. Too often, Singaporean SME managers purely associate productivity increases with the PIC rather than recognising that they are in the driving seat to increase productivity. This could be facilitated by a potential rating scheme that focuses on the companies' evolution along key performance indicators such as realised productivity gains (e.g., value add per employee over last five years), innovativeness (e.g., revenues by products introduced in last three years), financial performance, and strategic position (e.g., quality and potential of five to ten year strategic roadmaps). As a result, pressure on SMEs to improve on key performance dimensions would increase, resulting in higher competitiveness and potentially superior strategic positioning in the medium term. Needless to say, such required reforms are not likely to be very popular but may well be a necessary evil to keep Singaporean SMEs going.

Taking a step back and considering the industry mix, policymakers should — despite lower revenue per square meter figures — continue to promote manufacturing and SMEs. As part of an economy's transformation, manufacturing tends to reach its natural limit and the economy starts to shift its focus to services when manufacturing accounts for 25 to 30 percent of GDP. This transformation typically begins when per capita income is as low as US$10,000. Both Singapore and Switzerland have long passed this turning point. Even though this transformation seems to be inherent to the normal evolutionary path, a continued governmental focus on high-end manufacturing seems beneficial to the overall economy. Examples of countries with strong manufacturing powerhouses that have outperformed their peers are South Korea, Germany, and by far, Switzerland.

In addition, these countries have shown less liability to global downturns or external shocks given their strong reliance on SMEs. Promoting SMEs is particularly important to prepare an economy for downturns. A recent McKinsey study showed that family firms — of which most are SMEs — not only beat global stock market returns by an average of three percent a year between 1997 to 2009 but also came out of the 2008 crisis in much better shape than non-family rivals, with less debt, more cash, and higher R&D investments throughout the downturn.

References

Baeuml, M. The Impact of Strategic Performance Management on SME performance. Dissertation, St. Gallen, 2015.

Bast, A. In Hard Times, Family Firms Do Better. Newsweek, December 29, 2011. Retrieved from http://www.newsweek.com/family-owned-businesses-get through-hard-times-69069

Berry, M. Strategic planning in small high tech companies. Long Range Planning 31, no. 3 (1998), pp. 455–466

Chew, R., Chew, S. B. A study of SMEs in Singapore. Journal of Enterprising Communities 2, no. 4 (2008), pp. 332–347.

Christian, C., Dias, A.K., Elstrodt, H.-P. The Five Attributes of Enduring Family Business. McKinsey Quarterly, January 2010.

Chu, W. Family ownership and firm performance: Influence of family management, family control, and firm size. Asia Pacific Journal of Management 28, no. 4 (2011), pp. 833–851.

DP Information Group. Singapore 1000 family of rankings media conference 2012. Conference paper, February 9, 2012. Singapore: DP Information Group. Retrieved April 16, 2013, from http://www.dpgroup.com.sg/ Attachments/ 95_S1000%202012%20Media%20Slides%20FNL.pdf.

DP Information Group. SMEs embrace productivity to counter rising costs. Singapore: DP Information Group, press release, 2012. Retrieved April 29, 2014, from http://www.dpgroup.com.sg/Attachments/108_SMEDS%20 2012%20Media%20Release%20FNL.pdf

EDB Singapore. Report on the Census of Manufacturing Activities 2011, 2010, 2009, 2008, 2007, 2006.

Kwang, H. F., Ibrahim, Z., Chua, M. H., Lim, L., Low, I., Lin, R., Chan, R. Lee Kuan Yew — Hard Truths to Keep Singapore Going, Straits Times Press, 2011.

International Enterprise Singapore. Summary of small and mighty enterprises. IE Singapore Work Plan Seminar Report 2010. Singapore: IE Singapore.

Lee, B. L. Productivity, technical and efficiency change in Singapore's services sector, 2005 to 2008. Applied Economics 45, no. 15 (2013), pp. 2023–2029.

Ries, E. The Lean startup — How constant innovation creates radically successful businesses. London: Penguin Books, 2011.

Schwab, K. World Economic Forum: Global Competitiveness Report 2013–2014. Geneva: World Economic Forum, 2014. Retrieved April 23, 2014, from http://www.weforum.org/reports/global-competitiveness-report-2013–2014.

Schweizer Bundesamt für Statistik (BFS) Analysen zur Betriebszählung 2005: KMU–Landschaft im Wandel. Neuchâtel: Bundesamt für Statistik printing office, 2008. Retrieved May 01, 2014, from www.bfs.admin.ch/bfs/portal/de/ index/news/ publikationen.Document.105225.pdf.

Schweizer Bundesamt für Statistik (BFS). Statistik Schweiz — Arbeitsproduktivität: Methodologie und Analyse der wichtigsten Resultate von 1991 bis 2006. Neuchâtel: Bundesamt für Statistik printing office, 2008. Retrieved April 29, 2014, from www.bfs.admin.ch/bfs/portal/de/index/themen/04/22/ publ. Document.113305.pdf.

Schweizer Bundesamt für Statistik (BFS). Unternehmen — Indikatoren: Größe. Marktwirtschaftliche Unternehmen und Beschäftigte nach Größenklassen, 2008. Neuchâtel: Bundesamt für Statistik, 2010. Retrieved June 25, 2014 from www.bfs.admin.ch/bfs/portal/de/index/themen/06/02/blank/key/01/ groesse.html.

Schweizer Bundesamt für Statistik (BFS). Statistik Schweiz — Taschenstatistik der Schweiz: Statistische Grundlagen und Übersichten 021–1300. Neuchâtel: Bundesamt für Statistik printing office, 2010. Retrieved April 29, 2014, from www.bfs.admin.ch/bfs/portal/de/index/news/publikationen.Document. 176863.pdf.

Schweizer Bundesamt für Statistik (BFS). Produktionskonto — Daten, Indikatoren: Produktionskonto nach Branchen (aggregiert nach Abschnitten). Neuchâtel: Bundesamt für Statistik printing office, 2014. Retrieved May 1, 2014, from http://www.bfs.admin.ch/bfs/portal/de/index/themen/04/02/02/ key/ nach_branchen.html.

Schweizer Bundesamt für Statistik (BFS). Regionale Disparitäten in der Schweiz–Indikatorensystem. Wirtschaftsstruktur und wirtschaftliche Leistungsfähigkeit — Kleine und mittlere Unternehmen 2011. Neuchâtel: Bundesamt für Statistik printing office, 2014. Retrieved May 01, 2014, from http://www.bfs.admin.ch/bfs/portal/de/index/regionen/03/key/00/ind27.indicator.270107.2701.html.

Schweizer Eidgenössisches Department für Wirtschaft, Bildung (WBF). Die Politik des Bundes zugunsten der kleinen und mittleren Unternehmen (KMU). Bericht des Bundesrates in Schweizer Beantwortung des Postulats Walker (02.3702) und Evaluationsbericht zum Bundesgesetz über Risikokapitalgesellschaften vom 8. Juni 2007. KMU Portal. Bern: WBF, 2007. Retrieved April 29, 2014, from www.kmu.admin.ch/aktuell/00493/00494/00498/index.html?download=NHzLpZeg7t,lnp6I0NTU042l2Z6ln1acy4Zn4Z2qZpnO2Yuq2Z6gpJCDdX96fGym162epYbg2c_JjKbNoKSn6A--&lang=de.

Schweizer Eidgenössisches Department für Wirtschaft, Bildung (WBF), & Staatssekretariat für Wirtschaft SECO. Die Schweiz–Unternehmen sstandort mit Zukunft. Bern: WBF, 2012. Retrieved April 29, 2014 from www.kmu.admin.ch/kmu-gruenden/03476/03575/03578/index.html?download=NHzLpZeg7t,lnp6I0NTU042l2Z6ln1acy4Zn4Z2qZpnO2Yuq2Z6gpJCDfHx7fmym162epYbg2c_JjKbNoKSn6A--&lang=de.

Schweizer Eidgenössisches Department für Wirtschaft SECO. Kurzarbeitsentschädigung. Bern, 2015. Retrieved January 09, 2015 from http://www.seco.admin.ch/themen/00385/04770/04772/index.html?lang=de.

Sharma, R. Breakout Nations — In Pursuit of the Next Economic Miracles. W.W. Norton & Company, 2012.

Singapore Ministry of Manpower. Singapore Yearbook of Manpower Statistics 2012. Singapore: Manpower Research and Statistics Department, 2012. Retrieved January 15, 2014, from http://stats.mom.gov.sg/Pages/Singapore-Yearbook-of-Manpower-Statistics-2013.aspx.

Singapore Ministry of Trade & Industry. Yearbook of statistics Singapore 2011, 2012. Singapore: Department of Statistics, Ministry of Trade & Industry, 2012, 2013.

Singapore Ministry of Trade & Industry. Economic Survey of Singapore 2010, 2012. Singapore: Ministry of Trade & Industry, 2010, 2012.

Song, M., Im, S., Bij, H. V. D., & Song, L. Z. Does Strategic Planning Enhance or Impede Innovation and Firm Performance?. Journal of Product Innovation Management 28, no. 4 (2011) 503–520.

SPRING Singapore. Factsheet on new SME definition. Singapore: Singapore Ministry of Trade, 2011. Retrieved April 29, 2014 from http://www.spring. gov.sg/NewsEvents/PR/Documents/Fact_Sheet_on_New_SME_Definition. pdf?skw=Factsheet%20on%20new%20SME%20definition.

U.S. Department of Labour. Charting International Labour Comparisons — 2012 edition. Bureau of Labour Statistics, 2013. Retrieved May 13, 2014 from http://www.bls.gov/fls/#compensation.

Chapter 7

Recent Trends in First-Class World Competitiveness: Singapore and Switzerland in Global Entrepreneurship Rankings

Philippe Régnier[1] and Pascal Wild

Introduction

At first glance, it may sound a little strange to compare the entrepreneurship profiles of Singapore and Switzerland. For instance, both the economic geography and the industrial history of the two countries have little in common, and present rather different trajectories. Often, entrepreneurship surveys tend to compare two Asian city-states such as Hong Kong and Singapore, or two small European land-locked and mountainous economies such as Austria and Switzerland.

However, since the last decade and again in the year 2014, the prestigious *Global Competitiveness Report* (GCR, annual) has given much visibility to both Switzerland and Singapore by ranking them in first and second place ahead of the USA, Finland, Germany and Japan (Table 1)!

---

[1] Philippe Régnier has specialized in Southeast Asia's socio-economic development studies, and in particular on the economy of Singapore as a global and regional city-state, since the 1980s. His first book on Singapore was published in Geneva and Paris with the French University Press in 1987.

Table 1:   The Global Competitiveness Index 2014–2015

The Global Competitiveness Index 2014–2015:
Global Top 10

Country	Global Rank*
Switzerland	1
Singapore	2
United States	3
Finland	4
Germany	5
Japan	6
Hong Kong SAR	7
Netherlands	8
United Kingdom	9
Sweden	10

Source: (Schwab & Sala-i-Martin, 2014).
*2014–2015 rank out of 144 economies.

Therefore, in parallel to the different parameters used to build up this Global Competitiveness Index that classify Switzerland and Singapore at the top, this chapter aims to explore how their leading competitiveness classifications may be also explained by their respective entrepreneurial profiles, a subject not covered explicitly by the GCR.

The entrepreneurial capacity of a country refers to the notion of entrepreneurship, which was introduced as a new Anglo-Saxon concept derived from the neo-liberal globalisation discourse introduced in the early 1990s. Today, the promotion of entrepreneurship and of an eco-system conducive to entrepreneurial initiatives and start-ups ranks high on the priority agenda of most governments worldwide. Furthermore, entrepreneurship studies have developed as major training programs for both students and professionals in all leading business and management schools.

The definition of entrepreneurship is the individual or collective willingness and capacity to start and manage a business venture, and to create value for profit through an appropriate combination of factors of production (financial, human and technical capital). The entrepreneurial profile of a nation is characterised by its innovative and risk-taking spirit to succeed economically in an ever-changing and increasingly competitive global market place.

In this context, various initiatives have emerged during the last 20 years to measure and evaluate over time national economies, specific subnational locations, and public/private institutions in terms of their entrepreneurship capacities and/or enabling abilities.

Initiated in 1999 by the London Business School and Babson College, the *Global Entrepreneurship Monitor* has established itself as the world's largest survey of national entrepreneurship dynamics. The GEM project aims to conduct an annual assessment of entrepreneurial activity, aspirations and attitudes of individuals across a wide range of over one hundred countries as of today. With an annual budget of US$9 million (in 2014), it is led by national research teams as a global network of over 500 experts in entrepreneurship research. The central goal is to explore the role of entrepreneurship in national economic growth, and to collect and harmonise national data to facilitate cross-national comparisons. Three more specific objectives are:

- To measure differences in the level of entrepreneurial activity among countries,
- To uncover factors leading to appropriate levels of entrepreneurship,
- To suggest policies that may enhance the national level of entrepreneurship facilitation and implementation.

The GEM Global has established a compulsory rule that all national GEM surveys must use the same research methodology. It is divided into two types of surveys. A first one, called the APS (*Adult Population Survey*) is of a quantitative nature and conducts a minimum of 2,000 entrepreneurship-related interviews among local residents, which are analysed on a random basis. A second survey is of a qualitative nature (*National Expert Survey*) and consists of a number of in-depth interviews (a minimum of 36 interviews) with public and private sector experts in local and national entrepreneurship from various viewpoints.

The following pages present a selection of comparative research inputs derived from the *GEM Global Report 2014,* the *GEM Singapore 2014,* and *the GEM Switzerland 2014*. They are envisaged as entrepreneurship achievements that provide some contributions to the analysis and interpretation of Singapore's and Switzerland's global competitiveness successes. Since 2011, the GEM Singapore team has been based at the Nanyang Technological University (NTU). The GEM Switzerland team has been based at the Swiss School of Management in Fribourg. The second author of this chapter is one of the main researchers involved in the GEM Switzerland annual survey.

Singapore and Switzerland: Some Key Findings

The GEM methodology categorises the surveyed economies into factor-driven, efficiency-driven and innovation-driven economies (Table 2). Singapore and Switzerland are classified under a group of 29 countries belonging to the innovation-driven economies. In these economies, entrepreneurial framework conditions are important levers of economic development. They are more important than basic requirements such as infrastructure, macroeconomic stability or primary education (as in factor-driven economies), or efficiency enhancers like higher education systems, goods and labour markets and technological readiness (as in efficiency-driven economies). The outcome of good framework conditions

Table 2: The 29 Innovation-Driven Economies (Singer, Amoros, and Mosa, 2015)

Australia	Ireland	Slovakia
Austria	Italy	Slovenia
Belgium	Japan	Spain
Canada	Luxembourg	Sweden
Denmark	Netherlands	**Switzerland**
Estonia	Norway	Taiwan
Finland	Portugal	Trinidad & Tobago
France	Puerto Rico	United Kingdom
Germany	Qatar	United States
Greece	**Singapore**	

in innovation-driven economies should be national economic growth through, for example, job creation and technical innovation.

The total early-stage entrepreneurship activity indicator (TEA) measured by the GEM indicates the proportion of all residents in both countries having entrepreneurial activities or intentions. With 10.96 percent, Singapore ranks sixth in 2014, behind countries such as the United States, Australia and Canada, whereas Switzerland is 17th with 7.1 percent (Table 3).

On average (from 2011 to 2013), Singapore ranks second behind the United States in the percentage of early-stage entrepreneurs (9.6 percent) compared to Switzerland, which is ranked 11th (6.9 percent). Furthermore,

Table 3:   TEA Rate 2014 by Country

Rank	Country	TEA Rate 2014 (%)
1	Qatar	16.38
2	Trinidad & Tobago	14.62
3	United States	13.81
4	Australia	13.14
5	Canada	13.04
6	**Singapore**	10.96
7	Slovakia	10.90
8	United Kingdom	10.66
9	Puerto Rico	10.04
10	Portugal	9.97
11	Netherlands	9.46
12	Estonia	9.43
13	Austria	8.71
14	Taiwan	8.49
15	Greece	7.85
16	Luxembourg	7.14
17	**Switzerland**	7.12
18	Sweden	6.71

(Continued)

Table 3: (*Continued*)

Rank	Country	TEA Rate 2014 (%)
19	Ireland	6.53
20	Slovenia	6.33
21	Norway	5.65
22	Finland	5.63
23	Spain	5.47
24	Denmark	5.47
25	Belgium	5.40
26	France	5.34
27	Germany	5.27
28	Italy	4.42
29	Japan	3.83

Source: (Singer, Amoros, & Mosa, 2015).

Singapore ranks 11th in terms of intentions to start a business in the next three years, whereas Switzerland ranks 15th. This moderate intention to start a business may be attributed to the fact that employee positions are still perceived to be relatively attractive. In both countries, many multinational companies offer good career opportunities for their well-qualified workforce.

By observing the age distribution of the early-stage entrepreneurs, almost three-quarters of Swiss citizens tend to start their business between the ages of 35 and 64, whereas Singapore shows a relatively higher entrepreneurial activity among the 18-to-35 year-old age group (Figure 1). Switzerland ranks among the highest for entrepreneurship dynamics among the elderly age groups as well as for entrepreneurs' satisfaction and well-being (ahead of Norway, the Netherlands and Singapore). In Switzerland, women's entrepreneurship activities are more or less at parity with men, whereas in Singapore, male entrepreneurs are still in the majority.

Compared to its relative lower TEA (Figure 2), Switzerland, however, shows a higher indicator for established business ownership, and especially when the innovative orientation of new start-ups is measured.

Figure 1: The TEA 2014 distribution by age in Singapore and Switzerland

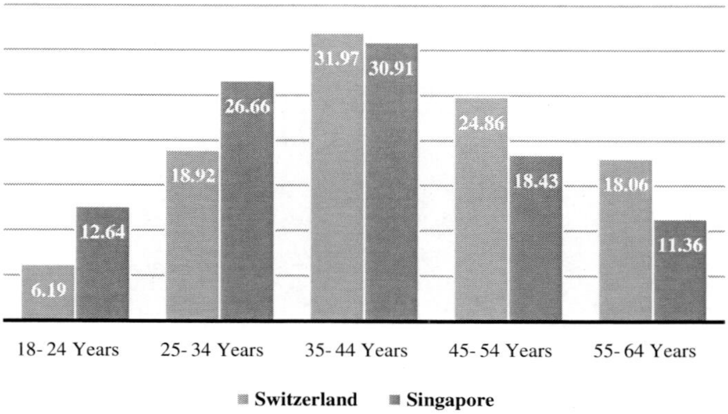

■ **Switzerland** ■ **Singapore**

Source: Analysis by the author with GEM 2014 data.

Figure 2: Average TEA rates from 2011–2013

Averge TEA rates (%) from 2011-2013

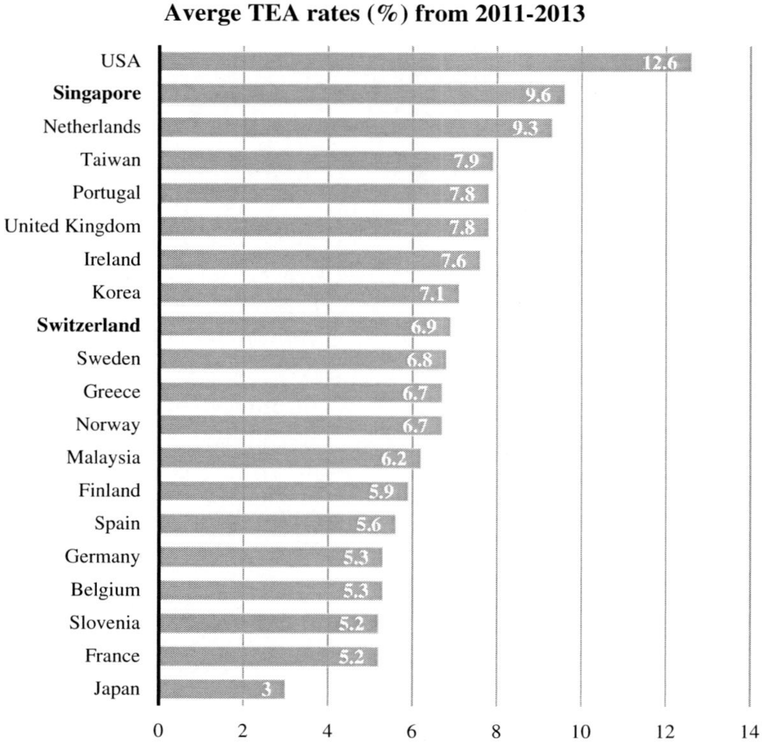

Source: (Chernyshenko, Calvin, and Ong, 2014).

Table 4:   Intentions to Start a Business

	Intent to Start a Business in the Next 3 Years				
Rank	**Country**	**Rate (%)**	**Rank**	**Country**	**Rate (%)**
1	Qatar	55.48	16	Netherlands	10.81
2	Trinidad & Tobago	33.68	17	Austria	10.69
3	Taiwan	28.09	18	Estonia	10.55
4	Puerto Rico	19.39	19	Greece	10.43
5	Slovakia	19.00	20	Sweden	10.07
6	Portugal	18.44	21	Finland	9.08
7	Canada	16.76	22	United Kingdom	8.92
8	Luxembourg	16.44	23	**Switzerland**	8.82
9	United States	16.23	24	Denmark	8.35
10	France	16.00	25	Ireland	8.30
11	**Singapore**	15.01	26	Germany	8.28
12	Italy	13.19	27	Spain	8.03
13	Belgium	12.36	28	Norway	6.21
14	Slovenia	12.31	29	Japan	5.29
15	Australia	12.05			

Source: Analysis by the author with GEM 2014 data.

On the one hand, the fear of business failure is higher in Singapore than in Switzerland (Figure 4). On the other hand, the city-state stands very low in terms of perceived skills and opportunities to start a business (Table 8), which may partly explain such fears.

Interestingly, the two countries show differences in the characteristics of early-stage businesses. Singapore clearly outperforms Switzerland in the field of new technology utilisation (Table 5) while both countries are somewhat equal in terms of innovation and new product or service differentiation from all existing businesses and potential customers (Figure 3).

National Eco-systems Conducive for Entrepreneurship

For the last fifteen years, Switzerland has continued to remain in the lead. The Swiss eco-system is perceived to be highly favourable, in particular,

Table 5:   Early-Stage Entrepreneurs and Technology Use in 2014

Latest Technology: Only Available Last Year			New Technology: Available in the Last 1–5 Years			No New Technology		
Rank	Country	Rate (%)	Rank	Country	Rate (%)	Rank	Country	Rate (%)
1	Qatar	32.54	1	**Singapore**	32.87	1	Norway	86.73
2	Slovakia	24.31	2	Qatar	32.23	2	Trinidad and Tobago	85.55
3	France	22.41	3	Luxembourg	29.72	3	Denmark	80.02
4	Greece	21.22	4	Italy	28.19	4	Austria	78.64
5	**Singapore**	19.31	5	Slovakia	27.06	5	Finland	78.22
6	Estonia	18.23	6	Belgium	26.47	6	**Switzerland**	77.44
7	Taiwan	15.78	7	Portugal	26.42	7	Germany	76.20
8	Luxembourg	15.76	8	United Kingdom	25.55	8	Slovenia	74.72
9	Portugal	15.21	9	United States	22.96	9	Australia	73.53
10	Puerto Rico	15.18	10	France	22.89	10	Canada	72.89
11	Italy	13.15	11	Ireland	22.21	11	Netherlands	72.51
12	Japan	13.13	12	Estonia	21.88	12	Puerto Rico	71.66
13	Sweden	12.67	13	Spain	21.67	13	United States	68.50
14	Belgium	11.69	14	Australia	21.53	14	Taiwan	67.96
15	Spain	11.60	15	Sweden	20.67	15	Japan	67.55
16	Netherlands	10.85	16	Canada	19.90	16	Ireland	67.42
17	Slovenia	10.37	17	Japan	19.32	17	United Kingdom	66.73
18	Ireland	10.37	18	Greece	16.72	18	Spain	66.73
19	United States	8.54	19	Netherlands	16.63	19	Sweden	66.67
20	**Switzerland**	8.09	20	Finland	16.46	20	Greece	62.06
21	Germany	7.74	21	Taiwan	16.26	21	Belgium	61.84
22	United Kingdom	7.72	22	Germany	16.06	22	Estonia	59.90
23	Canada	7.21	23	Denmark	15.54	23	Italy	58.66
24	Austria	6.24	24	Austria	15.11	24	Portugal	58.36
25	Finland	5.32	25	Slovenia	14.91	25	France	54.70
26	Norway	5.31	26	**Switzerland**	14.47	26	Luxembourg	54.53
27	Australia	4.94	27	Puerto Rico	13.16	27	Slovakia	48.62
28	Denmark	4.44	28	Trinidad and Tobago	11.38	28	**Singapore**	47.82
29	Trinidad and Tobago	3.07	29	Norway	7.96	29	Qatar	35.23

Source: Analysis by the author with GEM 2014 data.

Figure 3:   New products and new markets among the early-stage entrepreneurs

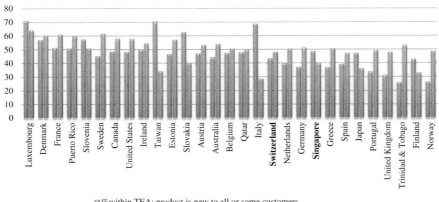

    %within TEA: product is new to all or some customers
    %within TEA: new market (few/no businesses offer the same product)

Source: Analysis by the author with GEM 2014 data.

with regards to access to research & development (R&D) and commercial infrastructure, especially transfers from educational institutions (such as the famous Swiss Federal Institutes of Technology in Lausanne and Zurich) to the private economy.

Derived from the NES (National Expert Survey) as one of the two pillars of GEM national reporting, the so-called "Framework Conditions" are considered to perform particularly well in both Singapore and Switzerland, but for different reasons.

Singapore ranks first for financial support to entrepreneurship as well as for the number and quality of entrepreneurship-oriented support policies and schemes, yet combined with more or less full market openness due to the status, location and size of the city-state.

Switzerland ranks first for the quality of its R&D and commercial transfers, as well as for socio-cultural norms and societal support (Tables 6 and 7).

Singapore is still facing some problems in smoothening R&D transfers to new start-ups or to serve corporate expansion, and new technologies are perceived to be rather costly, especially by local firms. Furthermore, Singapore still needs to fully encourage a domestic culture

Figure 4: Fear of failure rate among innovation-driven economies in 2014

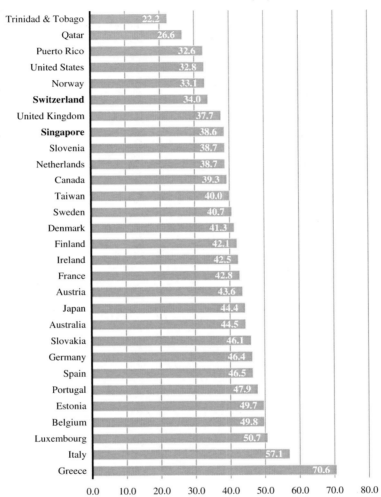

Fear of Failure (%)

Source: Analysis by the author with GEM 2014 data.

Table 6:   National Framework Conditions in Innovation-Driven Economies in 2014

	Finance	National Policy — General Policy	National Policy — Regulation	Government Programs	Education	Education — Post School
Australia	2.34	1.83	2.44	2.23	2.19	2.85
Austria	2.51	2.46	2.60	3.58	1.66	3.02
Belgium	3.38	2.62	1.98	2.71	1.95	2.75
Canada	3.10	2.50	2.85	2.86	2.32	3.14
Denmark	2.73	3.33	3.31	3.43	3.10	3.43
Estonia	2.86	2.43	3.58	3.39	2.63	2.99
Finland	2.82	3.17	2.95	2.77	2.28	2.70
France	2.77	2.99	2.96	3.17	1.75	2.92
Germany	2.84	2.93	2.87	3.46	2.13	2.81
Greece	2.11	2.07	1.74	1.95	1.50	2.31
Ireland	2.87	3.24	2.64	3.26	2.09	2.95
Italy	2.55	2.40	1.50	2.08	1.68	2.33
Japan	3.01	3.12	2.56	2.80	1.64	2.82
Luxembourg	2.76	3.41	3.22	3.47	2.13	2.90
Netherlands	2.81	2.59	3.13	3.15	2.85	3.17
Norway	2.58	2.49	3.18	3.18	2.48	2.56
Portugal	2.73	2.57	2.01	3.00	2.04	3.04
Puerto Rico	1.96	2.42	1.78	2.56	1.66	3.07
Qatar	2.72	3.15	2.95	2.90	2.72	3.33
Singapore	**3.56**	**3.48**	**3.98**	**3.68**	**3.02**	**3.34**
Slovakia	2.73	2.28	2.16	2.26	2.21	2.98
Slovenia	2.33	2.13	1.92	2.43	1.77	2.34
Spain	2.14	2.50	2.40	2.88	1.84	2.61
Sweden	2.63	2.74	2.53	3.00	2.55	2.75
Switzerland	**3.23**	**3.08**	**3.70**	**3.48**	**2.56**	**3.42**
Taiwan	2.98	2.71	2.91	2.73	2.19	2.77
Trinidad and Tobago	2.66	1.81	2.38	2.34	1.83	2.51

(Continued)

Table 6: (*Continued*)

	Finance	National Policy — General Policy	National Policy — Regulation	Government Programs	Education	Education — Post School
United Kingdom	2.77	2.90	2.33	2.62	2.44	3.02
United States	2.99	2.69	2.33	2.61	2.21	2.87
Average	**2.74**	**2.69**	**2.65**	**2.90**	**2.19**	**2.89**

Source: (Singer, Amoros, & Mosa, 2015).

Table 7: National Framework Conditions in Innovation-Driven Economies in 2014

	R&D Transfer	Commercial Infra-structure	Internal Market Dynamics	Internal Market Burdens	Physical Infrastructures and Services Access	Cultural, Social Norms and Society Support
Australia	2.18	3.42	3.03	2.79	3.91	3.19
Austria	2.82	3.40	2.49	3.33	4.12	2.46
Belgium	2.99	3.74	2.50	3.19	3.79	2.15
Canada	2.57	3.49	2.31	2.95	4.28	3.28
Denmark	2.77	3.56	2.43	3.44	4.49	2.82
Estonia	2.92	3.21	3.39	3.12	4.39	3.39
Finland	2.61	3.20	3.23	2.72	4.25	2.76
France	2.73	3.06	3.02	2.34	4.04	2.14
Germany	2.75	3.34	2.84	2.81	3.82	2.65
Greece	2.26	3.05	3.42	2.12	3.53	2.47
Ireland	2.82	3.29	2.59	3.13	3.71	2.95
Italy	2.18	2.83	3.50	2.61	2.92	2.22
Japan	3.15	2.44	3.92	2.85	4.47	2.58
Luxembourg	2.98	3.50	2.76	3.05	4.04	2.56
Netherlands	2.88	3.68	2.85	3.40	4.82	3.58
Norway	2.78	3.42	2.59	2.64	4.43	2.86
Portugal	2.76	3.34	2.40	2.75	4.43	2.55

(Continued)

Table 7: *(Continued)*

	R&D Transfer	Commercial Infra- structure	Internal Market Dynamics	Internal Market Burdens	Physical Infrastructures and Services Access	Cultural, Social Norms and Society Support
Puerto Rico	2.28	2.84	2.61	2.30	3.25	2.76
Qatar	2.41	2.95	3.25	2.08	3.44	2.89
Singapore	**3.17**	**3.23**	**3.42**	**3.04**	**4.45**	**3.16**
Slovakia	2.13	3.07	2.63	2.84	3.94	2.40
Slovenia	2.29	2.71	3.04	2.56	3.56	2.06
Spain	2.45	3.03	2.87	2.47	3.64	2.64
Sweden	2.65	3.28	3.13	2.80	4.25	3.07
Switzerland	**3.57**	**3.51**	**2.34**	**2.97**	**4.45**	**3.40**
Taiwan	2.68	2.65	3.86	2.78	3.90	3.26
Trinidad & Tobago	1.95	2.94	2.29	2.34	3.76	2.85
United Kingdom	2.20	2.95	3.28	2.73	3.54	2.83
United States	2.64	3.12	3.30	2.67	3.98	3.75
Average	**2.64**	**3.18**	**2.94**	**2.79**	**3.99**	**2.82**

Source: (Singer, Amoros, & Mosa, 2015).

of creativity and innovativeness. This may be a legacy of the predominant role of the state in industrial development, encouraging a culture of conformity and obedience.

Entrepreneurial Spirit

Entrepreneurship spirit refers to individual attitudes, behaviours and perceptions conducive to a variety of entrepreneurship initiatives at the national level.

In both countries, successful entrepreneurs benefit from high social status and recognition, particularly in Switzerland (Table 8).

Table 8:   Individual Attributes in the GEM Economies in 2014

Innovation-Driven Economies	Perceived Opportunities	Perceived Capabilities	Fear of Failure*	Entrepreneurial Intentions**	Entrepreneurship as a Good Career Choice	High Status to Successful Entrepreneurs	Media Attention for Entrepreneurship
Australia	45.7	46.8	39.2	10.0	53.4	67.1	72.6
Austria	44.4	48.7	34.9	8.1			
Belgium	35.9	30.4	49.4	10.6	52.4	51.7	50.8
Canada	55.5	49.0	36.5	12.0	57.2	69.7	67.7
Denmark	59.7	34.9	41.0	6.9			
Estonia	49.4	42.5	41.8	9.8	55.6	64.9	43.3
Finland	42.4	34.9	36.8	7.9	41.2	84.4	66.9
France	28.3	35.4	41.2	14.2	59.0	70.4	39.0
Germany	37.6	36.4	39.9	5.9	51.7	79.1	51.4
Greece	19.9	45.5	61.6	9.5	58.4	66.4	45.8
Ireland	33.4	47.2	39.3	7.2	49.4	76.9	75.7
Italy	26.6	31.3	49.1	11.4	65.1	72.1	48.3
Japan	7.3	12.2	54.5	2.5	31.0	55.8	58.7
Luxembourg	42.5	37.6	42.0	11.9	40.7	68.2	43.5
Netherlands	45.6	44.3	34.8	9.3	79.1	67.8	55.7
Norway	63.5	30.5	37.6	5.0	58.2	83.5	
Portugal	22.9	46.6	38.4	15.8	62.2	62.9	69.7
Puerto Rico	25.1	48.8	24.0	12.5	18.5	51.1	72.7
Qatar	63.4	60.9	25.5	50.4	75.8	87.1	76.8
Singapore	16.7	21.4	39.4	9.4	51.7	62.9	79.1
Slovakia	23.5	54.4	36.0	15.1	45.4	58.1	52.6
Slovenia	17.2	48.6	29.0	11.4	53.4	72.3	57.6
Spain	22.6	48.1	38.0	7.1	53.9	49.0	46.3
Sweden	70.1	36.7	36.5	8.5	51.6	70.9	60.3
Switzerland	43.7	41.6	29.0	7.1	42.3	65.8	50.4

(Continued)

Table 8: *(Continued)*

Innovation-Driven Economies	Perceived Opportunities	Perceived Capabilities	Fear of Failure*	Entrepreneurial Intentions **	Entrepreneurship as a Good Career Choice	High status to Successful Entrepreneurs	Media Attention for Entrepreneurship
Taiwan	33.5	29.0	37.4	25.6	75.2	62.6	83.5
Trinidad & Tobago	58.6	75.2	16.8	33.9	79.5	69.5	65.6
United Kingdom	41.0	46.4	36.8	6.9	60.3	75.0	58.4
United States	50.9	53.3	29.7	12.1	64.7	76.9	75.8
Average (unweighted)	**38.8**	**42.0**	**37.8**	**12.3**	**55.1**	**68.2**	**60.3**

* Fear of failure assessed among those seeing opportunities.
** Respondent expects to start a business within three years; currently not involved in entrepreneurial activity.
Source: Analysis by the author with GEM 2014 data.

This may partly explain why the media attention to entrepreneurship and new start-ups is much higher in Singapore, where the economic survival and prosperity of the city-state has often been presented by the government as a national security priority.

Switzerland presents indicators twice as high as those of Singapore in terms of perception of business opportunities and perception of entrepreneurship capacities among the respondents interviewed by GEM. The fear of business failure is consequently 10 percent higher in Singapore than in Switzerland.

Singapore shows higher indicators in terms of entrepreneurial intentions (15.1 percent against 9.8 percent), and in terms of entrepreneurship perceived as a good career choice (51.7 percent against 42.3 percent, see Table 6). However, such indicators have to be interpreted with caution, taking into consideration the context and availability of other equally-perceived professional opportunities in both countries.

International Orientation

Singapore ranks first, and Switzerland second, in the field of internationalisation of the corporate sector, defined as foreign customers representing 25 percent to 75 percent of total sales.

Switzerland lags far behind Singapore when full internationalisation is weighted in terms of foreign customers representing 75 to 100 percent of total sales. This is not surprising, since the city-state relies primarily on external markets. In contrast, although the Swiss domestic market is small (the size of Hong Kong), it still matters for a fair number of Swiss SMEs since Swiss purchasing power per capita stands above the EU average both in consumer products and capital goods.

Special Topics in Entrepreneurship

Education and training in entrepreneurship

Since 2013, the GEM Singapore has had a special emphasis on the education and training sector. Despite the overall high quality of this sector, the city-state is still characterised by a low concentration of entrepreneurship-driven programs and needs much more investment in this field compared to the other innovation-driven economies (Finland ranks no 1). Only 19.6 percent of GEM Singaporean respondents declare having received specific preparatory training in the acquisition of entrepreneurship skills (Table 9).

There is no specific Swiss data on this topic apart from the GUESS annual report focusing on the entrepreneurship activities of students at secondary and tertiary levels (Sieger, Fueglistaller and Zellweger, 2014). However, like in the case of Germany, the Swiss apprenticeship and dual education system is well-known internationally, and is often cited as a model of close links established between educational institutions and the real economy at local and national levels. In recent years, Singapore has expressed more interest in this Swiss system, and some new initiatives like the Singapore Institute of Technology (SIT) have been launched.

Gender and entrepreneurship

This issue has been present in the GEM Switzerland since 2013. The motivation was to explore whether and to what extent Swiss women had access to entrepreneurship activities, and in what proportion and positions.

Figure 5:   Entrepreneurship as a good career choice among innovation-driven economies in 2014

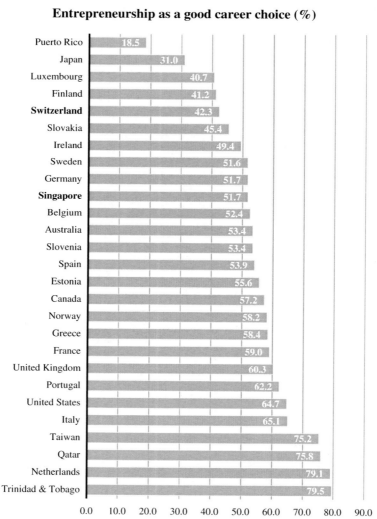

Entrepreneurship as a good career choice (%)

Source: Analysis by the author with GEM 2014 data.

Figure 6: Public opinion on whether successful entrepreneurs enjoy high status

Successful entrepreneurs enjoy high status (%)

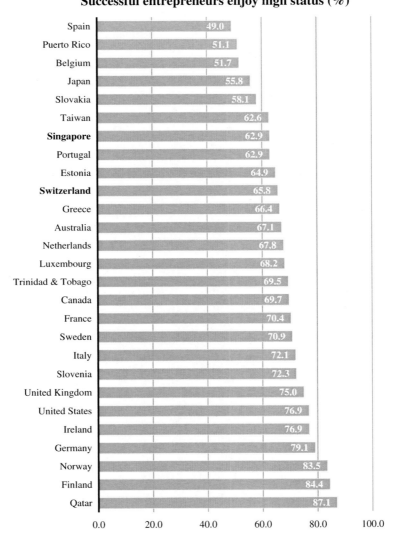

Source: Analysis by the author with GEM 2014 data.

Table 9: Prevalence Rate of Population Receiving Entrepreneurship Training (Comparison Between 2008 and 2013 Statistics).

Rank	Country	In-School Training	After-School Training	Either in- or after-School Training
1	Finland	16.5	40.4	48.0
2	Slovenia	22.8	22.6	35.7
3	Belgium	24.1	18.2	33.4
4	Iceland	11.2	17.7	26.7
5	Ireland	13.9	17.5	26.1
6	Denmark	9.4	14.1	22.2
7	Spain	11.7	14.6	21.9
8	Germany	12.1	13.2	21.0
9	**Singapore** (2013 data)	9.4	13.6	19.6
10	United Kingdom	8.9	13.8	19.5
11	France	9.9	12.4	18.1
12	Japan	4.7	15.7	17.4
13	Greece	6.1	12.8	17.0
14	Italy	10.0	9.1	16.5
15	Korea	5.6	9.2	13.5
16	Israel	5.8	8.5	12.7
	Average	**11.4**	**15.8**	**23.1**

Source: (Chernyshenko, Calvin, & Ong, 2014).

The first survey was quite a surprise for a country where women got the right to vote at the federal level only in 1971 and in all cantons only in 1990. While enterpreneurship is close to achieving gender parity in Switzerland, it is still dominated by males in Singapore. It is significant that Switzerland ranks first in this regard among the 25 innovation-driven economies of its surveyed group under the GEM Global.

Some surveys have been initiated recently to illustrate that Swiss women are not only active in retail businesses, but have become founders and CEOs of a variety of SMEs, especially in services, and are located in urban and peri-urban areas of the northern and western parts of Switzerland.

Seniors' entrepreneurship

Both the Singaporean and the Swiss societies are ageing rapidly. Yet, the proportion of entrepreneurial individuals between 18 and 24 years old is much higher in Singapore, whereas it is the reverse for the over-45 age group. As the Swiss economy is close to full employment, this result cannot be explained by senior executives losing their jobs in big numbers (like in neighbouring European countries), and creating their own businesses. It primarily reflects a Swiss propensity for senior entrepreneurship based on the valorisation of accumulated professional experiences in the creation of new businesses.

Foreign workers and entrepreneurship

The deliverance of working permits to foreign workers is a rather sensitive issue in both economies. On the one hand, the proportion of foreigners among total residents is already quite high in comparison to the regional averages in Southeast Asia and Western Europe respectively. This is aggravated by a strong interdependence with and substantial migration flows from large and heavily populated countries in the hinterlands of both Singapore (i.e., Indonesia; Philippines) and Switzerland (i.e., Germany, France, Italy). On the other hand, both economies are heavily dependent on foreign worker inflows to maintain their competitive profile and the operational functions of various sectors in manufacturing and services.

Multiculturalism and entrepreneurship

Interestingly enough, the study of possible sociological linkages (as suggested by Max Weber and his successors) between multiculturalism and entrepreneurship has not been covered by the GEM Singapore and Switzerland.

Yet, both countries have a high multicultural and multilingual profile leading to a variety of entrepreneurship modes (ethnic Chinese entrepreneurship for instance in Singapore), and to the openness of both economies to their respective regions and the global world.

In addition, both economies have been historically fertilised by various entrepreneurship migration inflows (foreign investors, for instance) bringing in differentiated cultural origins, traditions and modes of knowledge and transfer.

The continued openness of both countries to foreign cultural inflows is crucial for the continued competitiveness and renewed entrepreneurship capacity of both economies.

Discussion

The above findings have shown that Singapore and Switzerland rank first and second in the *Global Competitiveness Report (2014)*, but are differentiated from each other when considering a variety of entrepreneurial capacity indicators.

Table 10:   Singapore and Switzerland in GEM 2014

Innovation-Driven Economies	Singapore	Switzerland
Global Competitiveness Index Rank	2	1
TEA rate 2014	10.96	7.12
Intention to start a business in the next 3 years (%)	15.01	8.82
Perceived opportunities (%)	16.7	43.7
Perceived capabilities (%)	21.4	41.6
Fear of failure (%)	39.4	29
Entrepreneurial intentions (%)	9.4	7.1
Entrepreneurship as a good career choice (%)	51.7	42.3
High status to successful entrepreneurs (%)	62.9	65.8
Media attention to entrepreneurship (%)	79.1	50.4

Source: Analysis by the author with GEM 2014 data and Global Competitiveness Index data (Schwab & Sala-i-Martin, 2014).

Key findings

As shown, the TEA indicator does not totally reflect the real conditions of early stage entrepreneurship in the two countries. For demographic and sociological reasons, the youth seems more pro-active in Singapore, whereas it is the age group above 35 years old and the group of seniors which dominate in Switzerland. The entrepreneurial performance of Swiss seniors is rather high and may partly explain how Switzerland keeps an edge in terms of innovation and new product or service differentiation.

Singaporeans are keen to use new or very recent technologies brought from abroad, whereas Swiss technology is still highly regarded at home in a number of key industries and services.

Eco-systems

Switzerland and Singapore converge regarding the quality of their infrastructure, the nature of which, however, differs substantially, as Switzerland is not a city-state and has to cope with wide mountainous landscapes covering most of the national space.

Due to the developmental state context in Singapore, governmental schemes supporting entrepreneurship are numerous and influential, whereas both Swiss federal and provincial state interventions are limited and subsidiary. When the role of the private sector is dominant like in Switzerland, it may enable and enhance R&D commercialisation and transfers to the real economy. It seems more costly and problematic in Singapore, where the accumulation of corporate experience and know-how is limited among local firms to only a few decades since independence in 1965. In contrast, some of the most specialised Swiss SMEs, fairly internationalised, are still family-based businesses which have accumulated their *savoir-faire* over several generations.

Entrepreneurial spirit

There is no recipe to creating and boosting an enabling entrepreneurial environment. A variety of domestic and external ingredients deeply rooted in the local and national history of Switzerland may explain the entrepreneurial capacity of the Swiss since the late 19th-century.

Due to its colonial past and the absence of any manufacturing presence until the early 1970s, Singapore has come a long way on the entrepreneurship learning curve since its independence. Yet, the major industrialisation roles played by the state and foreign multinational corporations cannot be replaced overnight by individual or collective initiatives from within the new generations of Singaporeans and civil society at large.

Internationalisation

The GEM data does reflect the high global competitiveness rankings of both Singapore and Switzerland. However, the two economies are not fully comparable.

In the case of Singapore, foreign multinationals and only a few domestic firms are the major global traders and investors. In the case of Switzerland, Swiss multinationals and a high number of specialised SMEs are active both domestically and internationally, especially on European and other OECD markets.[2]

From another perspective, Singapore is classified internationally as a city-state and as a global city and global port. In the case of Switzerland, city-states like Geneva are creations of the past. Geneva and Zurich are ranked as global cities, an play an important role in international trade and finance, like Singapore does. Private banking, for instance, is an area of Swiss financial specialisation which has inspired Singapore considerably since the early 2000s. In 2014, total private assets managed in Singapore represented 30 percent of the equivalent managed in Switzerland.

Special topics

According to the GEM Singapore, entrepreneurship is still limited due to the rather unconducive role played by education and training. To respond to this challenge, Singapore has recently started to introduce dual and professional education after the successful German and Swiss models. However, the focus on education represents only one type of response, as its linkages with entrepreneurship creativity remains to be fully demonstrated. Entrepreneurship cannot be really taught, even if it is

---

[2] Baldegger, R. (2013). *Swiss International Entrepreneurship Survey*. Fribourg/Bern: Postfinance and Bisnode B&B Switzerland.

currently emphasised in the curriculum of most business and management schools including in Singapore and Switzerland.

On another note, the entrepreneurial profile of foreign migrants and workers has not been addressed in both the GEM Singapore and GEM Switzerland. It is a paradox when looking at the proportion of foreigners in both countries. The role of multiculturalism in both locations, and its entrepreneurial or industrial fertilisation capacities, has not been addressed by the GEM so far. However, one may observe that the high proportion of migrants devoted to entrepreneurial activities in comparison to national citizens is well-covered in the economic and management literature: the above-average proportion of entrepreneurs among migrants is analysed as a universal phenomenon.

In Singapore, the economic contribution of the Chinese business community in the city-state itself, and also among the 30 million overseas Chinese established in various ASEAN countries, is a major factor of Singapore's regional and global success in trade, finance and even manufacturing.

Challenges

The challenges regarding a full analysis and interpretation of the GEM data lie in the relative absence of entrepreneurship contextualisation for both countries. Such contextualisation is not included in the GEM survey methodology. However, the geo-economic situation of Singapore and Switzerland, and their industrial trajectories differ historically and, in recent years, rather substantially. This leads to various difficulties in comparing the GEM results in terms of entrepreneurship perceptions, behaviours and developments in both locations.

Singapore is basically a city-state, which is an island-state entity extremely rare on the global scene in the 21st century. First, its economic survival and development constraints are very specific, and induce a definite type of guided governance hardly replicable elsewhere. Furthermore, a city-state, with its former functions as a colonial emporium and port, offers primarily key regional and international services. In the absence of any manufacturing sector prior to independence, both government and foreign investors (primarily affiliates and subsidiaries of multinational corporations) replaced the lack of domestic entrepreneurs outside trade and finance. Therefore, Singapore's entrepreneurship characteristics can be compared to another city-state in East Asia, namely Hong Kong, but not so much to small performing European economies such as Denmark, Finland, Netherlands, Switzerland or Sweden.

Switzerland is classified among the so-called highly niche or specialised small economies of Europe having limited domestic markets and being therefore fairly (and early on) internationalised compared to larger neighbours. The Swiss geo-economic functions are partly derived from a good strategic location not at air and sea-route crossroads (like Singapore), but at the heart of road and water communication crossroads in continental Europe linking North and South in terms of cultures, languages, infrastructure and transportation. As a fragment of Alpine Europe, Switzerland was not absorbed or colonised by external powers, and proved early on her entrepreneurial resilience through trade, finance, and pre-industrial/manufacturing activities such as agro-food and forestry, precision machinery, and pharmaceuticals. Historically, business activities and the rise of entrepreneurial families flourished since the 18th to 19th centuries, and contributed to a rather dynamic private sector. This explains the early adoption of a pragmatic mode of confederal governance, and the subsidiary role played by government in the nation-building process and in the construction of a vibrant market economy. This is definitely a major difference compared to the governance and development of Singapore before and since independence.

Conclusion

Since independence, Singaporean leaders have regularly praised Switzerland as one of their most inspiring models of development and economic success. The "Swiss model", as often mentioned by the late Prime Minister Lee Kuan Yew, has remained in the official discourse and in the civil society mindset until now. The very concept of this book aiming to compare Singapore' achievements with only one foreign country, namely Switzerland, represents another illustration of this Singaporean mindset on the occasion of 50 years of independence.

After five decades, one can only express admiration and respect for Singapore's mode and pace of development, which has led the city-state to be able to catch up with Switzerland and all other OECD economies as well.

Even if Switzerland still ranks one seat ahead of Singapore in the Global Competitiveness Report, this difference is of limited significance. This chapter has therefore preferred to underline that the entrepreneurship capacities and paths of the two countries not only illustrate their equivalent competitiveness leadership, but also stresses quantitative and qualitative differences between Singapore and Switzerland by comparing their respective entrepreneurship performances derived from the GEM.

Such differences may lead to a final conclusion that Singapore should probably refrain from comparing the city-state with the "Swiss model". The Swiss should not compare themselves to Singaporeans either. The authors suggest that Singaporeans and Swiss should instead learn from their mutual entrepreneurial experiences and performances, and cultivate their complementarities for more bilateral cooperation in areas of common interest. This could provide a new and original impetus to socio-economic, financial, scientific and technological relations between the two countries in addition to their close links which already exist. Bilateral cooperation in entrepreneurship stimulation and in the design of joint R&D enabling instruments for the incubation and creation of business start-ups could be one of several new ventures between Singapore and Switzerland. Beyond their geographic distance, this objective could help both economies to sustain their first-class global competiveness rankings and to further assert their entrepreneurship capacities throughout the 21st century.

References

Asian Development Bank. (2014). *Key Indicators for Asia and the Pacific 2014.* Mandaluyong City, Philippines: Asian Development Bank.

Asian Development Bank. (2015). *Asian Development Outlook 2015, Financing Asia's Future Growth.* Mandaluyong City, Philippines: Asian Development Bank.

Baldegger, R. (2013). *Swiss International Entrepreneurship Survey.* Fribourg/ Bern: Postfinance and Bisnode B&B Switzerland.

Chernyshenko, A. S., Calvin, H. L. and Ong, C. H. (2014). *Global Entrepreneurship Monitor 2013 Singapore Report.* Nanyang: Nanyang Technological University.

Economic Development Board (EDB) Singapore. (2014). *Annual Report 2013/14.* Singapore: EDB Singapore.

GEM Consortium. (2015, 03 12). *The GEM Model.* Retrieved from http://www.gemconsortium.org/Model.

OECD. (1991). *Foreign Direct Investment and Industrialization in Malaysia, Singapore, Taiwan and Thailand.* OECD Publishing.

OECD. (2011). *OECD Territorial Reviews: Switzerland 2011, OECD Publishing.* OECD Publishing.

OECD. (2014). *OECD Factbook 2014 Economic, Environmental and Social Statistics.* OECD Publishing.

Schwab, K. and Sala-i-Martin, X. (2014). *The Global Competitiveness Report 2014–2015.* Geneva: World Economic Forum.

Sieger, P., Fueglistaller, U. and Zellweger, T. (2014). *Student Entrepreneurship Across the Globe: A Look at Intentions and Activities.* St. Gallen: Swiss Research Institute of Small Business and Entrepreneurship at the University of St. Gallen.

Singer, S., Amoros, J. E. and Mosa, D. (2015). *GEM Global Entrepreneurship Monitor 2014 Global Report.* Boston, USA: Global Entrepreneurship Reseaerch Association (GERA).

Chapter 8

Singapore and Switzerland: Success Stories in Education

Suzanne Hraba-Renevey and Yvonne Guo

Introduction

Both Singapore and Switzerland have scarce natural resources and invest heavily in education, with the objective of becoming and remaining knowledge-based societies. Both countries top rankings in innovation and competitiveness, PISA rankings, as well as numerous secondary-level and vocational education competitions, and their tertiary education is ranked among the best worldwide. However, the ways in which they have become the best in the class of worldwide education reflect almost diametrically opposed pathways.

In this chapter, we present a review of the educational history, politics, and policies of Singapore and Switzerland, comparisons between the two systems and finally, the challenges as well as opportunities of learning from each other.

Case of Singapore

History

The Singapore education system has gone through three phases: "survival-driven" (1959–1978), "efficiency-driven" (1979–1996) and "ability-driven" (1997 to present).

Singapore's "survival" phase emphasised raising enrolment as quickly as possible, so that every child had a place in school. One new school was built every month and the number of teachers doubled from 10,500 in 1959 to over 19,000 by 1968. This rapid expansion led to Singapore's achievement of near-universal primary education in less than two decades. In the 1960s, Singapore's bilingual policy was also introduced, with the learning of a second language made compulsory in all primary and secondary schools. Moreover, equal treatment for all four streams of education (Malay, Chinese, Tamil and English) and the teaching of mathematics, science and technical subjects was emphasised.[1]

Despite the changes made, significant problems persisted: 30% of primary school students did not go on to secondary school and English level standards remained low. Moreover, instructional materials were of poor quality, and teachers had low morale, creating problems in talent retention. From this unpromising starting point, Goh Keng Swee, then Minister for Education, argued in his 1978 'Goh Report' that a number of significant policy reforms had to be made.[2] For instance, one of the report's key recommendations was the introduction of 'streaming': students would be separated into different groups based on their academic abilities and different curricula would be customised to fit the needs of each group, helping them to learn at a pace most suitable for them.[3]

The implementation of the streaming reforms marked the start of the "Efficiency" phase, which emphasised the reduction of performance variation within the education system. The streaming of students was intended to reduce dropout rates and facilitate the workload of teachers, who could concentrate on teaching classes with similar ability levels. The creation of the Curriculum Development Institute of Singapore (CDIS) during this period helped standardise curricula across schools, and teachers were trained on how to use educational materials effectively. In the 1980s and 1990s, educational performance in Singapore improved

---

[1] Gopinathan, S. "The Development of Education in Singapore since 1965," 2006. http://siteresources.worldbank.org/EDUCATION/Resources/278200-1121703274255/1439264-1153425508901/Development_Edu_Singapore_draft.pdf.

[2] Goh, K. S. & Education Study Team. *Report on the Ministry of Education 1978*. Singapore: Singapore National Printers, 1979.

[3] Mourshed, Mona, Chinezi Chijloke, and Michael Barber. "McKinsey: World's Most Improved Education Systems," 2010. http://elibrary.kiu.ac.ug:8080/jspui/handle/1/1449.

significantly, and gaps in achievement between different ethnic groups were correspondingly reduced.[4]

By the end of the 1980s, Singapore was able to start introducing more flexibility within the education system, by measures such as the establishment of Independent Schools (1988) and Autonomous Schools (1994) that had greater autonomy than regular schools in terms of curriculum design, school fees or student selection. In this "Ability-Driven" phase, more emphasis was paid to recognising multiple types of intelligence, within a broader curriculum encompassing national education, creative thinking, collaborative learning as well as ICT literacy.

Politics

Singapore's only resource is its people, underscoring the importance of education in the country.[5] This section will discuss the political and administrative structures of Singapore which constitute the institutional foundations of Singapore's education system, and how they work together toward common policy goals, which will be covered in the next section.

The different ministries in Singapore are integrated, and each plays a part in establishing the link between education policy and workforce needs. For example, the Ministry of Manpower (MOM) and the Economic Development Board (EDB) collaborate in identifying manpower requirements and forecasting demands for skill sets, so that training programmes can be specifically designed for such needs. The Ministry of Education (MOE) and higher education institutions use these skill projections to inform their own education planning. This state-led manpower planning approach ensures a greater coherence between education and the job market, helping students to move faster into growing sectors, reducing oversupply in areas of declining demand more quickly, and targeting public funds more efficiently for post-secondary education.[6]

---

[4] *Ibid.*

[5] Singapore Government. "Singapore Budget 2015 — Developing Our People." Accessed October 29, 2015. http://www.singaporebudget.gov.sg/budget_2015/pc.aspx.

[6] OECD. "Singapore: Rapid Improvement Followed by Strong Performance," 2010. http://www.oecd.org/countries/singapore/46581101.pdf.

The MOE is in charge of building strategies and implementing processes, in collaboration with other ministries and agencies including the Ministry of Culture, Community and Youth (MCCY), the Ministry of Social and Family Development (MSF) and the Health Promotion Board (HPB). Moreover, there is a close tripartite relationship between MOE, the National Institute of Education (NIE), which trains teachers, and the schools, fostering both policy coherence and implementation consistency. Research conducted at NIE informs the policymaking process at MOE, so that NIE's work is easily aligned with ministry policies.[7]

Today, a wide range of educational choices is available in the Singaporean public education sector. These include a common trunk of pre-school and primary education, leading to a diversified secondary level (10 years in total), followed by a post-secondary education at junior colleges (an academic pathway to tertiary universities), polytechnics (set up to train middle-level professionals) and the Institutes of Technical Education (ITE) (established as a post-secondary technical institution). The system is permeable, allowing excellent ITE students to access polytechnics and polytechnic diploma holders to access universities. Currently, 31% of students enter junior colleges, while 43% go to polytechnics and 22% are admitted to ITEs.[8]

In addition to public schools, Singapore currently has more than 30 international schools. Three of Singapore's top public schools also offer the International Baccalaureate qualification in addition to the GCE 'A' Levels. Five autonomous universities, attended by 30% of the cohort in 2015,[9] exist in Singapore: the National University of Singapore (NUS), Nanyang Technological University (NTU), Singapore Management University (SMU), Singapore University of Technology and Design (SUTD), and the Singapore Institute of Technology (SIT). Some Singaporean students pursue their education abroad as they seek alternatives to local universities, while about 16% of university students in Singapore are foreigners.[10]

---

[7] *Ibid.*

[8] *Ibid.*

[9] Contact Singapore. "Living in Singapore — Education." Accessed October 29, 2015. https://www.contactsingapore.sg/en/professionals/why-singapore/living/education.

[10] OECD. "Singapore: Rapid Improvement Followed by Strong Performance."

Furthermore, a wide number of specialised and private institutions exist, such as Singapore Institute of Management, which offers continuous education; business schools such as INSEAD, IMD and ESSEC; and arts schools such as LASALLE College of the Arts and Nanyang Academy of the Arts (NAFA). Over 300 private education institutions exist in Singapore, providing a wide range of programmes.[11] Expenditure on education in 2015 amounted to $12.1 million, equivalent to 18% of government expenditure.[12]

Policies

Since Singapore's independence, government policy has dictated that education has to be closely tied to the needs of the economy. Singapore's education system has thus been highly responsive to its economic transition from a low-wage, labour-intensive manufacturing economy focusing on port and warehousing, to a capital and skill-intensive economy, and finally to a knowledge-intensive economy. The government's role in driving these changes cannot be understated, despite the increased autonomy devolved to schools. Planning at both macro and micro levels has enabled the continuous evolution of Singapore's education system to keep up with a rapidly-changing economic context.[13]

Singapore's education system is strongly tied to the principle of meritocracy, where academic grades are perceived to be objective measures of ability and effort, with curricula closely tied to examinable topics in schools. Bright students are identified at a young age and enrolled in special programmes such as the Gifted Education Programme (GEP). Moreover, top students graduating from junior colleges in Singapore are often offered scholarships to finance their university education locally or overseas in exchange for a 'bond' of up to six years in the Singapore civil service. The country's political and administrative 'elite' is therefore often drawn from the academic 'elite' at the pre-university level.

---

[11] Contact Singapore. "Living in Singapore — Education."

[12] Singapore Budget 2015 (PDF). Ministry of Finance, Singapore. Retrieved March 2, 2015.

[13] OECD. "Singapore: Rapid Improvement Followed by Strong Performance."

The legacy of streaming — the tailoring of programmes to fit the learning abilities of students — has given rise to concerns that the system may penalise late bloomers and those without the resources to excel at an early age. The private tuition industry — worth more than a billion dollars[14] and used by 70% of parents[15] — is an often-neglected, but no less important, factor of Singapore's educational achievements. While, in theory, parents cannot 'buy' their way into the top schools in Singapore due to the strictly meritocratic character of the national examinations, children whose parents can afford to send them for private tuition may have an advantage over their less privileged peers. Having good academic results is a direct determinant of success in the job market, with employers being very sensitive to the academic background of job candidates.

A cornerstone of the Singapore education system since 1966, bilingualism has had a dual purpose: to ensure that Singaporeans would be plugged into the global economy (with the use of English) and yet retain their cultural identity (with the learning of 'mother tongues', defined in Singapore as a second language taught after English, such as Chinese, Malay or Tamil).[16] Moreover, the promotion of English as a first language would promote harmony among the different ethnic groups in Singapore. With the closing of all vernacular schools in 1987, Singaporean children today are taught core subjects such as mathematics, science and the humanities in English, while also taking compulsory 'mother tongue' classes in primary school and up till, at least, the end of secondary school.

To ensure that education is equally provided to all students regardless of financial background, school fees in public schools are heavily subsidised. With the exception of miscellaneous fees, primary education is free, and low-income students can opt for a waiver of miscellaneous fees and

---

[14]Tan, Theresa. "$1 Billion Spent on Tuition in One Year, AsiaOne Education News." Accessed October 29, 2015. http://news.asiaone.com/news/education/1-billion-spent-tuition-one-year.

[15]Davie, Sandra. "7 in 10 Parents Send Their Children for Tuition: ST Poll." Straits Times. Accessed October 29, 2015. http://www.straitstimes.com/singapore/education/7-in-10-parents-send-their-children-for-tuition-st-poll.

[16]Iswaran, S. "Opening Address by Mr S Iswaran at the SIM University Public Forum: 'Crossing Cultures, Bridging Minds: A Role for Singapore's Languages and Literatures.'" Ministry of Education. Accessed October 29, 2015. http://www.moe.gov.sg/media/speeches/2009/08/15/opening-address-by-mr-s-iswara.php.

free textbooks, school attire and subsidised transport.[17] High-performing students (the top 25%) from families whose monthly household income does not exceed $6000 are also eligible for the Edusave Merit Bursary, providing up to $500 per year.[18] Other financial assistance schemes are provided by individual schools as well as by the government or welfare organisations.

In 2011, the MOE formed the Committee on University Education Pathways Beyond 2015 (CUEP) to come up with suggestions on how to improve and adapt the current education system. Ten actions were highlighted:

- Increasing publicly-funded university cohort participation rate (CPR) to 40% by 2020;
- Diversifying the university landscape to provide more opportunities;
- Introducing a new applied degree pathway with strong nexus with the economy;
- Establishing the Singapore Institute of Technology (SIT) as a new autonomous university;
- Conducting an in-depth study of the private education sector;
- Introducing publicly-funded full-time degree programmes at SIM University;
- Enhancing degree-level Continuing Education and Training programmes;
- Ensuring the affordability of university education; and
- Improving the provision of information to teachers, students and working adults.[19]

In summary, the changes are aimed at providing not only a new applied degree pathway, but also more publicly-funded university places, thus offering more opportunities and choices in a diverse university land-scape. At the time of writing, some of these recommendations, like the

---

[17]Ministry of Education, Singapore. "Financial Assistance and Bursary Schemes." Accessed October 29, 2015. http://www.moe.gov.sg/initiatives/financial-assistance/.

[18]Ministry of Education, Singapore. "Edusave Awards." Accessed October 29, 2015. http://www.moe.gov.sg/initiatives/edusave/awards/.

[19]Ministry of Education, Singapore. "Report of the Committee on University Education Pathways Beyond 2015 (CUEP)," August 2012.

establishment of the Singapore Institute of Technology (SIT), have already been implemented, while others, like raising the publicly-funded university cohort rate, are still being pursued. By 2020, it is expected that 40% of every cohort will enter university, while an additional 10% can receive degree education through publicly-funded part-time places. Therefore, half of each cohort in Singapore is projected to receive a government-subsidised degree education.[20]

Historically, Singapore based its educational system on the Anglo-Saxon theory-driven model. However, an increased global demand for deep and relevant skills has necessitated changes promoting a more skills-based system. In November 2013, ASPIRE — the Applied Study in Polytechnics and ITE Review — was introduced. In this context, the Ministry of Education (MOE) appointed a committee of experts (the ASPIRE Committee) from government, academia and industry sectors to propose solutions to better equip tomorrow's professionals. The review started in January 2014 by canvassing the views of about 20,000 people, including students, parents and polytechnic and as well as ITE staff. Leveraging on strong ties in education between Singapore and its partners, the ASPIRE committee visited several countries, including Switzerland, to meet with various stakeholders of vocational education.[21]

The 31-member ASPIRE team, led by Senior Minister of State for Education, Indranee Rajah, announced in August 2014 a list of 10 recommendations which the government has since accepted in full. ASPIRE's goal is to ensure that polytechnic and ITE students are highly employable with highly sought-after skills. The committee highlighted four elements to improve:

- Helping students make better education and career choices;
- Strengthening education and training in polytechnics and ITE;

---

[20] Ministry of Education, Singapore. "Greater Diversity, More Opportunities in Singapore's University Sector," August 28, 2012. http://www.moe.gov.sg/media/press/2012/08/greater-diversity-more-opportunities-in-singapores-university-sector.php.

[21] Ministry of Education, Singapore. "ASPIRE: Applied Study in Polytechnics and ITE Review." Accessed November 23, 2015. http://www.moe.gov.sg/aspire/.

Figure 1: Education pathways in Singapore from primary to tertiary levels.

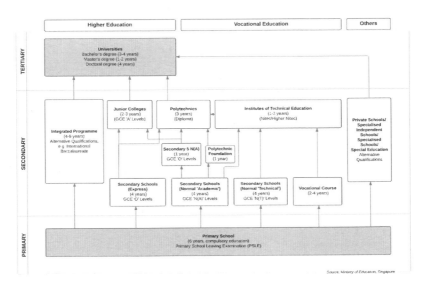

Note: Authors' illustration based on information from the Ministry of Education, Singapore.

Figure 2: Education pathways in Switzerland from primary to tertiary levels.

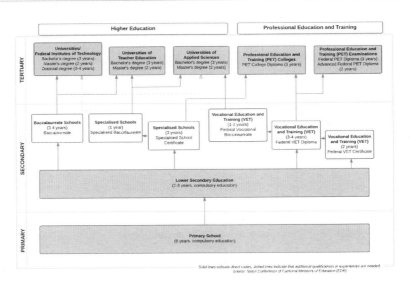

Note: Authors' illustration based on information from the Swiss Conference of Cantonal Ministers of Education (EDK).

- Helping polytechnic and ITE graduates deepen skills post-graduation;
- Helping polytechnic and ITE graduates progress in their careers.[22]

Finally, the SkillsFuture Council has been created to implement the recommendations of the ASPIRE report. Led by Deputy Prime Minister Tharman Shanmugaratnam, the council aims to help Singaporeans develop skills relevant to the future, and build a future based on skill mastery in every job.[23] The various SkillsFuture programmes and initiatives are targeted at students, employees (early- and mid-career), employers and training providers. Some highlights of the SkillsFuture initiatives include the SkillsFuture Credit — a credit of $500 offered to every Singapore citizen aged 25 and above to support his or her learning needs at every stage of life, including those seeking to re-enter the workforce, and SkillsFuture Study Awards, which is a cash award of $500 given to early and mid-career individuals to develop and deepen their skills in future growth clusters.[24]

Case of Switzerland

History

Because of the decentralised nature of the Swiss Confederation, the division of competencies between the federal and the cantonal governments is at the heart of much of Swiss education policy. As discussed in the introduction to this book, 1848 marked the year in which the Swiss Confederation adopted its Federal Constitution. In so doing, Swiss

---

[22]Ministry of Education, Singapore. "FY 2014 Committee of Supply Debate: Reply by SMS Indranee Rajah." Accessed November 23, 2015. http://www.moe.gov.sg/media/speeches/2014/03/07/fy-2014-committee-of-supply-reply-by-sms-indranee-rajah.php.

[23]Ministry of Manpower. "SkillsFuture." Ministry of Manpower Singapore. Accessed October 29, 2015. http://www.mom.gov.sg/employment-practices/skills-training-and-development/skillsfuture.

[24]SkillsFuture. "SkillsFuture Programmes and Initiatives." Accessed October 29, 2015. http://www.skillsfuture.sg/programmes-and-initiatives.html.

cantons transferred a number of their central rights and duties to the Federation. This transfer of competences had a number of implications for the Swiss education landscape, as will be discussed below.[25]

The 1848 Constitution laid the legal basis for the creation of a Federal Institute of Technology founded in Zurich (ETH Zurich) in 1855 and a federal university (which has never been set up). The 10 regional universities (the oldest being the University of Basel, created in 1460) remained under cantonal responsibility. The 1874 Constitution established the cantons as responsible for compulsory education, which had to be state-driven and free. The education-related task distribution and responsibilities between the federal state and cantons was a source of debate and political tensions for decades. A federal law establishing the position of an Education State Secretary at the federal level was rejected by a popular vote in 1882.

Apart from vocational education, which was always a responsibility of the federal government, education remained under the authority of the cantons until the 1970s. In view of growing population mobility and increasing education-related expenditure, the sole cantonal responsibility for education was increasingly questioned. The Intercantonal Agreement on Education Coordination of 29 October 1970 obliged the cantons to cooperate generally in the field of education and culture. However, a proposal of a new education-related article in the Constitution was rejected in 1973 and, in that context, the Swiss Conference of Cantonal Ministers of Education established a legal basis for inter-cantonal coordination in the field of education. In the 1990s, a number of inter-cantonal agreements were signed, relating to national-level recognition of degrees, among others.[26]

New articles on education (in Article 61 of the Federal Constitution), were adopted by the people and the cantons on 26 May 2006. Since then, the Confederation and the cantons have been obliged to work

---

[25] EUROPA. "Switzerland: Historical Development — Eurydice," August 22, 2012.

[26] Staatssekretariat fuer Bildung und Forschung SBF. "Aufbau des Bildungssystems und Bildungsverwaltung." Schweizerische Eidgenossenschaft, November 5, 2007. http://www.edk.ch/dyn/bin/12961-13431-1-eurydice_02d.pdf.

together within the scope of their responsibilities to ensure a higher quality and better permeability between school types.[27]

A number of major developments have taken place in the Swiss education landscape over the last 30 years. Some highlights include HarmoS, a national effort for harmonising compulsory education in terms of school starting age, duration of school levels, as well as objectives (education standards); a reform of the baccalaureate certificate and introduction of the professional baccalaureate certificate at the secondary level; alignment to the Bologna bachelor and master system of the universities, and the setting up of the universities of applied sciences, as well as universities of teacher education at the tertiary level.[28] The reforms at the tertiary level have notably created a growing competition between institutions, which face fundamental questions of relevance and resources in a globalised environment.

In 2012, the universities, universities of applied sciences and universities of teachers' education in Switzerland founded "swissuniversities", which merged the individual rectors' conferences that existed previously. "swissuniversities" works to strengthen and enhance collaboration among Swiss institutions of higher education and promotes a common voice on educational issues in Switzerland. It also coordinates and acts on the international level as the national rectors' conference for all universities, universities of applied sciences and universities of teacher education in Switzerland.[29] The Federal Act on the Funding and Coordination of the Higher Education Sector (Higher Education Funding and Coordination, HEdA) has been in force since 1 January 2015. This act serves as the basis for the new Rectors' Conference of Swiss Universities.[30]

Politics

In view of cantonal sovereignty in the education sector and the variety of levels of responsibility, there is a great need for coordination of Swiss

---

[27]EUROPA. "Switzerland: Historical Development — Eurydice."
[28]Swiss Coordination Centre for Research in Education. "Swiss Education Report 2014," 2014.
[29]Rectors' Conference of Swiss Universities. "Swissuniversities." Accessed October 29, 2015. http://www.swissuniversities.ch/en/organisation/.
[30]*Ibid.*

education between the Confederation and the cantons and between the cantons.[31] In the compulsory education sector (primary and lower secondary, lasting 11 years in most cantons), the cantons and their communes have regulatory and enforcement competencies, while in the post-compulsory education sector (upper secondary and tertiary), the cantons and the Confederation both have regulatory competencies. The federal institutes of technology as well as vocational training (vocational education and training, tertiary level professional education and training and job-related continuing education and training) are regulated by the Confederation. Except for the federal institutes of technology, the cantons are responsible for enforcement, in a strong interplay with the private sector.

In the majority of cantons, it is compulsory to attend pre-school for one or two years, primary school lasts six years, and lower-secondary education three years.[32] In lower-secondary education, teaching is carried out at different performance levels. Pupils complete compulsory education at the age of 15 or 16.

Upper-secondary education comprises both general education programmes and vocational education and training (VET) programmes. General education programmes include the Baccalaureate schools and the upper-secondary specialised schools, which prepare for tertiary-level education programmes. In the vocational programmes, adolescents learn a profession. Vocational education and training is mostly completed at training companies combined with teaching at a VET school. After lower-secondary education, about two-thirds of students commence vocational education and training and complete their upper-secondary education at the age of 18 or 19.

Tertiary-level education can be completed at tertiary institutions or within the framework of tertiary professional education and training (PET). The different types of tertiary institutions (universities, universities of applied sciences, and universities of teacher education) offer various academic and practice-oriented degree programmes. This enables experienced

---

[31] EUROPA. "Switzerland: Organisation and Governance — Eurydice." Accessed November 20, 2015. https://webgate.ec.europa.eu/fpfis/mwikis/eurydice/index.php?title=Special:PdfPrint&page=Switzerland%3AOrganisation_and_Governance.

[32] OECD. "Education Policy Outlook 2015: Making Reforms Happen." OECD Publishing, 2015.

professionals who have completed vocational education and training at the upper-secondary level to acquire more in-depth specialist knowledge.

According to Article 61a of the Swiss Constitution, permeability is a constitutional principle. Vertical permeability (no dead-end qualifications) means that those with a vocational education and training diploma at the upper secondary level can join matching programmes of professional education and training (PET) at the tertiary level. A vocational baccalaureate allows for admission to universities of applied sciences. An additional exam even allows for an admission to a university or federal institute of technology. Conversely, those with a baccalaureate in general education on upper secondary level can enter universities of applied sciences or PET programmes with additional practical experience on the labour market. Horizontal permeability guarantees a smooth transition between different programmes on the same level of education. This applies in particular to switching from one type of university to another, such as from a conventional university to a university of applied sciences or vice versa.[33]

A large majority of the Swiss population has attained at least upper-secondary education: 86% of 25–64 year-olds and 89% of 25–34 year-olds.[34] In contrast to Singapore, with its emphasis on traditional degree routes, vocational education in Switzerland plays a significantly larger role in the education system. More than 65% of Swiss students in upper secondary education are enrolled in pre-vocational or vocational programmes, while 93% of the latter are enrolled in joint vocational programmes combining school and work-based elements.[35]

Switzerland spends 16 percent of its total public expenditure on education at all levels combined, and international students make up 16% of all tertiary students. 75% of international students are pursuing Bachelor's or Master's programmes, or their equivalent, while 25% are in advanced research programmes.[36]

---

[33] OECD. "Education Policy Outlook 2015: Making Reforms Happen."

[34] OECD. "Switzerland: High Levels of Upper Secondary Attainment Predominated by Vocational Programmes," 2014. www.oecd.org/edu/Switzerland-EAG2014-Country-Note.pdf

[35] *Ibid.*

[36] *Ibid.*

Policies

For the Swiss Federal Council, education, research and innovation (ERI) is a priority policy sector. Swiss competitiveness is directly related to the fact that it is a knowledge-based society. Like in Singapore, the Swiss acknowledge the link between education, research and innovation and the preservation of social standards, social cohesion, sustainable development and Switzerland's appeal as a location. With the cantonal agreement and based on the strategic plans of grant funding recipients, the Swiss Federal Council has established three education, research and innovation policy guidelines, with the following objectives:[37]

- Education — "Satisfy the demand for workers with general education or VET/PET qualifications";
- Research and Innovation — "Consolidate the high level of grant funding awarded on a competitive basis and further strengthen Switzerland's internationally competitive position";
- General aspects of the ERI system — "Establish Switzerland as a location where research and economic activities are based on the principles of equal opportunity, sustainability and competitiveness".

Notably, the Federal Council has an international strategy for education, research and innovation (ERI) based on the intention to further develop an internationally competitive ERI system in Switzerland and to reinforce it over time by setting priorities and clear objectives.[38]

International cooperation in vocational and professional education is also a main objective of the federal government. The Swiss Confederation and the cantons agreed, on 30 May 2011, on common political objectives listed in a statement entitled "Making Optimal Use of Opportunities".[39]

---

[37] State Secretariat for Education, and Research and Innovation (SERI). "Promotion of Education, Research and Innovation for 2013–2016." Accessed October 29, 2015. http://www.sbfi.admin.ch/org/01645/index.html?lang=en.

[38] *Ibid.*

[39] Swiss Conference of Cantonal Ministers of Education (EDK). "Chancen Optimal Nutzen," 2014. http://skbf-csre.ch/fileadmin/files/pdf/bildungsmonitoring/Swiss_Education_Report_2014.pdf

The latter defines six main objectives of the Swiss education and training landscape:

- Harmonising compulsory education in terms of the age of enrolment, mandatory schooling, duration of education levels as well as transitions and objectives;
- Ensuring that 95% of all 25-year-olds hold an upper-secondary level qualification;
- Maintaining examination-free access to Swiss universities for baccalaureate holders;
- Achieving international comparability of PET qualifications;
- Sustainably enhancing the appeal of careers in research at Swiss tier-one universities;
- Establishing validation of prior learning (VPL) processes throughout the entire education system to enable the acquisition of formal qualifications on the basis of non-formal and informal learning.

The Swiss Confederation and the Cantons will also intensify their coordination efforts and cooperation in order to face current challenges. The policies proposed include the following:

- Coordinating and further developing language courses and exchange programmes between linguistic regions of Switzerland;
- Addressing shortages of skilled workers in the area of mathematics, IT, natural sciences and engineering as well as health care;
- Maintaining the quality of teaching at all levels within the education system through well-trained teaching staff, support for the development of specialised didactics centres and research in the field of specialised didactics;
- Supporting political education.[40]

In addition to the federal and the common federal-cantonal objectives, each canton has established its own targets in education.

---

[40] Swiss Coordination Centre for Research in Education. "Swiss Education Report 2014."

Challenges for Singapore and Switzerland

Despite its strengths discussed in previous sections, Singapore's education system is not without its limitations. The education system in Singapore has been criticised for not encouraging creativity and initiative, and reinforcing both exam-driven learning and ambitious, competition-driven achievements. Indeed, one constraint is Singapore's emphasis on assessments and results, which sets high standards but also inhibits innovation. Yet the culture of rigorous testing is so strongly ingrained that it is often challenging to find alternatives to cultivating and measuring more complex 'soft' skills relevant to the industries of the 21st century. Although changes have been made to the system to encourage creative thinking, a reluctance to 'think out of the box' is still an enduring consequence of the education system, as teachers may not be motivated to teach beyond a given syllabus, and students continue to be incentivised to think linearly and search for 'correct' answers rather than to find different interpretations of questions. This is tied up with students generally preferring to study the sciences and mathematics, with the comfort of having 'standard' answers, rather than more creative and subjective humanities subjects, deemed 'riskier' from a results perspective.

Moreover, despite Singapore's emphasis on meritocracy and the availability of financial support schemes, the success of the private tuition industry has widened the opportunity gap between the financially privileged and the less well-off, resulting in the persistence of correlations between socio-economic status and academic achievements.[41] Finally, the high proportion of degree holders in Singapore means that some graduates may not be employed in jobs requiring a tertiary degree, while some industries may find it increasingly challenging to recruit unskilled workers.

Another limitation in Singapore is the lack of recognition of skills compared to degrees. Although the route of skills-based learning has been recently taken by the government, the benefits and virtues of apprenticeships are not yet fully recognised by parents and employers. Singaporeans mostly consider tertiary education as the paramount way to achieve success professionally. Therefore, the government has increasingly acknowledged

---

[41] OECD. "Singapore: Rapid Improvement Followed by Strong Performance."

dual education, and more specifically, apprenticeships, as a form of education, to ensure a healthy economy, and has initiated a campaign to inform parents and students of its benefits. Besides conducting extensive study visits to understand the apprenticeship systems in both countries, Singaporean policymakers have also launched collaborations with vocational schools in both Switzerland and Germany.[42]

Given the results of the Swiss Education Report 2014, one can conclude that substantial progress has been observed, specifically at the level of national harmonisation of cantonal systems. However, most of the objectives stated in 2011 still constitute the major challenges of the Swiss education landscape as they have a long-term perspective and remain relevant for the future, while some new ones are coming into focus.

The limitations of the education system in Switzerland may be the interplay between cantons and the federal government, which slows down the overall decision-making and implementation process. Other challenges also include potential redundancy between the cantonal academic institutions seen from a global perspective, open access to universities which includes a costly first year selection and may lead to academic tourism, a slow process of internationalisation of some of the academic institutions, as well as a relatively low level of ambition and poor awareness by the students of the fiercely competitive global environment. Finally, highly subsidised fees, even for foreign students, raises the question of financial sustainability.

Collaboration Opportunities

During the last 10 years, many collaborations have developed between Swiss and Singaporean academic institutions, with a number of Swiss researchers becoming professionally active and some Swiss academic players creating an antenna in the Lion City. Indeed, the ETH-Singapore

---

[42]"Learning from Each Other." The Business Times, July 31, 2015. http://www. businesstimes.com.sg/hub/swiss-national-day-2015/learning-from-each-other; Ng, Jing Yng. "Swiss Model of Vocational Education Offers Lessons for Singapore." TODAYonline. Accessed April 29, 2016. http://www.todayonline.com/singapore/swiss-model-vocational-education-offers-lessons-singapore

Centre was established in Singapore in 2012, as well as the St. Gallen Institute of Management in Asia, which was set up in Singapore as an antenna of the University of St. Gallen. Finally, at the level of the universities of applied sciences, the École hôtelière de Lausanne has recently opened its Singapore entity. Moreover, the International Institute of Management Development (IMD), a private business school, has also grown stronger in Singapore with an executive education hub. These institutions have not only benefitted the local research scene, but thanks to synergies established with local academic players and other foreign players in Singapore, they have also enriched global research activities in key fields such as environmental sustainability. Furthermore, the local presence in Southeast Asia has enriched the Swiss entities with Asian perspectives, networks and economic opportunities.

The universities of applied sciences are also becoming stronger with summer university programmes initiated and supported by the Canton of Vaud, in fields as diverse as engineering, music and nursing. Singaporean academic institutions have also expressed a growing interest in Switzerland. A notable example is the setting up of an NUS overseas college in EPFL Lausanne in 2016, with a focus on engineering. Such initiatives will be strengthened with the launch of the Swiss Innovation Park in 2016, a national endeavour openly attracting major international academic and economic players to innovation hubs ensuring an optimal transfer of technologies. More collaborations have also taken place at the strategic level: common curricula, exchanges of best practices and a genuine willingness to learn from each other, as East meets West, bottom-up meets top-down, and the internationalisation of apprentices meets a journey towards the recognition of skills.

Lately, the role of Swiss expertise in the implementation of the apprenticeship system has been explored both by the Singapore government and its private sector. Switzerland's strong vocational education and training through apprenticeships ensures that a significant number of youths leave the education system with skills relevant to the market. "Switzerland stands out as a place of business thanks to low unemployment, high competitiveness and a strong innovation capacity. Our country owes this success, among others, to its much advanced education system, in which vocational and professional education and training allows for the creation of a hub of qualified professionals and managers and guarantees high employment and prosperity. Traditionally, the private and public sector share the responsibility for vocational and professional education and training. To enshrine this success as enduring, Switzerland depends on a prosperous and organised vocational and professional education and training based on this partnership," said Federal Councillor Johann N. Schneider-Ammann.[43]

While Singapore considers implementing the dual education system, Switzerland has been willing to share its expertise. Indeed, among a number of initiatives, the Swiss Confederation launched the first International Congress devoted exclusively to vocational education and training, focusing on image building, bilateral exchanges between the private sector and policymakers and the presentation of best practices in host companies as well as vocational education and training schools.[44]

In this context, the following domains, related to the ASPIRE committee recommendations, are a fertile ground for collaboration, as attested by the numerous official and study visits from Singapore to Switzerland:

- Counselling of students, enabling guidance in their studying and career decisions

Switzerland has strong cantonal and independent career guidance centres with their own mission, strategy and budget, acting in coordination with industry needs and education strategies.

- Connections with Swiss companies based in Singapore

For example, Nestlé and the Institute of Technical Education (ITE) launched a pilot project with a "test" classroom of 20 students from the

---

[43] Federal Department of Economic Affairs, Education and Research. "International Congress on Vocational and Professional Education and Training Skills for the Future." September 2014.

[44] International Congress on Vocational and Professional Education and Training. "2nd International Congress on Vocational and Professional Education and Training from 20–22 June 2016." Accessed October 29, 2015. http://www.vpet-congress.ch/. See also Rebecca Zay, "Implementation of the Vocational Training in Singapore, collaboration with Switzerland", *swissnex Singapore*, 2015.

School of Applied and Health Sciences hosted at Nestlé from July 2013 to December 2014.

- Educating the Educators

Among the many strengths of the Swiss vocational education and training system are the educators in companies who are well-prepared, trained and certified to convey their knowledge to the apprentices.

- Continuous education

Polytechnic and ITE students usually do not further their studies after graduation but integrate into the professional world; therefore Singapore wants to offer "industry-recognised modular courses that individuals can take to build up their skills in a targeted manner".[45] In that context, the SkillsFuture Program Earn and Learn for Food Manufacturing was launched at Nestlé in April 2015.[46] ITE will offer five new 'Place-and-Train' Diploma programmes for fresh polytechnic and ITE graduates, with overseas partners, starting from 2016.

- Exchanges at the apprenticeship level

The canton of Zug in Switzerland has offered the opportunity to launch an exchange of apprenticeship program with Singapore. Indeed, the canton welcomes a number of global companies and this is the reason why a unique apprenticeship programme in English was developed.

- Career development enhancement through better permeability

The ASPIRE Committee would like to implement industry-recognised modular courses for individuals to build up their skills in a targeted way.

---

[45]Ministry of Education, Singapore. "Better Choices, Deeper Skills, Multiple Paths: Government Accepts ASPIRE Committee's Recommendations." Accessed October 29, 2015. http://www.moe.gov.sg/media/press/2014/08/better-choices-deeper-skills-multiple-paths-government-accepts-aspire-committee-recommendations.php.

[46]"Poly Grads to Get Work Experience under SkillsFuture Programme." *TODAYonline*. Accessed November 23, 2015. http://www.todayonline.com/singapore/poly-grads-get-work-experience-under-skillsfuture-programme.

For example, "some courses could count as credits and/or be recognised for admission to other programmes offered by the universities and polytechnics or other training programmes provided or recognised by industry."

In Switzerland, flexible pathways have been introduced to allow mobility and avoid the risk of dead-ends.

Switzerland's education system is taken as an example in Singapore. Swiss government bodies, Swiss institutions, as well as Swiss companies are willing to support Singapore to reach its objectives. But there is a mutual interest in exchange and collaboration both in Singapore and in Switzerland. Indeed, numerous delegations from Switzerland come to Singapore as part of study trips to discover, understand and discuss with local institutions cross-cutting issues and challenges in education.

What can Switzerland learn from Singapore? Singapore is both a "rapid improver" and a "continuing high performer".[47] Within half a century, it has transformed its education system to one with high levels of illiteracy in the 1960s to the world's top performer in mathematics and science, as evidenced in the OECD's 2015 PISA rankings.[48] Singapore's educational achievements are testimony to the power of a singular vision emphasising the importance of continuous policy experimentation and improvement, with a clear focus on global standards. A combination of sound policy objectives, a comprehensive policy infrastructure that drives performance, and a high implementation capacity to deliver policy outcomes, the Singapore model can also be an inspiration to Switzerland in the force of its vision and its resolute willingness to study models that work and learn from other countries' successes.

Conclusion

Singapore, with its fast development since its birth as a nation, has opted for a top-down approach to education planning. Its achievements over the

---

[47]OECD. "Singapore: Rapid Improvement Followed by Strong Performance."
[48]Goy, Priscilla. "Singapore Tops Biggest Global Education Rankings Published by OECD." The Straits Times. Accessed October 29, 2015. http://www.straitstimes.com/singapore/education/singapore-tops-biggest-global-education-rankings-published-by-oecd.

years have been impressive. The Singapore experience illustrates the power of a singular vision in designing an education system flexible enough to adapt to economic needs, while at the same time fulfilling socio-cultural imperatives of integration between different ethnic groups. It also demonstrates the importance of strategic alignment between different government ministries, and between policy and practice. Finally, it shows the importance of cultivating and retaining teaching talent, of setting ambitious standards and rigorous testing, of making continuous improvements, and of benchmarking educational policies to global best practices.[49]

Inspired by successful economies enjoying a low unemployment rate such as Switzerland, Singapore presently engages in a more vocationally-driven, as well as sustained, continuous education, while ensuring that higher numbers of its citizens can access a diversified tertiary education landscape. Recent assessments and recommendations have indeed identified vocational and professional education and training as a key economic driver and speedy implementation of the recommendations takes place through programs such as SkillsFuture. Challenges, however, remain in building public-private partnerships, which seems to be one of the key success factors of vocational and professional education and training in Switzerland, as well as acceptance and recognition by the general public and industry of the value of vocational training and education.

Switzerland, on the other hand, with its history of tertiary education dating back a few hundred years, has taken a federalist and bottom-up approach in terms of policy implementation. The freedom of conducting blue-sky research at universities and a tight connection with industry at the Federal Institutes of Technology and the Universities of Applied Sciences, which nourishes the faculty with hands-on experience and provides the students with real-life projects, are some of the assets of Swiss higher education.

One additional highlight of the Swiss education system is its dual education system which offers an apprenticeship track. Giving young individuals who prefer a more practical education an alternative to an academic environment, where they have the option to develop skills in a

---

[49] OECD. "Singapore: Rapid Improvement Followed by Strong Performance."

process well regarded by society, provides a valuable alternative to the strictly academic curriculum of the universities. The numerous bridging options allow the same individual to pursue higher qualifications, up to the doctoral level, should his or her professional career and personal development guide him or her in such a pathway. Challenges, however, remain in the enduring complexity of the education landscape, the relevance of potentially redundant institutions subjected to higher competition and the process of internationalisation at the institutional and individual levels.

Both Singapore and Switzerland lack natural resources and invest heavily in education, sustaining knowledge-based economies. Similar in population size, they play a pivotal role in their respective regions. Although their systems have evolved from fundamentally different perspectives, both countries are world champions in education. These high performers have rather complementary approaches and it is precisely because of the varied routes they have taken that Singapore and Switzerland have a lot to learn from each other. Ensuring strong interplay between the different actors, sharing best practices in the globalized world, building up common strategies and establishing education hubs in their respective counterparts should ensure that synergies beneficial to both partners continue to blossom.

References

Centre on International Education Benchmarking. "NCEE » Singapore Overview." Accessed October 29, 2015. about:reader?url=http%3A%2F%2Fwww.ncee. org%2Fprograms-affiliates%2Fcenter-on-international-education-bench marking%2Ftop-performing-countries%2Fsingapore-overview%2F.

Contact Singapore. "Living in Singapore — Education." Accessed October 29, 2015. https://www.contactsingapore.sg/en/professionals/why-singapore/ living/education.

Davie, S. "7 in 10 Parents Send Their Children for Tuition: ST Poll." *Straits Times*. Accessed October 29, 2015. http://www.straitstimes.com/singapore/ education/7-in-10-parents-send-their-children-for-tuition-st-poll.

EDK. "Bildungssystem Schweiz." Accessed November 21, 2015. http://www. ides.ch/dyn/16600.php.

Eurydice. "Switzerland: Administration and Governance at Central And/or Regional Level." Accessed October 29, 2015. https://webgate.ec.europa.eu/

fpfis/mwikis/eurydice/index.php/Switzerland:Administration_and_ Governance_at_Central_and/or_Regional_Level#Administration_%20%20 and_governance_at_intercantonal_level.

Eurydice. "Switzerland: Historical Development." Accessed November 21, 2015. https://webgate.ec.europa.eu/fpfis/mwikis/eurydice/index.php/Switzerland: Historical_Development.

Eurydice. "Switzerland: Organisation and Governance." Accessed November 21, 2015. https://webgate.ec.europa.eu/fpfis/mwikis/eurydice/index.php/ Switzerland:Organisation_and_Governance.

Eurydice. "Switzerland: Organisation of the Education System and of Its Structure." Accessed November 21, 2015. https://webgate.ec.europa.eu/fpfis/ mwikis/eurydice/index.php/Switzerland:Organisation_of_the_Education_ System_and_of_its_Structure.

Federal Department of Economic Affairs, Education and Research. "International Congress on Vocational and Professional Education and Training Skills for the Future." September 2014. Gopinathan, S. "The Development of Education in Singapore since 1965," 2006. http://siteresources.worldbank.org/EDUCATION/ Resources/278200-1121703274255/1439264-1153425508901/Development_ Edu_Singapore_draft.pdf.

Goy, P. "Singapore Tops Biggest Global Education Rankings Published by OECD." *The Straits Times.* Accessed October 29, 2015. http://www.straitstimes. com/singapore/education/singapore-tops-biggest-global-education- rankings-published-by-oecd.

International Congress on Vocational and Professional Education and Training. "2nd International Congress on Vocational and Professional Education and Training from 20–22 June 2016." Accessed October 29, 2015. http://www. vpet-congress.ch/.

Iswaran, S. "Opening Address by Mr S Iswaran at the SIM University Public Forum: 'Crossing Cultures, Bridging Minds: A Role for Singapore's Languages and Literatures.'" *Ministry of Education.* Accessed October 29, 2015. http://www.moe.gov.sg/media/speeches/2009/08/15/opening-address- by-mr-s-iswara.php.

Kanton Bern. "Bildungsstrategie 2016," 2015.

Kanton Bern. "Bildungsstrategie (Die Direktion) Erziehungsdirektion." Accessed October 29, 2015. http://www.erz.be.ch/erz/de/index/direktion/ueber-die- direktion/dossiers/bildungsstrategie.html.

Khor, A. "Speech by Dr Amy Khor at the Launch of the Skillsfuture Earn and Learn Programme for Food Manufacturing." *Ministry of Manpower Singapore*, April 29, 2015. http://www.mom.gov.sg/newsroom/speeches/

2015/speech-by-dr-amy-khor-at-the-launch-of-the-skillsfuture-earn-and-learn-programme-for-food-manufacturing-29-april-2015-nestle-rd-centre.

McKinsey. "How Singapore School System Became Great: McKinsey." *Pressrun. net*. Accessed November 21, 2015. http://www.pressrun.net/weblog/2010/12/how-singapore-school-system-became-great-mckinsey.html.

Ministry of Education, Singapore. "ASPIRE: Applied Study in Polytechnics and ITE Review." Accessed November 23, 2015. http://www.moe.gov.sg/aspire/.

Ministry of Education, Singapore. "Better Choices, Deeper Skills, Multiple Paths: Government Accepts ASPIRE Committee's Recommendations." Accessed October 29, 2015. http://www.moe.gov.sg/media/press/2014/08/better-choices-deeper-skills-multiple-paths-government-accepts-aspire-committee-recommendations.php.

Ministry of Education, Singapore. "Bringing out the Best in Every Child." Accessed November 21, 2015. http://www.moe.gov.sg/about/files/moe-corporate-brochure.pdf.

Ministry of Education, Singapore. "Education Statistics Digest 2014." Accessed November 21, 2015. http://www.moe.gov.sg/education/education-statistics-digest/files/esd-2014.pdf.

Ministry of Education, Singapore. "Edusave Awards." Accessed October 29, 2015. http://www.moe.gov.sg/initiatives/edusave/awards/.

Ministry of Education, Singapore. "Financial Assistance and Bursary Schemes." Accessed October 29, 2015. http://www.moe.gov.sg/initiatives/financial-assistance/.

Ministry of Education, Singapore. "FY 2014 Committee of Supply Debate: Reply by SMS Indranee Rajah." Accessed November 23, 2015. http://www.moe.gov.sg/media/speeches/2014/03/07/fy-2014-committee-of-supply-reply-by-sms-indranee-rajah.php.

Ministry of Education, Singapore. "Greater Diversity, More Opportunities in Singapore's University Sector," August 28, 2012. http://www.moe.gov.sg/media/press/2012/08/greater-diversity-more-opportunities-in-singapores-university-sector.php.

Ministry of Education, Singapore. "Ministry of Education, Singapore: Applied Study in Polytechnics and ITE Review." Accessed November 21, 2015. http://www.moe.gov.sg/aspire/aspire-report/.

Ministry of Education, Singapore. "Ministry of Education, Singapore: Committee on University Education Pathways Beyond 2015." Accessed November 21, 2015. http://www.moe.gov.sg/feedback/2011/committee-on-university-education-pathways-beyond-2015/.

Ministry of Education, Singapore. "Ministry of Education, Singapore: Education System." Accessed November 21, 2015. http://www.moe.gov.sg/education/.

Ministry of Education, Singapore. "Ministry of Education, Singapore: Parliamentary Replies — Government Expenditure on Education." Accessed November 21, 2015. http://www.moe.gov.sg/media/parliamentary-replies/2013/10/government-expenditure-on-education.php.

Ministry of Education, Singapore. "Ministry of Education, Singapore: Parliamentary Replies — Percentage of International Students in Undergraduate Programmes (Major) at NUS, NTU And SMU." Accessed November 21, 2015. http://www.moe.gov.sg/media/parliamentary-replies/2013/07/percentage-of-international-students-in-undergraduate-programmes-at-nus-ntu-smu.php.

Ministry of Education, Singapore. "Report of the Committee on University Education Pathways Beyond 2015 (CUEP)," August 2012.

Ministry of Manpower. "SkillsFuture." *Ministry of Manpower Singapore.* Accessed October 29, 2015. http://www.mom.gov.sg/employment-practices/skills-training-and-development/skillsfuture.

Mourshed, M., C. Chijloke, and M. Barber. "McKinsey: World's Most Improved Education Systems," 2010. http://elibrary.kiu.ac.ug:8080/jspui/handle/1/1449.

OECD. *Education Policy Outlook 2015: Making Reforms Happen.* OECD Publishing, 2015.

OECD. "Singapore: Rapid Improvement Followed by Strong Performance," 2010. http://www.oecd.org/countries/singapore/46581101.pdf.

OECD. "Switzerland: High Levels of Upper Secondary Attainment Predominated by Vocational Programmes," 2014. http://www.oecd.org/edu/Switzerland-EAG2014-Country-Note.pdf.

Rectors' Conference of Swiss Universities. "Swissuniversities." Accessed October 29, 2015. http://www.swissuniversities.ch/en/organisation/.

Singapore Government. "Singapore Budget 2015 — Developing Our People." Accessed October 29, 2015. http://www.singaporebudget.gov.sg/budget_2015/pc.aspx.

SkillsFuture. "SkillsFuture Programmes and Initiatives." Accessed October 29, 2015. http://www.skillsfuture.sg/programmes-and-initiatives.html.

Staatssekretariat fuer Bildung und Forschung SBF. "Aufbau Des Bildungssystems Und Bildungsverwaltung." Schweizerische Eidgenossenschaft, November 5, 2007. http://www.edk.ch/dyn/bin/12961-13431-1-eurydice_02d.pdf.

State Secretariat for Education, Research and Innovation (SERI). "Promotion of Education, Research and Innovation for 2013-2016." Accessed October 29, 2015. http://www.sbfi.admin.ch/org/01645/index.html?lang=en.

State Secretariat for Education, Research and Innovation (SERI). "Strengthening the Position of Swiss VPET in an International Context." Accessed October 29, 2015. http://www.sbfi.admin.ch/themen/01369/01697/index.html?lang=en.

State Secretariat for Education, Research and Innovation (SERI). "Vocational Education and Training." Accessed November 21, 2015. http://www.sbfi. admin.ch/dokumentation/00335/00400/index.html?lang=en.

Swiss Conference of Cantonal Ministers of Education (EDK). "Chancen Optimal Nutzen," May 30, 2011. http://edudoc.ch/record/96061/files/erklaerung_30052011_d.pdf.

Swiss Conference of Cantonal Ministers of Education (EDK). "HarmoS." Accessed October 29, 2015. http://www.edk.ch/dyn/11659.php.

Swiss Conference of Cantonal Ministers of Education (EDK). "The Swiss Education System." Accessed October 29, 2015. http://www.ides.ch/dyn/16600.php.

Swiss Coordination Centre for Research in Education. "Swiss Education Report 2014," 2014. http://skbf-csre.ch/fileadmin/files/pdf/bildungsmonitoring/Swiss_Education_Report_2014.pdf.

Swiss Federal Council. "Switzerland's International Strategy for Education, Research and Innovation," June 30, 2010.

Tan, L. "The Development of Education in Singapore since Independence — A 40-Year Perspective." Accessed November 21, 2015. http://siteresources.worldbank.org/INTAFRREGTOPEDUCATION/Resources/444659-1204656846740/4734984-1204738243676/Session15-ProfLeoTan-OverviewofSingaporesMilestoneReforms.pdf.

Tan, T. "$1 Billion Spent on Tuition in One Year." Accessed October 29, 2015. http://news.asiaone.com/news/education/1-billion-spent-tuition-one-year.

TODAYonline. "Poly Grads to Get Work Experience under SkillsFuture Programme." *TODAYonline.* Accessed November 23, 2015. http://www.todayonline.com/singapore/poly-grads-get-work-experience-under-skillsfuture-programme.

Zay, R. "Implementation of the Vocational Training in Singapore, collaboration with Switzerland", *swissnex Singapore*, 2015.

Chapter 9

United in Diversity? Managing Multiculturalism in Singapore and Switzerland

Yvonne Guo

The central theme of this chapter is the comparison of multiculturalism, as a government policy, in Singapore and Switzerland. Singapore and Switzerland share many characteristics: both are small states surrounded by bigger neighbours and both have multicultural, linguistically diverse populations. Both countries have adopted models of ethnic and linguistic diversity that explicitly recognise the presence of different ethnic or linguistic groups in their societies (the Chinese, Malays, Indians and Others in Singapore, and the German-speakers, French-speakers, Italian-speakers and Romansch-speakers in Switzerland). At the same time, both models are being challenged by rising immigration, which alters the composition of different ethnic or linguistic groups within both societies, accompanied by a growing resentment of the 'native' population against foreigners, who often do not fit the labels inherent within the respective 'multicultural' frameworks. This chapter therefore seeks to understand the merits as well as the limits of the Singaporean and Swiss policies that deal with ethnic and linguistic diversity within their respective populations.

It is important to note that there are significant differences between the Singaporean and Swiss models of multiculturalism. The Singaporean model is one where the different ethnic groups are mixed and forced to live together; where 'ethnicity' is defined in racial as well as linguistic and cultural terms, and where cultural differences are accommodated rather than emphasised. The Swiss model is one of 'consociationalism', which involves different groups living in territorially segregated units within the same country, and 'ethnicity' is defined in linguistic and cultural terms, and regional or cultural differences are emphasised and even celebrated. In Switzerland, 'multiculturalism' is not even explicitly acknowledged as a policy. The political structures of both countries have directly determined the evolution of their multicultural policies, and both models, despite their historical success, are struggling to address the role of immigrants in society. While the economic openness of both countries has led to an increased reliance on immigrants, the existence of bottom-up pressures in both Singapore and Switzerland has generated a non-negligible degree of concern towards 'foreign' cultures and immigrants in general. How have Singapore and Switzerland attempted to manage these two opposing forces?

Review of the Literature

A great number of definitions of multiculturalism exist. Tracing its origins to the 1960s, Modood distinguished between American and European conceptions of the term. For Americans, multiculturalism was "a politics of identity: being true to one's nature or heritage and seeking with others of the same kind public recognition for one's collectivity". For Europe, multiculturalism was a political idea triggered by immigration — it was thus "the recognition of group difference within the public sphere of laws, policies, democratic discourses and the terms of a shared citizenship and national identity". While traditional immigrant societies, such as Canada, Australia and the US, were the first to call themselves 'multicultural' societies, other European societies, such as Britain, Sweden and the Netherlands, soon followed suit.[1] Yet recent years have witnessed a downscaling of multiculturalism in most European countries, and a renewed focus on 'civic integration', supported by the rise of far-right nationalist parties in Europe.

Contemporary theorists of multiculturalism, such as Kymlicka, have been particularly fascinated by its relationship with liberalism. Modood

---

[1] Modood, Tariq, *Multiculturalism*. John Wiley & Sons, 2013.

pointed out that what was new about contemporary multiculturalism was its emergence in contexts of liberal or social democratic egalitarianism and citizenship. While multiculturalism was founded upon liberal democratic institutions, it could also challenge some of these institutions. Therein lies the heart of the debate: to what extent is multiculturalism compatible with liberal democracy?

Academics have been divided over the use of multicultural policy prescriptions in democratic governance. On one hand, Kymlicka was optimistic that a liberal form of multiculturalism is successfully being practised, at least in Western liberal democracies.[2] He also argued that 'multiculturalists have won the day' in arguing for laws in liberal states that were accommodating of differences.[3] Besides Kymlicka, other political theorists such as William Galston, Bhikhu Parekh, Charles Taylor, and Iris Marion Young also supported state policies in support of cultural identities, including exempting groups from certain laws, affirming the value of different cultures, and providing them with special privileges or subsidies.[4]

On the other hand, Barry criticised the pro-multiculturalists, suggesting that they were guilty of misdiagnosing minorities' problems, and emphasising that equal rights had to be given priority as a universal standard of fairness. He also pointed to the inevitability of the fact that diverse beliefs would lead to different consequences under universal and equally applicable laws. Sartori distinguished between pluralism and multiculturalism, emphasising the voluntary and reciprocal nature of pluralism and the involuntary and one-sided nature of multiculturalism. Levy argued that multiculturalism could only be defended as a realistic

---

[2] Bruyneel, Kevin, "Multicultural Odysseys: Navigating the New International Politics of Diversity, Will Kymlicka, Oxford and New York: Oxford University Press, 2007, pp. vii, 374." *Canadian Journal of Political Science/Revue canadienne de science politique* 41, No. 04 (December 2008): 1044–46. doi:10.1017/S0008423908081274.

[3] Joppke, Christian, "The Retreat of Multiculturalism in the Liberal State: Theory and Policy". *The British Journal of Sociology* 55, No. 2 (1. June 2004): 237–57. doi:10.1111/j.1468-4446.2004.00017.x.

[4] Barry, Brian, *Culture and Equality: An Egalitarian Critique of Multiculturalism*. Harvard University Press, 2002.

'multiculturalism of fear', arguing that diversity had to be accepted as a fact of life rather than being promoted in state policy.[5]

Case of Singapore

Multiculturalism in Singapore has a long history that dates back to its past as a British colony. Early 19th-century town plans demonstrate the co-existence between the different ethnic and religious groups. Each group was allocated a specific area under the 1822 Raffles Town Plan and subsequent plans, giving rise to ethnic enclaves such as Chinatown, Kampong Glam and Little India. Former Chief Justice of Singapore, Chan Sek Keong, has attributed the success of multiculturalism in modern Singapore to the legacy of British institutions: both its legal system, which regulated the affairs of the various communities, and the English language, a common language which helped to unite all the communities in Singapore[6] without appearing to favour any of them. Besides the teaching of English as a first language, the bilingual policy, under which students had to learn their ethnic 'mother tongue' as a second language after English, helped younger generations to retain their cultural ties, in addition to being an economic asset when doing business with both regional and international companies.

Multiculturalism as a state policy continued to be practised by the Singaporean political leadership after independence. Legally, the Singapore Constitution contains provisions for the protection of minority communities, especially the Malays, and their religion and culture.

The official languages of Singapore recognised by the Singapore government are English, Malay, Mandarin, and Tamil. Malay is Singapore's ceremonial national language, and other vernaculars and dialects are also spoken. The four official languages were chosen to correspond to the major ethnic groups in Singapore, as were the 11 public holidays of Singapore, which include Buddhist, Islamic, Hindu and Christian holidays.

---

[5] Joppke, "The Retreat of Multiculturalism in the Liberal State: Theory and Policy".
[6] Chan, "Multiculturalism in Singapore — The Way to a Harmonious Society".

In 2014, Singapore had a resident population of 74 percent Chinese, 13 percent Malays, nine percent Indians, and three percent Others.[7]

Stipulating that "it shall be the responsibility of the Government constantly to care for the interests of the racial and religious minorities in Singapore", Article 152 of the Constitution specifically recognises "the special position of the Malays", while Article 153 provides for the establishment of a Muslim religious council.[8] Currently, the Islamic Religious Council of Singapore (MUIS) is given the mandate to administer the Muslim faith and affairs, while a Syariah Court adjudicates on disputes relating to family and inheritance in accordance with Muslim law and custom. For other groups with the exception of the Muslims, the principal family law statute is the Women's Charter.[9]

The inclusion of minority voices in the political process is explicitly provided for by the Constitution on a few levels. Within Parliament, Bills are reviewed by the Presidential Council for Minority Rights. If they disadvantage any racial or religious community in their practical application, they must be reconsidered by Parliament. Secondly, the electoral process guarantees a minimum level of minority representation in Parliament through the policy innovation of Group Representation Constituencies (GRCs), divisions of three to six candidates that must include one member from a minority race.

Due to the occurrence of major racial riots in 1950 and 1964, policymakers in Singapore have preferred to err on the side of caution by establishing targeted limits on freedom of expression with the objective of preserving racial and religious harmony. These include laws protecting

---

[7] Department of Statistics Singapore, Ministry of Trade and Industry, "Statistics Singapore: Population Trends 2015". Accessed June 11, 2016. https://www.singstat.gov.sg/docs/default-source/default-document-library/publications/publications_and_papers/population_and_population_structure/population2015.pdf.

[8] Singapore Statutes Online, "Constitution of the Republic of Singapore". Accessed June 11, 2015. http://statutes.agc.gov.sg/aol/search/display/view.w3p;page=0;query=DocId%3A%22cf2412ff-fca5-4a64-a8ef-b95b8987728e%22%20Status%3Ainforce%20Depth%3A0;rec=0.

[9] Chan, "Multiculturalism in Singapore — The Way to a Harmonious Society".

religion, and punishment for those defiling places of worship, disturbing religious assembly, trespassing on burial places, uttering words with deliberate intent to wound religious feelings, promoting enmity between different groups on grounds on race or religion, or distributing seditious publications. In recent years, since 2005, the Sedition Act has been used against individuals for racist postings online, including remarks critical of Malay–Muslims, evangelical tracts critical of Islam, and offensive cartoons of Jesus Christ.

Finally, multiculturalism also governs public housing in Singapore through the Ethnic Integration Policy. Implemented in 1989 to prevent the formation of ethnic enclaves and to promote racial harmony within HDB estates, the policy has ensured an even ethnic distribution throughout Singapore, at least within public housing estates. The maximum ethnic limits for a neighbourhood and a block respectively are 84 percent and 87 percent for Chinese, 22 percent and 25 percent for Malays and 12 percent and 15 percent for Indians/Others.

In Singapore, scholars have proposed that a realist framework of analysis, with an emphasis on national security, could explain why Singapore adopted the policy of multiculturalism. It is a small state surrounded by more powerful states with ethnic and cultural ties with different segments of their population. Geopolitical considerations seem to have made multiculturalism a necessity in the search for a national identity. For example, Brown argues that "geopolitical circumstances were the dominant considerations behind the governing People's Action Party (PAP) rationale for adopting a policy of multiracialism. Because the political consciousness of the Chinese majority in Singapore has historically been dominated by their self-consciousness as a minority within a Malay-dominated region, the PAP has assiduously cultivated a multiracial identity so that the Republic is not seen as a 'third China'".[10] Similarly, Tong Chee Kiong and Anne Pakir also note that "the survival motif runs through as a constant theme in Singapore's evolution. Singapore is often projected as a potentially vulnerable independent state, faced with both internal and external threats. The survival of

---

[10] Lian Kwen Fee and Michael Hill, The Politics of Nation Building and Citizenship in Singapore; New York: Routledge, 1995, pp. 91–112.

Singapore, according to this projection, rests not on any single ethnic group, but on all Singaporeans, working together to ensure the country's future".[11]

Other scholars of multiculturalism in Singapore have attributed the consensus surrounding multicultural policies to the political dominance of the governing party, but proposed different reasons for why this was done. As early as in 1976, Geoffrey Benjamin, a professor of sociology in Singapore, noted that a consequence of the "almost complete political hegemony of the People's Action Party" was that "although the discussion of social and political alternatives has not been a strong feature of Singapore life in recent years, neither has any serious criticism of the multiracial model arisen. There has instead emerged a widely accepted middle position, so widely accepted that it is rarely even discussed nowadays, somewhere between "chauvinism" — any militant adherence to one's race, culture or country of historical origin — and a totally diluted, "culture-less" state in which no one any longer knows their roots".[12]

In 1995, Lian Kwen Fee and Michael Hill argued that "what began as a political ideal for a group of English-educated intellectuals with strong 'Malayan' sentiments was later worked into a consistent political ideology which touched the heartstrings of a generation of Malayan-born, and was finally institutionalised through official policy".[13] They acknowledged that "the origins of multiracialism in Singapore are found in the political philosophy of English-educated middle-class intellectuals who dominated local politics, with the tacit approval of a colonial administration in the lead-up to independence. Such a philosophy was not only a reflection of the personal commitments of its exponents, but also of the political sensitivities in which the PAP found itself embroiled — namely, the need to simultaneously contain and appease the Chinese-educated whose growing

---

[11] Tong Chee Kiong and Anne Pakir, The Making of National Culture in Singapore, in Cultures in Asean and the 21st Century, edited by Edwin Thumboo, Singapore, UniPress, NUS, 1996.

[12] Geoffrey Benjamin, The Cultural Logic of Singapore's Multiculturalism. From Singapore: Society in Transition, ed. Riaz Hassan. KL: Oxford UP, 1976.

[13] Lian and Hill, "The Politics of Nation Building and Citizenship in Singapore"

influence on the island was felt through the ballot box".[14] Similarly, Carl Trocki emphasised that "multiculturalism was a defence against the masses of the Chinese-educated"[15] that Lee Kuan Yew distrusted.

In 2003, Chua Beng Huat went one step further, proposing that multiculturalism in Singapore was "an instrument of social control".[16] "Rather than resisting or denying the pressures generated by a multiracial society, the Singapore government's adoption of multiracialism as self-definition enabled it to incorporate the concept as a tool for governance… through all the multiracial practices of official and unofficial public institutions, 'race' is highly visible in the public sphere in Singapore. The high visibility of racial cultures, signifying the 'divisions' within the nation, is used to contribute directly to the formation of the Singapore state. The racial divisions enable, indeed require, the state to set itself structurally above race, as the neutral umpire that oversees and maintains racial peace and racial equality. This position enables the state to avoid being captured by the numerically dominant Chinese majority and becoming 'synonymous' with Chinese interests. The state thus achieves and retains a high level of autonomy in respect of the racial groups".[17]

Scholars such as Syed Farid Alatas have noted that the official discourse on multiculturalism does not necessarily reflect the social reality in Singapore. In his latest book, *Hard Truths to Keep Singapore Going*, founding prime minister Lee Kuan Yew defined the Singapore identity as follows: "An acceptance of multiracialism, a tolerance of people of different races, languages, cultures, religions, and an equal basis for competition". He said, "My definition of a Singaporean, which will make us different from any others, is that we accept that whoever joins us is part of us. And that's an American concept. You can keep your name, Brzezinski, Berlusconi, whatever it is, you have come, join me, you are American. We need talent, we accept them. That must be our defining attitude".[18] However, Alatas declares that "Singapore is not yet

---

[14] *Ibid.*

[15] Trocki, Carl A, *Singapore: Wealth, Power and the Culture of Control*. Routledge, 2006.

[16] Chua, Beng Huat, "Multiculturalism in Singapore: An Instrument of Social Control". *Race & Class* 44, No. 3 (1 January 2003): 58–77. doi:10.1177/0306396803044003025.

[17] *Ibid.*

[18] Lee Kuan Yew, *Hard Truths to Keep Singapore Going*, Straits Times Press, 2011.

truly multicultural". "We are not a multiculturalist society. We are multicultural in the sense that there are many cultures co-existing. But our orientation is not founded on the idea of multiculturalism. There isn't a celebration of being multicultural or developing an admiration and interest in other cultures. Our education system does not breed multiculturalism." He notes that "people in Singapore always talk about tolerance — but tolerance is a bad word. It's a grudging acceptance of the other".[19]

The new frontier pertaining to multiculturalism in Singapore has to do with the integration of minorities not included in the Chinese/Malay/Indian/Others framework, such as foreigners (who make up 38 percent of Singapore's population) and sexual minorities. Although concerns over ethnic harmony still exist, policymakers are now increasingly concerned about the integration of foreigners and new immigrants into Singaporean society in the context of an increased reliance on immigrants for both economic and demographic purposes. The interactions between Singaporeans and foreigners have been subject to some tensions due to perceptions that rapid immigration and an increasing cost of living were pricing Singaporeans out of their own home. Singaporeans were also upset at the perceived lack of public consultation over plans to increase the number of residents to a maximum of 6.9 million by 2030. The proposal, known as the Population White Paper, triggered an intense nationwide debate, including protests that drew thousands of people, but was ultimately passed by Parliament.[20]

Case of Switzerland

As a small open economy, Switzerland faces many of the same challenges Singapore does in dealing with a linguistically and increasingly ethnically diverse population. However, this has been more the result of bottom-up

---

[19] Lee Siew Hua, "Singapore is not yet truly multicultural", The Straits Times, November 9, 2011.

[20] Tan, Jeanette, "Population White Paper triggers nationwide debate". *Yahoo News Singapore*. Accessed June 11, 2015. https://sg.news.yahoo.com/-yir2013--population-white-paper-triggers-nationwide-debate-101840966.html.

movements rather than top-down initiatives, since policies to promote cultural integration at the federal level only emerged in the 1990s. Switzerland currently has a resident population of 8.14 million, with 23.8 percent foreigners, an increasing proportion of them from outside Europe.[21] The main language groups are German (63.5 percent), French (22.5 percent), Italian (8.1 percent) and Romansh (0.5 percent).[22] This section will address both linguistic and cultural integration from a historical and policy perspective.

Wimmer describes Swiss early civil society associations and state-building patriots as "ethnically indifferent, rather than consciously and programmatically multi-ethnic".[23] The growth of nationalism brought the different communities together; in 1882, in his famous speech *"Qu'est-ce qu'une nation?"*, Ernest Renan pointed out that "language is an invitation to union, not a compulsion to it. Switzerland, which came into being by the consent of its different parts, has three or four languages. There is in man something that ranks above language, and that is will." Till today, the Swiss still call themselves a nation built on will — a *Willensnation*.

Swiss consociationalism — power-sharing between its different communities — was further facilitated by what Lijphart called 'cross-cutting cleavages', in the sense that linguistic, religious, cantonal and economic cleavages are not parallel.[24] According to Mayer, "the Swiss 'miracle' of unity in diversity rests upon a particular equilibrium of cross-cutting cultural divisions which is historically unique." The fact that the political alliances of the elites controlling the nation-building project reached across an ethnic divide, and became institutionalised and

---

[21] Swiss Federal Statistical Office, "Swiss Statistics — Key figures". Accessed June 11, 2015. http://www.bfs.admin.ch/bfs/portal/en/index/themen/01/01/key.html.

[22] Swiss Federal Statistical Office, "Swiss Statistics — Languages". Accessed June 11, 2015. http://www.bfs.admin.ch/bfs/portal/en/index/themen/01/05/blank/key/sprachen.html

[23] Wimmer, Andreas, "A Swiss Anomaly? A Relational Account of National Boundary-Making: A Relational Account of National Boundary-Making". *Nations and Nationalism* 17, No. 4 (October 2011): 718–37. doi:10.1111/j.1469-8129.2011.00517.x.

[24] Pelinka, Anton, and Dov Ronen, *The Challenge of Ethnic Conflict, Democracy and Self-Determination in Central Europe*. Routledge, 2013.

organisationally stabilised, caused a pan-ethnic national identity to develop.[25] Political decentralisation also facilitated multiculturalism; Wolf Linder notes that federalism allows for a political and cultural autonomy that made it possible for various cultural, linguistic and religious groups to coexist in a common, shared space.

Swiss consociationalism was at the start informal and based on a shared understanding about the representation of the different language groups. For example, in the Swiss Federal Council, at least two councillors had to come from the French and Italian communities, and until 1999 they had to come from different cantons.[26] Since 1999, the Swiss Constitution has provided for an equitable distribution of seats among the cantons and language regions of the country, without setting concrete quotas.[27]

However, a key concept that is associated with the Swiss consociational model is 'balance'; there is an assumption that members of the national language communities will not actually need to meet "while they can still live the image of their communion".[28] Thus the policy of 'linguistic territoriality' that exists in Switzerland means that Swiss cantons decide on their official languages for the purposes of administration and education.[29]

In 1996, a national vote led to the inclusion of an article in the Swiss Federal Constitution dealing with language rights and obligations, which was subsequently revised in 2000. The Constitution currently states that the "national languages are German, French, Italian and Romansh" (Article 4); but also clarifies that the *official* languages are German, French and Italian, with Romansh as an official language "when communicating

---

[25] Wimmer, Andreas, "A Swiss Anomaly? A Relational Account of National Boundary-Making: A Relational Account of National Boundary-Making".

[26] Weller, Marc, and Katherine Nobbs, *Political Participation of Minorities: A Commentary on International Standards and Practice*. Oxford University Press, 2010.

[27] Wouters, Jan, Van Kerckhoven, Sven, and Maarten Vidal. "The Dynamics of Federalism: Belgium and Switzerland Compared." SSRN Scholarly Paper. Rochester, NY: Social Science Research Network, April 30, 2014. http://papers.ssrn.com.libproxy1.nus.edu.sg/abstract=2431193.

[28] *Ibid*.

[29] Stotz, Daniel, "Breaching the Peace: Struggles around Multilingualism in Switzerland". *Language Policy* 5, No. 3 (13 July 2006): 247–65. doi:10.1007/s10993-006-9025-4.

with persons who speak Romansh" (Article 70).[30] Cantons designate their own official languages, respecting the traditional territorial distribution of languages and taking into account indigenous linguistic minorities.

Stotz has identified elements of the 'confederate discourse on multilingualism', including little spontaneous interaction among speakers across the language borders, the prevalence of ethnification (especially the Swiss German preference to use dialect rather than Standard German) and globalisation (resulting in the increasing use of English). Moreover, one subject that is the focus of much debate today is the role of the second national language, the language taught in schools after the mother tongue. The decision of the canton of Zurich to introduce the teaching of English at the primary school level in 1998 constituted "a clear disruption in educational language policy", accentuated by the fact that other cantons had not been consulted. The teaching of French was moved to the fifth year of primary school. Zurich's initiative demonstrated the existence of a tension between multilingualism (as it was understood by the Swiss Confederation) and globalisation, with businesses and parents themselves expressing a preference for the prioritisation of English over the national languages.[31] The current national debate over the use of English, then, focuses on whether it contributes to enhancing intracultural communication and Swiss multilingual identity, or risks undermining Swiss identity and the nation-state itself.[32]

Immigration is another factor that has contributed to the re-shaping of the Swiss cultural identity. Having already earned a reputation as a haven for religious exiles in the 16th century, Swiss industrialisation in the late 19th century accentuated this trend, attracting intellectuals and workers from other European countries. By the time World War One broke out, Switzerland had 14.7 percent foreigners. It is notable that the emergence of anti-immigration sentiment around this time resulted in the development

---

[30] Swiss Confederation, "Federal Constitution of the Swiss Confederation". Accessed 11 June 2015. https://www.admin.ch/opc/en/classified-compilation/19995395/201405180000/101.pdf.
[31] Stotz, Daniel, "Breaching the Peace: Struggles around Multilingualism in Switzerland".
[32] Demont-Heinrich, Christof, "Language and National Identity in the Era of Globalization: The Case of English in Switzerland". *Journal of Communication Inquiry* 29, No. 1 (1 January 2005): 66–84. doi:10.1177/0196859904270001.

of a new Constitutional article in 1925 giving the federal government the power to address immigration issues at the national level. Prior to this article, every canton was responsible for its own immigration policy. This article led to the creation of the *Fremdenpolizei* (Federal Aliens Police) and the Law on Residence and Settlement of Foreigners, with the assumption that foreigners would leave the country rather than settle permanently.[33] In 1948, Switzerland signed an agreement with the Italian government to recruit Italian guest workers, a policy which was later extended to other Europeans. Guest workers made up 17.2 percent of the population in 1970. Their residence period varied from five to 10 years and carried restrictive conditions on family reunion. This was known as the 'rotation model' as new workers could be brought in after the old workers left. However, the 'rotation model' was gradually replaced by an 'integration-oriented' model when it became clear that state support had to be provided for the guest workers that had settled in the country, as well as for asylum-seekers.

In the 1990s, new immigrants coming from outside Europe were perceived to be problematic due to their 'cultural distance' from the predominant Swiss culture, as proposed by leading migration researcher Hoffman-Nowotny. He thus proposed the imposition of immigration limits from countries that were culturally different. This culminated in the 'two circles' policy in the late 1990s, prioritising immigration from Europe over immigration from the rest of the world. Swiss integration policy in the 1990s was characterised by a double reading: encouragement to integrate (*Fördern*) or necessity to comply (*Fordern*).[34] Immigration also increased after the Balkan Wars of 1995 and the 2002 agreement of free movement of persons with the European Community, which increased the number of high-skilled immigrants in Switzerland. Between 2000 and 2013, Switzerland experienced a net immigration of 75,000 persons per year. In 2013, 29 percent of people were born abroad.

But the rapidly growing population also raised challenges of infrastructure, land-use, and social cohesion. The electoral gains of the

---

[33] D'Amato, Gianni, "Switzerland: A Multicultural Country Without Multicultural Policies?" In *Multiculturalism Backlash: European Discourses, Policies and Practices*. Routledge, 2010.

[34] *Ibid.*

Swiss People's Party, which became the largest political party in Switzerland in 2003, reflected the fact that the party's nationalist and anti-immigrant political rhetoric was gaining ground. The party successfully launched a number of popular initiatives aimed at restricting the number of foreigners in Switzerland and at 'protecting' Swiss culture from foreign influences, including the tightening of asylum and immigration laws (in 2006, with 68% approval), a ban on the construction of minarets (in 2009, with 57.5% approval), the expulsion of criminal foreigners (in 2010, with 52.3% approval), and the limitation of immigration through quotas (in 2014, with 50.3% approval). Due to the outcome of the 2009 referendum, the Swiss Constitution currently states (in Article 72) that 'the construction of minarets is prohibited'.[35] Moreover, at the time of writing, the Swiss Confederation is still negotiating with the European Union over how to implement the result of the 2014 referendum restricting immigration without contravening the existing bilateral agreements between Switzerland and the European Community, which allow, among other things, the unrestricted movement of people between the European Union and Switzerland.

The debate on multiculturalism in Switzerland, therefore, is not over: it has shifted from discussions about established minorities to the rights of new minorities, particularly immigrants and religious minorities. D'Amato points out that although Switzerland is seen by foreign scholars as a successful example of peaceful coexistence of different ethnic groups, with the tools to equilibrate potential ethnic tensions within the country, "this optimistic assumption misreads the fact that public talk on multiculturalism is only referring to the established minorities. For a majority of Swiss citizens, it is completely self-evident that labour migrants are not part of multicultural Switzerland".

Suggesting that Switzerland is currently a "multicultural country missing politics of diversity",[36] he points out that "Switzerland is more homogeneous than the usual talk on Swiss cultural diversity suggests. This homogeneity is given by the reality that people with different languages, religious beliefs, mentalities, and economic structures are living in one territory with a common history, side by side. For more conservative

---

[35] Swiss Confederation, "Federal Constitution of the Swiss Confederation".

[36] D'Amato, Gianni, "Switzerland: A Multicultural Country Without Multicultural Policies?"

observers, the condition that makes cultural diversity possible in Switzerland is linked to the principle of territoriality. For them, there is no Swiss multiculturalism in a strict sense since each cultural group is living in their own territory, the cantons, preventing in this respect an overlapping of other groups or a spill-over of their cultural influence".[37]

Comparisons, Discussions and Challenges

Both Singapore and Switzerland's relatively robust models of cultural diversity notwithstanding, the evolution of both societies has led to the emergence of new minorities and new forms of defining identity. First, from a linguistic perspective, Singapore and Switzerland have had to grapple with the distinction between standard and vernacular forms of some of their spoken languages. In Singapore, Chinese dialects were banned in 1981 on television based on the belief that it would impair the mastery of Mandarin and English. The widely-spoken Singlish vernacular has also been discouraged, the government's official stand being that "using Singlish will make it harder for Singaporeans to learn and use standard English."[38] In their place, the "Speak Good English" and "Speak Mandarin" campaigns were launched, thus effectively isolating a generation of older dialect-speakers. Although some exceptions to the 'no-dialect' policy have been made in recent years, with the government realising the need to explain policies to the elderly in dialect, the ban on dialect media broadcasts remains largely in effect. Here the Singapore government's policy of discouraging, and even banning, the use of certain vernaculars and dialects can be contrasted with the Swiss desire to protect and promote the use of their dialects, as evidenced in a 2011 referendum making the teaching of Swiss German compulsory in Zurich kindergartens. The trade-off can be framed as one pitting cultural heritage, social integration (and to some extent, national pride) against the perceived economic or cultural benefits of speaking a 'standard' variant of the language.

A related point is both countries' relationship with English. In Singapore as in Switzerland, English was a foreign language to all

---

[37] *Ibid.*
[38] Chang, Li Lin. "The Reality Behind Singlish." The New York Times, May 23, 2016. http://www.nytimes.com/2016/05/23/opinion/the-reality-behind-singlish.html.

speakers merely fifty years ago; yet today English has become the native language of 32.3 percent of Singaporeans and the most widely spoken language in Singapore.[39] In Switzerland, meanwhile, the spread of English has not gone unchallenged. Some scholars have been wary of English's role in displacing the national languages and thus a threat to national cohesion, although its value in building intercultural dialogue between different communities has also been acknowledged. According to Knuesel, "Resorting to English, a foreign language to all speakers, is undoubtedly an acknowledgement of failure. Even if it allows elites to engage in a dialogue among equals, it nevertheless reduces the specific features of the other cultures". Pitsch asserts that English is not a threat to the Swiss multilingual ideal "as long as the intention does not exist to introduce English as the lingua franca of the country".[40]

Moreover, both Singapore and Switzerland have witnessed the dominance of two of their four national languages at the expense of speakers of the minority languages. In Singapore, ethnic minorities have expressed concern at the increased immigration of native Chinese speakers, an intentional government policy to maintain the ethnic proportion and compensate for the lower fertility rate among the Chinese population. In Switzerland, the Italian-speaking Ticino also voted massively for the restoration of immigration quotas. The use of Romansh, Switzerland's fourth national language, has declined significantly; it is spoken by merely 0.5 percent of the population and ranks only as the 11th most widely spoken language in the country.[41]

From a cultural perspective, the question of *who* qualifies as a minority has also been posed with greater frequency. Multiculturalism in Singapore has been framed ethnically and in Switzerland linguistically, providing protection to groups defined along these terms but not to other minority groups. In Switzerland, the 2009 referendum banning the

---

[39] Singapore, ed. *Census of Population 2010*. Singapore: Singapore Department of Statistics, 2010.

[40] Watts, Richard J., and Heather Murray, *Die fünfte Landessprache?: Englisch in der Schweiz*. vdf Hochschulverlag AG, 2001.

[41] Swiss Federal Statistical Office, "Swiss Statistics — Languages". Accessed June 11, 2015. http://www.bfs.admin.ch/bfs/portal/en/index/themen/01/05/blank/key/sprachen.html.

construction of minarets was seen to infringe on the rights of religious minorities; this was followed up in 2013 by a popular initiative banning burqas in Ticino and proposals to ban headscarves in the Valais. Whether such initiatives are contrary to the Swiss Constitution's Article 15 on the freedom of religion has been subject to considerable debate.[42] In Singapore, the retention of Section 377A of the Penal Code, which criminalises sex between men, is seen to be discriminatory against sexual minorities. There has been calls among academics and civil society activists in Singapore to redefine the country's so-called 'monolithic multiculturalism' in a more inclusive and cosmopolitan manner.[43]

Finally, the ambivalence of both the Singaporean and Swiss populations towards rising immigration can be witnessed in the outcome of recent policy initiatives, including the re-introduction of immigration quotas in Switzerland, protests against the Population White Paper in Singapore, the creation of a "Singaporeans First" political party and even government-sanctioned "Singaporeans First" policies in housing, education and jobs.[44] As both countries project themselves as competitive, cosmopolitan global hubs for talent, tensions between the needs of international business and the demands of the locals are inevitable, while the question of integration frequently surfaces. Ironically, although a majority of Singaporeans live in HDB estates with their ethnic proportions tightly controlled, foreign worker and expatriate communities often live in their own 'enclaves' — upscale condominiums in the city centre, or worker dormitories in the outskirts of the country. The rights of foreign workers and domestic workers in Singapore on fixed-term contracts are also strictly curtailed.

Perhaps both Singapore and Switzerland's similar economic structures have given rise to the similar immigration pressures they are currently facing. For example, both countries have strong financial services sectors

---

[42] Amnesty International, "Switzerland minaret ban would breach freedom of religion obligations". Accessed June 11, 2015. https://www.amnesty.org/articles/news/2009/11/switzerland-minaret-ban-would-breach-freedom-religion-obligations-20091125/.

[43] Bahwari, Nazry, "Is Singapore truly multicultural?". *TODAYonline*. Accessed 11 June 2015. http://www.todayonline.com/singapore/singapore-truly-multicultural.

[44] Wong, Alicia, "PM Lee unveils new 'Singaporeans-first' policies". *Yahoo News Singapore*. Accessed June 11, 2015. https://sg.news.yahoo.com/blogs/singaporescene/gov-t-puts-poreans-first-pm-lee-175645736.html.

that tend to be more cosmopolitan in nature due to the globalised nature of finance. Overall, both have relied on their positions as global cities to survive and compensate for their smallness and lack of natural resources, and both have benefited greatly from flows of people and capital. Yet in an increasingly globalised world, the question is how to strike a balance between domestic stability and external economic forces.

Conclusion

The above analysis has shown that there is a gap between the official discourses and images of both countries as sites of multicultural, cosmopolitan openness, and the growth of nationalist and occasionally xenophobic discourse that has gained ground among certain segments of the population. Direct democracy in Switzerland provided pathways for nationalist parties to gain political influence and portray the increased diversity of Swiss society as a threat. In Singapore, the government's decade-long pro-immigration policy culminated in their 2011 electoral setback. Immigration was blamed for the rise in living costs, and the suppression of wages. Foreigners were perceived to be better treated than Singaporeans, since they had rights but no obligations, such as mandatory National Service. Despite the different political structures of both countries, official discourse in favour of multiculturalism, cultural diversity and openness to immigration was undermined to some extent by bottom-up pressures by nationalist groups. As a consequence, both in Singapore and Switzerland, policies have been implemented to compel companies to give citizens of both countries priority for job openings.[45] Therefore, growing nationalism in both countries could reinforce a type of exclusive multiculturalism, in which benefits and privileges are extended only to people from certain 'native' cultural backgrounds but not to others.

---

[45] Gough, Neil, "Singapore to Give Citizens Priority for Job Openings". *The New York Times*, 23 September 2013. http://www.nytimes.com/2013/09/24/business/global/singapore-seeks-to-put-locals-first-in-line-for-jobs.html; Summermatter, Stefania, and Armando Mombelli, "Immigration: one vote, many questions". *Swissinfo.ch*. http://www.swissinfo.ch/eng/vote-faqs_immigration--one-vote--many-questions/38007016.

Ultimately, the Singaporean and Swiss experiences are also a reminder that majoritarianism can come at the expense of minority rights. The wishes of the majority have been invoked to justify legislation that discriminates against religious minorities in Switzerland, sexual minorities in Singapore, and certain groups of foreigners in both countries, from a social justice perspective. While policies that discriminate against minority groups may be politically popular with the majority, such discrimination can come at the cost of a multicultural society's inclusiveness by rendering some members of society politically and socially vulnerable, and accentuating the power differences between advantaged and disadvantaged groups in society.

References

Amnesty International. "Switzerland Minaret Ban Would Breach Freedom of Religion Obligations." Accessed June 11, 2015. https://www.amnesty.org/articles/news/2009/11/switzerland-minaret-ban-would-breach-freedom-religion-obligations-20091125/.

Bahwari, N. "Is Singapore Truly Multicultural?" *TODAYonline*. Accessed June 11, 2015. http://www.todayonline.com/singapore/singapore-truly-multicultural.

Barry, B. *Culture and Equality: An Egalitarian Critique of Multiculturalism.* Harvard University Press, 2002.

Bruyneel, K. "Multicultural Odysseys: Navigating the New International Politics of Diversity, Will Kymlicka, Oxford and New York: Oxford University Press, 2007, p. Vii, 374." *Canadian Journal of Political Science/Revue Canadienne de Science Politique* 41, no. 04 (December 2008): 1044–46. doi:10.1017/S0008423908081274.

Chan, S. K. "Multiculturalism in Singapore — The Way to a Harmonious Society." *Singapore Academy of Law Journal* 25 (2013): 84.

Chang, L. L. "The Reality Behind Singlish." The New York Times, May 23, 2016. http://www.nytimes.com/2016/05/23/opinion/the-reality-behind-singlish.html.

Chua, B. H. "Multiculturalism in Singapore: An Instrument of Social Control." *Race & Class* 44, no. 3 (January 1, 2003): 58–77. doi:10.1177/0306396803044003025.

D'Amato, G. "Switzerland: A Multicultural Country Without Multicultural Policies?" In *Multiculturalism Backlash: European Discourses, Policies and Practices*. Routledge, 2010.

Demont-Heinrich, C. "Language and National Identity in the Era of Globalization: The Case of English in Switzerland." *Journal of Communication Inquiry* 29, no. 1 (January 1, 2005): 66–84. doi:10.1177/0196859904270001.

Department of Statistics Singapore, Ministry of Trade and Industry. "Statistics Singapore: Population Trends 2014." Accessed June 11, 2015. http://www.singstat.gov.sg/docs/default-source/default-document-library/publications/publications_and_papers/population_and_population_structure/population2014.pdf.

Gough, N. "Singapore to Give Citizens Priority for Job Openings." *The New York Times*, September 23, 2013. http://www.nytimes.com/2013/09/24/business/global/singapore-seeks-to-put-locals-first-in-line-for-jobs.html.

Hassan, R. *Singapore: Society in Transition.* Oxford University Press, 1976.

Hill, M., and Kwen F. L. *The Politics of Nation Building and Citizenship in Singapore.* London; New York: Routledge, 1995. http://public.eblib.com/choice/publicfullrecord.aspx?p=166746.

Joppke, C. "The Retreat of Multiculturalism in the Liberal State: Theory and Policy." *The British Journal of Sociology* 55, no. 2 (June 1, 2004): 237–57. doi:10.1111/j.1468-4446.2004.00017.x.

Modood, T. *Multiculturalism.* John Wiley & Sons, 2013.

Pelinka, A., and D. Ronen. *The Challenge of Ethnic Conflict, Democracy and Self-Determination in Central Europe.* Routledge, 2013.

Singapore, ed. *Census of Population 2010.* Singapore: Singapore Department of Statistics, 2010.

Singapore Statutes Online. "Constitution of the Republic of Singapore." Accessed June 11, 2015. http://statutes.agc.gov.sg/aol/search/display/view.w3p;page=0;query=DocId%3A%22cf2412ff-fca5-4a64-a8ef-b95b8987728e%22%20Status%3Ainforce%20Depth%3A0;rec=0.

Stotz, D. "Breaching the Peace: Struggles around Multilingualism in Switzerland." *Language Policy* 5, no. 3 (July 13, 2006): 247–65. doi:10.1007/s10993-006-9025-4.

Summermatter, S., and A. Mombelli. "Immigration: One Vote, Many Questions." *SWI Swissinfo.ch.* Accessed June 12, 2015. http://www.swissinfo.ch/eng/vote-faqs_immigration--one-vote--many-questions/38007016.

Swiss Confederation. "Federal Constitution of the Swiss Confederation." Accessed June 11, 2015. https://www.admin.ch/opc/en/classified-compilation/19995395/201405180000/101.pdf.

Swiss Federal Statistical Office. "Swiss Statistics — Key Figures." Accessed June 11, 2015. http://www.bfs.admin.ch/bfs/portal/en/index/themen/01/01/key.html.

Swiss Federal Statistical Office. "Swiss Statistics — Languages," May 28, 2015. http://www.bfs.admin.ch/bfs/portal/en/index/themen/01/05/blank/key/ sprachen.html.

Tan, J. "Population White Paper Triggers Nationwide Debate." *Yahoo News Singapore*. Accessed June 11, 2015. https://sg.news.yahoo.com/-yir2013-- population-white-paper-triggers-nationwide-debate-101840966.html.

Thumboo, E. *Cultures in ASEAN and the 21st Century*. Published by UniPress, Centre for the Arts, National University of Singapore for ASEAN-COCI, 1996.

Trocki, C. A. *Singapore: Wealth, Power and the Culture of Control*. Routledge, 2006.

Watts, R. J. and H. Murray. *Die fünfte Landessprache?: Englisch in der Schweiz*. vdf Hochschulverlag AG, 2001.

Weller, M., and K. Nobbs. *Political Participation of Minorities: A Commentary on International Standards and Practice*. Oxford University Press, 2010.

Wimmer, A. "A Swiss Anomaly? A Relational Account of National Boundary-Making: A Relational Account of National Boundary-Making." *Nations and Nationalism* 17, no. 4 (October 2011): 718–37. doi:10.1111/j.1469-8129. 2011.00517.x.

Wong, A. "PM Lee Unveils New 'Singaporeans-First' Policies." *Yahoo News Singapore*. Accessed June 11, 2015. https://sg.news.yahoo.com/blogs/ singaporescene/gov-t-puts-poreans-first-pm-lee-175645736.html.

Wouters, J., S. Van Kerckhoven, and M. Vidal. "The Dynamics of Federalism: Belgium and Switzerland Compared." SSRN Scholarly Paper. Rochester, NY: Social Science Research Network, April 30, 2014. http://papers.ssrn. com.libproxy1.nus.edu.sg/abstract=2431193.

Chapter 10

Migration Policies: Lessons from the Singaporean and Swiss Experiences

Hui Weng Tat and Cindy Helfer[1]

Introduction

The economic development of Singapore and Switzerland has been closely intertwined with immigration. Both countries are exceptions in their own regions. Despite being situated at the heart of Europe, Switzerland, which has been sheltered from major wars and economic crises of the last century, has flourished economically with consistently low unemployment rates. Likewise, Singapore is a prosperous island in the middle of a less advanced and wealthy region. The favourable economic conditions of each country present strong pull-factors to inflows of migrant labour which has become a key factor that shapes economic and political developments in both countries. This paper will examine Switzerland's long experience with migration and the lessons that it can provide for Singapore's public policies to deal with the challenges triggered by labour migration. To do this, it will first examine the similarities and differences between Singapore and Switzerland to better understand how their respective labour markets are affected by migration. The state and impact of migration in Singapore and the current migration-related challenges facing the island, as well as the policy responses adopted by the

[1] Funding support from the Ministry of Education AcRF Tier 1 grant R-603-000-136-112 is gratefully acknowledged.

government, will be reviewed. Finally, the paper will examine Swiss policies on immigration adopted over the last 40 years and the relevance of Switzerland's experience and challenges for Singapore.

Overall Macro Situation

Singapore and Switzerland are both relatively small countries, with population sizes of 5,399,200 (2013)[2] and 8,014,000 people (2012),[3] respectively. Their economic successes are not due to the presence of rich natural resources, as none of the two countries are endowed with such resources (except for water in Switzerland). Trade is, however, a key component of both countries' success. Singapore is one of the most important ports of transit in Southeast Asia, from where its success originates. In 2012, Singapore was ranked as the 14th largest country by international trade in goods, with a total volume of US$788.1 billion amounting to more than two percent of world trade.[4] Switzerland is the world's 20th largest exporter and the 18th largest importer,[5] mainly exporting high-tech, luxury or innovative finished products, produced by a skilled labour force. Both countries are important tourism destinations[6] and also regional hubs for wealth management,[7] and the financial sector is in both places an important economic sector, accounting for

---

[2]"Population & Land Area Statistics (Mid-Year Estimates)." *Statistics Singapore*, June 2013. http://www.singstat.gov.sg/statistics/latest-data#16.

[3]Swiss Federal Statistical Office, "Recent monthly and quarterly figures: provisional data". Population and Households Statistics (STATPOP), Neuchâtel, Retrieved 16 June 2013.

[4]"Short-Term Trade Statistics." *World Trade Organization.* Accessed April 28, 2013. https://www.wto.org/english/res_e/statis_e/statis_e.htm.

[5]"Switzerland." *CIA World Factbook.* Accessed April 28, 2013. https://www.cia.gov/library/publications/the-world-factbook/geos/sz.html.

[6]Switzerland and Singapore are ranked first and 10th in the Travel and Tourism Competitiveness Report 2013. See Blanke, Jennifer, and Thea Chiesa. "Reducing Barriers to Economic Growth and Job Creation." *The Travel & Tourism Competitiveness Report 2013*, Geneva 2013.

[7]UBS, "Wealth Management". Retrieved 18 April 2013 https://www.ubs.com/global/en/wealth_management.html.

approximately 11.6 percent of Switzerland's GDP and 11.9 percent of Singapore's GDP (2013).[8]

Low unemployment

Singapore has enjoyed virtually full employment for long periods of time. Amid an economic slump, the unemployment rate rose beyond 4.0 percent from 2002 to 2004.[9] The resident unemployment rate has since declined to 2.8 percent in 2013.

Switzerland has had a lower unemployment rate than many other European states, as can be seen in Figure 1 below.

Figure 1: Unemployment rates in Singapore and Switzerland

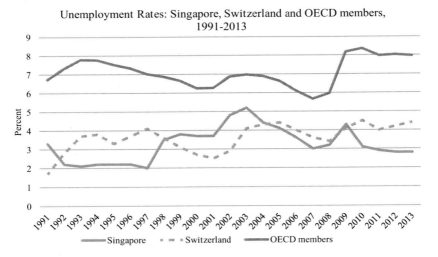

Unemployment Rates: Singapore, Switzerland and OECD members, 1991-2013

Source: The World Bank, World Development Indicators.

---

[8] Department of Statistics Singapore, Share of GDP per industry, http://www.singstat.gov.sg/statistics/visualising_data/chart/Share_Of_GDP_By_Industry.html

[9] Ramesh, S. "Singapore's Q3 Jobless Rate Remains Low, but Employment Growth Slows." *Channel NewsAsia*, October 31, 2012. http://archive.is/puRLZ.

High GDP per capita

Singapore and Switzerland are two developed economies with very high GDP per capita: according to World Bank data, in PPP terms, Singapore is ranked as the country with the 4th highest GDP per capita, with $78,763 PPP (2013), while Switzerland is ranked 7th, with $56,950 PPP (2013).[10] In current US$ terms, Singapore is ranked 9th with $55,182 while Switzerland ranks 7th with $60,380.[11]

Labour shortage

With a falling fertility rate in an ageing society, the relative small domestic populations of those two small countries cannot provide all the required manpower needed to sustain their consistently strong economic

Figure 2:   GDP per capita in Singapore and Switzerland 1990–2013 (PPP $)

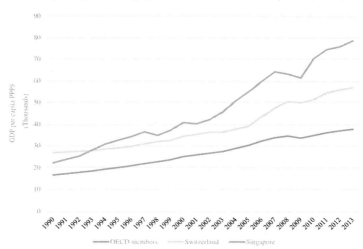

Source: The World Bank, World Development Indicators.

---

[10]"GNI, PPP (Current International $)." *The World Bank*. Accessed May 14, 2015. http://data.worldbank.org/indicator/NY.GNP.MKTP.PP.CD/countries.

[11]"GDP per Capita, PPP (Current International $)." *The World Bank*. Accessed May 14, 2015. http://data.worldbank.org/indicator/NY.GDP.PCAP.PP.CD.

growth. Both Singapore and Switzerland have experienced shortages of labour in many sectors of the economy and therefore are in need of foreign labour to meet demand. Both nations therefore cannot afford to sustain their growth without the intake of migrants, especially those who are highly-skilled.

Diversity of the population and relative openness

As discussed in the previous chapter, a common trait of the Swiss and Singaporean populations is their diversity. In Switzerland, the population comprises four main groups, defined by their language: French, German, Italian, and Romansh. Singapore is also divided into three main groups of different language and culture: Chinese, Tamil, and Malay, speaking four national languages, including English.

Switzerland can be considered an exception among European countries: it has the highest foreign population share, and, at the same time, it has long been the most open country towards foreigners.[12] Switzerland has absorbed a great number of immigrants in the 20th century, even after 1974, when most European countries switched to a restrictive immigration policy.[13]

Therefore, in addition to good job opportunities, high incomes, well-developed infrastructure, and stable and safe political and social environments, Singapore and Switzerland are also regarded as desirable destinations by potential migrants due to the ease of assimilation into their diverse populations.

Foreign worker classification in Singapore and Switzerland

To understand the differences and similarities between foreign workers in Singapore and Switzerland, one needs to know the categories and classifications of migrants in both countries. Singapore and Switzerland use different terminologies and classifications for migrants.

---

[12] De Melo, Jaime, Florence Miguet, and Tobias Müller. "The Political Economy of Migration and EU Enlargement: Lessons from Switzerland." *CESifo*, May 2002.
[13] *Ibid.*

Singapore has a dual policy on migration: one for skilled workers, commonly referred to as *foreign talents*, and another for unskilled workers, who are usually referred to as *foreign workers*. Permits are divided into categories, for which different rules apply: P and Q for skilled professionals, S for the semi-skilled and R for low-skilled migrants expecting lower salaries. Migrant workers are classified under two major categories:

a. *Non-residents*: immigrants who are in Singapore temporarily on the following work passes:

i.   The *P and Q Pass*, or employment pass (*EP Pass*), for professionals, managers and administrator positions with a minimum basic monthly salary of $3,300 and a degree or other professional qualifications;

ii. The *S Pass*, for mid-level associate professionals and technicians positions with a minimum basic monthly salary of $2,200, with the payment of an employer levy and subject to a firm-level quota of 20 percent of the total workforce;

iii. The *R Pass* or work permit, for unskilled or semi-skilled workers with a basic salary of less than $2,200, with the payment of an employer levy and subject to a firm-level quota depending on the industry sector;

b. *Permanent residents (PR)*: for investors or entrepreneurs, spouses and unmarried children of a citizen/PR, and P, Q or S work pass holders who have worked for at least six months in Singapore.

In Switzerland, the classification by the Swiss authorities dates back to 1948, but has been adjusted since:[14]

a. *Frontier worker*: a wholly non-resident worker who commutes daily to Switzerland;

b. *Seasonal workers*: workers with a residence permit for a maximum of nine months, and are employed (most often in the construction or hotel sectors). These are not counted as residents;

---

[14] White, Paul. "Switzerland: From Migrant Rotation to Migrant Communities." *Geography* 70, no. 2 (1985): 168–71.

c. *Annual workers*: workers with limited social security rights, who may bring in dependents after 15 months. Until the mid-60s, annual status was often accorded to new workers on their first trip, but such generosity was abandoned in the face of public opinion. Annual permits are renewable depending on the labour market conditions;

d. *Established status*: holders with full social security benefits, including both unemployment and pension rights. This status can be obtained after 10 years as an annual permit holder on renewable three-year terms.

In both Singapore and Switzerland, immigration policies are balanced between economic interests, on one hand, which favour more liberal immigration policies; and public opinion, on the other hand, which favours stricter regulation of migration, for concerns of national identity, job competition and for other social reasons.

Composition of migrants

Singapore has traditionally been the destination of choice for labourers from China, India, and the Malay Archipelago. While Singapore favours migrants from these traditional countries to preserve the ethnic composition of the island,[15] an increasing number of migrants now come from other countries, such as Thailand or Myanmar, in order to meet the Singaporean demand for workers. Singapore pays relatively high salaries, which attract skilled migrants from all over the world. However, the majority of the foreign workforce in Singapore comprises lower-skilled workers. For example, of the 1,321,600 foreigners working in Singapore at end 2013, 74 percent of them are holders of lower-skilled work permits (*R Pass*).

Switzerland has been a destination primarily for employment-seeking Italians, French and Germans and then for Portuguese and Turks (including Kurds), as well as Eastern European dissidents such as Yugoslavians and Albanians. Switzerland is also a destination for asylum-seekers from all

---

[15] In 2010, compared to 2000 (figures in parenthesis), the racial composition was as follows: 74.1% (76.8%) Chinese, 13.4% (13.9%) Malay, 9.2% (7.9%) Indian and 3.3% (1.4%) of other races. Singapore Census of Population (2010).

over the world. The largest immigrant groups in Switzerland are those from Italy, Germany, the Former Yugoslavia, Albania, Portugal, and Turkey which, together, account for about 1.5 million people (60 percent of the Swiss population with an immigrant background), or close to 20 percent of the total Swiss population. About two-thirds of foreign workers (69 percent in 2011) are citizens of an EU or EFTA country. Half of them come from either Germany (27 percent) or Italy (23 percent).[16]

The migrant populations are large mainly because of the pull factors created by networks of migrants already established in Switzerland. Networks create information streams and support groups that induce migrants to move. As an example, in 1998, 50 percent of immigrants entered as workers and 45 percent for family reunification purposes.

Immigrants generally have lower skill levels than native Swiss. Moreover, even in cases of comparable skill levels, they usually have salaries and occupational status below those of natives, and smaller chances of reaching high hierarchical positions.[17]

Public concerns with migrants

In both Singapore and Switzerland, there is popular demand to stabilise the number of foreigners. In Switzerland, a number of popular initiatives — a tool of direct democracy which allows the Swiss people to suggest law in Switzerland — have demonstrated the concerns of the Swiss people about the number of immigrants entering the country, and portrayed the disagreement of the Swiss people with the public policy responses by the government to this influx. The extreme-right has repeatedly suggested limiting the number of migrants in the total population.[18] On the other hand, leftist parties have proposed equality of rights (except for political rights)

---

[16] Federal Statistical Office, *Employment and Income from Employment*, Panorama, February 2013.

[17] Müller, Tobias, and José V. Ramirez. "Wage Inequality and Segregation between Native and Immigrant Workers in Switzerland: Evidence Using Matched Employee-Employer Data." SSRN Scholarly Paper. Rochester, NY: Social Science Research Network, January 1, 2009. http://papers.ssrn.com.libproxy1.nus.edu.sg/abstract=1703013.

[18] One of the most famous campaigns by the Swiss people's party (UDC) painted foreigners as a black sheep, expelled from the Swiss territory by white sheep; this campaign triggered massive reactions within Switzerland, and international outrage.

between migrants and locals. Even though those initiatives have rarely been confirmed through popular votes, they have influenced the policies of the government.

In Singapore, while public opinion is generally less vocal, Singaporeans have also manifested their concerns and fears towards the increasing presence of migrants in Singapore such as during the 2013 announcement of the Population White Paper, which projected a population of 6.9 million by 2030.

Differences between Singapore and Switzerland

Singapore and Switzerland are situated in opposite parts of the world. They have a very different history and contrasting political systems and relationships with democracy. The Singaporean and Swiss populations are different in terms of ethnicity, and also cultural and political sensibilities. Moreover, Singapore's population is fully urban, which is not the case with Switzerland. Switzerland also has a longer history of industrial and economic development. The labour migrant policies of the two countries are also dissimilar: for example, a major difference is that Switzerland does not impose a levy system as implemented in Singapore.

Foreign labour in Singapore

In Singapore, migrants form a very important part of the labour force. In 1970, foreign labour numbered about 21,000, or 3.2 percent of the total workforce. This increased almost four-fold to 80,000 or 7.4 percent of the workforce in 1980.[19] By end-2013, there were 1.322 million foreign workers in Singapore, constituting 37.8 percent of the total employment. By composition, 42.9 percent of the general population of Singapore was not born on the island, placing it among the top 10 countries in the world with the highest share of international migrants in their total population. The growth of Singapore's foreign workforce is due to the small domestic labour force and the rapid economic growth of Singapore's city-state, which resulted in the need for foreign labour inflow to relieve the acute shortage of labour. The strong economic growth is supported by the fact

---

[19]"Census of Population." *Statistics Singapore*. Accessed April 28, 2013. http://www.singstat.gov.sg/statistics/browse-by-theme/census-of-population.

Figure 3:   Foreigners as proportion of population in Singapore, 1980–2014

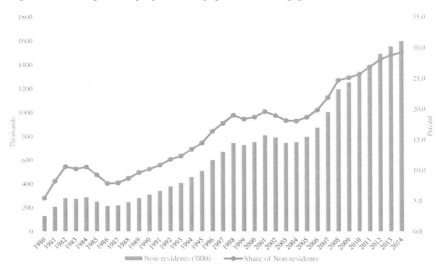

Source: Singapore Department of Statistics.

that Singapore's labour force has a very high percentage of proficient English-language speakers, making it an attractive place for investments by multinational corporations.

The share of foreigners in Singapore's population has rapidly increased over the last decades. As of June 2014, more than 29 percent of Singapore's population of 5.4 million people comprised foreign-born temporary residents (Figure 3). When foreign-born permanent residents are included, the share increases to about 39 percent.[20] This figure was 26 percent in 2000 and only 9 percent in 1980, indicating the significant surge in the non-citizen population over the past three decades.

Immigration policies in Singapore

Until the 2011 general elections, Singapore had a very liberal immigration policy, allowing the country to bring in much of the manpower that helped

---

[20]"Department of Statistics: Key Demographic Indicators." *Statistics Singapore*. Accessed September 30, 2014. http://www.singstat.gov.sg/statistics/browse-by-theme/population-and-population-structure.

fuel its rapid economic growth over the past decade. This boosted its population by nearly 32 percent since 2000.[21]

The number of migrants allowed to enter the country is determined by market demand driven by the growth of the economy. Controls take the form of minimum qualifying salaries for the P and Q passes, and levies and maximum shares of foreigners in a company's total employment, or dependency ratios, for the more restrictive R permits. The S Pass has requirements for minimum salaries, levies and dependency ratios. The dependency ratios vary across industrial sectors with higher quotas for construction, followed by manufacturing, and then by the service industry. These quotas have evolved over time based on the ability of companies to fill vacancies with local employees.

As shown in Table 1, a substantial proportion of foreign labour in Singapore comprises the lower-skilled workers in the R category.

The government also makes a distinction between traditional and *non-traditional* countries of emigration, and favours the first category based on the argument that migrants from "traditional" countries of immigration, such as neighbouring Malaysia, integrate more easily in the Singaporean society than those from "non-traditional" countries (India, China, Philippines, Thailand, Bangladesh, Sri Lanka and Myanmar, for example). Moreover, because of its history and geopolitical position, Singapore is also sensitive to keeping a stable ethnic composition through the years, which influences its immigration policies and its preference of migrants from "traditional" lands.

The relatively liberal policy changed after the 2011 general elections, when a tightening of migration policies was effectively implemented as a result of Singaporeans' discontent towards immigration policies that have boosted the number of foreign residents. Many citizens blamed the influx of workers for overcrowding in public transport, soaring home prices and depressed low-end pay. The unhappiness was reflected in the final election results which showed an erosion of the general population's support of the

---

[21] Wong, Chun Han. "Singapore Tightens Hiring Rules for Foreign Skilled Labor." *Wall Street Journal*, September 23, 2013. http://www.wsj.com/articles/SB10001424052702303 75960457909286388803466.

Table 1: Foreign Workforce in Singapore

	2007	2008	2009	2010	2011	2012	2013	2014
Total Foreign Workforce Number	900,800	1,057,700	1,053,500	1,113,200	1,197,900	1,268,300	1,321,600	1,355,700
Pass Type Share								
P & Q Pass	11.0	10.7	10.8	12.9	14.6	13.7	13.2	13.2
S Pass	4.9	7.0	7.9	8.9	9.5	11.2	12.2	12.5
Work Permit (R)	84.0	82.3	80.8	77.7	75.2	74.3	73.7	73.1

Source: Singapore Ministry of Manpower.

governing party, the People's Action Party (PAP), to a level which was the lowest since 1965.[22]

To further placate public discontent, as well as to reduce employer discrimination against locals, new rules, in the form of the 'Fair Consideration Framework,' were implemented in 2014. Employers who intend to apply for foreign work passes or permits must first consider Singapore citizens for the job in question and the position must be advertised in a government job bank portal for at least two weeks.

The impact of migration in Singapore

The main impacts of migration on Singaporean economy and society can be felt in the following areas: economic and entrepreneurship development, productivity growth, unemployment, work discipline, income disparities, the fiscal budget, and property prices, among others.[23] It is instructive to analyse these by classifying them according to their positive and negative economic impacts. Immigration to Singapore has had the following positive results:

Economic development. Migrants have helped Singapore sustain its high growth rates[24] since independence, providing the city-state with requisite manpower and skills to alleviate its labour force shortage. Low-skilled migrants have benefited businesses and exports, and contributed to the construction of the nation's infrastructure. High-skilled migrants have provided Singapore with knowledge and expertise, essential to the shift in Singapore's economy from labour-intensive to capital-intensive industries and enhancing economic growth through higher productivity and innovation. The ready availability of labour augmented by the inflow of migrants in Singapore has minimised the risk of labour shortages, thereby helping to attract foreign investments.

---

[22] *Ibid.*

[23] Hui, Weng Tat. "Foreign Manpower Policy in Singapore." In *Singapore Economy in the 21st Century: Issues and Strategies.* McGraw-Hill, 2002.

[24] Singapore growth was been between 8–10 percent in the 80s, between 6–11 percent in the 1990s (except 1998: -2.2 percent) and between 2–15 percent in the 2000s.

Entrepreneurship. Generally, migrants, by self-selection, tend to have a greater appetite for risk-taking due to their stronger aspirations and motivation to succeed. Moreover, because being self-employed is a way to avoid discrimination or cultural difficulties faced when one has to adapt to a foreign working environment, the proportion of migrants who are entrepreneurs is higher than among locals, especially for migrants with higher skills. In 2004, as part of Singapore's overall plan to become a regional business hub and attract the best business and entrepreneurial minds to the country,[25] the Entrepreneur Pass (EntrePass) scheme was introduced to lure foreign entrepreneurs with innovative business proposals wishing to start a business in Singapore with least a 30 percent ownership of company shares.

Buffer against cyclical fluctuations. Migrant workers act as a buffer to protect the local workforce in the case of an economic downturn. For example, during the 1985 economic recession in Singapore, employers chose to retrench the foreigners first, sparing local workers. However, even though this argument is used by Singapore political leaders to justify the continuing presence of many foreigners, there is no law or obligation that compels firms to terminate the employment of foreign workers before that of locals. Although it might be argued that foreigners are likely to be fired first, as firms usually invest less in training them than in locals, they might be retained as their wages are usually lower than locals.

Work discipline. Migrants are usually very motivated to succeed, which is the objective of their journey. Therefore, foreigners often work harder than locals, leading to increased competition among workers, which in turn leads to increased workforce productivity. For example, Hong Kong professionals who migrated to Singapore in large numbers in the 1990s brought with them a positive and competitive work ethic which helped Singapore develop, and instilled similar productive traits in the local workforce. This is seen as a factor which could help sustain Singapore's competitive position in the region.

---

[25] "Singapore Entrepreneur Visa." *Guide Me Singapore*. Accessed April 28, 2013. http://www.guidemesingapore.com/relocation/work-pass/singapore-entrepreneur-pass-guide.

Immigration to Singapore has also had mixed or even negative consequences:

Income inequality. The influx of foreign workers has been cited as one of the contributing factors to worsening income inequality in Singapore. This deteriorating disparity in income may be attributed to the depression of wage levels and the dampening of wage increases of the unskilled and semi-skilled workers; this is a result of a ready pool of foreign workers who are prepared to work at wages substantially below those for local workers. Hui and Toh,[26] for example, show that prior to 2005, the wage disparity in Singapore actually narrowed or remained stable. However, with the surge in foreign worker inflow from 2006, the wage disparity in Singapore began to increase significantly. Wage depression has four major consequences within society: first, it makes low-wage jobs unattractive to locals, and lowers full-time employment for local workers. Second, it triggers the need for subsidies to locals and for the creation and improvement of a social support scheme. Third, low wages have an adverse impact on workers' perception of fairness, affecting their morale and productivity. Finally, all those adverse effects lead to a potential fracture of social cohesion.

Lower productivity. Although Singapore welcomes lower-skilled foreign workers, they are discouraged from permanent migration as they are only allowed to renew their work permits up to a certain number of years. Employers therefore find it necessary to replenish this revolving pool of workers with fresh foreign workers to replace those who have reached their maximum duration of stay. There are productivity downsides associated with the revolving pool of lower-skilled foreign workers. This constant attrition effectively represents a depletion of trained human capital which results in lower productivity for the workers in aggregate. The adverse effect of foreign labour on productivity is most apparent in the construction sector, where the ready access to foreign labour has resulted in the reluctance of contractors to invest in skills upgrading and

---

[26]Hui, Weng Tat, and Ruby Toh. "Growth with Equity in Singapore: Challenges and Prospects" Conditions of Work and Employment Series No. 48, Conditions of Work and Employment Branch, International Labour Office, Geneva, March 2014.

labour-saving techniques, contributing to persistent negative or low productivity growth in this sector. Low wages resulting from the presence of migrants also depress the morale of workers. If perceived to be unfairly treated due to low wages, workers are likely to lack motivation to give their best effort, and would instead perform at a lower level of productivity in their jobs.

Fiscal implications. Wage depression caused by the influx of low-skilled foreign migrants has also meant that new social protection measures have to be put in place to support the meagre income of low-wage Singaporeans. From 2007, the Workfare Income Supplement Scheme (WIS) was introduced as a new pillar in the social safety net system in Singapore. Under the WIS, low-wage workers aged 35 earning less than $1,900 per month receive payouts every quarter to supplement their wages and retirement savings. This scheme cost about $650 million per year in 2013 and was expected to benefit up to 480,000 local workers.[27]

Low-skilled migrants, because of their very low pay, also tend to place a relatively higher demand on public services. This is especially evident on weekends where large numbers of foreign workers congregate in various areas in Singapore, creating congestion in public transport systems and public spaces. This in turn requires additional public investment spending in social services and infrastructural investments in buses and the mass rapid transport system. Land on which special housing dormitories could be built also had to be set aside to house over 900,000 work permit holders. For the smaller number of high-skilled foreign talent who have access to well-paid jobs, they are generally net contributors to the fiscal budget.

Property price escalation. While foreign construction workers have contributed immensely towards the building of homes for residents, the effect of skilled foreigners on housing prices has also been an issue. During 1992 to 1996, escalating property prices left many Singaporeans worried and resentful that private properties might eventually be priced beyond their affordability. It heightened public awareness and concern

---

[27]"Singapore Budget Speech 2013." *Ministry of Finance*. Accessed April 28, 2013. http://www.singaporebudget.gov.sg/budget_2013/budget_speech.html.

over the increased pressures that foreign buyers might exert on housing prices. Calls for restrictions on home ownership by foreigners led to the introduction of measures in May 1996 which targeted property speculation by non-citizens. These include restricting access to Singapore-dollar loans for foreigners wishing to buy residential properties. Non-resident sellers also had to set aside withholding taxes for properties that are resold within three years. Under the new guidelines, foreign investors seeking permanent residence in Singapore, who formerly could invest up to 50 percent of their $1 million deposit in residential properties, were required to invest the full amount of a higher $1.5 million deposit in productive economic ventures. Since 2009, due to quantitative easing measures and the low interest rate environment in other countries, restrictions on property purchases by foreigners in the form of an additional buyer stamp duty of up to 15 percent imposed on foreign nationals have been introduced in addition to other cooling measures to ward off potential inflationary pressures in the property market.

Political tensions. Singapore has been criticised by migrants' home countries for its poor treatment of their nationals in Singapore. Scandals, such as the death of many Thai workers in the 1990s, or the inability of migrants to withdraw their Central Provident Fund (CPF) savings, created some political tensions with Thailand, Malaysia, and other countries. These could potentially have an adverse impact on the economic front.

Nation building and identity. In the 1960s, most migrants came from neigbouring Malaysia, and had no problems with assimilation. But as the supply from Malaysia dried up, migrants increasingly hailed from countries with a bigger cultural gap, such as Thailand and Myanmar. With a higher proportion of migrants, Singaporean society is suffering from a loss of its own identity. This problem has increased during the last decades, as more and more migrants come from countries that are culturally different from Singapore.

Discrimination. Male Singaporeans are required to attend mandatory annual reservist training in the uniformed services. They thus have to be released from regular work for a few weeks every year, after their compulsory two years of full-time national service at age 19. This has caused discontent among Singaporean employees who fear being subject to discrimination by employers, as they may hire equally qualified foreigners with no national service liability and who are therefore potentially more attractive due to their less disrupted work schedule.

Economic restructuring. The availability of low-skilled, low-paid migrant workers risks hindering economic restructuring. It is argued that Singapore has missed out on potentially beneficial restructuring in the past two decades.[28] Instead of moving towards capital-intensive methods of production and shifting out labour-intensive industries, many Singaporean firms are still stuck in the cycle of labour-intensive methods of production. Singapore therefore has "missed the train" to economic modernisation, unlike some advanced European countries and South Korea, a situation that Singapore is now trying to remedy.

The benefits of migration generally outweigh the costs, according to policymakers. The official policy stance is that Singapore should continue to fine-tune the calibration of its inflow of foreigners as the country continues to face an ageing population and a shrinking workforce. The Singapore government asserts that the current overall foreign workforce helps companies greatly, as they raise productivity through business restructuring and workforce retraining.[29] The foreign workforce should complement the local resident workforce and not replace Singaporean citizens.[30]

Since its independence, Singapore has relied on economic growth to produce its wealth. This impressive growth has been made possible by massive immigration to the city-state. However, now that Singapore is a developed state, it cannot reasonably aim at growing at an annual rate of

---

[28]Ngiam, Tong Dow. "Singapore must achieve more with less." *The Business Times.* March 14, 2012,

[29]"MTI Occasional Paper on Population and Economy." *Ministry of Trade and Industry.* September 25, 2012. https://www.mti.gov.sg/mtiinsights/pages/mti-occasional-paper-on-population-and-economy.aspx.

[30]"National Population and Talent Division." *Government of Singapore.* Accessed April 28, 2013. http://www.nptd.gov.sg/ and Singapore Workforce Development Agency (WDA)." *Government of Singapore.* Accessed April 28, 2013. http://www.wda.gov.sg/.

above five percent. Reasonable estimates forecast that the domestic labour force can only grow at approximately 1–1.5 percent, and consequently, that Singapore cannot expect more than a three to four percent GDP growth to be sustainable.

Policymakers have been trying to strike a balance in keeping Singapore a top destination for foreign investors and new immigrants — seen as a way to offset the low birth rate — while containing the anti-foreigner sentiment. The government has, in recent years, tightened immigration controls, including increasing financial barriers for foreign workers seeking entry, and handing Singaporeans more benefits in areas like education and healthcare.[31]

The government has adopted measures to wean Singapore off a growth model that has been heavily dependent on labour force expansion. In recent years, efforts have been made to cut Singapore's dependence on skilled and unskilled foreign labour by increasing the foreign worker levy for the lower-skilled and imposing higher qualifying salaries. For example, in January 2014, the minimum monthly compensation threshold that companies had to pay individuals on employment passes (work permits issued to foreign executives and managerial professionals) was raised to S$3,300 (US$2,636) from S$3,000. And starting from August 2014, through the Fair Consideration Framework, companies with more than 25 employees have had to advertise all positions with fixed monthly salaries of less than S$12,000 dollars for a minimum of two weeks on a government-run job bank. These are also part of the efforts to curb discriminatory hiring practices and to encourage employers to give Singaporeans a fair chance at job opportunities.

Despite these policies and efforts to cope with the challenges triggered by migration, Singapore has not yet overcome them all. This paper will now turn to the Swiss example and experience. We will study how Switzerland has coped with migration challenges since the end of World War Two (WWII). Then we will assess if some of these lessons learnt can be inferred from the Swiss experience to help the Singaporean government shape its future labour market policies.

---

[31] Wong, Chun Han. "Singapore Tightens Hiring Rules for Foreign Skilled Labor."

Foreign Labour in Switzerland

Switzerland has had a substantial share of migrant workers for more than a century. The number of foreigners has been on the rise in the early years after WWII, when Switzerland attracted a significant number of immigrants. However, the situation began to change after the 1960s when the country started to adopt more restrictive immigration policies.[32] Despite migration barriers and a slight adjustment following the 1973 oil crisis, the foreign population has grown more sharply than the Swiss population, rising to 20 percent of the total population by 2000.[33] For the second part of the 20th century, the stock of foreigners in Switzerland has more than tripled,[34] placing Switzerland among the countries with the highest proportion of foreign residents in Europe. The population growth in Switzerland is driven mainly by immigration: for example, of the population growth rate of 1.1 percent during 2009, about 0.2 percent is due to births, and 0.9 percent due to immigration.

Immigration policies in Switzerland from 1945

Swiss immigration policy has been shaped by economic interest groups which are opposed to tight quotas and parts of the population who favour immigration control. Switzerland's long history with immigration started in the late 19th century when the country became prosperous through its industrialisation and banking activities. From that time until the 1960s, Switzerland established liberal policies, keeping its borders wide open.

In the post-WWII period, Switzerland experienced strong economic growth. This was due to the opportunity for Switzerland's intact industry (an exception to European war destruction) to meet rising domestic and regional demand for goods. During this period of growth, labour shortages

---

[32] De Melo, Jaime, Florence Miguet, and Tobias Müller. "The Political Economy of Migration and EU Enlargement: Lessons from Switzerland."

[33] Tai, Silvio H. T. "Market Structure and the Link between Migration and Trade." *Review of World Economics / Weltwirtschaftliches Archiv* 145, no. 2 (2009): 225–49. http://www.jstor.org/stable/40441179.

[34] De Melo, Jaime, Florence Miguet, and Tobias Müller. "The Political Economy of Migration and EU Enlargement: Lessons from Switzerland."

Figure 4: Switzerland — permanent foreign residents as a percentage of total population, 1900–2011

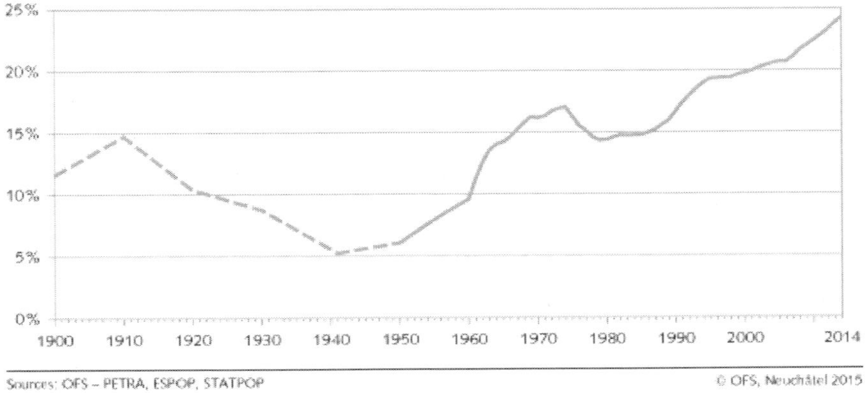

Sources: OFS – PETRA, ESPOP, STATPOP   © OFS, Neuchâtel 2015

Source: Swiss Statistics: Migration and integration. Retrieved 10 June 2016. http://www.bfs.admin.ch/ bfs/portal/fr/index/themen/01/07/blank/key/01/01.html

in Switzerland were filled by immigrants attracted to Switzerland's economic health. The share of foreigners in the population increased from 5.8 percent to 9.1 percent between 1950 and 1960.[35]

In the 1950s, Switzerland adopted a *laissez-faire* strategy, and regarded immigration as temporary.[36] A system of seasonal workers, involving workers coming for a short period of time, was established. This policy aimed to create a "rotation" system, with migrants providing labour supply to Swiss industries for a short period only, discouraging the workers from establishing roots in Switzerland. In 1948, Switzerland signed a bilateral recruitment agreement with Italy to be provided with a foreign labour force, which was the beginning of a massive immigration trend, mainly consisting of seasonal workers (working under a "permit A", valid for nine months).[37] This system is similar to Singapore's current

---

[35] *Ibid.*

[36] Piguet, Etienne, and Hans Mahnig. *Quotas d'immigration: l'expérience suisse*. Bureau international du travail, 2000. http://www.karch.ch/repository/default/content/sites/sfm/ files/shared/pub/o/o_03.pdf.

[37] Permit B was valid annually and could be renewable, and permit C was a long-term permit.

policy for short-term low-skilled migrants, whose permits cannot be renewed indefinitely.

In the early 1960s, the Swiss economy over-heated, and tensions regarding the large number of migrants arose.[38] The Federal Council, the executive branch of the Swiss government, started implementing admission restrictions aimed at limiting the inflow of immigrants. The 1963 and 1964 federal orders established a system of foreign/local workforce quotas at the firm-level. Companies required the government's permission to recruit foreign workers, and migrants were not to exceed an additional three percent of the firm's existing percentage of migrants in the workforce. This firm-based quota is similar to the current practice in Singapore.

However, this policy was a failure due to many Swiss workers moving from secondary to tertiary jobs at that time. In 1964, Italy pressured Switzerland to renegotiate the 1948 bilateral recruiting agreement, leading to important improvements in the legal situation of Italian immigrants in Switzerland. Italy asked for the "residence permit" procedures and family reunification to be eased, and for better unemployment and health insurance for guest workers. This renegotiation aroused opposition in Switzerland, triggering the creation of several anti-immigration movements.[39]

In 1970, the Swiss population rejected a rather xenophobic proposal, termed the *Schwarzenbach* initiative, which aimed to limit foreign workers to Switzerland to 10 percent and required the deportation of up to 300,000 foreigners over four years. This initiative, even after it was rejected by 45 percent of votes cast, pushed the government to adopt a policy of stabilisation. In the 1970s, the government shifted from a firm-based cap to a federal cap on the numbers of migrants allowed to enter Switzerland to work — a system that is partly still in force today.[40] The annually-set federal quotas aimed at controlling the number of migrant

---

[38] De Melo, Jaime, Florence Miguet, and Tobias Müller. "The Political Economy of Migration and EU Enlargement: Lessons from Switzerland."

[39] *Ibid.*

[40] Chancellerie fédérale. "Message relatif à l'initiative populaire «Contre l'immigration de masse»," December 7, 2012. https://www.admin.ch/opc/fr/federal-gazette/2013/279.pdf.

inflow to the country, while also providing certain industries and regions with the labour force they needed. This quota-based policy was successful as it diminished the numbers of migrants from 70,000 to 50,000 in its first year of implementation; as a result, xenophobia declined as well.[41] Initially, the mobility of migrants was restricted and they could not change their employer for the first year of employment. This is somewhat similar to Singapore's current policy which prohibits any changes of employers for foreign workers.

In 1975, when the oil crisis struck Switzerland, the government used migrants as a cyclical buffer by refusing to renew their work permits. In addition, immigrants were the first ones to be fired. Switzerland therefore managed to "export" unemployment during this economic downturn.

In the 1980s, the favourable economic conditions in Switzerland brought about a renewed demand for labour, which was filled by a massive influx of foreign workers.[42] This period saw the diversification of immigration motives through an increasing number of asylum-seekers, which were not included in the quotas; it also saw a major change in the political context, with Switzerland getting closer to the European Union (EU).

In 1991, the Federal Council adopted a new admission policy to the Swiss labour market called the "three circles model",[43] and distinguished or discriminated between migrants from different countries of origin, according to their "cultural proximity"[44] to Switzerland Such discrimination is similar to Singapore's preference towards migrants from the so-called "traditional" countries.

In 1996, the Federal Council established a commission on immigration, the Hug Commission, to establish a new policy on immigration, which ultimately resulted in the drafting of a new law on immigration. In 1998, the

---

[41]De Melo, Jaime, Florence Miguet, and Tobias Müller. "The Political Economy of Migration and EU Enlargement: Lessons from Switzerland."

[42]Chancellerie fédérale. "Message relatif à l'initiative populaire «Contre l'immigration de masse»."

[43]The first circle is made of EU/EFTA countries, the second includes Canada, the US and Eastern European countries and the third includes all other countries.

[44]De Melo, Jaime, Florence Miguet, and Tobias Müller. "The Political Economy of Migration and EU Enlargement: Lessons from Switzerland."

Swiss government abandoned the system of three circles[45] and considered a system based on points, like that in Canada and Australia, but eventually decided against its adoption. Instead, the system adopted distinguishes between migrants from member states of the EU/EFTA and those from all other countries (two-circle policy). This system has the benefit of lowering xenophobia while satisfying the needs of the economy. The government also abolished the seasonal worker status that became impracticable with the increasingly close relations with the EU. This triggered some discontent among a large part of the Swiss population, including in the construction and hotel industries, where many of such seasonal workers were employed.[46] With continuing strong labour demand in the 1990s, the proportion of foreigners continued to rise to reach more than 20 percent of the population.[47]

In 2002, a bilateral agreement with the EU on the free movement of people was implemented after its approval by the Swiss people, through a national referendum (67.2 percent voted in favour). This was later complemented by the Swiss entry into the Schengen zone (2004) and the signature of the Dublin agreements on asylum-seekers (2008).[48] Under this free movement agreement, individuals from EU or EFTA member states, regardless of their qualifications, were granted easy access to the Swiss labour market.

In January 2008, the current Swiss federal law on foreigners, the Foreign Nationals Act,[49] came into force. This law replaced the Federal Act on the Residence of Foreigners of 1931. It restricted the admission of people from non-EU/EFTA countries (so-called "third states") to skilled workers who were urgently required and were likely to integrate successfully in the long term. These quotas were decided nationally and yearly, and were adjusted to take into account economic fluctuations as well as public opinion (e.g., waves of xenophobia).[50] De facto, the possibility of recruiting unskilled workers from outside of Europe was abolished, with the exception of

---

[45] *Ibid.*

[46] *Ibid.*

[47] De Melo, Jaime, Florence Miguet, and Tobias Müller. "The Political Economy of Migration and EU Enlargement: Lessons from Switzerland."

[48] *Ibid.*

[49] This is the federal law of 16 December 2005 on foreigners.

[50] White, Paul. "Switzerland: From Migrant Rotation to Migrant Communities."

family reunification and asylum applications. The law not only limits the "third state" citizens to a certain category (skilled workers), but it also puts a cap on their number by establishing yearly quotas. In 2012, this was set at 3,500 residency permits and 5,000 short-term permits.[51]

Coping with Migration–Related Issues and Challenges in Switzerland

Poverty and low wages

Just as in Singapore, the presence of migrant workers also exerts a downward influence on wages. A job is usually considered a "low-wage job" (or at the low end of the wage scale) if the wage (calculated on the basis of a full-time job of 40 hours per week) amounts to less than two-thirds of the gross median wage. In 2010, this corresponded to a wage of less than CHF3,986 per month (S$5,423) in Switzerland and included some 275,000 low-wage jobs, accounting for 10.5 percent of all jobs in the labour market. Half of these low-wage jobs are found in the "retail trade" sector, food and beverage service activities and services to buildings and landscape activities. The share of low-wage workers is much lower than in Singapore. This may be attributed to the social contract in Switzerland with strong union representation against low-wage exploitation and poor working conditions.[52] Low-wage incidence also presents a less serious issue in Switzerland than in Singapore (Figure 5) because Switzerland has more extensive welfare provisions than Singapore. Switzerland's public social spending as a share of GDP was about 20 percent in 2013, just slightly below the OECD average of 22 percent.[53] The absolute poverty rate in Switzerland decreased from 12.5 percent pre-welfare, to 3.8 percent post-welfare, in the period of 1960 to 1991 — a relatively low rate compared to most developed

[51] *Ibid.*
[52] Alleva, Vania, and Mauro Moretto. "Domestic Workers in Switzerland Protected by the Country's First Sectoral Employment Contract." *Global Labour Column*, February 2011. http://www.global-labour-university.org/fileadmin/GLU_Column/papers/no_47_Alleva___Moretto.pdf.
[53] "Social Expenditure — Aggregated Data." *OECD Statistics*. Accessed April 28, 2013. http://stats.oecd.org/Index.aspx?datasetcode=SOCX_AGG.

Figure 5:   International comparison of low-wage incidence, 2012

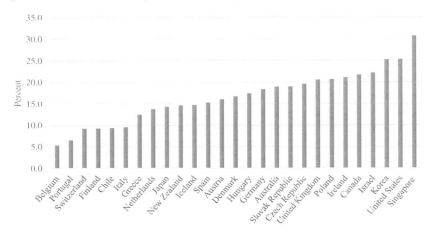

Source: OECD Stats and Ministry of Manpower Singapore.[56]

countries.[54] The risk of falling in the poverty zone is lower in Switzerland than in Europe on average.[55]

Income inequality

In Switzerland, income inequality is also less pronounced. The Gini coefficient after taxes and transfers of Switzerland is 0.28 (2012), much lower than Singapore's 0.46 (Figure 6). The income disparity before taxes and transfers has, however, been rising. Top salaries at the largest Swiss companies stood at 93 times those of the lowest-paid workers in 2011, according to the Swiss Federation of Trade Unions. In 1998, the ratio was just 14 times.[57]

Pay differences have also increased at small and mid-sized companies, although not as quickly. Including all Swiss companies, the ratio between

---

[54] Kenworthy, Lane. "Do Social-Welfare Policies Reduce Poverty? A Cross-National Assessment." *Social Forces* 77, no. 3 (March 1, 1999): 1119–39. doi:10.1093/sf/77.3.1119.

[55] "Poverty Remains a Threat in Land of Plenty." *SWI swissinfo.ch*, December 18, 2012. http://www.swissinfo.ch/eng/struggle-street_poverty-remains-a-threat-in-land-of-plenty/34447884.

[56] The data for OECD is based on 2/3 of the median in 2011 and 2012. For Singapore, it is estimated using data of full-time resident workers (excluding employer CPF).

[57] Revill, John. "Swiss to Vote on Executive Pay." *Wall Street Journal*, March 20, 2013. http://www.wsj.com/articles/SB10001424127887324103504578372203886463598.

Figure 6: International comparison of income inequality, 2012

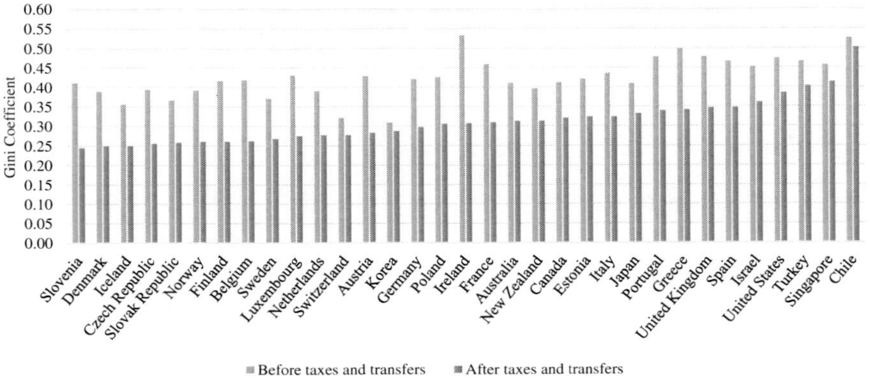

■ Before taxes and transfers   ■ After taxes and transfers

Source: OECD Statistics.

the median wages of the highest and lowest earners grew from 7.6 times in 1996 to 8.5 times in 2010 (Swiss Federal Statistics Office).[58] The Swiss are therefore increasingly concerned about the gap between a wealthy executive class and average workers. While the wages of employees were traditionally established during salary negotiations between unions and management, acting as social partners, a substantial part of the population wished to see the government's involvement in the process, in order to further reduce salary inequalities. An initiative was launched by the youth socialist movement to implement a "fairer salary system", in which top managers could earn a maximum of 12 times the lowest paid employee of their company. This initiative, which was named "1:12", reflected the belief that no one in a Swiss company should earn more in a month than what someone else makes in a year. This proposal to limit executive pay was an effort to govern corporate compensations, after Switzerland had approved one of the world's strictest say-on-pay[59] rules.[60] With more than 100,000 signatures collected in support of this initiative (the

[58] *Ibid.*

[59] The Swiss initiative "against rip-off salaries" of March 2013 was a successful popular initiative to control executive pay of companies listed on the Swiss stock market, and to increase shareholders' say in corporate governance. The vote passed with a majority of 67.9%, with a 46% turnout.

[60] *Ibid.*

threshold to call for a public vote), the initiative was presented to the people in November 2013, but it was ultimately defeated by 65 percent of the votes cast.

Avoiding structural unemployment

Until the beginning of the 1990s, unemployment was not a problem in Switzerland. Since 1940 it had generally been under one percent. This stability was attributable to various factors, including the Swiss brand of industrial peace, in which firms refrained from firing workers during economic downturns, together with the use of immigration policy, in which the foreign workforce was used as a buffer to stabilise cyclical fluctuations in the labour market.

However, from the 1990s, cyclical fluctuations have had a much stronger effect on unemployment in Switzerland as migrant workers were no longer seasonal, and could not be expelled from the country, which is different from previous crises. Since 2008, 16 percent of economically active persons in Switzerland have experienced unemployment, often for a short time.[61] Labour force participants who are most seriously affected by unemployment in Switzerland include low-skilled persons, young people (aged 15–24), women, inhabitants of the Lake Geneva and Ticino regions, and foreigners (on average less qualified than the Swiss).[62]

By international comparison, Switzerland has a relatively low unemployment rate. This has been made possible through the flexibility of its labour market,[63] the development and growth of companies in high technology and knowledge-based production, and a highly developed service sector generating demand for skilled jobs, which is supported by the supply from quality education and training systems. In addition to its renowned high schools and universities, Switzerland has invested in

---

[61] *Employment and income from employment, Panorama,* Swiss Federal Statistical Office, February 2013.

[62] *Ibid.*

[63] Straubhaar, Thomas, and Heinz Werner. "Arbeitsmarkt Schweiz - ein Erfolgsmodell?" *Mitteilungen aus der Arbeitsmarkt- und Berufsforschung* 36, no. 1 (2003): 60–76.

developing high quality industry-relevant skills through its dual-track vocational and professional apprenticeship-based educational systems.

Maintaining national identity

Just like in Singapore, the Swiss population is very diverse with four national languages and different religions, customs and lifestyles. Despite this fact, the Swiss national identity is strongly established. This might be the result of Switzerland's long history dating back to the formation of the old Swiss Confederation in 1291. The Swiss' peculiar form of quasi-direct democracy and its neutrality might also be uniting factors of Swiss identity. However, Swiss nationals are also afraid that the large number of migrants entering the country will "denature" and threaten the Swiss national identity. There has been a number of ballot proposals and votes to restrict immigration in Switzerland; however, many of these were rejected by popular vote.[64] Between 1993 and 2010, 18 referendums were held on topics related to the foreign population. These were approved in 11 cases, and rejected in seven.[65] For example, on 24 September 2000, a national vote was organised on an initiative[66] proposed by the right-wing party, the Swiss People's Party (*Schweizerische Volkspartei*) to include in the constitution a clause limiting the number of foreigners living in Switzerland to 18 percent of the population. The result was 36 percent of the votes in favour of and 64 percent against the initiative (with a participation rate of 45 percent of the population).[67]

Further, studies have shown that — despite the image given by the Swiss extreme-right — Swiss nationals are relatively more open to migration than neighbouring European countries. In the recent 'Mass

---

[64]Chancellerie fédérale. "Message relatif à l'initiative populaire «Contre l'immigration de masse»."

[65]Skenderovic, Damir. "Xénophobie." *Dictionnaire historique de la Suisse*. Accessed April 28, 2013. http://www.hls-dhs-dss.ch/textes/f/F16529.php.

[66]A popular initiative is proposition made by citizens, which is submitted to the vote of the population to the condition that it previously collects 100,000 signatures.

[67]Epstein, Gil S., and Shmuel Nitzan. "The Struggle over Migration Policy." Journal of Population Economics 19, no. 4 (2006): 703–23.

Immigration initiative' on immigration controls held in February 2014, Switzerland voted by a narrow margin of 50.4 percent, with a voter turnout of 56 percent, to re-introduce immigration quotas from EU countries within three years. While this effectively ends its 2002 acceptance of the free movement of people within the EU's Schengen visa-free travel zone, the more recent November 2014 initiative to drastically reduce net immigration to 0.2 percent of the population from about 80,000 to 16,000 was rejected by 74.1 percent of votes. This indicates that while the Swiss are fearful of overcrowding stress, there is nevertheless a recognition that immigration will continue to be important for economic development in this interconnected global market.

Illegal immigration and treatment of foreign workers

Switzerland has worked in cooperation with the European Union to find solutions to counter illegal immigration. However, having its borders completely open to the rest of Europe (through the Schengen agreement), there is no easy solution to control illegal migration.

With regard to the treatment of migrants, Switzerland subscribes to and monitors closely all its national and international engagement on human rights, such as the two 1966 International Covenants on Human Rights, as well as the International Convention on the Protection of the Rights of All Migrant Workers and Members of Their Families.

Dealing with growth challenges

Switzerland has dealt with the growth challenge of a small population by being one of the first countries to change the nature of its production from labour-intensive to high-technology and capital-intensive methods, ensuring a slow but sustainable growth of the Swiss economy. The tertiary sector (services) of the economy represents 71 percent of the Swiss workforce in 2012, followed by the secondary sector (manufacturing), with 27.7 percent. Switzerland has world-renowned companies in capital-intensive industries such as chemicals (for industrial and construction use, e.g., Sika AG), pharmaceuticals (Novartis, Roche) and food processing

Figure 7:   Growth of the Swiss economy

GDP of Switzerland (current U.S. dollars), 1980-2014

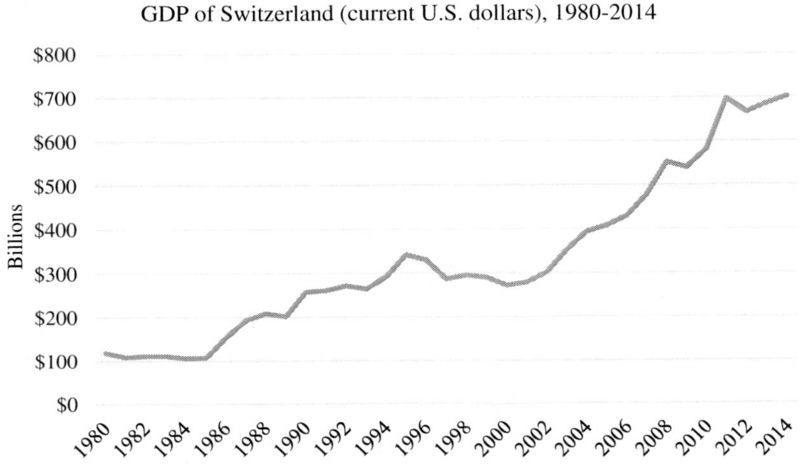

Source: The World Bank.

(Nestlé). The primary sector (agriculture) represents a very small minority with 1.3 percent of the workforce.[68]

Switzerland's growth over the last 50 years has been relatively steady, except for some periods such as the beginning of the 1990s, when Switzerland experienced a tough three-year recession (Figure 7). In 2012, the growth of the Swiss economy was one percent.[69]

Swiss Lessons for Singapore

To a large extent, Singapore's immigration experience exhibits many similarities with that of Switzerland. Both countries are regarded as

---

[68]"Statistik Schweiz - Kennzahlen." *Swiss Federal Statistical Office*, 2013. https://web. archive.org/web/20130117065126/http://www.bfs.admin.ch/bfs/portal/de/index/ international/laenderportraets/schweiz/blank/kennzahlen.html.

[69]"GNI, PPP (Current International $)." *The World Bank*. Accessed May 14, 2015. http:// data.worldbank.org/indicator/NY.GNP.MKTP.PP.CD/countries.

'islands' of prosperity surrounded by less prosperous neighbours and have benefited from inflows of talented foreigners. The scale of immigration, both in terms of size and proportion, is, however, much larger in the case of Singapore, especially in the period from 2004 to 2010 when the size of the workforce increased by about 600,000. Both countries have experienced significant increases in foreign population inflows in recent years, leading to growing resentment among the citizen population. Singapore's immigration inflows are also overwhelmingly skewed towards lower-skilled workers who constituted about three-quarters of the foreign workforce. There are several lessons that can be gleaned from the Swiss experience with foreign labour. These are:

a. *Reducing wage depression and wage disparity.* Inflows of foreign labour will depress local wages, especially in a situation where no minimum wage is in place. The avoidance of wage depression will reduce the excess dependence on unskilled workers, which has a detrimental effect on economic restructuring and the upgrading of skills in the longer term. Although there is no statutory minimum wage in Switzerland, there are binding collective agreements providing de facto minimum wages for certain industries under the Swiss social contract. The Swiss parliament had also considered the introduction of a minimum wage for foreigners to prevent wage dumping. In the case of Singapore, there is no official policy or union support on lifting wages for unskilled foreign workers and improving the contract terms for them.

b. *Removing wage discrimination of lower-skilled workers.* In Switzerland, highly-skilled foreigners earn higher wages than highly-skilled Swiss workers, while lower-skilled foreign workers get paid slightly lower wages than Swiss workers in similar positions (refer to Table 2). This is not a recent phenomenon and Muller *et al.* has found similar evidence that this averaged about a 12 percent premium for the high-skilled and a six to 15 percent discount for the unskilled.[70]

---

[70] Müller, Tobias, and José V. Ramirez. "Wage Inequality and Segregation between Native and Immigrant Workers in Switzerland: Evidence Using Matched Employee-Employer Data."

Table 2:   Gross Monthly Median Wage by Professional Position, 2012 (in CHF)

Position	Swiss	Foreigners	Foreigner to Swiss
All Positions	6,369	5,655	0.89
Top, Upper and Middle Management	9,683	11,250	1.16
Lower Management	7,884	8,314	1.05
Lowest Management	6,689	6,370	0.95
No Management Function	5,729	5,226	0.91

Source: Swiss Federal Statistical Office, Swiss Earnings Structure Survey.

In Singapore, the use of the foreign worker levy for the lower-skilled foreign workers has significantly reduced foreign workers' pay compared to that of locals. Such pay discrimination has the effect of not only reducing foreign workers' morale and overall productivity, but it also reduces the local public perception of the value of the jobs, further aggravating the difficulty of recruiting locals for such jobs. There should be a greater appreciation for the social value of these jobs and the role played by these workers. The public attitude cultivated towards foreign workers should be one of appreciation and not simply of tolerance. There should be a greater realisation that low-skilled migrant workers are a long-term indispensable factor of the Singapore economy, and therefore greater efforts should be made to improve their working and living conditions. Since the mid-1960s, Switzerland has progressively acknowledged that migration is not a transient phenomenon but an indispensable factor of its economic development in the long run. Political tensions with external actors arising from migrant workers need to be skillfully managed. The Swiss experience shows us that countries will increasingly exercise greater pressure to secure rights for its nationals working in Switzerland; Italy exercised such pressure in the 1960s, and Portugal and Spain in the 1980s. Singapore has experienced some frictions in bilateral relations with Malaysia since the 1990s over concerns raised by the Malaysian government on Malaysian workers' right to withdraw their CPF savings after ceasing work in Singapore. It should be expected that foreign neighbours will exercise a strong pressure on the small island in the future in order to see improvements in the living conditions of their nationals.

c. *Maintaining strong social safety nets.* Fears that new foreign migrants may deprive locals of job opportunities are real. The fact remains, however, that in both countries, the local population will have to be complemented by foreign inflows to support economic growth. The displacement of some local employment may be inevitable given the structural adjustments to new business opportunities in the fast-changing global economy. To facilitate these adjustments and acceptance of the necessary complementary foreign labour inputs, it is imperative for Singapore to have stronger social safety nets to help locals tide over the period of transitions. Increased welfare transfers and social services would also be needed to lower the extent of income inequality that accompanies such changes. In this process of redistribution, migrants should not be left aside, and should benefit from basic rights and benefits.

d. *Increasing productivity by moving up the value chain.* Singapore should continue to move up the value chain in high-tech manufacturing and high-value service sectors and should turn its economy away from lower-value labour-intensive production. The current tightening of lower-skilled foreign inflows is painful but necessary in this regard. Even as the number and proportion of high-skilled foreign talents increase, it is necessary to improve the quality and skills of the foreign work permit holders by offering them some form of subsidised training schemes. This is consistent with the recommendation of the Report of the Economic Strategies Committee, which recommends that Singapore "shift to achieving GDP growth by expanding productivity rather than the labour force" and boost productivity in order to stay competitive, upgrade the quality of jobs, and raise Singaporeans' incomes. This shift to productivity-driven growth will require "major new investments in the skills, expertise and innovative capabilities of our people and businesses over the next decade."[71]

---

[71]"Report of the Economic Strategies Committee." *Ministry of Trade and Industry,* February 1, 2010. https://www.mti.gov.sg/ResearchRoom/Pages/Report-of-the-Economic-Strategies-Committee.aspx.

e. *Removing the efficiency of the quotas system based on firm-level employment to one based on a national cap on migrants.* In Switzerland in the 1960s, two successive firms-based policies of quotas adopted by the government failed. They did not lead to a decrease of the foreign population, and also harmed the Swiss economy, limiting the expansion of successful firms. The system of national quotas adopted in the 1970s was more successful in stabilising the migrant population in Switzerland: it even led to a decrease in the absolute number of migrants (for the first time since 1945). Singapore's firm-based quotas do not take into consideration the different needs of the companies and the most efficient allocation of the stock of migrants. A national quota would allow more efficient firms to bargain for migrants, while maintaining a control on the stable number of migrants in the country.

f. *Preserving a strong national identity and societal peace and stability, by paying more attention to public opinion.* Even if Singaporeans' opinion does not resonate as loudly or openly as their Swiss counterparts because of the peculiarity of Swiss direct democracy, the public opinion of Singaporeans would ultimately validate the legitimacy of the government. The Swiss experience reminds us that immigration policies cannot only be dictated by economic interests. Although Swiss policies were dictated by economic considerations right after WWII, this quickly changed. Relationships with origin countries and public opinion rapidly became major considerations in the drafting of Swiss immigration policies.

Concluding Remarks

Singapore's economic development strategies have facilitated its successful transition from third-world developing status to its current position as a first-world country with a high GDP per capita. However, Singapore is now facing fundamental challenges in its next phase of economic transformation. In the past two decades, Singapore has increased its total population by one million every decade compared to Switzerland, which has experienced the same increase in population every two decades. Given that Switzerland's land area is 56 times that of Singapore, this effectively means that Singapore has increased its population density by an amount that is 110 times that of Switzerland. This is clearly an unsustainable policy for Singapore given its already high population density and very limited land area. The recent widespread opposition and concerns about the rate of immigration inflows to fuel economic growth effectively sets the boundary for employment expansion as the driver of future growth in Singapore. Productivity-led quality growth through continuing education, skills development and innovation is an integral part of the process. Critical to this are policy measures that are directed at improving the productivity of the current stock of foreign workers. The comparison of the immigration policies of Singapore and Switzerland has highlighted important differences in the impact of policy on the labour market and the incentive effects that they could have on firms' restructuring activities and the work motivations of the lower-skilled workers in particular. A key difference lies in the redistributional effects of taxes and transfers in reducing inequality in disposable incomes in these countries.

The share of foreigners in the labour force and the mean wages are other major contrasts worthy of note. Switzerland, despite its relatively high share of foreigners, has an average wage which is more than twice that of Singapore. The median wages of foreign workers are on average about 89 percent of local Swiss wages. This highlights the importance for Singapore to transition away from growth that is dependent on the continued use of cheap foreign labour, which can have detrimental effects on productivity performance, towards a system that can sustain increasing productivity through higher wages backed by adequate social security protection. These key labour market reforms would ultimately determine the successful transition of the Singapore economy from a factor-driven economy to an efficient innovation-driven economy with higher living standards for its residents.

References

Alleva, V., and M. Moretto. "Domestic Workers in Switzerland Protected by the Country's First Sectoral Employment Contract." *Global Labour Column*, February 2011. http://www.global-labour-university.org/fileadmin/GLU_Column/papers/no_47_Alleva___Moretto.pdf.

Blanke, J., and T. Chiesa. "Reducing Barriers to Economic Growth and Job Creation." *The Travel & Tourism Competitiveness Report 2013*, Geneva 2013.

"Census of Population." *Statistics Singapore*. Accessed April 28, 2013. http://www.singstat.gov.sg/statistics/browse-by-theme/census-of-population.

Chancellerie fédérale. "Message relatif à l'initiative populaire «Contre l'immigration de masse»," December 7, 2012. https://www.admin.ch/opc/fr/federal-gazette/2013/279.pdf.

De Melo, J., F. Miguet, and T. Müller. "The Political Economy of Migration and EU Enlargement: Lessons from Switzerland." *CESifo*, May 2002. http://archive-ouverte.unige.ch/unige:35481/ATTACHMENT01.

"Department of Statistics: Key Demographic Indicators." *Statistics Singapore*. Accessed September 30, 2014. http://www.singstat.gov.sg/statistics/browse-by-theme/population-and-population-structure.

"Employment and income from employment", *Panorama*. Swiss Federal Statistical Office, February 2013.

Epstein, G. S., and S. Nitzan. "The Struggle over Migration Policy." *Journal of Population Economics* 19, no. 4 (2006): 703–23.

"GDP Growth (Annual %)." *The World Bank*. Accessed April 28, 2013. http://data.worldbank.org/indicator/NY.GDP.MKTP.KD.ZG.

"GDP per Capita, PPP (Current International $)." *The World Bank*. Accessed May 14, 2015. http://data.worldbank.org/indicator/NY.GDP.PCAP.PP.CD.

"GNI, PPP (Current International $)." *The World Bank*. Accessed May 14, 2015. http://data.worldbank.org/indicator/NY.GNP.MKTP.PP.CD/countries.

Hui, W. T. "Foreign Manpower Policy in Singapore." In *Singapore Economy in the 21st Century: Issues and Strategies*. McGraw-Hill, 2002.

Hui, W. T., and R. Toh. "Growth with Equity in Singapore: Challenges and Prospects." *Conditions of Work Employment Series*, no. 48 (2014). http://natlex.ilo.ch/wcmsp5/groups/public/---ed_protect/---protrav/---travail/documents/publication/wcms_244819.pdf.

Kenworthy, L. "Do Social-Welfare Policies Reduce Poverty? A Cross-National Assessment." *Social Forces* 77, no. 3 (March 1, 1999): 1119–39. doi:10.1093/sf/77.3.1119.

"MTI Occasional Paper on Population and Economy." *Ministry of Trade and Industry*. September 25, 2012. https://www.mti.gov.sg/mtiinsights/pages/mti-occasional-paper-on-population-and-economy.aspx.

Müller, T., and J. V. Ramirez. "Wage Inequality and Segregation between Native and Immigrant Workers in Switzerland: Evidence Using Matched Employee-Employer Data." SSRN Scholarly Paper. Rochester, NY: Social

Science Research Network, January 1, 2009. http://papers.ssrn.com.libproxy1. nus.edu.sg/abstract=1703013.

"National Population and Talent Division." *Government of Singapore*. Accessed April 28, 2013. http://www.nptd.gov.sg/.

Ngiam, T. D. "Singapore Must Achieve More with Less." *The Business Times*. March 14, 2012.

Piguet, E. and H. Mahnig. *Quotas d'immigration: l'expérience suisse*. Bureau international du travail, 2000. http://www.karch.ch/repository/default/content/sites/sfm/files/shared/pub/o/o_03.pdf.

"Population & Land Area Statistics (Mid-Year Estimates)." *Statistics Singapore*, June 2013. http://www.singstat.gov.sg/statistics/latest-data#16.

"Poverty Remains a Threat in Land of Plenty." *SWI swissinfo.ch*, December 18, 2012. http://www.swissinfo.ch/eng/struggle-street_poverty-remains-a-threat-in-land-of-plenty/34447884.

Ramesh, S. "Singapore's Q3 Jobless Rate Remains Low, but Employment Growth Slows." *Channel NewsAsia*, October 31, 2012. http://archive.is/puRLZ.

"Recent Monthly and Quarterly Figures: Provisional Data." *Swiss Federal Statistical Office*, June 16, 2013. http://www.bfs.admin.ch/bfs/portal/en/index/themen/01/02/blank/key/bevoelkerungsstand/01.html.

"Report of the Economic Strategies Committee." *Ministry of Trade and Industry*, February 1, 2010. https://www.mti.gov.sg/ResearchRoom/Pages/Report-of-the-Economic-Strategies-Committee.aspx.

Revill, J. "Swiss to Vote on Executive Pay." *Wall Street Journal*, March 20, 2013. http://www.wsj.com/articles/SB10001424127887324103504578372203886463598.

"Share of GDP by Industry." *Statistics Singapore*. Accessed April 28, 2013. http://www.singstat.gov.sg/statistics/visualising-data/charts/share-of-gdp-by-industry.

"Short-Term Trade Statistics." *World Trade Organization*. Accessed April 28, 2013. https://www.wto.org/english/res_e/statis_e/statis_e.htm.

"Singapore Budget Speech 2013." *Ministry of Finance*. Accessed April 28, 2013. http://www.singaporebudget.gov.sg/budget_2013/budget_speech.html.

"Singapore Entrepreneur Visa." *Guide Me Singapore*. Accessed April 28, 2013. http://www.guidemesingapore.com/relocation/work-pass/singapore-entrepreneur-pass-guide.

"Singapore Workforce Development Agency (WDA)." *Government of Singapore*. Accessed April 28, 2013. http://www.wda.gov.sg/.

Skenderovic, D. "Xénophobie." *Dictionnaire historique de la Suisse.* Accessed April 28, 2013. http://www.hls-dhs-dss.ch/textes/f/F16529.php.

"Snapshot." Accessed April 28, 2013. https://www.mti.gov.sg/ResearchRoom/Pages/Report-of-the-Economic-Strategies-Committee.aspx.

"Social Expenditure — Aggregated Data." *OECD Statistics.* Accessed April 28, 2013. http://stats.oecd.org/Index.aspx?datasetcode=SOCX_AGG.

"Statistik Schweiz — Kennzahlen." *Swiss Federal Statistical Office*, 2013. https://web.archive.org/web/20130117065126/http://www.bfs.admin.ch/bfs/portal/de/index/international/laenderportraets/schweiz/blank/kennzahlen.html.

Straubhaar, T., and H. Werner. "Arbeitsmarkt Schweiz — ein Erfolgsmodell?" *Mitteilungen aus der Arbeitsmarkt- und Berufsforschung* 36, no. 1 (2003): 60–76.

"Switzerland." *CIA World Factbook.* Accessed April 28, 2013. https://www.cia.gov/library/publications/the-world-factbook/geos/sz.html.

Tai, S. H. T. "Market Structure and the Link between Migration and Trade." *Review of World Economics/Weltwirtschaftliches Archiv* 145, no. 2 (2009): 225–49.

"Wages and Income from Employment." *Swiss Federal Statistical Office*, February 19, 2013. http://www.bfs.admin.ch/bfs/portal/en/index/themen/03/04.html.

"Wealth Management." *UBS.* Accessed April 18, 2013. https://www.ubs.com/global/en/wealth_management.html.

White, P. "Switzerland: From Migrant Rotation to Migrant Communities." *Geography* 70, no. 2 (1985): 168–71.

Wong, C. H. "Singapore Tightens Hiring Rules for Foreign Skilled Labor." *Wall Street Journal*, September 23, 2013. http://www.wsj.com/articles/SB10001424052702303759604579092863888803466.

Chapter 11

Power Resources and Income Inequality in Singapore and Switzerland

Mehmet Kerem Çoban

> *"[We]conclude that the concentration of wealth is natural and inevitable, and is periodically alleviated by violent or peaceable partial redistribution. In this view all economic history is the slow heartbeat of the social organism, a vast systole and diastole of concentrating wealth and compulsive recirculation."*
>
> Durant (1968: 57)

Introduction

In the aftermath of the global financial crisis in 2008, both the public and policymakers have become increasingly aware of rising income inequality in both developed and developing countries. Piketty's controversial book reignited the debate about why inequality has been rising, and how to react with proper policies to minimise the social, economic, and political by-products of rising inequality.[1] At the same time, many existing theories about inequality have also been challenged. For example, Kuznets' inverted U-shape curve, which illustrates the hypothesis that as an economy develops, market forces first increase and then decrease economic inequality

---

[1] Piketty, T. *Capital in the Twenty-First Century*. Cambridge, MA: Harvard University Press, 2014.

can no longer be observed, particularly in developed countries.[2] It has transformed into a horizontal S-curve, showing that instead of decreasing, inequality increases after a certain level of economic development.

This chapter attempts to explain rising inequality in Singapore and Switzerland through a political economy approach, by using the framework of power resource theory and focusing on the relative political strength of trade unions. The change in the relative political strength of the trade unions and labour movement is hypothesised to be one of the determining factors leading to rising or declining inequality. This chapter explains why both of these countries have taken different trajectories since the 1990s, when the Swiss government began to allocate more funds to social spending.

Power Resources and a Trilemma in a Service Economy

How the fruits of economic activity are distributed according to "who gets what, when and how"[3] is a political problem stemming from a series of political decisions. This problem requires an analysis of where actors are located in the political decision-making process. Moreover, their relative strength in convincing other actors to comply with their causes depends on their relative positioning in this bargaining game.

Framed in this light, rising income inequality, as explained cogently by Piketty,[4] is a phenomenon of the dominance of capital *vis-à-vis* labour. As the share of wage in the gross domestic product (GDP) has declined in recent years,[5] the relative political influence of the labouring classes[6] is

---

[2] Galbraith, J. K. *Inequality and Instability: A Study of the World Economy Before the Great Crisis*. New York: Oxford University Press, 2012.

[3] Lasswell, H. *Politics: Who Gets What, When, How*. New York: McGraw–Hill.

[4] Piketty, *Capital in the Twenty-First Century*, 1958.

[5] Stockhammer, E. Wage-led Growth: An Introduction. *International Journal of Labour Research* 3, no. 2 (2011): 167–187.

[6] In this chapter, I refer to "labouring classes" as a generic concept to define labour as forming a "class" on its own, for the sake of simplicity, without further discussion of how classes are formed or if labour includes all working classes. Interested readers can read a Marxist interpretation of social classes in Poulantzas (1973), and a discussion of the formation of class structure according to the Weberian tradition, the social democratic interpretation, and others in Esping-Andersen (1985: 26–36).

assumed to have declined with the "rise of capital" and its power to exit[7] as global capital mobility has increased significantly since the 1980s.

Korpi's analysis on class struggle, particularly in Western capitalist democracies, shows that the relative bargaining power of the labouring classes rests upon power resources, in particular the emergence of trade unions.[8] According to Esping–Andersen, political representation (as opposed to revolution) has become one of the major paths for the labouring class to influence the political bargaining process from within the parliament.[9] Consequently, as Korpi points out, any change in relative strength can change the outcome of the bargaining and the functioning of the bargaining system,[10] but it all depends on how power resources are divided between actors.[11]

Here, it is important to briefly mention why we may need to analyse the role and impact of trade unions on income inequality. In a recent study, the International Monetary Fund (IMF) argues that since the 1980s, rising income inequality in high-income countries is highly associated with a declining union density rate.[12] Keeping in mind that unions' activism in early 20th century led to the development of a social welfare state, particularly in Western Europe,[13] the declining union density rate can explain about half of the rise in the share of the top five and 10 percent in high-income countries in the sample since the 1980s.

---

[7] Hirschmann, A. O. *Exit, Voice, and Loyalty: Responses to Decline in Firms, Organisations, and States*. Cambridge, MA: Harvard University Press, 1970.

[8] Korpi, W. *The Democratic Class Struggle*. London: Routledge and Kegan Paul, 1983.

[9] Esping-Andersen, G. *Politics Against Markets*. Princeton: Princeton University Press 1985. Galbraith, *Inequality and Instability: A Study of the World Economy Before the Great Crisis*, 2012.

[10] This undoubtedly depends on various politico-economic ecosystems in which each actor is positioned according to the unique experiences of a given country. This is in line with the "varieties of capitalism" literature (Hall and Soskice, 2001) which gives way to dissimilar wage-setting institutions, either centralised or decentralised (Wallerstein, 1999).

[11] Esping–Andersen, *Politics Against Markets*, p. 19.

[12] Jaumotte, F. and Buitron, C. O. Power from the People. *Finance and Development* 52, no.1 (2015): 29–31.

[13] Acemoglu, D. The World Our Grandchildren will Inherit: The Rights Revolution and Beyond. Mimeo, MIT, 2012. Available at: http://economics.mit.edu/files/7742, accessed on November 10, 2014.

The unexplained part in the power resources theory is the role of the State. According to Iversen and Wren, the State faces a trade-off between three factors: earnings equality, (full) employment, and (public) budgetary restraint.[14] When it chooses fiscal discipline, it has to either choose earnings equality or employment growth. If it combines fiscal discipline with employment growth, it tolerates depressing wages in what the authors call the "neo-liberal model". The second combination is fiscal discipline accompanied with earnings equality, labelled as the "Christian democratic model". Finally, if earnings equality is accompanying employment growth, it is labelled as the "social democratic model."

We can assume that the power resources of parties engaged in the political decision-making process determine the choice of the model. The relative strength of the labouring class to influence the political decision-making process determines the outcome of the bargaining process. What it can gain will purely depend on its influential power. This chapter will assume power resources as given, so it is not concerned with how resources are divided *ex ante*. Nevertheless, in line with Korpi's arguments,[15] we can expect that the division of power resources does in fact determine the process. Furthermore, the trilemma presented by Iversen and Wren[16] shows that one of the three models is adopted in the bargaining process within their respective borders. By mobilising these two analytical frameworks for the Swiss and the Singaporean cases, we should expect to observe that some sort of "neo-liberal" model has been adopted in Singapore, whereas the Swiss case shows first a pattern of a "Christian democratic" model until the 1990s, which then evolves into more of a "social democratic" model in the aftermath of the long recession in the early 1990s. The relative strength of the labouring class that is mobilised through trade unions and/or leftist parties determines the choice of these models in the two cases. The highly centralised government

---

[14] Iversen, T. and Wren, A. Equality, Employment, and Budgetary Restraint: The Trilemma of the Service Economy. *World Politics* 50, no. 4 (1998): 507–546.

[15] Korpi, *The Democratic Class Struggle*.

[16] Iversen and Wren, *Equality, Employment, and Budgetary Restraint: The Trilemma of the Service Economy*.

system in Singapore,[17] and its unique history with unions and a story of independence and survival, contrasts sharply with the highly decentralised federal system in Switzerland[18] and its different political system and political institutions to form one critical explanatory variable in income distribution and the evolution of social policies in both countries.

Case of Singapore

In terms of earnings inequality, Singapore ranks ahead of Switzerland. This is not limited to a short period of time but is reflected throughout the history of the city-state. The average income share of the top 10 percent income level has almost never been less than 30 percent and it has reached historical record levels since the late 1990s. The income disparity between the top 10 percent and the bottom 90 percent income levels has also widened, reflecting the rising share of the top 10 percent (Figure 1). In comparison to Switzerland, this historically stable income disparity presents a unique case in a small country context. It is also unique in terms of general government spending (Figure 2).

Government consumption seems to be anchored at 10 percent of GDP, although several times the government had to spend more. However, the statistics signal that the Singapore government has chosen the "neo-liberal" model of Iversen and Wren, which includes fiscal discipline and full employment. The aspect of full employment in this policy mix will be discussed below when we touch upon flexible wage determination and the non-existence of minimum wage in the country.

The annual percentage growth of government expenditure paints a mixed picture because several economic shocks have driven the government to respond to these crises through expansionary policies. Health expenditure seems to have recovered during the last decade. Concessions for the "Pioneer Generation" are expected to rise in the

---

[17] Régnier, P. T. *Singapour et son environnement régional: etude d'une cité-État au sein du monde malais*. Paris: Presses universitaires de France 1987.

[18] Linder, W. *Swiss Democracy: Possible Solutions to Conflict in Multicultural Societies*. New York: St. Martin's Press, 1994; Obinger, H. Federalism, Direct Democracy, and Welfare State Development in Switzerland. *Journal of Public Policy* 18, no. 3 (1998): 241–263.

Figure 1:   The income disparity between the top 10 percent and the bottom 90 percent of income levels, Singapore.

Top 10% income share (left axis)

Top 10% average income / Bottom 90% average income ratio (right axis)

Source: World Top Incomes Database, http://topincomes.g-mond.parisschoolofeconomics.eu/, accessed on April 24, 2014. Data from 1992 is absent in the original dataset.

Note: Top 10 percent and bottom 90 percent average income are in real 2014 Singapore dollars.

Figure 2:   General government expenditure and health expenditure, Singapore

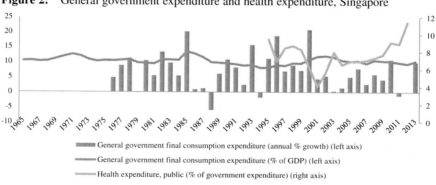

General government final consumption expenditure (annual % growth) (left axis)

General government final consumption expenditure (% of GDP) (left axis)

Health expenditure, public (% of government expenditure) (right axis)

Source: World Development Indicators, the World Bank, accessed on April 18, 2014.

Figure 3: Net union membership as a proportion of wage and salary earners in employment (%), Singapore

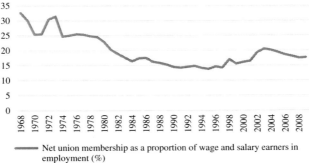

Net union membership as a proportion of wage and salary earners in employment (%)

Source: ICTWSS Database, http://www.uva-aias.net/208, accessed on April 18, 2014.

future, which will probably increase government social spending. Although changes to the welfare regime are expected to benefit Singaporeans, more has to be achieved to reduce income inequality in the country by reconsidering the growth model, minimum income, immigration, and even public housing.[19]

With respect to the role of trade unions, although there have been several upward shifts in union density (i.e., membership of wage and salary earners), Figure 3 shows that even if the trend has recorded a recovery in the mid-2000s, it has declined again and we need to see how it will evolve in the coming years. As mentioned above, the decline in unionism is a contemporary phenomenon and Singapore is not an outlier in reflecting this.

Consequently, we can assume that in smaller political units where trade unions might need to cope with fewer limitations, welfare policies can be more easily channelled. In Singapore, the unique experience of a highly centralised political system, scepticism about the potential of a communist movement[20] and the tripartite coordinated wage-setting

---

[19] Low, D. and Vadaketh, S. T. *Hard Choices: Challenging the Singapore Consensus.* Singapore: NUS Press, 2014.
[20] Lee, K. Y. *The Battle for Merger.* Singapore: Straits Times Press; Mahbubani, K. 2014. Lee Kuan Yew's Complex Legacy. In Shashi Jayakumar and Rahul Sagar (eds.) *The Big Ideas of Lee Kuan Yew.* Singapore: Straits Times Press, 2014.

framework which includes the representatives of the labouring class, the National Trades Union Congress (NTUC), the government, and the business sector, posed impediments in its own nature in the city-state. The remaining part of this section will discuss the role of the centralised political regime and the role of trade unions in accessing the political arena to push for a better welfare regime in Singapore.

The wage-setting institution in Singapore is a tripartite body called the National Wage Council. The Council is headed by a chairman who is expected to be neutral to three parties. As the Founding Chairman of the tripartite Council, Lim Chong Yah explains, the Council operates on two major principles; (a) unanimity; (b) the Chatham House rule.[21] The former requires unanimous decision-making in the Council, so each party has to agree on the terms. The latter indicates that whatever is discussed inside the meeting room is not disclosed so that each party does not have to be worried about their positions being publicly known. They can protect themselves against a backlash if their position during the meeting differ significantly from their public position. When discussing wages, the Council considers a guideline composed of quantitative and qualitative items. The quantitative guidelines start off with a benchmark annual percentage increase with respect to macroeconomic conditions, and the annual percentage increase was between two percent and six percent.[22] The qualitative guideline is more about the wording and punctuation, showing how the ultimate decision is disclosed. Since the introduction of the minimum wage is still controversial in the city-state, Lim mentions that he dropped the idea because he thought it would not be beneficial for Singapore.[23] Above all, he mentions that he was inspired by Milton Friedman's seminal book *Free to Choose* that made him reconsider the unintended consequences of passing stringent (economic) laws could may cause unemployment. Putting aside the ideological orientation of key policymakers, Lim also argues that firms do not have to obey national

---

[21] Lim, C. Y. *Singapore's National Wage Council: An Insider's View*. New Jersey: World Scientific, 2014, pp. 8–9.

[22] *Ibid*, pp. 17–18.

[23] *Ibid*, p. 19.

guidelines provided by the Council.[24] They are flexible enough to negotiate with sectoral and/or firm-level trade unions. Even though a centralised wage-setting institution can provide favourable terms from the perspective of the labouring class, the flexibility enjoyed by the private sector seems to leave the labouring class at the mercy of the employers.[25]

In such a centralised wage-setting institutional context that is complemented with a flexible and a decentralised bargaining context, the role of the unions and thereby the labouring class can be expected to be marginal.[26] Besides limitations on the role of unions to have a greater hand on policies, the history of the experience of trade unions in Singapore since colonisation did not provide favourable conditions and a solid background on which industrial relations would have been established. Rosa draws a clear picture of a turbulent history of the role of unions, and how and why they were incorporated in the National Wage Council later on following independence. Her study shows that the predecessors of modern unions had been formed previously as trade guilds in the 1930s. After the Second World War, the relative strength of the labouring class increased mainly due to a high demand to reconstruct the demolished

---

[24] *Ibid*, p. 22.

[25] To the best of my knowledge, there has not been any systematic study on whether the business sector complies with the guidelines of the Council. It seems to be a fruitful area for further research, which could be on the rate of compliance of the business sector to the guidelines of the Council, and to control for the effect of this particular exemption on earnings inequality.

[26] Barr (2000) points out that the "inclusionary corporatist state" proposes several nuances for us not be misled by the structural setting of the institutions. Even though the author agrees that the upper ranks in the hierarchy of NTUC are filled with PAP MPs, the Secretary General of NTUC, Lim Boon Heng was involved with NTUC since the 1980s. His case can be interpreted as a career path starting with a role in NTUC to being a PAP MP. The so-called symbiotic relationship between NTUC and the government is well known, but it signals another important aspect of that special relationship such that the MPs can be both insiders and outsiders in NTUC as well as in the government. They can wear both "hats" in different institutional contexts. Due to the fact that these officials and politicians can have such dual roles, the author concludes that trade unions — as well as the labouring class — can protect their interests, or at least expect to be protected by the government. Nevertheless, the structure could be interpreted in a way that co-opting unions may work in a way that unions conceive themselves as "responsible" and try not to upset social harmony.

infrastructure.[27] The General Labour Union of Singapore, established in 1945, and the Pan-Malayan General Labour Union, established in 1946, can be conceived as the origins of current unionism in the region and in Singapore. In the mid-1940s, unions were reported to cause disruptions through engaging in militancy; the government felt obliged to co-opt unions to reduce militancy among the unions. Hiok highlights, for instance, that the Singapore Factory and Shop Workers' Union was one of these unions which was involved in strikes that hit the operations of the colonial administration and the business sector.[28] The experience with militant unionism paved the way to the so-called "responsible unionism" which resulted in the launch of the Singapore Trade Union Congress in 1950.[29]

In the aftermath of the People's Action Party's (PAP) seizure of the government in 1959, left-wing leaders were arrested. Following the independence of Singapore from Malaysia, Rosa claims that the PAP had to put immense pressure on the labour movement that was conceived as a militant group which could have made foreign capital wary of investing in the small city–state.[30] Given the non-existence of a local bourgeois class with which the labour movement could establish an alliance *vis-à-vis* the government, the PAP found itself in a good position to limit the role of the unions. The strategy of the PAP to incorporate unions such that they would operate under the auspices of the government was the formation of the tripartite council. However, before that, the government also "injected" civil servants by seconding them to the NTUC when they were preparing for wage claims in the tripartite council.[31] Besides the role of the civil servants, Hiok argues that five out of 21 members of NTUC were also PAP Members of Parliament.[32] As far as these conditions and industrial relations are concerned, the historical evolution

---

[27] *Ibid*, p. 489.

[28] Hiok, L. B. Trade Union Growth in Singapore. *Asian Journal of Political Science* 3, no. 2 (1995), p. 92.

[29] Rosa, *The Singapore State and Trade Union Incorporation*, p. 490.

[30] *Ibid*, p. 491.

[31] *Ibid*, p. 492.

[32] Hiok, *Trade Union Growth in Singapore*, p. 93.

of unionism, and the way in which unions were incorporated into the system under the control of the government, leads us to conclude that unions were, and still are, subordinated to government control. It seems very challenging for the labouring class to have its voice heard at the higher levels of the decision-making process, especially when it is facing restrictions on mass mobilisation. As discussed previously, the threat of communism and militant unionism persuaded the political elite, namely the PAP, to be wary of not allowing greater space for the unions to manoeuvre.

As a small country, Singapore has always been an open economy. The intensification of economic internationalisation, and the deregulation of its labour market,[33] can be traced back to the 1980s. The deregulation of the labour market, which has become more friendly to low-skilled and highly-skilled migrants,[34] has had several implications on earnings equality[35] and on the role of the trade unions.[36] With respect to higher trade liberalisation, structural shifts in demand for highly-skilled labour have been shown to have a significant effect on the polarisation in income distribution.[37] The recession in the 1980s, rising wages, and concerns about competitiveness in a region mainly dominated by countries where costs related to investment and operations are lower, caused Singapore to opt for a deregulated labour market which welcomes a massive influx of low-skilled and high-skilled migrants, alongside pressure on wages to

---

[33] Ching, Y. C., and Lim G. S. Globalization, Labour Market Deregulation and Trade Unions in Singapore. *Asia Pacific Business Review* 6, no. 3–4 (January 1, 2000): 154–73. doi:10.1080/13602380012331288512.

[34] In order not to make a distinction between what Singaporeans call "foreign talent" to represent high-skilled labour; and "migrant workers" to represent low-skilled labour, the author will refer to them as "low-skilled" and "high-skilled" migrants respectively, because all migrants share the same identity of being a migrant regardless of their skills.

[35] Low and Vadaketh, *Hard Choices: Challenging the Singapore Consensus.*

[36] Ching and Lim, *Globalization, Labour Market Deregulation and Trade Unions in Singapore*, p. 164.

[37] Toh, R, and Hui, W. T. Trade Liberalization, Labour Demand Shifts and Earnings Inequality in Singapore. *Review of Urban & Regional Development Studies* 24, no. 3 (2013): 65–82.

moderate.[38] As for the role of the Council and the guidelines it provides to the whole economy with regard to wage policy, Ching and Lim report that firstly, the wage council would no longer provide guidelines with certain percentage increases but rather wage increases in percentages; secondly, it would underline changes in the way the labouring class would be remunerated. The remuneration would consist of individual payments but it would reflect the health of the national economy, the performance of the firm, and the performance of the labourer.[39] The employer's contribution to the Central Provident Fund (CPF) would reflect the performance of Singapore's economy. This means if the economy is underperforming, employers have the flexibility to contribute less to their employees' CPF accounts.

The evolution of the role of trade unions and their space to play a greater role seems to have implications on the wage disparity in the country. As one may intuitively expect, even social policies might be related to the rising earnings inequality, echoing the institutional environment. Asher and Nandy argue that the government cannot measure poverty because there is no single statistical method to detect poverty.[40] Moreover, Singapore's tax regime favours firms and high-level income earners, for whom tax rates have declined from 26 percent to 18 percent, and 28 percent to 20 percent respectively, from 2000 to 2007. If we consider health policies, Asher and Nandy report that almost 70 percent of health spending is privatised, which means that individuals are responsible for taking care of themselves, even if Figure 6 indicates a major upward shift in government spending on financing health expenses of the whole society.[41] However, it is questionable if the unions were pushing the case because we need evidence of their proactive

---

[38] Rao, V. V. B., Banerjee, D. S. and Mukhopadhaya, P. Earnings Inequality in Singapore. *Journal of the Asian Pacific Economy* 8, no. 2 (2003): 210–228.

[39] Ching and Lim, *Globalization, Labour Market Deregulation and Trade Unions in Singapore*, p. 164.

[40] Asher, M. and Nandy, A. Singapore's Policy Responses to Ageing, Inequality and Poverty: An Assessment. *International Social Security Review* 61, no. 1 (2008): 41–60.

[41] Asher, M. G., and A. Nandy. Health Financing in Singapore: A Case for Systemic Reforms. *International Social Security Review* 59, no. 1 (January 1, 2006): 75–92. doi:10.1111/j.1468-246X.2005.00234.x.

engagement in the shifts in the policy process. It seems more to be a case of government responsiveness to demands in the public sphere.[42]

Even the controversy about the question of minimum wage could well be explained with the power resources the labouring class holds to influence the policy process on the question of the potential benefits of the minimum wage.[43] Because they are not holding much resources, they have a lower degree of influence on this question as well so the public cannot be fully informed about the costs and benefits of the minimum wage. Although it may sound like a stretched version of the power resources theory, the role of the NTUC in influencing the political decision-making process on minimum wage is limited due to the centralised political institutional environment, and also the symbiotic relationship between the Singapore government and the NTUC. The NTUC Secretary-General Lim Swee Say declared in 2013 that "[Minimum] wage can be a "zero-sum game".[44] Based on that view, the NTUC came up with the proposal of a multi-tiered progressive (minimum) wage policy, as the Secretary-General explained in 2013. The policy aims at increasing wages in the lower segments of the labouring class. If the workers are more productive and gain more skills, they may expect to earn more. The weakest part of the policy is that it does not introduce a compulsory minimum wage on the whole economic activity in the country. Since a compulsory minimum wage policy is conceptualised as a

---

[42] Government responsiveness may not be evidence of power resource theory since it focuses on the relationships between the State, the labouring class and capital. The State, in theory, should be responsive to citizens' demands. Housing policy since independence reflects the degree of responsiveness of the government, which is labelled by Tremewan (1998) as "governance through welfare." The only concern in Singapore would be leaving the labouring class at the mercy of market forces through decentralised wage bargaining. The State should be more active in providing mandatory guidelines to the private sector.

[43] Hui, W. T. Economic Growth and Inequality in Singapore: The Case for a Miminum Wage. *International Labour Review* 152, no. 1 (2013): 107–123.

[44] The speech of the NTUC Secretary-General is available at on the website of the NTUC, http://www.ntuc.org.sg/wps/portal/up2/home/aboutntuc/newsroom/newshighlights/ newshighlightsdetails?WCM_GLOBAL_CONTEXT=/content_library/ntuc/home/ about+ntuc/newsroom/news+highlights/ace700004ecfeb748666af093c42a226, and on Channel News Asia, http://www.channelnewsasia.com/news/specialreports/parliament/news/ singapore-s-model-of-mini/596974.html. Accessed on April 2, 2015.

"zero-sum game" by the NTUC, it seems very difficult to overcome such ideational impediments for the trade unions to mobilise the labouring class for the introduction of the minimum wage. In Singapore, the role of trade unions on minimum wage policy, compared to that of in Switzerland seems, at first glance, to be more influenced by ideology rather than institutions. However, as argued earlier in this section, the policies of the Singapore government are mostly adopted by the NTUC due to its close ties with the government; as a result, a deeper understanding would still tell us that the process is still determined by the very centralised political environment in the country.

Finally, it would be important to touch upon recent measures taken by the Singapore government with the 2015 Budget which introduces higher taxation to higher income levels, and increased public spending on health and education.[45] The measures are welcomed, especially those on more public spending on social security, health, and education. With respect to higher taxation of higher levels of income, the Singapore government has pledged to start implementing these measures in 2016. Whether these measures would help Singapore reduce income inequality would depend on several different, but interlinked factors, such as economic models, political dimensions, and immigration policy, among others. Additionally, it might be delusional to expect to observe an impact of these policies in the short run, because there is always a time lag between implementation and observation of the outcome. Last but not least, public policies tend to produce beneficiaries. The Singapore government reacted to a public debate on low public spending and low taxation of higher levels of income. It will need to control the process if it does not want to (over)stretch itself with more pledges. This is important given the trilemma in a service-dominated economy. As argued earlier, a shift from a "neoliberal" stage to some sort of a "social democratic" stage will require some compromises in fiscal discipline.

To sum up, this section has endeavoured to highlight that a centralised and tripartite wage-setting institutional setting which is accompanied by a

---

[45] For further information about these recent measures, the readers may refer to the website of the 2015 Budget available at: http://www.singaporebudget.gov.sg/budget_2015/BudgetMeasures.aspx, accessed on April 2, 2015.

flexible and decentralised wage-setting environment at the firm-level does not give the labouring class a greater role to effectively channel demands for better working and salary conditions. Due to the militancy of unions and the efforts to confront a communist threat, the government incorporated the labour movement in the tripartite Council. The government also seconded the NTUC by putting PAP MPs on the board of NTUC. One can suspect that the cultural orientation of "responsible citizens"[46], who are at the same time "responsible" union members, would cause them to be careful not to upset the delicate balance between economic performance, societal relations, and the social fabric in the tiny city-state. The city-state can be considered to be vulnerable to foreign corporations, and more or less to mobile human capital. One important implication we can derive from the influx of migrant workers might be their impact on the role of unions. Migrants, if they wish to be granted nationality in the future, may solely be motivated by their material well-being; as a result they may not be engaged in the labour movement that can channel their demands to the government too. From the perspective of the government and the private sector, a higher number of foreigners may put pressure on the local labour class. If the foreign labour force is more productive than the local labour force, the locals might be forced to catch up with the foreigners. If this can be proven, then the power resources of the labouring class should not be expected to be higher *vis-à-vis* the other two actors in wage determination, since they can be increasingly marginalised due to the lower wages a migrant may ask.

Case of Switzerland

The unique political institution of direct democracy plays a critical role in policymaking in Switzerland. Wagschal points out that direct democracy requires the mobilisation of different actors to change the course of a policy at the federal level.[47] In order to change policies, the Swiss have three

---

[46] Nasir, K. M. and Turner, B. S. Governing as Gardening: Reflections on Soft Authoritarianism in Singapore. *Citizenship Studies* 17, nos. 3-4 (2013): 339–352.

[47] Wagschal, U. Direct Democracy and Public Policymaking. *Journal of Public Policy* 17, no. 2 (1997): 223–245.

options: (a) a constitutional referendum — which requires a double majority of citizens' and cantons' votes; (b) an optional (facultative) referendum — which requires the signatures of 50,000 voters, but can be challenged by a counter-initiative; (c) a popular initiative — to amend the constitution or changing current provisions in the constitution; and requires the signatures of 100,000 voters.[48] Even if the labouring class is successful in mobilising voters to alter provisions in the favour of expansionary welfare spending, the result of voting may not guarantee expansion in spending. Wagschal provides evidence on referenda in Switzerland from 1848 until 1996. 19 referenda out of 40 rejected an increase in taxation, and 28 out of 42 referenda resulted in the rejection of increasing expenditure.[49] Consequently, climbing up from a decentralised and a local context of a cantonal level to a federal level demands great effort from the labouring class to influence policies; and, as the historical evolution shows, country-wide initiatives are generally rejected.

The dynamics of direct democracy generated difficulties in the mobilisation of groups to alter the terms and conditions of social spending at the federal level. Bertozzi and Bonoli show that high costs of mobilisation paved the way to local arrangements at the cantonal level.[50] They present varying degrees of social welfare policies in 26 cantons. None of them provide the 'full menu' of social policies such as aid to families with children, allocation of individual housing, and life-long social security;[51] however, they provide several of these policies at differing degrees. Obinger *et al.* argue that 'local pre-emption' at the cantonal level to introducing social welfare policies was mainly driven by the non-existence of these policies at the federal level.[52] The authors argue that the labour movement called for improvements to the conditions of the labouring class in 1893, but it was rejected at the federal level under

---

[48] *Ibid*, pp. 228–229.

[49] *Ibid*, Table 2.

[50] Bertozzi, F. and Bonoli, G. Fédéralisme et protection sociale en Suisse: entre immobilisme et innovation. *Sociétés contemporaines* 51(2003): 13–33.

[51] *Ibid*, Tableau 3.

[52] Obinger, H. *et al.* Switzerland: The Marriage of Direct Democracy and Federalism. In Herbert Obinger, Stephan Leibrief and Francis G. Castles (eds.) *Federalism and the Welfare State*, pp. 263–304. Cambridge: Cambridge University Press, 2005.

the influence of the so-called bourgeois government.[53] Additionally, in the early 20th century, the Radical and Social Democratic parties presented a law on the general pension scheme, and it was rejected by the federal government due to fiscal costs. The presented data and historical evidence can be interpreted according to power resource theory: the relative strength of the labouring class in influencing politics and political decision-making on social welfare policies was stronger at the local level than at the federal level.

The strong presence of the "third sector" in the country has played its role in complementing private and public spending on social welfare. Butschi and Cattacin argue that industrialisation in Switzerland raises questions on how to take care of the labouring classes.[54] The Church, family and solidarity organisations constituted the first pillar of the social welfare system in the country. As the authors explain, industrialisation changed the conditions the labouring class was facing, so the political elite became cognizant of the potential of its social and economic aspects. The State was forced to engage in the social welfare system later on, as shown by Armingeon and Katzenstein, who define Switzerland as a "laggard" in developing a social welfare system.[55] Cattacin underlines the evolving role of solidarity organisations: although they were first utilised as a subsidiary to the State, their role is now complementary, since the State is much more involved in the social welfare system.[56]

Finally, with respect to political parties representing the labouring class and their relative strength and positioning, the bourgeois government has mostly positioned itself to protect the interests of business, preferring

---

[53] *Ibid*, p. 276.

[54] Butschi, D. and Cattacin, S. The Third Sector in Switzerland: The Transformation of the Subsidiarity Principle. *West European Politics* 16, no. 3 (1993): 362–379.

[55] Armingeon, K. Institutionalising the Swiss Welfare State. *West European Politics* 24, no. 2 (2001): 145–168; Katzenstein, P. J. *Small States in World Markets: Industrial Policy in Europe*. Ithaca: Cornell University Press, 1985.

[56] Cattacin, S. Retard, Rattrapage, Normalisation. L'Etat social suisse face aux défis de transformation de la sécurité sociale. *Studien und Quellen — Etudes et Sources* 31(2006): 49–78. Available at: http://www.idheap.ch/idheap.nsf/webvwFichier/17522B21105ECF0 AC1257782004997CC/$FILE/RPL+2007+texte+10.pdf, accessed on November 11, 2014.

the public to self-regulate and be self-reliant.[57] The federal political institutional environment created a fragmented and relatively weak labour movement that could hardly mobilise its representatives at the federal level, despite having some achievements at the cantonal level.[58] The dominance of the bourgeois governments since 1975 until today has been recorded in Beck *et al.*[59] The Social Democrats were only dominant in the 16 years between 1975 and 2012. The majority of the 'winning coalition' was the right-wing parties such as the Radicals and currently the Swiss People's Party. Both of them follow similar policies such as fiscal discipline, low tax rates, self-dependence, and also a lower dependence on subsidies.

All of these factors have played their respective roles in the development of the Swiss welfare state throughout history. As Figures 1 and 2 show, recent years, since the early 1990s, have witnessed the development of the Swiss welfare state with a greater involvement of the Swiss government through expansion in public social spending. Trampusch calls this era the "post-liberal" welfare regime[60] because the "liberal" regime was similar to the "neo-liberal" model of Iversen and Wren discussed above. The author argues that trade unions have increasingly started to use popular initiatives to mobilise the labouring class and to influence federal level politics. For instance, trade unions were successful in countering amendments in labour law and unemployment benefits in 1997.[61] Switzerland's strong economic performance, and favourable fiscal position, allowed the country to enjoy the benefits of low levels of

---

[57] Obinger, H. Minimum Income in Switzerland. *Journal of European Social Policy* 9, no. 1 (1999): 29–47.

[58] Katzenstein, *Small States in World Markets: Industrial Policy in Europe;* Obinger, *Federalism, Direct Democracy, and Welfare State Development in Switzerland.*

[59] Beck, T. *et al.* New Tools in Comparative Political Economy: The Database of Political Institutions. *World Bank Economic Review* 15, no. 1 (2001): 165–176.

[60] Trampusch, C. The Welfare State and Trade Unions in Switzerland: A Historical Reconstruction of the Shift from a Liberal to a Post-Liberal Welfare Regime. *Journal of European Social Policy*, no. 1(2001): 58–73.

[61] *Ibid.*, p. 68.

unemployment even without the greater engagement of the federal State in providing social welfare until the early 1990s.

The decentralised, individualised, and company-level wage determination is argued to be no longer benefitting the labouring class because economic distress hurt the labouring class in the early 1990s.[62] As a result, Oesch underlines that a "process of learning" among the trade unions motivated them to overcome the fragmented union system in the country by merging several unions with one another. By doing so, their collective strength was boosted countrywide.[63] However, Armingeon argues that this was also led by the efforts of the federal State.[64] It started balancing demands from capital and the labouring class. To give an example, women's retirement age was increased, as that would result in a longer working life, which could benefit employers. By merging these two policy instruments to balance demands from the remaining two parties, the State attempted to search for opportunities to be the broker between capital and labour.

In light of the major potential determinants of income inequality, Switzerland does not seem to be an outlier among developed countries, where earnings inequality is declining. Figure 4 shows that the share of the top 10 percent income level reached its historically highest point in the last decade. The ratio of the top 10 percent to bottom 90 percent levels of income had reached a level close to 4.5 before the Second World War, but it then declined and remained at a relatively stable level. The ratio started to go up again in the late 1990s, and it recently reached the level of 4.46 in 2009. The share of the top 10 percent income level in the whole "cake" reached its historically highest point of 33.15 percent in 2009. In brief, earnings inequality has been increasing in Switzerland particularly since the early 1990s, as shown in Figure 4.

---

[62] Oesch, D. Swiss Trade Unions and Industrial Relations after 1990: A History of Decline and Renewal. In Christine Trampusch and André Mach (eds.) *Switzerland in Europe: Continuity and Change in the Swiss Political Economy*, pp. 82–102. Oxon: Routledge, 2011.

[63] Trampusch, *The Welfare State and Trade Unions in Switzerland: A Historical Reconstruction of the Shift from a Liberal to a Post-Liberal Welfare Regime*, p. 69.

[64] Armingeon, K. Institutionalising the Swiss Welfare State. *West European Politics* 24, no. 2 (2001): 145–168.

Figure 4:   The income disparity between the top 10 percent and the bottom 90 percent of income levels, Switzerland

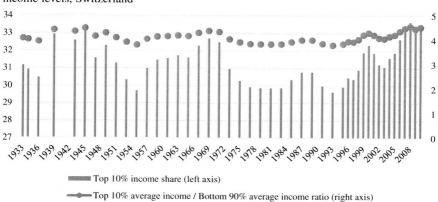

Top 10% income share (left axis)

Top 10% average income / Bottom 90% average income ratio (right axis)

Source: World Top Incomes Database, http://topincomes.g-mond.parisschoolofeconomics.eu/, accessed on April 24, 2014.

Note: Top 10 percent and bottom 90 percent average income is in real 2010 Swiss francs.

With respect to government expenditure on subsidies and other transfers, the Swiss government has been spending around 65 percent of its total government expenses on those items since the early 1990s onwards for which data is available (Figure 5). Figure 6 indicates that the share of general government spending was very low, less than 10 percent of GDP; however, it has gone up from that level since the mid-1970s, and has remained steadily above 10 percent of GDP. While it has stayed at a level above 10 percent of GDP, the yearly growth rate of government spending shows that since the 1990s, fiscal discipline, which can be defined here as lower growth rates compared to previous performance, has slowed down. However, the upward shift after the global financial crisis in 2008 is a global phenomenon as many countries around the globe have resorted to expansionary fiscal and monetary policies. In the meantime, government health expenditure has gone up due to two major drivers: (a) ageing in the Swiss population; (b) increasing levels of social security spending since the early 1990s.

These indicators show that the Swiss government has been expanding its social expenditure, at least since the early 1990s. It should be noted here that as Figure 7 depicts the story of the evolution of unionisation in

Figure 5:   Subsidies and other transfers, percentage of government expenses, Switzerland

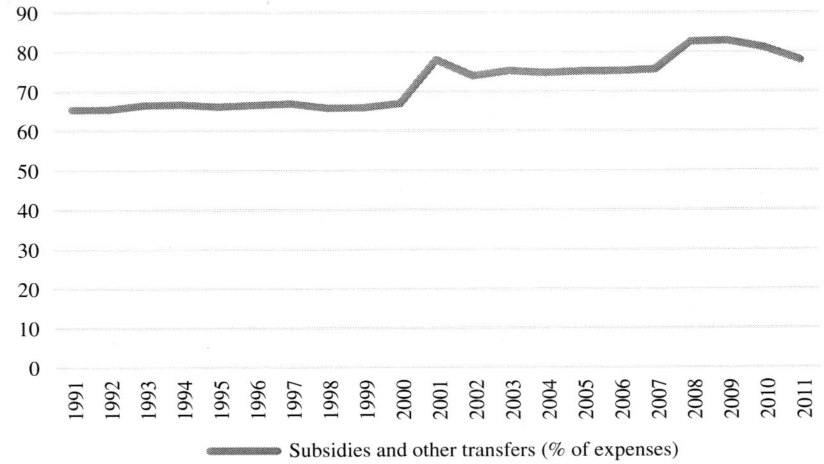

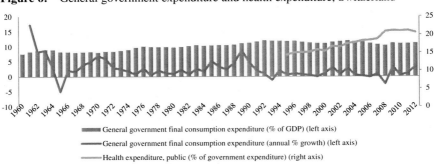

Source: World Development Indicators, the World Bank, accessed on April 18, 2014.

Figure 6:   General government expenditure and health expenditure, Switzerland

Source: World Development Indicators, the World Bank, accessed on April 18, 2014.

Switzerland, net union membership among the wage and salary earners has been declining since the late 1970s. According to collective action theory and power resource theory, we would expect to observe a different causal link between increasing government social spending and the strength of unions; however, the declining membership overlaps with an increasing level of social spending. We will try to answer the trend that is contradictory to our intuition by looking at the relative strength of the labour movement, and the political institutions in the country.

Figure 7: Net union membership as a proportion of wage and salary earners in employment (%), Switzerland[65]

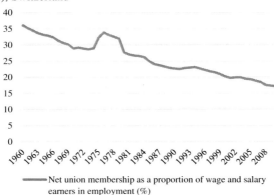

Net union membership as a proportion of wage and salary earners in employment (%)

Source: ICTWSS Database, http://www.uva-aias.net/208, accessed on April 18, 2014.

Lipset mentions that Switzerland has never witnessed radical mass mobilisation[66] firstly due to the introduction of political rights in relatively earlier periods, and secondly because industrialisation had not led to the massive urbanisation[67] that could have eroded social ties and rural institutions of communal cooperation and redistribution.[68] The non-existence of such radical movements resulted in the absence of radical labour unions, which could have translated into higher expectations for social transfers and scepticism of a strong federal State *vis-à-vis* the cantons.[69]

---

[65] According to the Amsterdam Institute of for Advanced Labour Studies ICTWSS database, union density rate is equal to NUM*100/WSEE where *NUM* is "net union membership"; and *WSEE* is "wage and salary earners in employment." Net union membership is calculated as follows: (total union membership) — union members outside active, dependent and employed labour force. WSEE is equal to employed wage and salary workers whose data is gathered from OECD, Labour Force Statistics. The ICTWSS Codebook is available at: http://www.uva-aias.net/208, accessed on April 18, 2014.

[66] Lipset, S. M. Radicalism or Reformism: The Sources of Working-class Politics. *The American Political Science Review* 77, no. 1 (1983): 1–18.

[67] Obinger, *Federalism, Direct Democracy, and Welfare State Development in Switzerland*.

[68] Polanyi, K. *The Great Transformation*. New York: Octagon Books, 1975.

[69] Linder, W. and Vatter, A. Institutions and Outcomes of Swiss Federalism: The Role of Cantons in Swiss Politics. *West European Politics* 24, no. 2 (2001): 95–122.

Baur *et al.* underline that "the federal government levies around one-third of total taxes and, likewise, accounts for approximately that proportion of total public expenditure."[70] The cantons shy away from giving up their internal independence to the federal State. As a result, the fragmented and relatively less developed federal governmental functions make it harder for the labouring class to influence federal level social security policies that would reduce inequality country-wide. The federal political institutional setting has been shown to impede the development of a welfare state in Switzerland. Obinger argues that the number of "veto players" and multi-tiered negotiations to change federal policies resulted in a particular type of "path dependence", halting the process of increasing welfare spending at the federal level.[71] Pierson also shows for the Canadian and the United States cases that the development and management of social welfare in federal political systems is likely to be more challenging than in non-federal systems, mainly due to competition between local political entities, and the influence of business interest groups at the federal level.[72]

In recent years, with the recognition of the benefit of collective effort to bring issues to general concern at the federal level, trade unions seem to be more active in bypassing multi-tiered negotiations from the cantonal level to the federal level. A good example is the recent attempt of the collective effort of unions and several affiliated non-profit organisations to bring the issue of the minimum wage to a popular vote on May 18, 2014.[73] The Swiss Union of Syndicates,[74] which is an umbrella organisation of many trade unions, had headed the group in this initiative. The initiative

---

[70] Baur, M., Bruchez, P. and Schlaffer, B. Institutions for Crisis Prevention: The Case of Switzerland. *Global Policy* 4 (Supplement 1, 2013): 10–21.

[71] Obinger, *Federalism, Direct Democracy, and Welfare State Development in Switzerland.*

[72] Pierson, P. Fragmented Welfare States: Federal Institutions and the Development of Social Policy. *Governance* 8, no. 4 (1995): 449–478.

[73] For further reference to that particular initiative, the readers may refer to website of the initiative that is available online at: http://www.salaires-minimums.ch/linitiative/, accessed on April 2, 2015.

[74] For more information about the union, readers can refer to the website of the Swiss Union of Syndicates, available at: http://www.uss.ch/luss/qui-sommes-nous/, accessed on April 2, 2015.

campaigned for a minimum wage of CHF4,000 (i.e., CHF22 per hour) applicable at the federal level. The popular initiative was rejected with little support since 76 percent of the Swiss voted "no" for the initiative.[75] The results show a dramatic "death" of the initiative as the percentage of electorate saying "no" to the initiative was remarkably higher than that of those saying "yes" (i.e., 76 percent versus 24 percent). When the result is analysed with some attention to the federal political institutional context, and the declining union density rate, trade unions seem to make attempts to address rising income inequality. However, the multiple "veto players" on the road to get the issue formally recognised as an agenda item at the federal level are stuck with the result of the popular initiative in May 2014. This example shows that although trade unions might be more willing to work within this political-economic structure to influence wage policies at the federal level, the structure itself may prove challenging for influencing the process.

In brief, as trade unions have become more centralised, and presumably started to influence employers and the State through collective bargaining in recent decades, we can interpret the current rise in social welfare spending in Switzerland through the lens of power resource theory, expecting them to have gained relatively higher levels of resources to project power in the political decision-making process. Throughout the history, the federal political institutional environment, fragmented trade unionism, and the dominance of bourgeois governments in the Swiss politico-economic system, have set up high barriers to the maturation of the welfare regime in the country. With the economic distress in the early 1990s, and a "learning process" among the trade unions, Switzerland recognised the need for a social welfare regime during the "hard times" in previous decades. Although unions seem to have difficulty having their concerns recognised by the federal State and a larger segment of the population, as was the case in the latest minimum wage initiative in 2014, we should expect income inequality to remain where it is today. This is a fair assumption given several conditions argued in this chapter, namely a decentralised political-economic institutional

---

[75] The results and the distribution of votes based on the cantonal level is available on the website of *Tribune de Genève*, http://www.tdg.ch/suisse/salaire-minimum-rejete-77-suisses/story/10325405, accessed on April 2, 2015.

structure, and the declining rate of union density, even if trade unions seem to have recognised the benefits of collective efforts in carrying issues of general concern to the federal level.

Conclusion

Income inequality has become a global concern. The Singaporean and Swiss cases in this chapter show that it has had an upward trend in these two countries as well. This chapter has endeavoured to explain the rise in income inequality with respect to the relative strength of trade unions, as representatives of the labouring class when political decisions on wage policies, and related social policies are negotiated with the State and capital-owners. The power resource theory predicts that the more power resources unions accumulate *vis-à-vis* other actors, the more they would exert an influence on policies which improve the socio-economic conditions of the labouring class, so that inequality is reduced. If they do not hold a certain level of power resources, one could expect to see the dominance of the preferences of the State and capital-owners.[76] The aim of this chapter is very focused and does not engage in a "horse race" presenting different determinants of rising income inequality in Singapore and Switzerland. It rather aims to show the reader that the relative power of trade unions in an era of declining union density might be an important indicator for better understanding one of the determinants of the recent phenomenon. One might well come up with other determinants such as collective bargaining coverage,[77] trade openness

---

[76] This should not be understood as the State not desiring to play a constructive role or be responsive to the demands of the labouring class. Populist regimes, and political concerns especially before elections, etc. are well known determinants of expansionary spending in developing countries as well as developed countries where it is a rare case due to established rules and practice in macroeconomic management. However, as Iversen and Wren (1998) predict, the State may not be able to spend beyond its budgetary limits, and thus, may need to resort to fiscal discipline. As a result, the labouring class cannot force the State to adopt more expansionary spending to reduce inequality if the labouring class has a relatively lesser degree of power resources.

[77] Salverda, W. and Mayhew, K. Capitalist Economies and Wage Inequality. *Oxford Review of Economic Policy* 25, no. 1 (2009): 126–154; Bosch, G. Shrinking Collective Bargaining

and financial deregulation resulting in premiums for skilled labour[78] or even differences in occupational wages and so on. These are assumed to be somehow intertwined, and they require a holistic assessment, which is out of the scope of this chapter.

Keeping in mind the limitations and the narrow scope of this chapter, we can observe that in Switzerland, the institutional structure built upon on a federal social welfare system accompanied by the unique institution of direct democracy did not allow the fragmented labour union movement to influence policy-making at the federal level. The lack of a militant labour movement, the strong presence of a third sector, and the long-time dominance of the so-called bourgeois governments resulted in lower levels of social spending and an increasing income inequality. The recession in the early 1990s, which had hit the labouring classes hard, set the stage for the labouring class to mobilise through centralising the unions across the cantons. As the labouring class overcame its own collective action problem by reforming the unions to be more centralised and more active at the federal level, they have become more influential in receiving concessions from the capital-owners and the State on wage policies and other social policies. The Swiss case, at least partially, shows that the higher degree of power resources the labouring class has accumulated has enabled them to influence the decision-making process. Although one may claim that their attempt with the recent popular vote on minimum wage is contradictory to the conclusion presented above, it should be noted that in such multi-tiered decision-making systems, reaching a consensus is a slow process. It is emphasised in this chapter that the recognition of the benefits of collective effort is notable despite the need to observe how this process will evolve.

Coverage, Increasing Income Inequality: A Comparison of five EU Countries. *International Labour Review* 154, no. 1 (2015): 57–66.

[78] Krugman, P. Growing World Trade: Causes and Consequences. *Brookings Papers on Economic Activity* 26, no. 1 (1995): 327–377; Goldberg, P. K. and Pavcnik, N. Distributional Effects of Globalisation in Developing Countries. *Journal of Economic Literature* 45, no. 1 (2007): 39–82; Jerzmanowski, M. and Nabar, M. Financial Development and Wage Inequality: Theory and Evidence. *Economic Inquiry* 51, no. 1 (2013): 211–234.

In the Singaporean case, the centralised wage determination, the tripartite institutional context within the National Wage Council, and probably the most important factor of a one-party dominated political system did not allow — and still does not allow — the labouring class to mobilise itself to have a greater say in the decision-making process. The ideological orientation of the key decision-makers such as founding Prime Minister Lee Kuan Yew, and the first Chairman of the National Wage Council Lim Chong Yah, reflects why they were sceptical of passing rigid wage policies, or letting the militant unions have more space in the political arena. In Singapore, it seems evident that the centralised political institutional context did not open enough space for the labouring class and its representatives to hold a greater amount of power resources.

To sum up, as power resource theory predicts, the cases tell us that the relative strength of the labouring class does matter in their role and reach in the political decision-making process of wage and social policies. A centralised or decentralised political structure poses different challenges for the labouring class. The initial point at which the labour movement is positioned may not matter much. In the Swiss case, however, as the context changed in the 1990s, the Swiss unions were able to overcome their collective action problem in a decentralised political structure. However, the Singaporean case is a tricky case insofar as the role of the centralised political structure limits the space for the unions to play a constructive role in policy decision-making process. The evolution of income inequality shows that it will all depend on how responsive the Singaporean government is to the demands of the population, rather than to the potential mobilisation of the labour movement, compared to the Swiss case.

References

Acemoglu, D. The World Our Grandchildren will Inherit: The Rights Revolution and Beyond. Mimeo, MIT, 2012. Available at: http://economics.mit.edu/files/7742, accessed on November 10, 2014.

Armingeon, K. Institutionalising the Swiss Welfare State. *West European Politics* 24, no. 2 (2001): 145–168.

Asher, M., and Nandy, A. Health Financing in Singapore: A Case for Systemic Reforms. *International Social Security Review* 59, no. 1 (January 1, 2006): 75–92. doi:10.1111/j.1468-246X.2005.00234.x.

Asher, M. and Nandy, A. Singapore's Policy Responses to Ageing, Inequality and Poverty: An Assessment. *International Social Security Review* 61, no. 1 (2008): 41–60.

Barr, M. D. Trade Unions in an Elitist Society: The Singapore Story. *Australian Journal of Politics and History* 46, no. 4 (2000): 480–496.

Baur, M., Bruchez, P. and Schlaffer, B. Institutions for Crisis Prevention: The Case of Switzerland. *Global Policy* 4 (Supplement 1, 2013): 10–21.

Beck, T. *et al.* New Tools in Comparative Political Economy: The Database of Political Institutions. *World Bank Economic Review* 15, no. 1 (2001): 165–176.

Bertozzi, F. and Bonoli, G. Fédéralisme et protection sociale en Suisse: entre immobilisme et innovation. *Sociétés contemporaines* 51 (2003): 13–33.

Bosch, G. Shrinking Collective Bargaining Coverage, Increasing Income Inequality: A Comparison of five EU Countries. *International Labour Review* 154, no. 1 (2015): 57–66.

Butschi, D. and Cattacin, S. The Third Sector in Switzerland: The Transformation of the Subsidiarity Principle. *West European Politics* 16, no. 3 (1993): 362–379.

Cattacin, S. Retard, Rattrapage, Normalisation. L'Etat social suisse face aux défis de transformation de la sécurité sociale. *Studien und Quellen/Etudes et Sources* 31 (2006): 49–78. Available at: http://www.idheap.ch/idheap.nsf/webvwFichier/17522B21105ECF0AC1257782004997CC/$FILE/RPL+2007+texte+10.pdf, accessed on November 11, 2014.

Ching, Y. C., and Lim G. S. Globalization, Labour Market Deregulation and Trade Unions in Singapore. *Asia Pacific Business Review* 6, no. 3–4 (January 1, 2000): 154–73. doi:10.1080/13602380012331288512.

Durant, W. and Durant, A. *The Lessons of History*. New York: Simon and Schuster, 1968.

Dutt, P. and Mitra, D. Inequality and the Instability of Polity and Policy. *The Economic Journal* 118, no. 531 (2008): 1285–1314.

Esping–Andersen, G. *Politics Against Markets*. Princeton: Princeton University Press, 1985.

Galbraith, J. K. *Inequality and Instability: A Study of the World Economy Before the Great Crisis*. New York: Oxford University Press 2012.

Goldberg, P. K. and Pavcnik, N. Distributional Effects of Globalisation in Developing Countries. *Journal of Economic Literature* 45, no. 1 (2007): 39–82.

Hiok, L. B. Trade Union Growth in Singapore. *Asian Journal of Political Science* 3, no. 2 (1995): 90–111.

Hirschmann, A. O. *Exit, Voice, and Loyalty: Responses to Decline in Firms, Organisations, and States*. Cambridge, MA: Harvard University Press, 1970.

Hui, W. T. Economic Growth and Inequality in Singapore: The Case for a Miminum Wage. *International Labour Review* 152, no. 1 (2013): 107–123.

Iversen, T. and Wren, A. Equality, Employment, and Budgetary Restraint: The Trilemma of the Service Economy. *World Politics* 50, no. 4 (1998): 507–546.

Jaumotte, F. and Buitron, C. O. Power from the People. *Finance and Development* 52, no. 1 (2015): 29–31.

Jerzmanowski, M. and Nabar, M. Financial Development and Wage Inequality: Theory and Evidence. *Economic Inquiry* 51, no. 1 (2013): 211–234.

Kaldor, Nicholas. Alternative Theories of Distribution. *The Review of Economic Studies* 23, no. 42 (1956): 83–100.

Katzenstein, P. J. *Small States in World Markets: Industrial Policy in Europe.* Ithaca: Cornell University Press, 1985.

Krugman, P. Growing World Trade: Causes and Consequences. *Brookings Papers on Economic Activity* 26, no. 1 (1995): 327–377.

Korpi, W. *The Democratic Class Struggle.* London: Routledge and Kegan Paul, 1983.

Lasswell, H. *Politics: Who Gets What, When, How.* New York: McGraw–Hill, 1958.

Lee, K. Y. *The Battle for Merger.* Singapore: Straits Times Press, 2014.

Lim, C. Y. *Singapore's National Wage Council: An Insider's View.* New Jersey: World Scientific, 2014.

Linder, W. *Swiss Democracy: Possible Solutions to Conflict in Multicultural Societies.* New York: St. Martin's Press, 1994.

Linder, W. and Vatter, A. Institutions and Outcomes of Swiss Federalism: The Role of Cantons in Swiss Politics. *West European Politics* 24, no. 2 (2001): 95–122.

Lipset, S. M. Radicalism or Reformism: The Sources of Working-class Politics. *The American Political Science Review* 77, no. 1 (1983): 1–18.

Low, D. and Vadaketh, S. T. *Hard Choices: Challenging the Singapore Consensus.* Singapore: NUS Press, 2014.

Mahbubani, K. Lee Kuan Yew's Complex Legacy. In Shashi Jayakumar and Rahul Sagar (eds.) *The Big Ideas of Lee Kuan Yew.* Singapore: Straits Times Press, 2014.

Meltzer, A. and Richard, S. A Rational Theory of the Size of Government. *Journal of Political Economy* 89, no. 5 (1981): 914–927.

Nasir, K. M. and Turner, B. S. Governing as Gardening: Reflections on Soft Authoritarianism in Singapore. *Citizenship Studies* 17, nos. 3-4 (2013): 339–352.

Obinger, H. Federalism, Direct Democracy, and Welfare State Development in Switzerland. *Journal of Public Policy* 18, no. 3 (1998): 241–263.

Obinger, H. Minimum Income in Switzerland. *Journal of European Social Policy* 9, no. 1 (1999): 29–47.

Obinger, H. *et al.* Switzerland: The Marriage of Direct Democracy and Federalism. In Herbert Obinger, Stephan Leibrief and Francis G. Castles (eds.) *Federalism and the Welfare State*, pp. 263–304. Cambridge: Cambridge University Press, 2005.

Oesch, D. Swiss Trade Unions and Industrial Relations after 1990: A History of Decline and Renewal. In Christine Trampusch and André Mach (eds.) *Switzerland in Europe: Continuity and Change in the Swiss Political Economy*, pp. 82–102. Oxon: Routledge, 2011.

Piketty, T. *Capital in the Twenty-First Century*. Cambridge, MA: Harvard University Press, 2014.

Pierson, P. Fragmented Welfare States: Federal Institutions and the Development of Social Policy. *Governance* 8, no. 4 (1995): 449–478.

Polanyi, K. *The Great Transformation*. New York: Octagon Books, 1975.

Poulantzas, N. On Social Classes. *New Left Review* 78 (1973): 27–54.

Rao, V. V. B., Banerjee, D. S. and Mukhopadhaya, P. Earnings Inequality in Singapore. *Journal of the Asian Pacific Economy* 8, no. 2 (2003): 210–228.

Régnier, P. T. *Singapour et son environnement régional : étude d'une cité-État au sein du monde malais*. Paris: Presses Universitaires de France, 1987.

Rosa, L. The Singapore State and Trade Union Incorporation. *Journal of Contemporary Asia* 20, no. 4 (1990): 487–508.

Salverda, W. and Mayhew, K. Capitalist Economies and Wage Inequality. *Oxford Review of Economic Policy* 25, no. 1 (2009): 126–154.

Stockhammer, E. Wage-led Growth: An Introduction. *International Journal of Labour Research* 3, no. 2 (2011): 167–187.

Toh, R, and Hui, W. T. Trade Liberalization, Labour Demand Shifts and Earningsss Inequality in Singapore. *Review of Urban & Regional Development Studies* 24, no. 3 (2013): 65–82.

Trampusch, C. The Welfare State and Trade Unions in Switzerland: An Historical Reconstruction of the Shift from a Liberal to a Post-Liberal Welfare Regime. *Journal of European Social Policy* 20, no. 1 (2010): 58–73.

Tremewan, C. Welfare and Governance: Public Housing under Singapore's Party-State. In Roger Goodman, Gordon White and Huck-ju Kwon (eds.) *The East Asian Welfare Model: Welfare Orientalism and the State*, pp. 77–105. London & New York: Routledge, 1998.

Wagschal, U. Direct Democracy and Public Policymaking. *Journal of Public Policy* 17, no. 2 (1997): 223–245.

Wallerstein, M. Wage-Setting Institutions and Pay Inequality in Advanced Industrial Societies. *American Journal of Political Science* 43, no. 3 (1999): 649–680.

Conclusion

The book ends, as it began, on a pensive note: given the divergent political systems and experiences of the two small states, what can Singapore and Switzerland learn from each other? From the Singapore perspective, the answer is perhaps clearer. Singapore has always prided itself on being a 'learning state', and attributed its success to its ability to study, copy and adapt best practices from around the world. So it has been with Swiss policy innovations. Beyond the "Swiss standard of living" ideal proclaimed by former Prime Minister Goh Chok Tong in 1984, one example of a lesson drawn from Switzerland was the strategy of "Total Defence", based on the recognition that military defence was not enough — a resilient civilian population and infrastructure was needed to defend against threats. A more recent lesson drawn from Switzerland was in reforms to national service — allowing servicemen to choose their vocations, certifying their skills to employers, and expanding the current volunteer scheme. Currently, Singapore policymakers are also studying with great interest Switzerland's work-and-study model which combines vocational education and training with career counselling and the permeability of the Swiss education system, with equal merit accorded to both vocational and academic routes.[1]

The chapters in this book have focused on other things Singapore can learn from Switzerland from a broader level. In terms of land transport

---

[1] "Swiss Model of Vocational Education Offers Lessons for Singapore". *TODAYonline*. Accessed June 21, 2015. http://www.todayonline.com/singapore/swiss-model-vocational-education-offers-lessons-singapore.

policy, Singapore can certainly take a leaf out of Switzerland's book in terms of prioritising the needs of pedestrians over automobiles, in its quest to design a more 'liveable' city that caters to the needs of public transport users. The Swiss experience of reducing wage disparity, providing stronger social safety nets and according adequate social protection to migrant workers is also instructive to Singapore, given recent studies highlighting food quality issues affecting a significant number of foreign workers in Singapore.[2] Singapore can also look to the Swiss experience in successful branding, both at the country level as well as at the level of its SMEs, which have achieved much success internationally.

In Switzerland, as befitting of its 'bottom-up' policymaking style, the impetus to study and 'learn' from Singapore also comes from domestic actors such as the economically liberal think-tank *Avenir Suisse*, which has researched Singapore in great depth, paying close attention to the pragmatic policy proposals that are a hallmark of Singapore's governance. But as has been discussed at length in this book, the direct democratic character of the Swiss policymaking process means that 'learning' must take place in a more gradual and piecemeal manner.

Singapore and Switzerland's destinies as small states, however, often put them in positions where international and domestic forces are in tension. Although from a geopolitical perspective, Switzerland's regional environment is more stable than Singapore's, Swiss neutrality has come at the cost of it having to accept decisions made by the European Union (the *acquis communautaire*) without having a seat at the table. But what Switzerland has is the certainty that no matter what happens in Europe, the country will still exist centuries from now. Meanwhile, Singapore's strategy of 'balancing' is driven by deep-seated existential insecurities, although some analysts predict that as its geopolitical context changes, Singapore may eventually also have to commit to international neutrality,

---

[2] "More than 9 in 10 Bangladeshi Foreign Workers Say They Are given Unclean and Unhygenic Food: NUS Survey". Accessed June 22, 2015. http://www.straitstimes.com/ news/singapore/more-singapore-stories/story/more-9-10-bangladeshi-foreign-workers-say-they-are-given.

relying, as Switzerland does, on international law and soft power to project influence.[3]

Both Singapore and Switzerland are also going through periods of gradual political transition. The 50th anniversary of Singapore's founding was marked by the demise of its founding Prime Minister, and amidst calls for greater political liberalisation, its political leaders are keenly aware of the demand for greater public consultation in policymaking. Lim Siong Guan, a former head of the Singapore civil service, thus argued that the Singapore government had to take on the new role of "convening and aggregating" ground-up energies, with the confidence to put resources behind new ideas. In Switzerland, the increasing influence of nationalist political groups, coupled with their use of the popular referendum to advance their political agenda, has reignited debate as to whether this process should be subject to stricter limits.[4]

Social integration is a third issue both countries have to face, reflecting the fact that immigrants currently make up 27 percent of Switzerland's population and almost 38 percent of Singapore's. A Swiss referendum held in February 2014, initiated by the populist Swiss People's Party, reflected a slight majority of the population voting for caps on immigration. In Singapore, immigration has been a highly charged issue even before the last general election in 2011, and popular discontent subsequently reached a high point at the release of the government's Population White Paper in 2013. The Singapore government, together with the National Integration Council and grassroots organisations, have crafted a coherent, nation-wide response to social integration. This has included policies to preserve a Singaporean core in various economic sectors; a ramp-up in infrastructural development to ease congestion; and programmes to facilitate cross-cultural understanding at schools, workplaces and in the heartlands. In

---

[3] Skilling, David, "Will Small Still Be Beautiful in 2065?" Accessed June 21, 2015. http://www.straitstimes.com/news/opinion/more-opinion-stories/story/will-small-still-be-beautiful-2065-20150615.

[4] "2014 IPS-AS Seminar on 'Singapore and Switzerland: Learning from Each Other' | Institute of Policy Studies". Accessed June 21, 2015. http://lkyspp.nus.edu.sg/ips/event/2014-ips-as-seminar-on-singapore-and-switzerland-learning-from-each-other.

Switzerland, integration policies have been delegated to individual cantons, but is financially supported by the federal government. Thus, according to Professor David Chan of the Singapore Management University, both Switzerland and Singapore "need to integrate the cosmopolitan openness goals of a global city and the national solidarity goals of a cohesive country".[5]

As countries with small domestic markets, both Swiss and Singaporean companies have been forced to be outward-looking, adapting to various demands and flexibly catering to global consumer needs. Swiss SMEs maintain a strong presence outside of Switzerland, allowing them to carve out a market niche. Similarly, Singaporean corporations have sought to expand their reach, although the majority of these corporations are government-linked (GLC) and are focused on developmental concerns such as financial sector development, water and urban development. As a "global brand", Switzerland stands for the values of freedom, tolerance, transparency and environmentalism,[6] while Singapore is known for its policy efficiency, transparency, attractiveness to businesses, and environmental liveability.[7]

In conclusion, the contrasting and complementary experiences of Switzerland and Singapore provide illuminating insights to each other. While Singapore's top-down solutions display the visionary foresight of government policymakers and help ensure predictability and long-term planning, bottom-up solutions demonstrated by the Swiss are able to secure consensus between the stakeholders of every policy decision and bestow upon citizens a sense of empowerment and responsibility for their individual and collective lives. Yet each of them seems to desire a

---

[5]"2014 IPS-AS Seminar on 'Singapore and Switzerland: Learning from Each Other' | Institute of Policy Studies". Accessed June 21, 2015. http://lkyspp.nus.edu.sg/ips/event/2014-ips-as-seminar-on-singapore-and-switzerland-learning-from-each-other.

[6]Smith, Jacquelyn, "Switzerland Tops Ranking of 25 Best Country Brands". *Forbes.* Accessed June 21, 2015. http://www.forbes.com/sites/jacquelynsmith/2012/10/24/switzerland-tops-ranking-of-25-best-country-brands/.

[7]Lee, Marissa, "Singapore beats NYC, London, Hong Kong in Global Liveable Cities Index". *Straits Times.* 12 December 2014; Weizhen, Tan, "Singapore still 3rd in world competitiveness ranking: Study". *Today.* 28 May 2015.

little bit more of what the other has mastered.[8] Both countries, while still being focused on making sure that bigger powers have a vested interest in their survival, can continue pursuing the vision of being hubs, pace-setter, and innovators, and through their different pathways, countries that get things right.[9]

In *Small States and World Markets*, Peter Katzenstein famously compared small states to frogs, emphasising their flexibility in adapting to change. "Although they appear to land on their stomachs, in fact they always land on their feet and retain the ability to jump again and again in different directions, correcting their course as they go along"[10]. Small states such as Singapore and Switzerland owe their survival and success to constant learning and innovation in the face of significant environmental and resource constraints. In this respect, they have much to offer their counterparts from all over the world.

---

[8] "2014 IPS-AS Seminar on 'Singapore and Switzerland: Learning from Each Other' | Institute of Policy Studies". Accessed June 21, 2015. http://lkyspp.nus.edu.sg/ips/event/2014-ips-as-seminar-on-singapore-and-switzerland-learning-from-each-other.

[9] Guo, Yvonne, and Jun Jie Woo, "The Secrets to Small State Survival". Accessed June 21, 2015. http://www.straitstimes.com/the-big-story/case-you-missed-it/story/the-secrets-small-state-survival-20130923.

[10] Katzenstein, Peter J, *Small States in World Markets: Industrial Policy in Europe*. Cornell University Press, 1985.

About the Authors

Editors

Yvonne Guo is a PhD candidate at the Lee Kuan Yew School of Public Policy, National University of Singapore, where she is writing her thesis on small state responses to international financial regulatory pressures, focusing on the cases of Singapore and Switzerland. She previously studied in Sciences Po Paris, Peking University, and the University, of St. Gallen, Switzerland. She obtained a dual Master of Arts degree in International Affairs and Governance from Sciences Po and the University of St. Gallen.

J.J. Woo is Assistant Professor in the Department of Public Policy and Global Affairs, Nanyang Technological University. He holds a PhD from the Lee Kuan Yew School of Public Policy, National University of Singapore and a Master of Science in International Political Economy from the S. Rajaratnam School of International Studies, Nanyang Technological University. His research interests include Singapore politics, international financial centres, and the political economy of finance.

Authors

Andreas Ladner is Professor of political institutions and public administration at the Swiss Graduate School of Public Administration (IDHEAP) at the University of Lausanne. His areas of research include the quality of democracy, local government, institutional change, political parties and voting advice applications. He has conducted several major research projects for the Swiss National Science Foundation and authored books and articles on these topics. He has published, among others, in Local Government Studies, International Review of Administrative Sciences, International Political Science Review, Environment and Planning C, International Journal of Electronic Governance, Environmental Politics, European Journal of Political Research, West European Politics, Electoral Studies and Party Politics, and is the editor in chief of the Handbook on Public Administration in Switzerland. He also regularly comments on Swiss politics in the media.

Bruno Wildermuth, born in 1936 in Zurich, Switzerland, studied Civil Engineering and holds a Masters of City and Regional Planning from University of California, Berkeley. His first assignment in Singapore was to plan the initial MRT System. In the 1970s, he played a key role in the MRT Debate, persuading Singapore policymakers on the feasibility of the MRT system, and subsequently was involved in building it. He also established TransitLink, the World's first integrated ticketing system. More recently, he formulated the distance-based through fares for public transport.

Cindy Helfer is a graduate student of international affairs at the Graduate Institute for International and Development Studies (Geneva), and holds a BA in international relations from the University of Geneva. She studied as an exchange student at the Lee Kuan Yew School of Public Policy in 2013. Her areas of interest cover three disciplines: public international law, politics and economics. She is interested in the ethics of migration policies and on the economic effects of migration, in Switzerland, her home country, and abroad.

Hui Weng Tat is Associate Professor at the Lee Kuan Yew (LKY) School of Public Policy, National University of Singapore (NUS). He specialises in the impact of globalisation on labour markets, economic issues of migration, education, ageing and retirement, and labour market policies in Singapore. He has also taught in the NUS Department of Economics before joining the LKY School in 2004. He has published in international labour and public economics journals and teaches graduate courses on Economics and Public Policy, Public Policy Research and Evaluation, and Labour Market Policy Issues at the LKY School.

Manuel Baeuml works in strategy development, product development and performance improvement for a top management consultancy. He was previously a Research Fellow at the St. Gallen Institute of Management in Asia where he wrote his PhD thesis on SME management in Switzerland and Singapore. Prior to joining the University of St. Gallen, he studied Industrial Engineering at the Technical University of Darmstadt.

Mehmet Kerem Çoban is a PhD candidate at the Lee Kuan Yew School of Public Policy, National University of Singapore (NUS). His research interests include the political economy of development, financial liberalisation and regulation, and development aid. Prior to his PhD studies, he interned in the Global Risk Identification Programme (GRIP) at the UNDP Office in Geneva, where he worked on the designing and editing of publications, and at the General Consulate of Turkey in Geneva. He obtained his Master's Degree in Development Studies at the Graduate Institute of International and Development Studies (IHEID), Geneva in 2013, and his Bachelor's Degree in International Relations at Kadir Has University, Istanbul in 2011.

Michel Anliker is a Customs and International Trade Senior Manager at PricewaterhouseCoopers (PwC), with a strong background in Indirect Taxes. He holds a Master of Law from the University of Fribourg (lic. iur.), Switzerland, and is an Attorney-at-Law (Swiss Bar Exam). Out of his nine years at PwC, he worked at PwC WMS Singapore between 2012 and 2015, helping companies various with customs and trade questions, and developing strategies to reduce landed costs and improve duty reduction and competitiveness through the usage of Free Trade Agreements. He assisted multinationals in strategic regional customs planning in Asia, customs valuation, import licensing, tariff classification, streamlining import/export activities in Asia and supply chain optimisation. Since July 2015 he has been based in Switzerland with PwC's Customs and International Trade team.

Pascal Wild holds a BSc and an MSc in entrepreneurship and management, and is currently a PhD candidate in international business management and the socio-economics of development at the University of Geneva, Switzerland. In his capacity as assistant professor and research assistant at the tri-lingual School of Management, Fribourg/Freiburg, Switzerland, he is one of the major research contributors to the Global Entrepreneurship Monitor (Switzerland), published by that school on an annual basis since 2009.

Philippe Régnier holds a PhD in development economics from the University of Geneva, Switzerland, and specialised in applied development economics of Southeast Asia, and Singapore in particular. His focus is in entrepreneurship, small business and development, and he has devoted most of his career to consulting, research, teaching and training in the field of private sector development in East and South Asia. After 20 years at the Graduate Institute of Development Studies, Geneva, until 2008, he continued as a full professor at the University of Ottawa, Canada. Since early 2015, he has been the recipient of a Swiss research chair in entrepreneurship and appropriate technologies in developing and emerging economies, in cooperation with the Swiss University of Applied Sciences, Western Switzerland. He is also a contributor to the diffusion of the Global Entrepreneurship Monitor in several developing economics of Northern and Western Africa, promoted by the Swiss School of Management Fribourg together with Canadian research institutions specialising in entrepreneurship and development.

Suzanne Hraba-Renevey is founder and CEO of "Hraba-Renevey Consulting" in Switzerland which connects stakeholders in research, education and entrepreneurship with a focus on Asia. She was awarded a PhD in Molecular Biology from the University of Geneva, Switzerland, and spent several years in academia and research. She created the position of Science Counsellor at the Embassy of Switzerland in Singapore and was instrumental in the implementation of *swissnex* Singapore, a platform of the Swiss government connecting the dots in science, education and innovation, which she led for 11 years.

Index

Free Trade Agreements (FTAs), ix,
44, 51–52, 54–58, 60–71
  bilateral, 53–55, 57–59, 61, 63,
  67
  multilateral, 52–53, 57, 65–66
  implementation, 63, 68
French invasion of Switzerland, xxvii,
xl, 40

G

General Agreement on Tariffs and
Trade (GATT), 61, 65
Geneva, xxvii, xlii, 7, 41–42, 84, 117,
137, 242
Gifted Education Programme, 169
Global Competitiveness Index,
xxxv, 12–13, 117, 137–138, 158,
163
Global Entrepreneurship Monitor
(GEM), xliii, 139–141, 145–146,
151–153, 155, 157, 160–161
Global financial crisis, 78, 81, 87,
131, 255, 274
Global Governance Group (3G), 30,
44, 45
Goh Keng Swee, xxiv, xxxvi, 166
Government Parliamentary
Committees (GPCs), 18–19
Group Representation Constituencies
(GRC), xxx–xxxii, 19, 197

H

Health expenditure, 259–260, 266,
268, 274–275
Helvetic Republic, xxvii, 40
High Net Worth Individuals, 77
Housing and Development Board
(HDB), xxiv, 198, 209

I

Immigration, x, xviii, xxii–xxiii,
xlii, 22–23, 59, 84, 193–194, 201,
204–206, 208–210, 215
  anti-immigration, xxxiv, 204,
  206, 225, 236, 243
  illegal immigration, 244
  nationalism, xxiii, xxxiv, 21,194,
  202, 206, 210, 287
  to Singapore, xxiii, 201, 208,
  210, 215, 220–221, 223,
  225, 227–229, 230–233,
  245–250
  to Switzerland, xxxiv, xlii,
  22–23, 59, 84, 205–206, 208,
  216, 219, 234–239, 242–244,
  247, 249
Income inequality, 227, 229, 240,
246, 255–257, 259–261, 266, 268,
273–274, 277–281, 286
Independence of Singapore, ix, xiii,
xxiv–xxv, xxix, xxxvi, 8, 29, 38,
44, 47, 79, 159, 161, 162, 169,
196, 199, 227, 232, 259, 263–264,
267
Independence of Switzerland, xxvii,
40, 46–47
Input legitimacy, xliii, 2, 10–11,
13–14, 21–24
Institutes of Technical Education
(ITE), 168, 172, 174, 184–185
Intercantonal Agreement on
Education Coordination, 175
International law, 31, 40, 46, 287

J

Japanese occupation of Singapore,
xvii, xxii–xxiii
Junior colleges, 168–169

Reviews of the Book

In this useful compendium, the editors have succeeded in assembling a team of authors who offer well-informed surveys of a broad range of topics and policy issues. Cross-regional work is rare in comparative politics and unique in the case of arguably the two most successful, conservative small states in the developed world.

Peter J. Katzenstein
Walter S. Carpenter, Jr. Professor of International Studies, Cornell University

This book continues in the best tradition of Katzenstein's path-breaking study *Small States in World Markets*. It presents a high-quality set of theoretically-informed case and comparative studies of Singapore and Switzerland, two countries with very different histories which have developed some very similar, and some very different policies and practices in coping with their status and location in the world order. The essays explore why this is the case, shedding light on how these two countries are likely to move forward into the future.

Michael Howlett
Burnaby Mountain Chair, Department of Political Science, Simon Fraser University
Yong Pung How Chair Professor, Lee Kuan Yew School of Public Policy, National University of Singapore

Small is indeed beautiful; it is amazing to see what two successful countries can learn from each other and how much they have in common.

Stefan Morkötter
Managing Director, St. Gallen Institute of Management in Asia
Assistant Professor, University of St. Gallen